地中海与东方学国际研究协会　　　　　北京大学考古文博学院

INTERNATIONAL ASSOCIATION FOR　　SCHOOL OF ARCHAEOLOGY AND MUSEOLOGY,
MEDITERRANEAN AND ORIENTAL STUDIES　　　　PEKING UNIVERSITY

丛书名称
亚欧丛书 EurAsia Series

Founded by 发起人

尼奥利（意大利亚非研究院）
GHERARDO GNOLI (Istituto Italiano per l'Africa e l'Oriente)

赵辉（北京大学考古文博学院）
ZHAO HUI (School of Archaeology and Museology,
Peking University)

Directed by 执行干事

魏正中（北京大学考古文博学院）
GIUSEPPE VIGNATO
(School of Archaeology and Museology, Peking University)

达仁利（地中海与东方学国际研究协会）
FRANCESCO D'ARELLI
(International Association of Mediterranean and Oriental Studies)

亚欧丛书　EurAsia Series

———————— 9 ————————

Architecture and Art
in Sasanian Iran

Pierfrancesco Callieri

伊朗萨珊时期的
建筑与艺术

〔意〕卡列宁　/ 著

吴筱　/ 译　〔意〕魏正中　/ 审校

上海古籍出版社
SHANGHAI CLASSICS PUBLISHING HOUSE

原书前言

尽管萨珊帝国在古典时期和中世纪早期的历史全景中占有一定的篇幅和地位，但对其与同时期罗马和拜占庭世界相比更为隐秘的历史和艺术材料，当今学界的认识仍然存在空白。大量语史学、历史学、历史宗教学和古币学研究都不足以解释的关键问题，只有考古学研究可以阐明。

与此同时，在对萨珊时期整体，尤其是其考古学的研究中，却缺乏可与法兰西学院布里昂的"阿契美尼德王朝和亚历山大帝国的历史与文明"教席相媲美的学术协作，即组织一系列会议，出版特定主题的重要汇编著作，并创立Achemenet网络项目，该项目如今在新加入的卢浮宫和芝加哥大学东方研究所继续进行。

关于萨珊时期，大西洋彼岸有一项值得称赞的创举，即创建sites.uci.edu/sasanika网站，但其仅致力于科学成果在网络上的传播，因而在协作研究上作用有限。这一项目亦由独立学者开展，因美国自诩在伊朗时期的萨珊考古发掘传统最为悠久，而遗憾的是部分成果尚未出版。自20世纪80年代以来，美国学者尤其注重以革新的方法研究萨珊时期的艺术史。

在欧洲，以丛书合集等出版物为核心，以伊朗研究发展协会为主导的学术活动，具有重大科学意义。该协会最初由吉钮领导，后由吉钮与吉塞莲共同领导，出版了一系列萨珊时期考古学的基础性著作。《萨珊钱币汇编》是法国、奥地利和德国博物馆机构合作的心血，由法国国家科研中心的吉塞莲和奥地利科学院钱币委员会的阿尔朗共同推进，在钱币领域取得了出色的成绩。

20世纪的主要的田野考古发掘集中于上半叶，之后的数十年中并未取得更多进展，直至近年才重启田野考古发掘。这一工作主要由伊朗考古学家进行，亦有若干国际合作，如伊朗—英国对戈尔甘城的发掘、伊朗—波兰对帕萨尔加德附近坦格·博拉吉的萨珊乡村遗址的发掘等。

囿于信息传播以及物质、语言的可及性，大部分伊朗学者的重大发现仅面向伊朗伊斯兰共和国境内及伊朗读者。这些成果主要通过布沙拉和《伊朗研究》期刊在国际上进行微乎其微的推广，而无法为学界充分利用。

正因如此，尽管哈珀已于1997年伦敦举办的会议中发表有关萨珊时期的演讲，演讲内容于2006年出版，我在受拉蒂菲与伊赫桑·亚尔夏特讲座科学委员会邀请参加此次会议时，仍不怯于借此盛会贡献微薄之力。

与美国学者不同，他们的科学研究大多着眼于萨珊艺术，并取得了若干重要成果，而我除了一组在印度次大陆西北部发现的印章外，从未直接研究过萨珊时期的艺术品，亦未主持过萨珊遗址的田野工作。但在从事前伊斯兰时期的伊朗考古研究时，不可避免地对萨珊时期格外关注（可参见我前后发表的关于萨珊考古关键主题的若干文章）。我在博洛尼亚大学开设的部分课程正是关于萨珊时期的。没有什么，比向具有批判精神的年轻人传授我对其他学者成果的思考，更能启迪智慧的了，他们对参考书目中的矛盾与论证不充分之处总是一丝不苟。从事教学的同僚对此应有同感。

故就萨珊时期而言，我所处的"局外"立场有利于我采取批判性方法展开研究。那些期冀从我的演讲中获取新信息、新发现或个人发现的，只会感到失望。相反，他们会看到呈批判性的整体见解（我充分意识到了自身局限性，却也不愿错过为辩论作出贡献的机会）。另一方面，该主题适合以系列讲座的形式组织内容。我力求相对浅显易懂，但材料的复杂性常使我背离初衷：受限于法语水平，我不得不照读优美的译文，并尽可能减少即兴发挥。

讲座内容基于我在伊朗的实地工作以及对波斯语文献的了解。希望这五次讲座不仅能从统一角度为论点提供框架，也能展示伊朗同仁在过去10年中的考古发现。在伊朗的工作中，我结识了以非凡热忱致力于这一广袤国家各个地区萨珊考古工作的志士。

我将在随后的章节中不止一次地回顾萨珊与安息王朝之间物质文化延续性的重要性。

不同于阿尔达希尔一世及其谋臣在政治宣传中表明的意识形态，萨珊波斯的艺术实际上建立于对安息王朝艺术品与手工艺品的延续上，而中断更多体现在作为君王象征的若干王朝图像的选择中，如钱币和摩崖浮雕。因哈珀的第一次演讲题目即为"延续性"，故这种观点并不新鲜，但我认为仍需重新说明这一点。

古典时期与中世纪之交见证了罗马政治和宗教的明显断代，而在萨珊帝国漫长的历史进程中，这一转折期亦体现在与委托制作的社会息息相关的艺术品与手工艺品中。此后，萨珊波斯晚期的艺术和建筑进入新的阶段，迎来伊斯兰中世纪的繁盛，再次呈现出独立于政权和意识形态的文化连续性。

因此，这五次讲座将借由伊朗近年来出版的新发现，在对已知建筑与艺术材料有总体新认识的基础之上，考察萨珊波斯建筑文化与形象艺术问题。目的并非详尽无遗地展示材料，而是更好地理解建筑空间的使用、表达与视觉交流的形式以及生产技术机制。我选取了五个需从根本上重新思考的主题。其中两个与建筑相关，尽管胡夫已在此领域做了基础性研究，但在我所期望贡献之处远没有达到普遍一致。一个是与建筑联系紧密的艺术品,即灰泥装饰。其余两个分别为摩崖浮雕和印章生产的技术—风格问题的深化研究上,因迄今为止的研究多从图像学角度切入。

首先,我要感谢向"大伊朗与印度次大陆"合作研究单位提出组织两年一度会议的伊赫桑·亚尔夏特,亦要感谢会议组织委员会给我难得的机遇。

其次,我要感谢"伊朗与印度次大陆"合作研究单位及其主管教授萨姆韦良对这次会议的成功组织与管理。感谢伊朗研究发展协会《伊朗研究手册》的主管吉钮先生和吉塞莲女士对本书出版的帮助。

感谢以不同方式促使我精进学识、提升能力的同侪,尤其是与我共享工作成果的伊朗学者。特别感谢在亚尔夏特会议科学委员会中展现协调才能的吉塞莲女士。她孜孜不倦地研究萨珊时期的印章与钱币,倘若没有她,关于印章与钱币的完整分类就不会为人熟知。她亦负责了本书细致的编辑工作。

在准备演讲的过程中,我有机会与一些同僚讨论我的观点。尤其是布沙拉,他仔细阅读了宗教建筑部分,提出了宝贵的建议,还校阅了法语文本。感谢西尼西和菲利真齐在最终定稿前修正文本。同样要感谢阿马多里、查韦尔迪、卡内帕、弗兰克、加尼马提、贡代、吉塞莲、凯姆、塔巴索、洛穆齐奥、拉赫巴尔、雷兹瓦尼、索埃。还应感谢参与讨论的广大巴黎听众。

感谢我在拉文纳课堂上的所有学生,他们的批判性观点常启发我做出新的阐释。

感谢巴塞洛、梅乌奇和亚兹丹尼为我提供了部分独家照片,也感谢所有允许我引用照片和平面图的作者和编辑。

尤其要感谢朱埃尔,他在从意大利语译成法语的艰巨任务中付出了大量心血与时间,以求忠实地还原我的想法。

最后要感谢恩里卡、米凯莱和伊雷妮,在过去两年中,他们耐心地陪伴在一个经常缺席、神游于泰西封和菲鲁扎巴德之间的丈夫(父亲)身边。

文本中对不同术语和语言采用了不同的转录方式。现代伊朗地名除标明元音长度外,均按照拉扎尔的标准。其他现代波斯语手写体亦遵循了同样的规则,标明了元音长度。中古波斯语则采用麦肯齐的转录系统[1]。国王与历史人物的名字采用了不同于中古波斯语的简化版本。

---

[1] Mackenzie, *A Concise Pahlavi Dictionary*, London, 1971.

中文版前言

编写《伊朗萨珊时期的建筑与艺术》中文版的想法始于2013年。其时，笔者受北京大学考古文博学院的邀请，开设了一门介绍从阿契美尼德至萨珊时期的伊朗考古入门课程。

鉴于萨珊时期（224—651年）中国与伊朗间密切的文化联系，该课程聚焦于这一时期的考古学。2014年，笔者有幸受邀在巴黎法兰西学院参加著名的"伊赫桑与拉蒂菲·亚尔夏特伊朗研究会议"，由伊赫桑·亚尔夏特教授赞助，"大伊朗与印度次大陆"合作研究单位主办。笔者决定借此良机，在诸多关于萨珊考古的开放性问题中选取五个作深入报告，即宫殿建筑、宗教建筑、灰泥装饰、摩崖浮雕及印章。其中，宫殿建筑、宗教建筑与摩崖浮雕在北京开设的课程中亦有涉及。关于这五个主题，笔者力求对现有研究与观点进行批判性评述，提取关键问题，并适时提出自己的阐释，以求触及问题的本质，而非泛泛描述。魏正中教授提议，亚尔夏特五次报告的文本若能译成中文出版，将对中国学者拓宽关于萨珊时期的伊朗的知识面大有裨益。

然而，要想掌握这五次报告的内容，需了解萨珊建筑与艺术的基础知识。故笔者基于在博洛尼亚大学的长期教学实践，为本书撰写了第一部分的导论。导论不仅涵盖五次报告的主题，亦包括相关研究屈指可数的其余伊朗萨珊时期的考古资料，为读者充分理解五次报告中提出的问题提供认知工具。导论亦包含主要的参考文献，以便读者深入研究，而正文中则列有更具体的索引。

特别感谢魏正中教授，他既是项目的发起人，也是法译中、英译中工作的指导者。没有他的付出与贡献，就不会有中译本的问世。还应感谢自愿承担重任的译者吴筱女士。承蒙《伊朗研究手册》编委会、伊朗研究发展协会主席丽卡·吉塞莲博士同意将法译本译成中文，谨致谢忱。

目 录

原书前言 ·· i
中文版前言 ·· i

上篇　导　论

序 ·· 3
领土：水利工程、防御工事 ·· 6
城市规划 ·· 9
宫殿建筑 ·· 13
民居建筑 ·· 28
宗教建筑 ·· 28
丧葬建筑 ·· 35
绘　画 ·· 39
灰泥装饰 ·· 40
马赛克 ·· 44
雕塑与摩崖浮雕 ·· 46
金属器 ·· 60
玻璃器 ·· 62
陶　器 ·· 62
纺织品 ·· 62
印　章 ·· 63
钱　币 ·· 65

下篇　专题

第一章　宫殿及贵族府邸 69
　　前　言 69
　　建筑单元 99
　　建筑类型 101
　　结　论 106

第二章　萨珊时期的火神庙 107

第三章　从新发现看灰泥工艺 136

第四章　萨珊时期的摩崖浮雕：艺术中心 161

第五章　萨珊时期的印章风格与技术：生产中心 202

附录1　萨珊世系 222
附录2　人名对照表 223
附录3　地名对照表 225
附录4　术语词汇 228

插图索引 231
参考文献 239
英文摘要 270
译后记 299

上篇 导论

序

自马其顿、塞琉古及安息帝国后，伊朗于萨珊时期（224—651年）再次被来自法尔斯地区，即阿契美尼德帝国（前550—前330年）发源地的王朝统治（图1—3）。

萨珊开国君主阿尔达希尔一世的登基之路，似在其建筑中得到了反映。他任法尔斯总督时在卡拉·杜赫塔尔所建的宫殿前卫而不甚稳定，即位后在菲鲁扎巴德附近所建的宫殿则形状规则、更为坚固；早期的阿尔达希尔—花拉为独特而有标志性的辐射型同心圆城市，而韦—阿尔达希尔亦为圆形平面，但布局更合理，内部为正交街道系统。萨珊王朝在鼎盛时期大兴土木，如公元3、4世纪沙普尔一世与沙普尔二世营建的宫殿与城市（比沙普尔、容迪·沙普尔），以及公元6、7世纪库思老一世、库思老二世开展的建造活动。5世纪至6世纪初，波斯人臣服于一支定居在巴克特里亚的中亚伊朗游牧民族，即在拜占庭文献中被称为"白匈奴"的嚈哒人，学界对这一漫长的危机时期知之甚少。

尽管与王朝发源地，即沿袭了阿契美尼德辉煌的伊朗传统的法尔斯地区联系紧密，萨珊亦将首都泰西封所在的美索不达米亚地区，以及控制东部边疆、屡受游牧民族侵犯的梅尔夫要塞视作核心领土。

萨珊王朝垄断了当时唯一广为流传的雕塑形式——摩崖浮雕，现仅有初期及末期遗存。摩崖浮雕影响了最成功的手工艺品，即人像及动物像银器，无论是产自"都城"作坊还是"外省"作坊，其主题多为皇家狩猎与国王坐朝。尽管数量有限，在当今伊朗（哈吉阿巴德、查拉·塔尔汉、雷伊、达姆甘）与美索不达米亚（泰西封、启什）的宫殿与贵族宅邸中，均发现了丰富的灰泥墙饰与壁画遗存。唯一一例马赛克发现于法尔斯的比沙普尔，与沙普尔一世驱逐的叙利亚安条克工匠有关。因艺术遗存稀少，有观点认为萨珊时期的伊朗缺乏图像艺术，或由王室及"国教"琐罗亚斯德教神职人员的直接控制所导致。然而近年来发现的遗迹似乎表明，所谓匮乏更多是出于考古资料的不足。在主要的私人艺术形式——印章中出现的大量图像亦可证实这一点。

伊朗萨珊时期的建筑与艺术

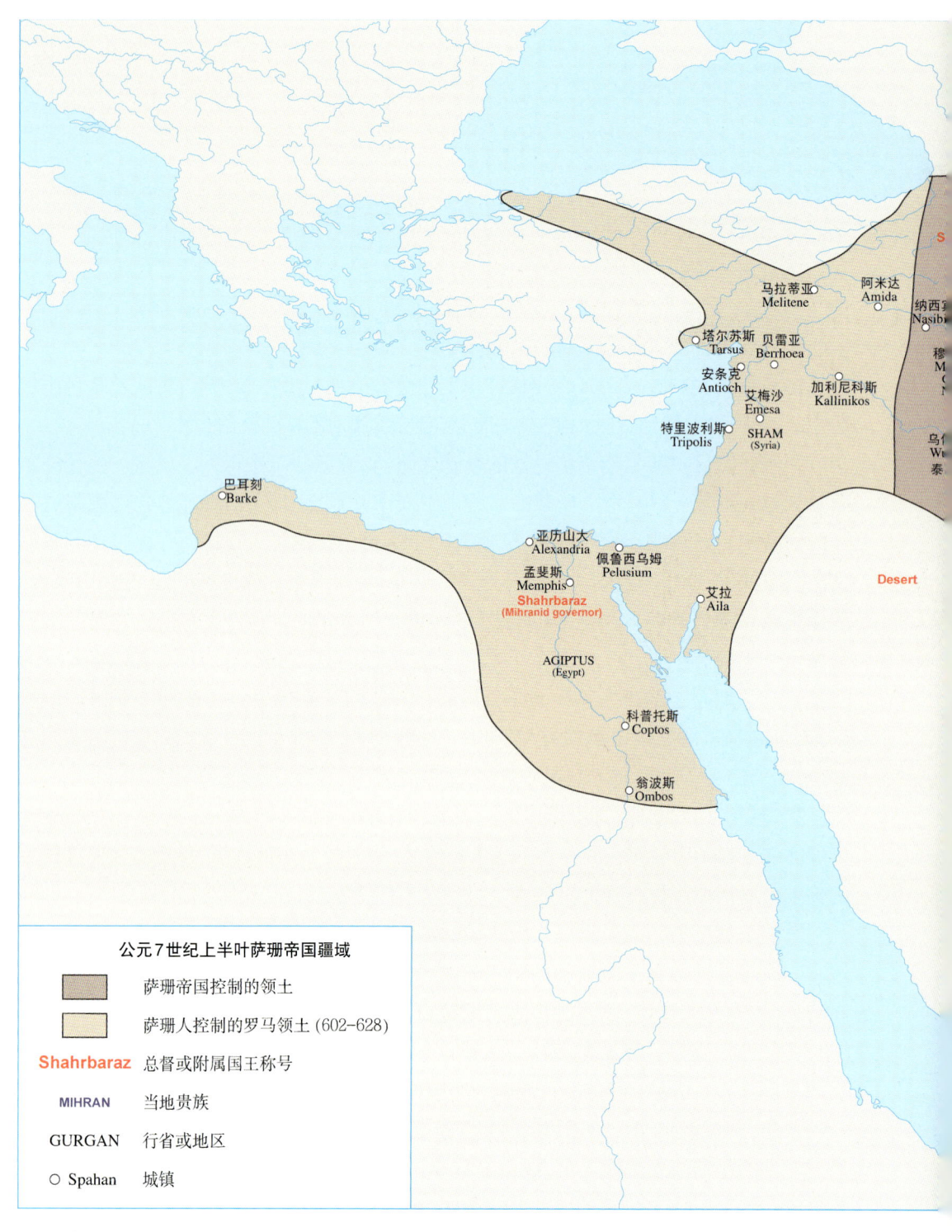

图1　库思老二世时期的萨珊帝国疆域图（图片来源于网络）

上篇 导论

伊朗萨珊时期的建筑与艺术

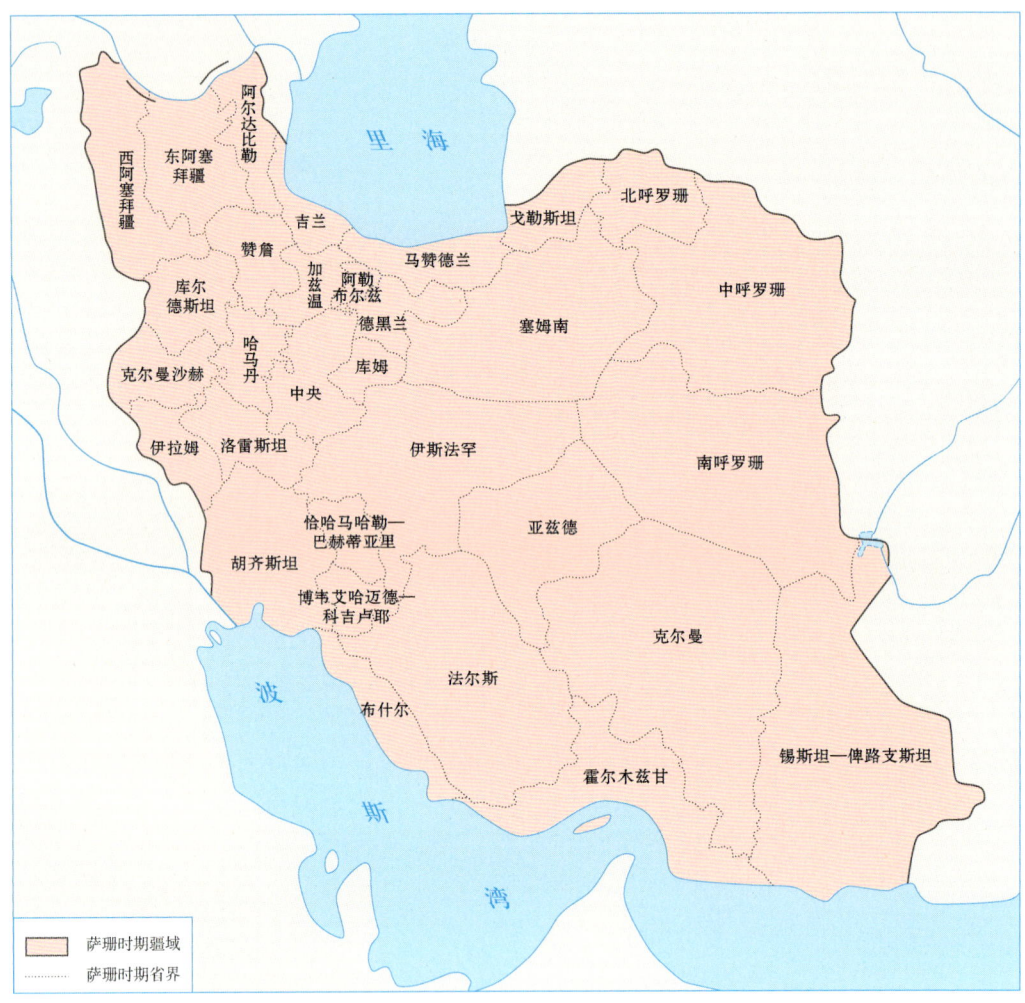

图2 伊朗萨珊时期的行政分布图（A. Eghra绘图）

领土：水利工程、防御工事

在伊朗部分地区开展的为数不多的实地调查表明，萨珊时期的聚落数量的增加得益于王朝发展经济的政策。

灌溉对于伊朗高原这类干旱地带至关重要。其时，窄长的传统地下水渠（坎儿井，图4）以及地面的小型水源均投入使用。在广袤丰饶的美索不达米亚平原，则可利用大江大河进行精耕细作，其灌溉工程的性质大不相同。以胡齐斯坦为例，由水坝、运河及堰组成的大型水利工程，或由被沙普尔一世驱逐的罗马技工参与修建。该地区最重要的实例是被称作班迪凯撒（意为"凯撒的水坝"）的舒什塔尔水坝桥（图5）。

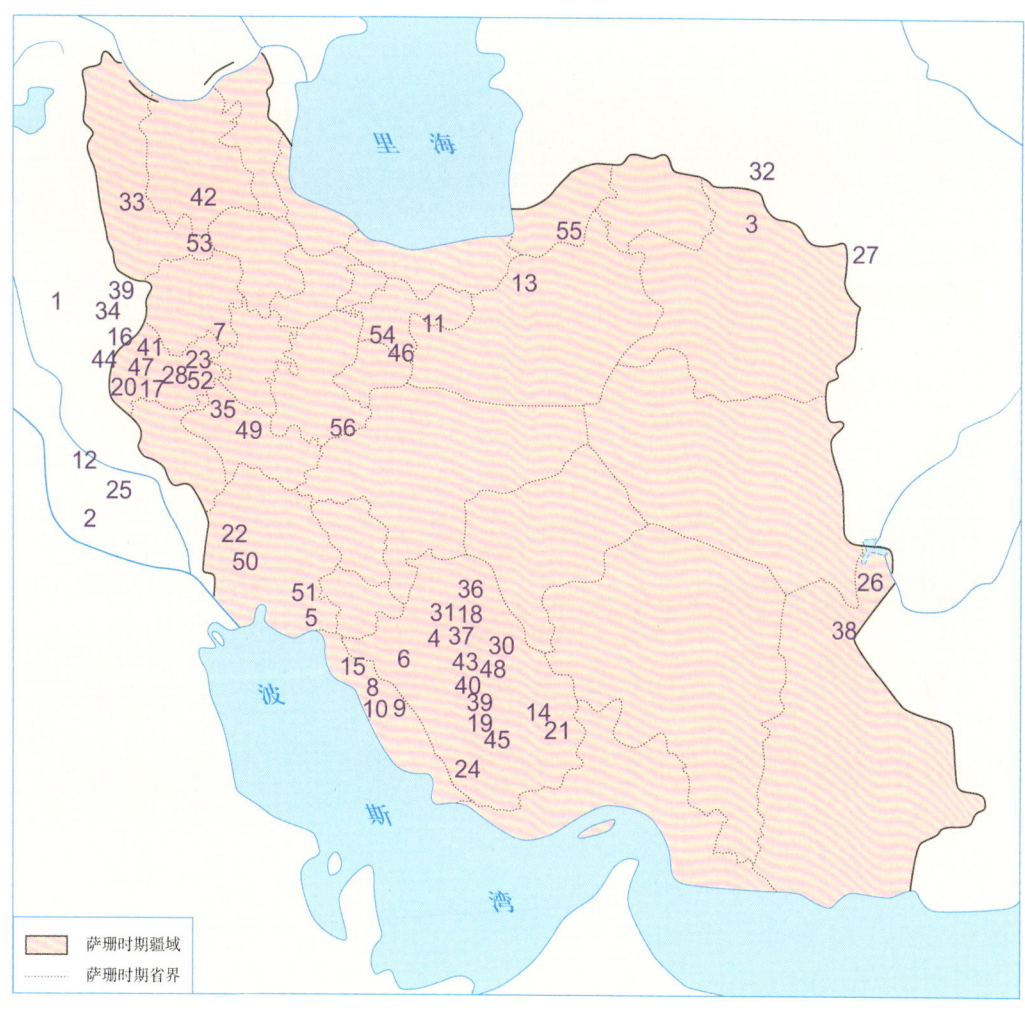

图3 萨珊时期伊朗主要遗址分布图（A. Eghra 绘图）

1. 亚述
2. 巴比伦
3. 班迪扬
4. 贝萨
5. 贝赫贝汗
6. 比沙普尔
7. 比索通
8. 博拉兹詹
9. 博兹帕尔
10. 布什尔
11. 查拉·塔尔汉—埃什加巴德
12. 泰西封
13. 达姆甘
14. 达拉卜·盖尔达
15. 德赫卡伊德
16. 伊马拉特·库思老
17. 西伊斯兰阿巴德
18. 伊斯塔尔
19. 菲鲁扎巴德
20. 西吉兰
21. 哈吉阿巴德
22. 卡尔萨伊万
23. 坎加瓦尔
24. 萨夫耶
25. 启什（美索不达米亚）
26. 库赫·哈加
27. 米勒·哈拉姆
28. 麦尔·麦拉吉
29. 米尔盖里
30. 纳赫拉克
31. 纳克什·鲁斯塔姆
32. 尼萨
33. 奥鲁米耶
34. 派库里
35. 帕朗盖尔德
36. 帕萨尔加德
37. 波斯波利斯
38. 卡拉·瑙
39. 卡拉·杜赫塔尔
40. 卡拉·沙内辛
41. 卡拉·亚兹德格德
42. 卡拉·扎哈克
43. 喀斯尔·阿卜纳斯尔
44. 喀斯尔·席林
45. 吉尔·卡尔珊
46. 拉伊—瓦拉明
47. 萨尔·波勒·扎哈卜
48. 萨尔韦斯坦
49. 希扬
50. 苏萨
51. 坦格·萨尔瓦克
52. 塔克·格拉
53. 塔克斯特·苏莱曼
54. 泰佩·米勒
55. 托尔让塔卜
56. 维什纳维

伊朗萨珊时期的建筑与艺术

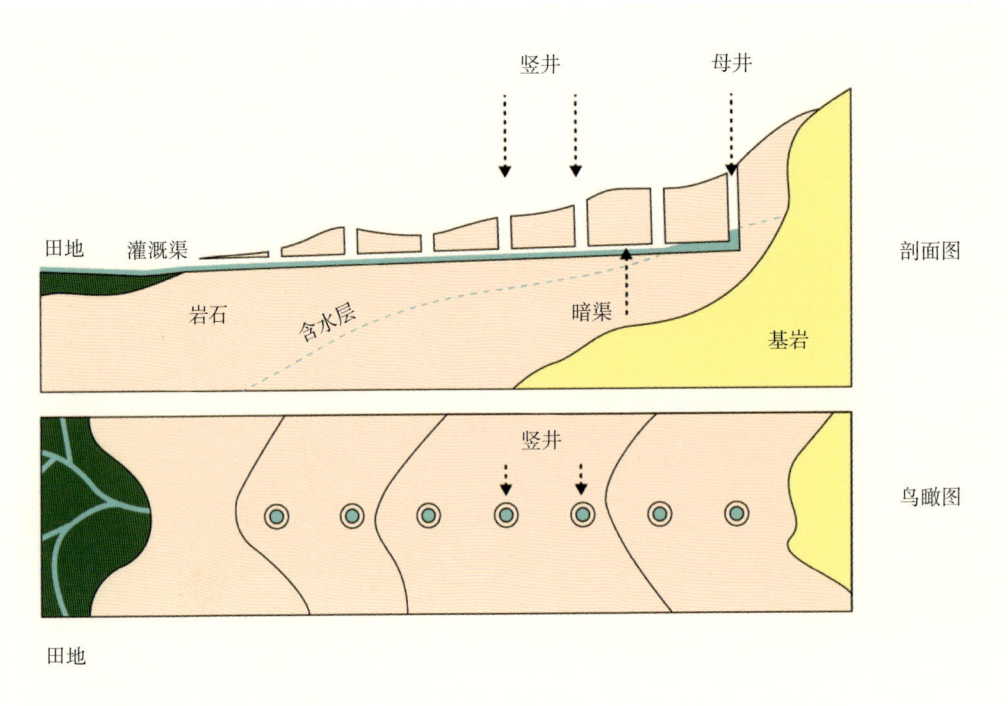

图4 坎儿井功能示意图（感谢俄克拉何马州立大学的Dale Lightfoot教授提供）

图5 舒什塔尔水坝桥（A. Eghra供图）

8

图6 德尔本特：城市防御工事南部（感谢UNESCO提供）

在筑防方面，除以圆形马面为特点的城墙外，亦在东部（锡斯坦边墙）、西部，尤其是北部边界建立了大型防御工事。里海以西为德尔本特城墙（位于今俄罗斯联邦达吉斯坦共和国），从海滨的同名港口要塞城市（图6）向内延伸了40千米。东北方则为"亚历山大城墙"，长达180千米。伊朗与苏格兰的联合研究表明，里海城墙水下部分的年代可追溯至6、7世纪。"塔米沙城墙"亦位于该地区。

城市规划

萨珊早期（3—4世纪）大举兴建城市，以阿尔达希尔一世、沙普尔一世及沙普尔二世最为典型。

阿尔达希尔一世在法尔斯的阿尔达希尔—花拉（意为"阿尔达希尔的荣耀"，后称古尔或菲鲁扎巴德）建立了标志性的放射型同心圆城市（图7、8）。城市直径2千米，被两条主轴线和八条次轴线分为二十个扇形区域，又被三个同心圆分为四环，最中心为官署，其中蒂尔巴尔塔和塔克斯特·内辛尤为重要（图9）。据称该城市受帕提亚的达拉

9

图7　菲鲁扎巴德：阿尔达希尔—花拉圆形城市鸟瞰图（A. Eghra 供图）

卜·盖尔达影响（图10），但后者最初为三角形平面，至萨珊末期才变为圆形，因此阿尔达希尔—花拉的创新平面或源自与太阳相关的理念。在菲鲁扎巴德（阿尔达希尔—花拉）被联合国教科文组织列入世界遗产名录后，伊朗与意大利的新联合项目开展了地球物理勘探，并详细记录了中世纪伊斯兰时期的地面遗存。

被称为"阿尔达希尔之最"的韦—阿尔达希尔位于帕提亚泰西封（今伊拉克中部），亦为圆形平面，内部为正交街道系统，城市规划更为合理。

阿尔达希尔的继任者则采用希腊化—罗马传统的棋盘式道路系统，或与被罗马帝国俘虏的工匠有关。

在法尔斯，沙普尔一世建立了带有围墙的不规则长方形城市比沙普尔（图11）。城市防御工事由石头筑成，有半圆形马面；南—北轴线与东—西轴线相交的城中心处，有一个受罗马传统影响的纪念堂，包含两根科林斯式立柱（其一刻有中古波斯语铭文），柱前为国王雕像的基座（图12、13）。在胡齐斯坦，沙普尔一世兴建了平面相似的城市贡德·沙布尔。在拜占庭帝国的异教徒学院停办后，继承了亚里士多德传统的哲学院避难于此，该城市因此而闻名。亦是在胡齐斯坦，沙普尔二世建立了被横向城墙分为三个区域的窄长方形城市伊万·卡尔卡（图14）。

上篇　导论

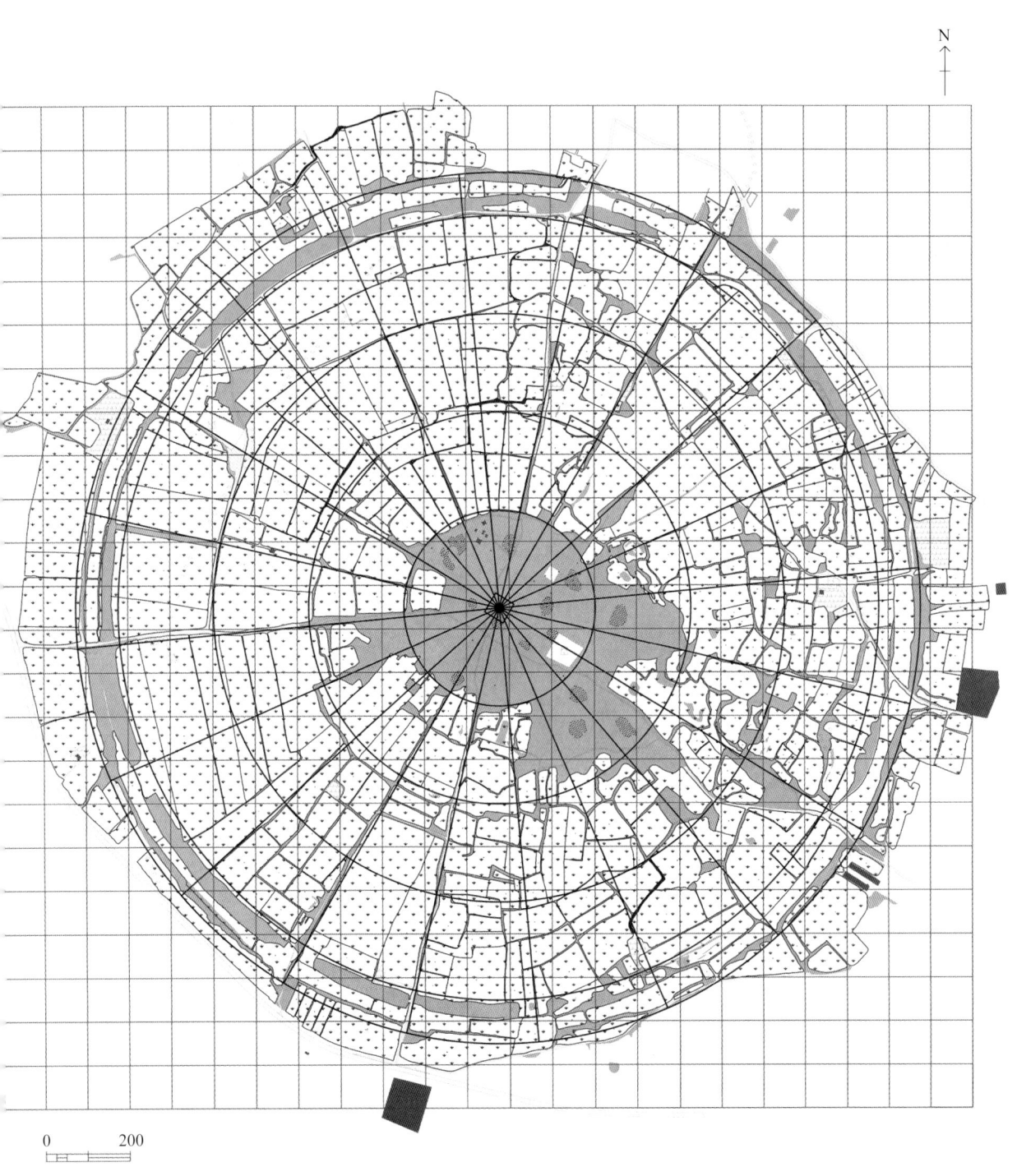

图8　菲鲁扎巴德：阿尔达希尔—花拉圆形城市平面图（A. Eghra绘图）

图9 菲鲁扎巴德:阿尔达希尔—花拉中塔克斯特·内辛(前景)及蒂尔巴尔塔鸟瞰图(A. Eghra供图)

图10 达拉卜·盖尔达平面图(A. Eghra绘图)

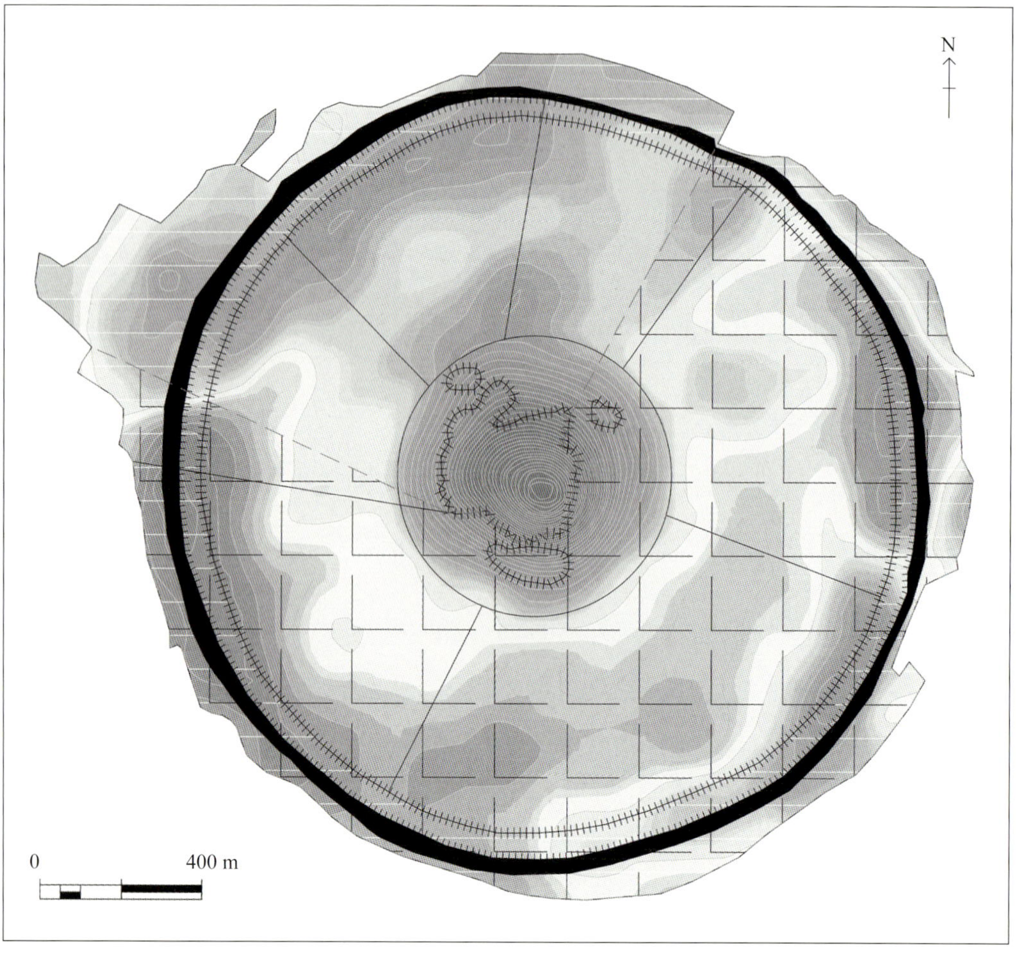

上篇　导论

图11　比沙普尔城及其周边鸟瞰图（SALF供图）

上述建于公元3、4世纪的城市直至萨珊末期及其后的伊斯兰时期仍在使用，至少延续至12、13世纪。其中最古老的城市为伊斯塔尔（图15、16），位于波斯波利斯以北5千米，或由安息时期的法尔斯地方王朝所建。该城市亦以其上层的中世纪遗迹著称。

除上述古城外，历任萨珊国王均进行新建或重建，如6、7世纪的黏土封泥上行政戳印中的诸多地名所示。

宫殿建筑

探讨萨珊时期建筑的难题在于确定目前已知建筑群的功能。萨珊时期宗教建筑的研究十分棘手，因表明功能的元素较少。此外，尽管著述众多，抛开经文、即并不符合社会经济现实的神职人员的表述，琐罗亚斯德教在萨珊社会中的实际意义仍令人费解。德国考古研究所的建筑学家胡夫试图提取区分伊朗萨珊时期的宫殿与宗教建筑的整体特征，寻求可应用于所有遗迹的统一标准，而避免对单个建筑群的孤立解读。

13

图12 比沙普尔城平面图（SALF绘图）

图13　比沙普尔中心纪念堂（@ Callieri）

图14　伊万·卡尔卡老城（感谢ITTO提供）

伊朗萨珊时期的建筑与艺术

图15 伊斯塔尔城鸟瞰图（A. Eghra 供图）

图16 伊斯塔尔城平面图（A. Eghra 绘图）

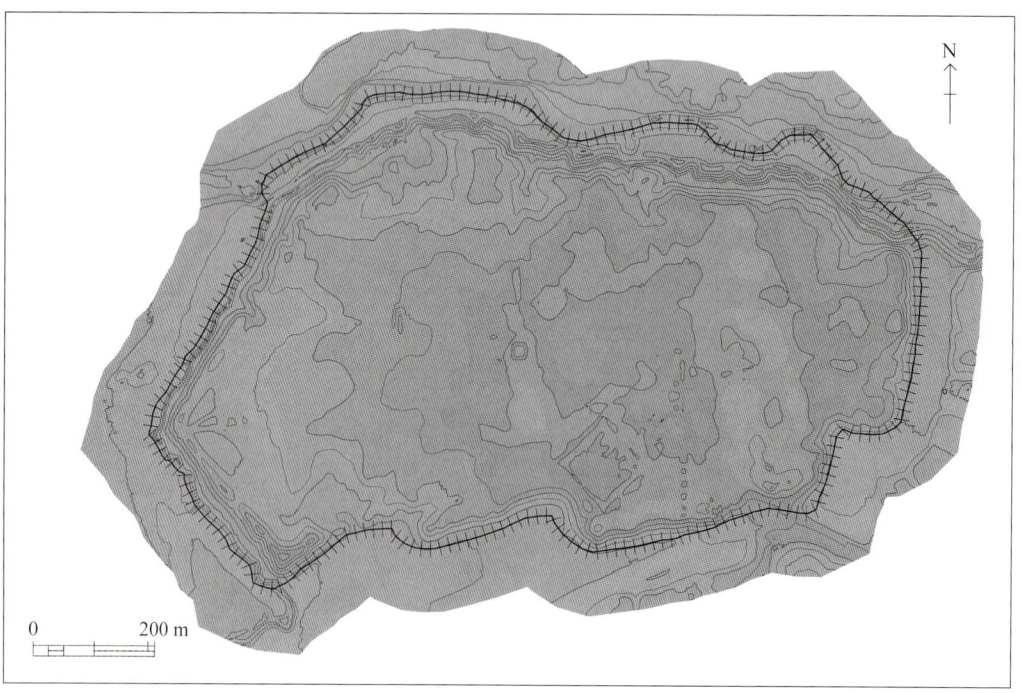

胡夫强调，部分建筑平面表现为房间沿单一轴线分布，与其他无突出轴线的复杂建筑平面形成对比。他又指出多层建筑与单层建筑的差异。质言之，平面简单的建筑为多层立面，而平面复杂的建筑为单层立面。依据可由文献确定功能的重要建筑群特征，胡夫提出，因承担琐罗亚斯德教祭司所需的众多功能，宗教建筑平面较为复杂，而宫殿建筑平面则沿单一轴线分布。

本书第二部分第一章《宫殿及贵族府邸》意在对胡夫所研究的及其后发现的考古资料作批判性回顾。

阿尔达希尔一世在法尔斯的卡拉·杜赫塔尔建立了第一所宫殿（图17），位于离菲鲁扎巴德平原不远处的山嘴之上，其时他仍对安息人称臣。宫殿沿单轴线分布，沿倾斜山嘴分为三层（图18）：下层前院（A）；中层庭院，内含高台与两侧各一列房间（B）；上层国王专属区域（C），内含一个长伊万（20），伊万后为正方形突角拱穹隆顶房间（23），周接圆墙。由正方形房间外的螺旋楼梯（53）可到达穹隆顶两侧的房间，即建筑上层。圆墙与正方形房间之间为更小的房间（24、25）。建筑设计前卫，开口相较墙体厚度过大，导致结构断裂，不得不将大部分小侧间填充，作为支撑穹隆顶的扶壁。伊万壁龛上饰有灰泥假额枋，上有埃及凹弧饰。该母题亦出现在大流士一世的波斯波利斯宫殿中。

图17　菲鲁扎巴德：卡拉·杜赫塔尔堡鸟瞰图（A. Eghra供图）

伊朗萨珊时期的建筑与艺术

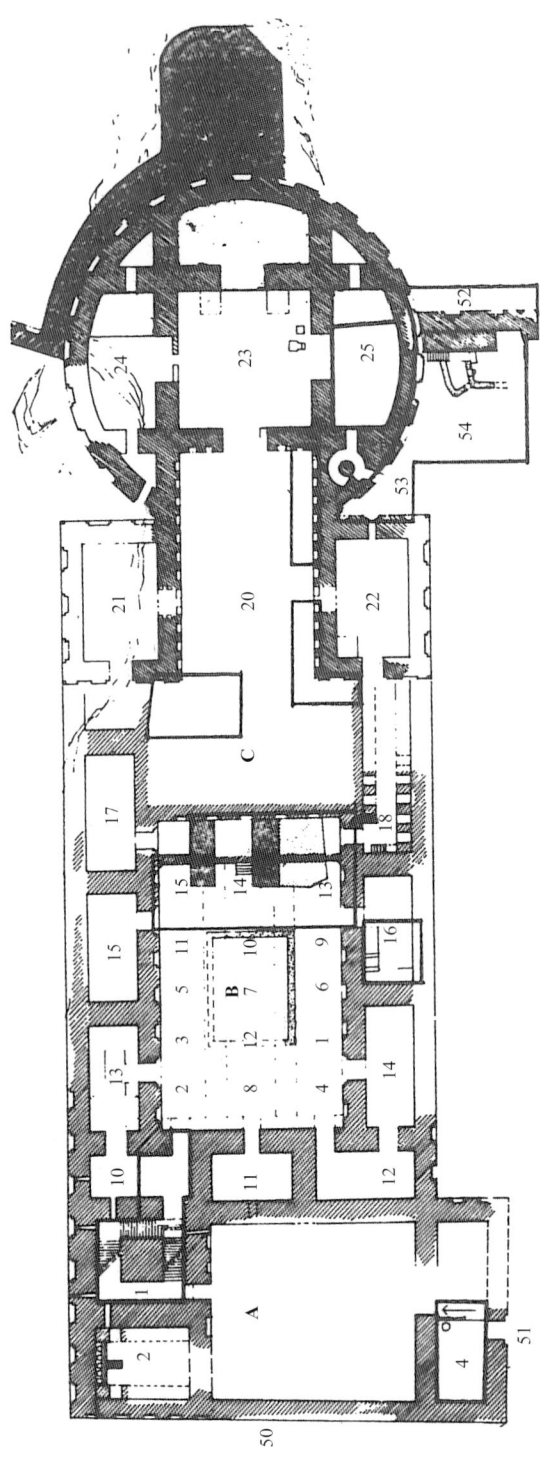

图18 菲鲁扎巴德：卡拉·杜赫塔尔堡平面图（A. Eghra 在 D. Huff 的基础上绘制，感谢德黑兰德国考古研究院提供）

阿尔达希尔一世在菲鲁扎巴德平原新建的宫殿则解决了上述技术问题（图19），墙体更厚，门更窄，穹隆顶加高，呈抛物线型。四个横向伊万朝前侧伊万敞开，前为正方形庭院，俯瞰小型圆形湖泊，湖水引自四季不断的泉水，以料石砌筑边缘。主伊万正壁上的门通往中央正方形穹隆顶大殿，两侧房间相似（图20）。通过突角拱实现从正方形房间到圆形穹隆顶的过渡，为萨珊原创，不同于罗马及随后的拜占庭穹隅。国王可在离地面5米高处的展望台上，从大殿望向伊万。三个穹隆顶大殿之后为一个大庭院，周绕房间，互不相连。该区域通常被定为私人区，但胡夫将其定为非正式办公区，而私人区应是位于穹隆顶之间空隙处的二、三层的小房间（图21）。穹隆顶大殿的壁龛上为埃及凹弧饰灰泥假额枋（图22），已出现在卡拉·杜赫塔尔宫殿中，体现出阿契美尼德艺术的影响。

比沙普尔宫殿位于山丘上（卡拉·杜赫塔尔）（图23），而非其下方原假设为宫殿、今确定为神庙的遗址。尚未被发掘的巨大建筑群由房间组成，铺地或与神庙一样为马赛克。该宫殿十分宜居，与世隔绝，俯瞰城市，沿袭阿尔达希尔一世的做法，亦与希腊化—罗马的宫殿传统相同。

萨珊晚期的宫殿实例之一为位于今伊拉克泰西封的塔克·基斯拉（图24、25），由库思老一世所建，上层与菲

图19 菲鲁扎巴德：阿尔达希尔一世宫殿鸟瞰图（A. Eghra供图）

图20 菲鲁扎巴德：阿尔达希尔一世宫殿中央正方形大殿（@ Callieri）

伊朗萨珊时期的建筑与艺术

图21 菲鲁扎巴德：阿尔达希尔一世宫殿上层，穹隆顶之间空隙处的房间（@ Callieri）

图22 菲鲁扎巴德：阿尔达希尔一世宫殿，阿契美尼德灰泥假额枋，上有埃及凹弧饰（@ Callieri）

上篇　导论

图23　比沙普尔：卡拉·杜赫塔尔（@Callieri）

图24　塔克·基斯拉（感谢UNESCO提供）

鲁扎巴德宫殿相似。伊万中有现存最大的无支架倾斜式抛物线拱，宽25.6米；立面有仅用于装饰的假半柱和圆拱。这一时期，穹隆顶大殿消失，其功能似被伊万取代。

阿塞拜疆的塔克斯特·苏莱曼神庙中有一座萨珊晚期的宫殿（西建筑群），或为国王朝圣所建（图25、26）。位于库尔德斯坦、喀斯尔·席林的伊马拉特·库思老通常被

21

图 25 塔克斯特·苏莱曼西伊万(@ Callieri)

图 26 塔克斯特·苏莱曼西伊万平面图(A. Eghra 在 W. Kleiss 的基础上绘制,感谢德黑兰德国考古研究院提供)

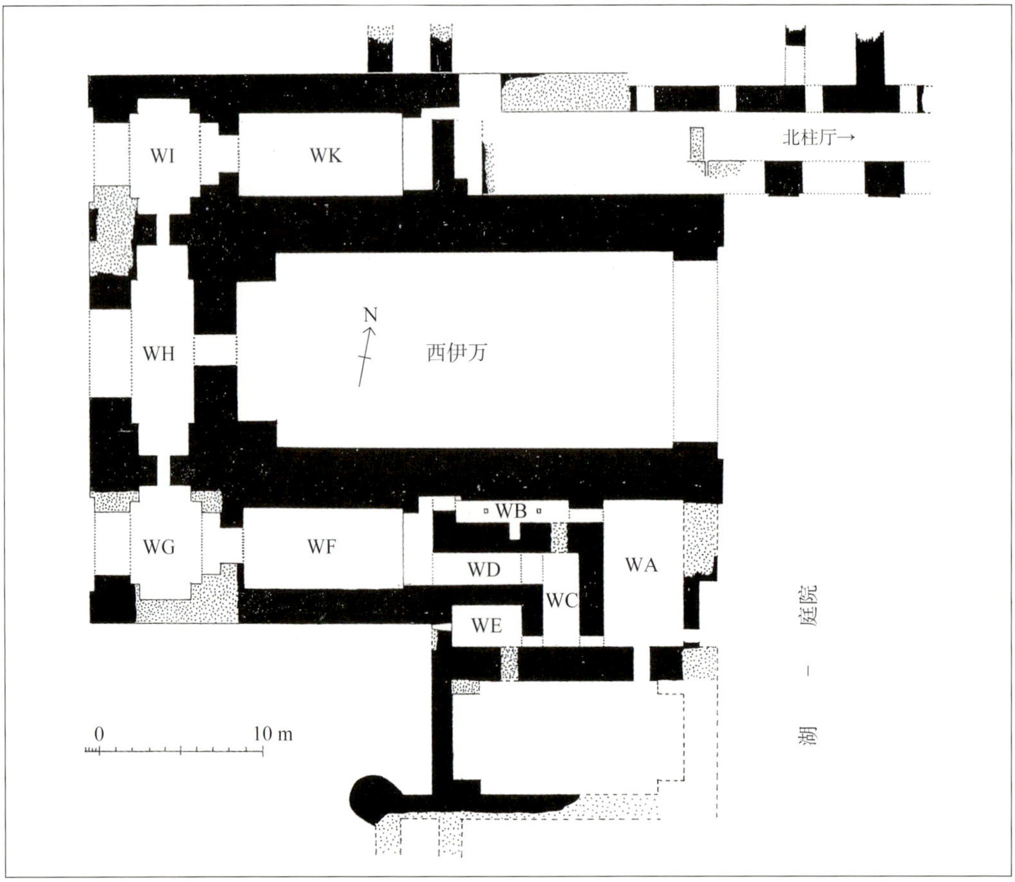

图27 萨尔韦斯坦鸟瞰图（A. Eghra 供图）

视作库思老二世的宫殿。位于法尔斯的萨尔韦斯坦似建于萨珊之后（图27、28），拱顶形状可追溯至伊斯兰时期（图29），而平面布局与萨珊时期的建筑没有可比性，或为伊斯兰神庙。

在伊朗北部达姆甘、查拉塔尔汉、雷伊，以及美索不达米亚的启什、达斯特盖尔德与泰西封，均发现被称作宫殿的建筑群，但具体功能难以确定。其共同之处为繁复的灰泥墙饰，集中分布于多柱大殿与伊万中。据克勒格尔关于萨珊建筑灰泥装饰位置的观点，多柱大殿与伊万可能用于举办琐罗亚斯德教宴饮。功能阐释的问题在于，上述均建于5世纪后的建筑结构，究竟是世俗建筑群中的神殿，还是整座建筑群都具有宗教功能？

20世纪70年代末，发现于哈吉阿巴德（法尔斯东部）的一座建筑群被定为庄园（图30）。建筑群分为居住区、接见区及礼拜区。礼拜区为十字形平面，与查哈尔·塔克相似，故宗教功能确凿。前两区的性质并不明确，但上述推测可作为参考。

位于库尔德斯坦的塔克·波斯坦大伊万（参见《雕塑与摩崖浮雕》一节）为复原宫殿建筑外观的重要依据（图31）。大伊万为石质仿凉亭建筑，其立面建筑框架采用了地面建筑中的元素，如阶梯金字塔顶饰，源自波斯波利斯，而出现在伊朗萨珊时期的塔克·格拉石质纪念碑中（库尔德斯坦，图32、33）。同样，伊万墙上的两幅大型猎鹿、猎野猪图亦表明，地面伊万中有丰富的绘画或灰泥装饰。

伊朗萨珊时期的建筑与艺术

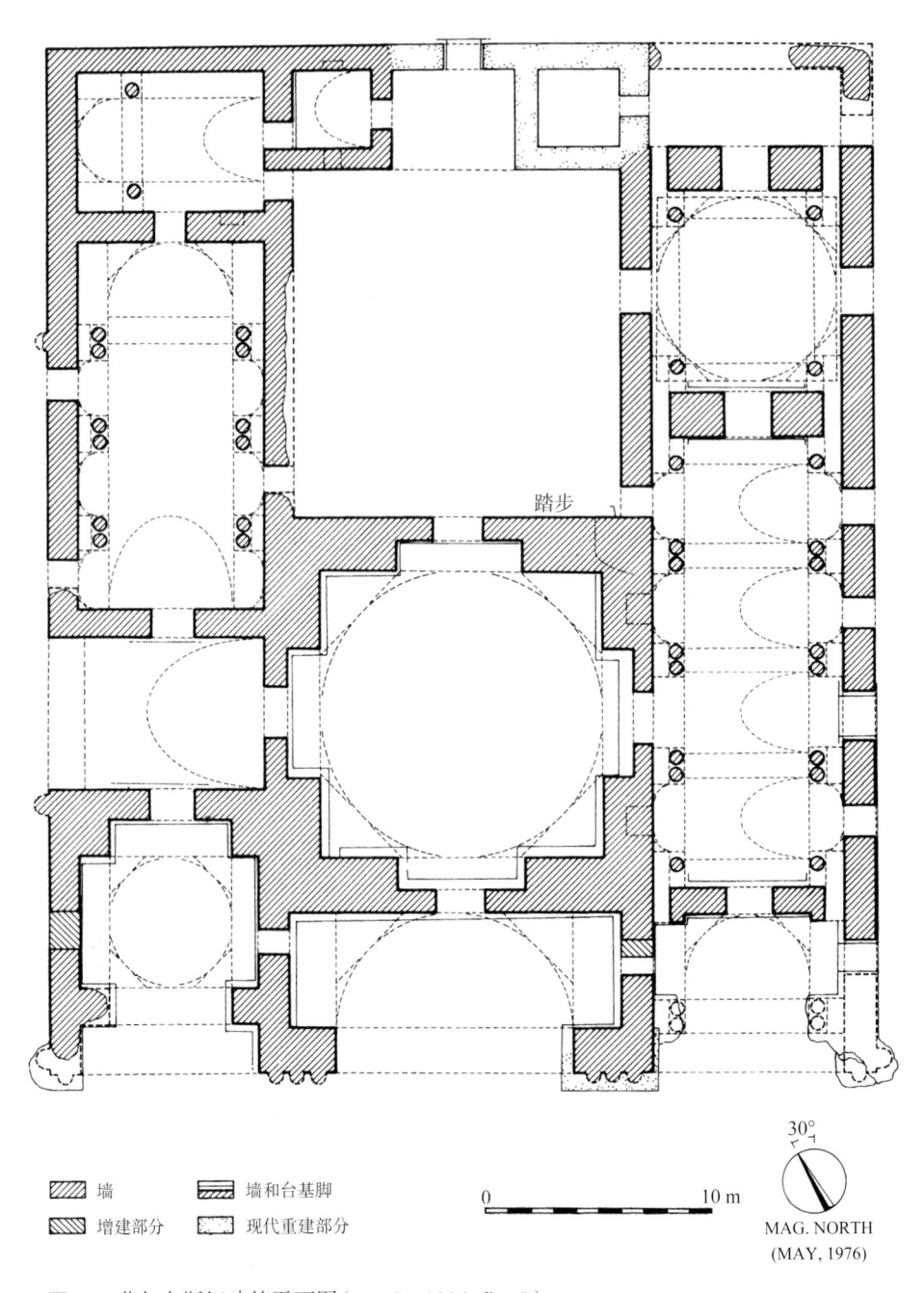

图28 萨尔韦斯坦建筑平面图（L. Bier 1986: fig. 5）

图29 萨尔韦斯坦10号房间方柱所支撑的穹隆顶（@ Callieri）

图30　哈吉阿巴德：L.178庭院（Azarnoush 1994, fig. 1）

图31　塔克·波斯坦大伊万（A. Eghra供图）

图32 塔克·格拉（A. Eghra 供图）

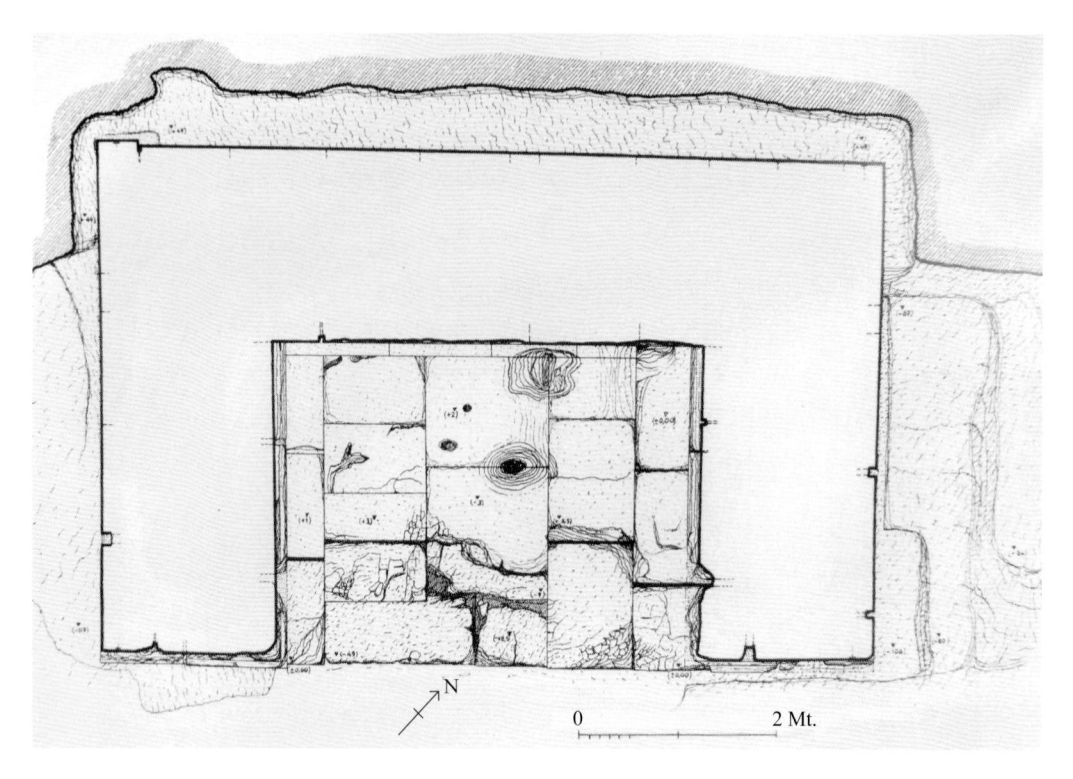

图33 塔克·格拉：平面图（G. Tilia绘图）

民居建筑

学界对伊朗萨珊时期的私人住宅所知甚少，城市内的发掘活动多在美索不达米亚及中亚开展，而伊朗高原的少量资料显示，私人住宅主要与当地建筑传统相关。

宗教建筑

琐罗亚斯德教以火祭神，因此萨珊时期的琐罗亚斯德圣火并不是崇拜的对象，而是纯洁神性的象征。圣火亦（通过持续使用余烬）被带到私人住宅中敬奉，保持长明。

火亦与萨珊王朝相联系，阿尔达希尔一世即位后，消灭了除王朝圣火外所有贵族世家的火种，以彰显其至高无上。

鉴于上述原因及宗教与政权之间的密切联系，火神庙在萨珊时期成为琐罗亚斯德教的最高礼拜场所。除拜火礼所需的空间（"火神殿"）外，火神庙中通常还包括为神职人员所设的具有祭拜或行政等功能的房间。

萨珊的不同阶层对应三级圣火（似与杜梅吉尔的印欧社会三功能假设相符）：国王与贵族的圣火为阿杜尔·古什纳斯普，位于阿塞拜疆（伊朗西北）的塔克斯特·苏莱曼神庙中；神职人员的圣火为阿杜尔·法恩巴格，可能位于喀布尔地区或法尔斯南部；农民的圣火为阿杜尔·布尔赞米赫，据文献记载位于呼罗珊（伊朗东北）。20世纪40年代，戈达尔与埃德曼各自提出了神庙由两座不同建筑组成的相同结论：

1）阿泰什伽或阿泰什卡代，即保存圣火的封闭之处；

2）查哈尔·塔克（字面含义为"四道拱券"），即穹隆顶礼拜场所，圣火将传至此处举行典礼。

考古发掘证实了赫兹菲尔德在20世纪20年代基于文献提出的假设，即火神殿一定是封闭式建筑。因为支撑穹隆顶的四道拱券被墙体封砌，或由于拱廊、向外延伸的伊万、正方形或十字形穹隆顶房间（查哈尔·塔克）而与外界隔绝。

建筑遗迹（参见下文）之间的重大差异或与琐罗亚斯德教文献证实的圣火等级相关，或符合信众的文化背景。遗憾的是，考古调查所揭露的两座最著名的建筑群，即塔克斯特·苏莱曼与托尔让·泰佩，其规模与布局复杂性分属两个极端。而数量众多、中等大小的查哈尔·塔克仍不明确。只有对主体周边区域进行考古调查，才能判断是否原存在有边墙。胡夫提出，许多遗迹可能属于埃马扎代类的伊斯兰圣人陵墓。研究伊朗宗教建筑的难题仍然在于缺少大量详尽的考古证据。倘若文献记载的宗教意识形态与祭祀活动的变革必然对建筑造成影响，那么只有通过完整、正确地复原建筑的布局与年代，方可解决与功能相关的诸多问题。

第二部分第二章《萨珊王朝的火神庙》将对照胡夫的建筑论述与克勒格尔的装饰论述，并进行批判性讨论。

最早的萨珊火神庙为菲鲁扎巴德的塔克斯特·内辛，位处阿尔达希尔—花拉城中心。建筑中央为穹隆顶大殿，轴向上的四扇门通向保存状况不佳的四个伊万，形成十字形平面，以满足琐罗亚斯德教对查哈尔·塔克的纯洁性的要求。

20世纪30年代及70年代，法国与伊朗考古学家相继发掘了比沙普尔建筑群。发掘者将其定为沙普尔一世的宫殿，包含若干房间，与其他宫殿不同之处在于有多条轴线及走廊（图34）。依据阿扎尔诺什提出、后为胡夫所采纳的假设，被定为沙普尔一世宫殿的2号大殿（图35），实际应为文献记载的沙普尔火神庙中的查哈尔·塔克。大殿外发现的祭坛石板可证实上述假设。查哈尔·塔克两侧的3号房间（"马赛克庭院"，图36）与4号房间（"马赛克伊万"）内发现了女性人物、酒神母题等马赛克装饰。若宗教功能属实，3、4号房间与琐罗亚斯德教宴会的关联，便可解释建筑中出现的马赛克装饰。神庙中极可能存在用于集体庆祝琐罗亚斯德教历节庆的场所。

5号半地下式建筑被定为阿纳希德（阿纳希塔的中古波斯语名称，水神）神殿（图37），

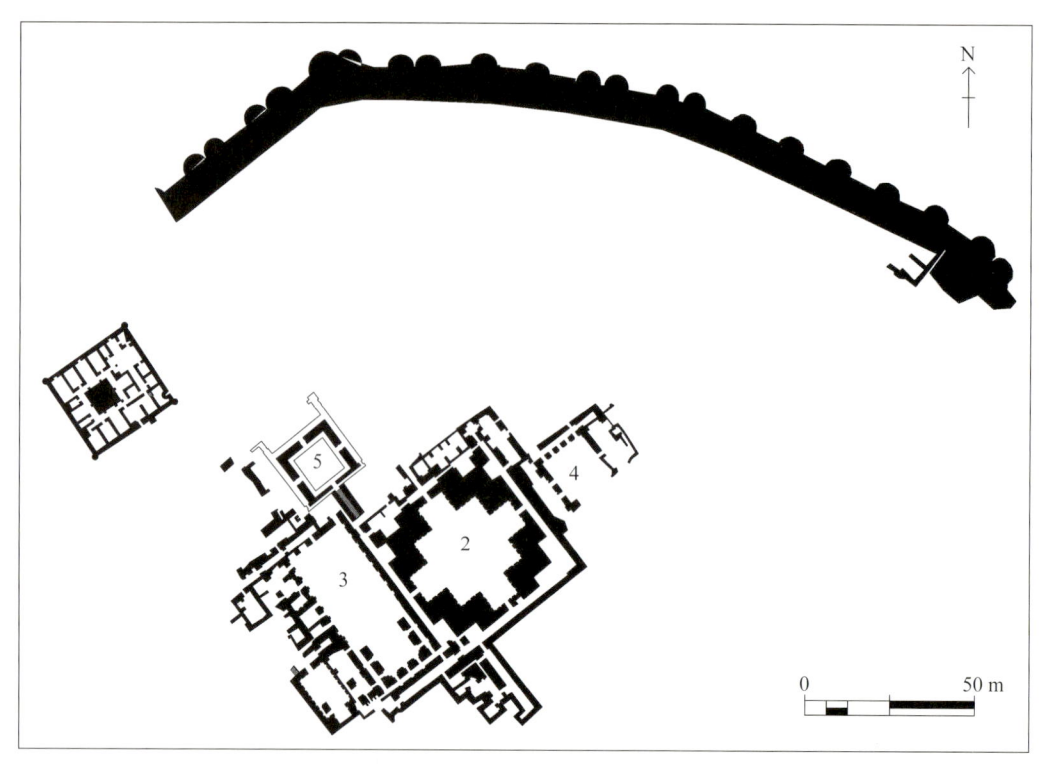

图 34 比沙普尔：火神庙平面图（A. Eghra 在 D. Huff 的基础上绘制，感谢德黑兰德国考古研究院提供）

图 35 比沙普尔：火神庙 2 号大殿（@ Callieri）

图36　比沙普尔：火神庙3号房间（@ Callieri）

图37　比沙普尔：火神庙5号半地下式建筑（@ Callieri）

墙体外为方形料石,内为石块与黏土。其中的管道系统与邻近河流相连,可通过入口处的移动隔板将中部灌满。而弗赖伊却认为,有水的背阴环境表明整座"宫殿"应为世俗建筑。

依据地表构造,10号似为"神庙"前的大庭院。7号为"瓦勒良宫殿"(图38),得名于被沙普尔一世俘虏的罗马皇帝,因其子加里恩努斯未能支付赎金而死于狱中。命名纯属臆造,但7号房址十分重要,因在其中发现了萨珊时期唯一的雕刻人像中楣(图39)。

图38 比沙普尔:"瓦勒良宫殿"(@ Callieri)

图39 比沙普尔博物馆:"瓦勒良宫殿"的雕刻人像中楣(A. Eghra供图)

塔克斯特·苏莱曼即"所罗门的宝座"（俗称），坐落于伊朗一座死火山口湖畔（图40）。该建筑为萨珊晚期神庙，部分结构在蒙古统治时期用于行政与居住。神庙四周被带马面的防御墙体包围。信众由北门进入，而南门则为君主专设。神庙布局较复杂，无上层结构，恰好印证了胡夫的阐释（图108）。

建筑群南边为一座伊万，俯瞰湖泊（S）。伊万所在轴线上有一座查哈尔·塔克（A），周绕回廊；其东边有另一座查哈尔·塔克（B），中央为储存祭祀余烬的火盆。继续向东，则为两个狭长房间（C、D），东北方有一个被狭长房间包围的方形柱廊庭院（E）。

另一区域以一座小查哈尔·塔克（PD）为中心，或为国王私人所有（图41）。PB、PA为圆柱或方柱大殿。对三者的解读大不相同。由于没有发现祭坛，PD中或无圣火。但其在德国考古队发掘前曾被盗，故无法确定。

库赫·哈加琐罗亚斯德教神庙位于锡斯坦（伊朗东部）哈姆湖的一座小岛上，历经若干建造阶段，年代尚有争议（图42）。最后阶段无疑为萨珊晚期，而倒数第二个阶段为安息晚期或萨珊早期。建筑现被视为埃贝德斯坦，即琐罗亚斯德教神学院。

图40 塔克斯特·苏莱曼：遗址鸟瞰图（A. Eghra供图）

伊朗萨珊时期的建筑与艺术

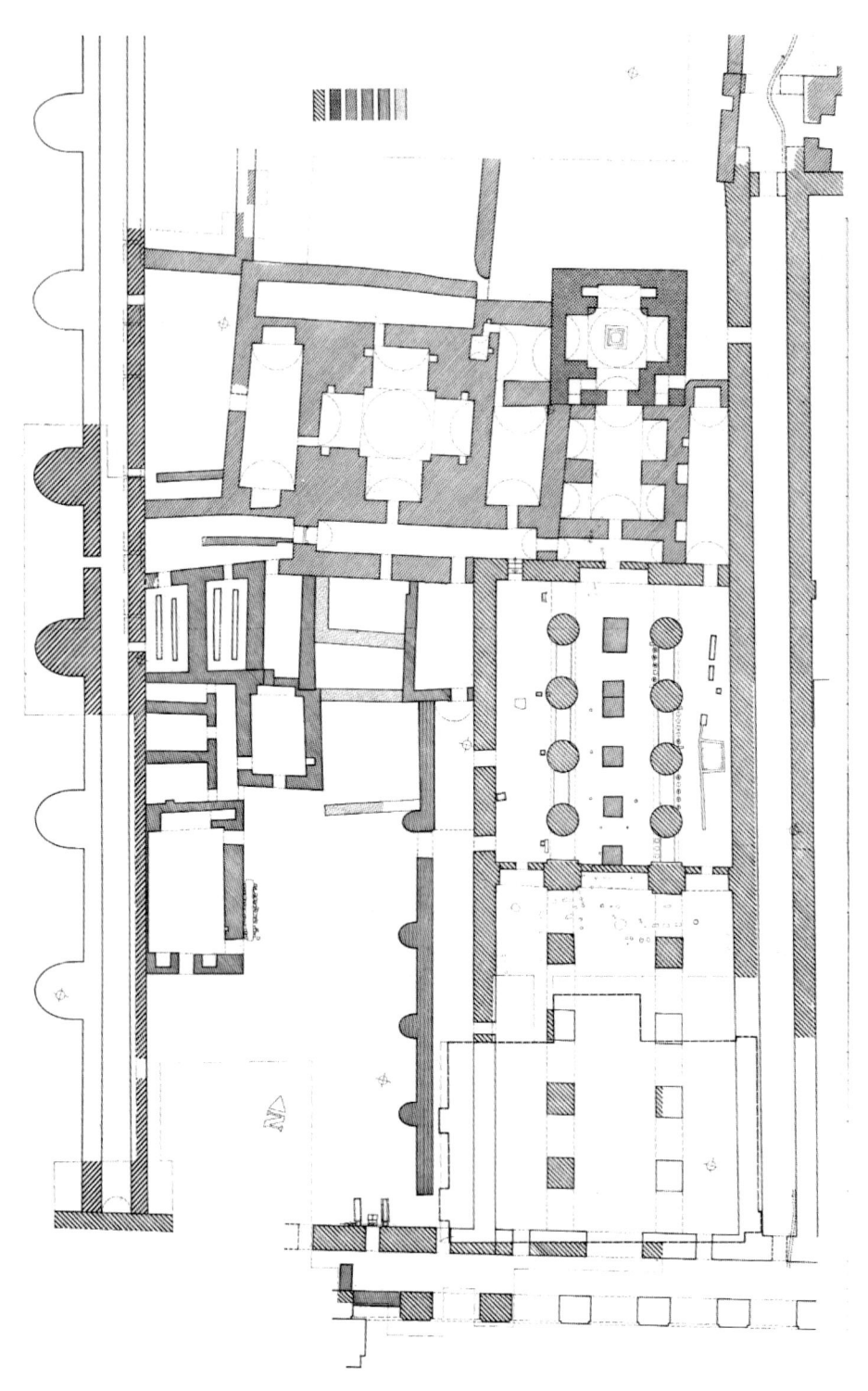

图41 塔克斯特·苏莱曼：查哈尔·塔克（PD）所在火神庙平面图（A. Eghra 在 Naumann 1977，图37 的基础上绘制）

图42　库赫·哈加主要建筑群（A.M. Naderi Bani 供图）

年代最晚的萨珊神殿是喀斯尔·席林（伊朗西部）的查哈尔·卡卜。建筑群中心为正方形穹隆顶结构，位于非对称轴线的一端，前为带侧间与走廊的两个庭院。我认同比尔的观点，即萨尔韦斯坦建筑群为伊斯兰早期的琐罗亚斯德教建筑。

丧葬建筑

萨珊时期，丧葬建筑受到广泛传播的琐罗亚斯德教习俗影响。教义规定，为清除尸体造成的自然元素污染，应于高处曝尸，猛禽食肉后归拢遗骨，存放在种类丰富、尺寸较小的奥斯托丹（"纳骨器"）中。

根据斯特拉波（XV, 3, 20）的论述，可知该习俗直至公元1世纪仍为祭司阶级所独有，而只是在萨珊晚期才变得普遍。

萨珊国王的葬仪尚不明确。唯一被定为陵墓的考古遗迹为比沙普尔的穆旦洞穴，内有沙普尔一世圆雕（图43）。

特林佩尔曼假设，阿尔达希尔一世与沙普尔一世以降，直至霍尔木兹二世，纳克什·鲁斯塔姆的阿契美尼德陵墓曾被重复利用（图44），改造内部并在岩壁上刻出现今所见陵墓下方的浮雕，亦即丧葬浮雕。阿尔达希尔一世选择邻近菲鲁扎巴德的卡拉·杜赫塔尔宫殿下葬。沙普尔一世原定葬于穆旦洞穴，但依据国王本人与大祭司卡提尔的两道铭文，最后葬于卡巴耶·扎尔达什特。纳塞赫的陵墓应当为派库里塔，亦在

图43 比沙普尔：穆旦洞穴（@ Callieri）

图44 纳克什·鲁斯塔姆：东南方视角（@ Callieri）

图 45 比索通：塔拉什·法尔哈德
（@ Callieri）

此处发现了该国王的铭文。依据一份伊斯兰年谱，萨珊晚期的国王应葬于泰西封，尽管位于米底地区比索通的塔拉什·法尔哈德被视作库思老二世未建成的丧葬建筑（图45）。笔者认为，上述观点缺乏客观因素支持，仍有待证实。

直至近期，伊朗及印度的琐罗亚斯德教众仍将尸体放置于"寂静塔"中，但伊斯兰时期之前未见这一类型的遗迹，而是曝尸于岩壁最高处凿出的洞穴中。特林佩尔曼提出，位于法尔斯南部萨尔·马沙德，直径80米、高7米、名为坎达克的圆形结构，是最早的"寂静塔"，为大祭司卡提尔下令建造。公元3世纪末，卡提尔已建立曝尸制度，下令将尸骨存放在同样位于萨尔·马沙德的石龛中，距离长铭文不远处。但上述解读亦未被证实。

在萨珊时期的伊朗，尤其是法尔斯中西部，常见岩壁凹处及水平凿石而成的墓穴，后者边缘突出，以安放棺盖，防止雨水与尸体接触（图46）。依据尺寸大小，可作为藏骨处或用于曝尸，亦可作非琐罗亚斯德教众的坟墓。萨珊时期，伊朗多教并行，使辨认工作变得更复杂，只在部分情况下可借助铭文。同时亦发现石质或陶质纳骨器，置于可能刻有纪念丧葬铭文的矮柱上。纳克什·鲁斯塔姆的两个祭坛形建筑物较为特殊（图47）。有学者将其定为火坛，但其上部边缘突出的凹槽或用于安放棺盖，表明可能为琐罗亚斯德教藏骨处。

圆形或椭圆形石墩（石冢）广泛分布在法尔斯东部至莫克兰，内有一个或多个墓室，可能为随葬明器的简单墓葬，年代为11—16世纪。

在波斯湾哈尔克岛上发现了以岩石凿成的两个大型多室地下墓穴，其中之一的宏伟建筑立面上饰有科林斯式方壁柱与假窗。因与巴尔米拉坟墓相似，墓穴应为巴尔米拉人所用，年代或为安息时期。

37

图46 阿霍尔·鲁斯塔姆(法尔斯中部):岩壁凹处墓穴(@ Callieri)

图47 纳克什·鲁斯塔姆:祭火坛形状的纳骨器(@ Callieri)

绘 画

在前伊斯兰时期的伊朗,尽管遗存较少,但绘画仍是最重要的艺术形式,一如古代其他地区。绘画的天然颜料及灰泥或织物载体本身不易保存,而雕塑所使用的石头、金属等材料较持久。伊朗萨珊时期的绘画遗存十分稀少,多为壁画,亦有少量分布于陶器上。建筑灰泥通常由细颗粒黏土构成,有时上部会覆盖一层薄薄的石膏。因此除极少数情况外,墙壁坍塌将导致壁画崩解。颜料由植物或矿物色素组成,以"丹培拉"技艺施在干灰泥上,故不如"湿壁画"耐久。

绘画遗存分布在法尔斯东部的哈吉阿巴德宫殿(图48)及苏萨古城。2005年,在阿尔达希尔—花拉城中部发现了属于丧葬建筑的壁画残片(图49),但至今未出版,亦无年代判定。

图48 哈吉阿巴德绘画遗存(A. Eghra供图,依据Azarnoush 1994, pl. XXXII)

图49 菲鲁扎巴德:阿尔达希尔—花拉中心区域出土的绘画场景(@ Callieri)

萨珊时期陶器上所绘的装饰通常较为简单，而在伊朗西南及美索不达米亚地区则逐渐被施釉技术所代替。在马尔吉亚那发现绘有形象的陶罐。在木鹿现存两座佛塔，发掘其中一座公元6世纪的佛塔时，出土了一个与该城市墓地常见的骨灰罐形制相似的大陶罐（图50）。罐内有古印度俗语写本，外有四幅以黑线与明亮色彩绘制的叙事画，表现一名贵族的生平，包含狩猎、患病、死亡与丧葬画面。此外，在巴克特里亚（阿富汗北部）古尔比扬的一个洞穴内发现了大量具有仪式性质的绘画。

图50 木鹿（马尔吉亚那）：绘有形象的纳骨罐（Koshelenko 1977）

灰泥装饰

萨珊时期的绘画遗存十分稀少，而灰泥装饰则遗留较多。

为免误解，从生产技艺上说，"灰泥"的定义为"除黏土以外的塑性材料制成的浮凸墙饰"。故"灰泥"多用于表示一种装饰，而非某种具体的材料。在英语中，墙上的保护层通称"plaster"，可为黏土或灰泥，而"stucco"则指灰泥装饰。在伊朗，通常使用石膏砂浆来粘结石质建筑材料，灰泥装饰亦以石膏塑性材料制成，而不同于以石灰为基材的西方传统。

灰泥装饰大多采用希腊—罗马式典型母题，由手工或模具制成。模具可使图像母题保存更久，成本更低、制作更快，即使在工匠去世后仍可继续使用。

萨珊时期，使用模具量产的可拆卸预制构件变得普遍，包括可组合成大型图案的方板，以及嵌在几何或植物背景中的圆板。萨珊时期的灰泥装饰仅分布于特定空间，即多柱大殿或伊万，或为琐罗亚斯德教举办大型重要会议或宴饮的场所。

克勒格尔基于20世纪70年代末的资料、于1981年出版的论著，堪称萨珊灰泥研究的典范。其后出土的众多发现拓宽了阐释角度，表明灰泥装饰技艺在萨珊广泛传播，但未推翻其结论。第二部分第三章《从新发现看灰泥工艺》，旨在将克勒格尔的成果与新发现进行比对。

年代最早的灰泥装饰之一位于比沙普尔的查哈尔·塔克（3世纪），该建筑或为火神殿。壁龛所在的墙上饰有受古典风格影响的植物母题，包括涡卷藤纹与希腊回纹（图51、52）。

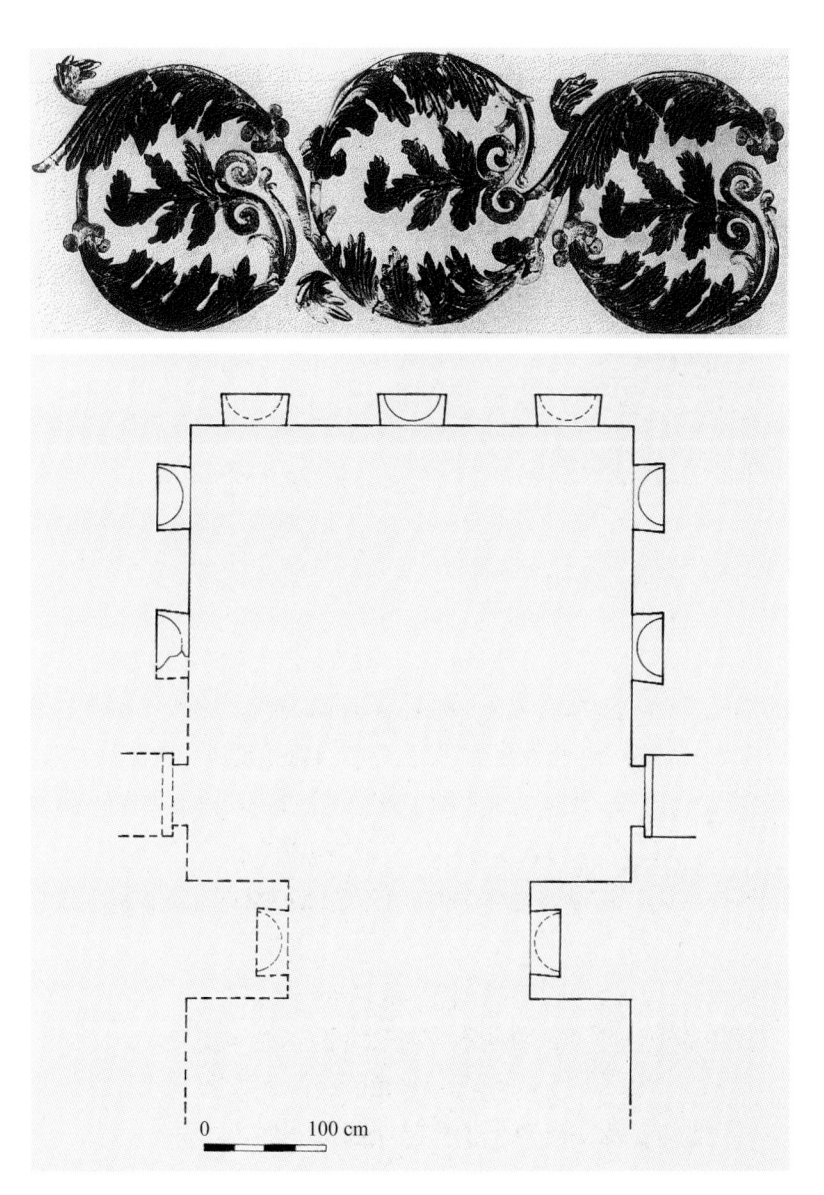

图51　比沙普尔：2号大殿查哈尔·塔克灰泥装饰细节（依据Kröger 1981, pl.90, 4绘制）

伊朗萨珊时期的建筑与艺术

哈吉阿巴德宫殿建筑群位于法尔斯东部，在农业活动中偶然被发现，是萨珊建筑最重要的实例之一。1978年考古队开展了唯一一次抢救性发掘，简报虽有收获，但在方法论上仍有欠缺。发掘者阿扎尔诺什将建筑群定为当地领主的府邸（"庄园"），分为三个部分：办公区、居住区及礼拜区。灰泥装饰集中分布于办公区的大庭院及礼拜区的一个房间L.114（图53）。阿扎尔诺什指出，与后者相邻的十字形平面房间与比沙普尔大殿有相似之处。依据出土的灰泥残片，阿扎尔诺什复原了房间内的装饰构图：正壁上有三个壁龛，内有着衣女性人像；两侧壁上各有两个

图52 比沙普尔：2号大殿查哈尔·塔克灰泥装饰的复原，现藏于巴黎卢浮宫博物馆（图片来源于Wikimedia Commons）

壁龛，壁龛间为狮首装饰；其上为叠戴两条项链的裸体女性人像，一侧头发为厚重的大波浪卷，盘圆髻，头部以简约线条彩绘而成。墙壁上方还饰有葡萄叶拱，拱下为持葡萄串的裸体孩童，从图像学角度看，该母题与酒神相关。上述复杂的表现形式在萨珊艺术中绝无仅有。

整体而言，灰泥装饰可归为"酒神"题材范畴。阿扎尔诺什将装饰空间的功能定为敬奉水神阿纳希塔，即壁龛内的女性人像，和比沙普尔的半地下神殿一致，而后者以水

图53 哈吉阿巴德庄园：L.114房间就地保存的灰泥装饰（Azarnoush 1994, Pl.XXVII Unit 114）

代表水神。矛盾之处则是无法解释水神为何以完全相同的女性形象出现七次。

希腊化影响仅限于若干母题,但其主题具有特定风格,因此并非模仿,而是原创。

此外,还有大型国王半身像灰泥圆板,阿扎尔诺什依此来确定建筑群年代。其中一个圆板为贵霜沙赫(即东部行省)的总督(其铸币与萨珊不同),由于哈吉阿巴德与该贵霜沙赫有关,建筑年代存在问题。萨珊侵略印度西北部,即贵霜沙赫的领地的时间,约在公元3—4世纪之间。阿扎尔诺什辨认出编号20的半身像为沙普尔二世。他认为此像由一位总督在沙普尔在任时下令制作,并将其置于庄园中。但哈吉阿巴德"庄园"的先祖走廊中包括沙普尔二世,圆板亦可能为庄园主人所制。相比将半身像视作在世国王的象征,以示称颂,后一种解释更符合逻辑。

迈赫迪·拉赫巴尔发现的班迪扬遗址位于呼罗珊东北部,与土库曼斯坦边境相距数千米,由伊朗文化遗产组织发掘。其中有一座萨珊中期(5世纪)的建筑,原址保存了丰富的灰泥装饰,集中分布于一面敞开的四圆柱大殿的墙上(图54)。在伊斯兰时期,建筑遭到破坏,仅余墙体下部。尽管如此,其遗存仍极大地丰富了萨珊时期的图像艺术。几何与植物边框内为男性、女性人物及中古波斯语铭文(图140—142),在图像与风格上都与同时期相距不远的中亚绘画十分相似,而灰泥刻划较浅,更接近绘画,而非雕塑。

图54 班迪扬:建造固定住所后的A遗址全景图(@ Callieri)

在萨珊帝国的另一端,美索不达米亚地区的启什,出土了植物形装饰及公元5世纪的国王半身像。在泰西封王城中发现了年代较晚(6世纪)的大型圆板,饰有花、棕榈叶及狩猎场景。王城周边房址中有几何及植物母题装饰,内为人像及小型动物像圆板。

在现伊朗境内,灰泥分布于东北部达姆甘及西北部塔克斯特·苏莱曼(6世纪?),后者的彩绘灰泥人像遗存出土于皇家火神殿的中心,即PD房间。

在查拉·塔尔汉、泰佩·米勒及雷伊附近的纳济马巴德建筑群中同样发现了灰泥装饰,年代约在7世纪,包括半身像及接近倭马亚风格的骑士像灰泥板。

克勒格尔注意到,灰泥装饰仅分布于建筑的部分空间:向庭院敞开的伊万,如哈吉阿巴德、启什及泰西封;圆柱或方柱大殿,如启什、塔克斯特·苏莱曼、达姆甘、查拉·塔尔汉与泰佩·米勒。塔克斯特·苏莱曼遗址对于解读至关重要,饰有灰泥的圆柱大殿无疑为第二座火神殿的一部分,故有礼拜功能。据此,克勒格尔对所有发现灰泥装饰的空间进行了分析。他强调,虽然灰泥装饰极少出自火神殿本身,但往往分布于与火神殿相连的大殿中。

在神殿布局中,走廊显然用于隔绝圣火存放处,而水池则与特定宗教功能相关。启什的两座主建筑似为仪式大殿,达姆甘的火神殿旁亦有一座圆柱大殿,均发现宗教功能的灰泥装饰遗存。

在属于今德黑兰的雷伊地区,查拉·塔尔汉遗址的一座建筑内出土了记录以大麦、葡萄酒等实物交税的"陶片"。克勒格尔认为,与其说上述物品是税收经济的实证,不如说是神殿祭品,由祭司准备并自己享用。他指出,神殿是集礼拜、行政管理与节庆功能于一身的大型建筑群,图像灰泥装饰所描绘的正是节庆空间。对克勒格尔而言,行政与宗教功能的房间难以区分,尽管后者更为常见。萨珊时期饰有灰泥的建筑群应具有宗教功能,许多宫殿等建筑实际上应为火神庙。据此,克勒格尔提出灰泥装饰与琐罗亚斯德教节庆相关。

马赛克

在比沙普尔,出土了伊朗高原唯一一例玻璃或石质镶嵌片制成的马赛克,即罗马时期叙利亚及巴勒斯坦的常见装饰。沙普尔一世占领安条克后,马赛克制作亦受到安条克的直接影响,或与水利工程一样由被放逐的工匠完成。

比沙普尔的马赛克集中分布于马赛克伊万和马赛克庭院的外围,构图较特殊,主要分为两类场景:

1)龛内场景:表现人像全身的镶板。通常为女性,如舞者、乐师、艺伎等(图55)。

1

2

图 55 比沙普尔"马赛克庭院":壁龛中的两幅马赛克画面(Ghirshman 1956)

伊朗萨珊时期的建筑与艺术

2）外围饰带：用于狭小的空间。白色背景上有无颈人头，多为正面或四分之三侧面，少数为侧面（图56）。上述头像应属酒神题材，因为发现了松果杖，即图像学中队伍领头人所持的标识。

音乐与舞蹈主题装饰适用于世俗及宗教节庆大殿。从图像学角度看，比沙普尔的马赛克十分独特，尤其是像面具一样的单体头像。在尼萨的安息来通杯中有凸出的单体头像。在哈特拉的一个安息晚期遗址中，若干建筑的墙上亦饰有凸出的头像，表明该装饰母题同时出现在伊朗与闪米特地区。

图56 比沙普尔"马赛克庭院"：沿墙分布的两幅马赛克装饰带（Ghirshman 1956）

比沙普尔的全身人像及单体头像的风格偏向自然主义，尽管也存在程式化的女性人像。衣物为紧贴身体、下摆变宽的典型萨珊类型。马赛克或出自安条克工匠，或出自向罗马人学习技艺的萨珊工匠，但无论如何，图像程序均为萨珊传统。

雕塑与摩崖浮雕

在形象艺术中，雕塑受萨珊王朝及琐罗亚斯德教会控制的影响最大，与绘画、银器有所不同：绘画遗存过于稀少，难以与同时期其他文化进行对比；银器生产从最初王朝垄断，逐渐发展为量产，脱离直接控制。而雕塑的发展一直受到琐罗亚斯德教"圣像毁坏"与萨珊王朝专属特权的双重限制。

玛丽·博伊斯指出，琐罗亚斯德教反对偶像，原因在于他们惧怕"无形"的、被剥夺了"活的"或"实体"性质的邪恶力量，会占据与阿胡拉·马兹达创造的生灵相似的无生命物质形式，并将之转化为邪恶的生物。故琐罗亚斯德教并非反对阿胡拉·马兹达或神祇的图像，而是反对一切圆雕，即准确模仿人体的唯一艺术形式。圣像的传播始于阿契美尼德晚期，由阿尔塔薛西斯二世将阿纳希塔的形象传遍帝国全境，并在塞琉古及希腊化时期延续。随后在标准化进程中，圣像逐渐式微并被圣火所取代，直至萨珊晚期，正如与圣像毁坏相关的大量法律文件所示。古代文明大多有丰富的宗教图像，并且将塑像视作最重要的艺术创作机会，而伊朗萨珊时期的神祇图像极其稀少，几乎没有圣像。

即便是受宗教限制更少的雕像艺术，如摩崖浮雕，亦被萨珊王朝所垄断，因而不难理解现存雕像资料的稀少。

除少数王室或贵族人物小铜像及一个沙普尔二世的银质头像外，穆旦洞穴内的沙普尔一世大雕像是唯一一座遗留的圆雕，位于比沙普尔附近、沙普尔河谷发源地的高崖峭壁上（图57）。以洞穴内的天然岩柱雕出，尺寸大于真人，呈现正面、程式化的国王站姿。头戴绶带王

图57　穆旦洞穴：沙普尔一世雕像（@ Callieri）

冠，脸侧垂下两大束头发，蓄络腮胡，着斗篷、束腰外袍与宽松长裤，穿鞋，佩剑，均为萨珊国王典型发型与服饰。雕像功能尚不明确，鉴于洞穴类型接近阿契美尼德国王的石墓及萨珊时期的藏骨堂，或为国王陵墓中的丧葬图像。

如前文所述，萨珊时期最典型的雕塑形式是摩崖浮雕。

伊朗高原上的雕塑传统可追溯至公元前3千纪，发源于卢路比的阿努巴尼尼国王浮雕，延续至阿契美尼德时期比索通的大流士一世浮雕。与其一脉相承，萨珊早期国王选择将家族浮雕刻在高不可攀的岩壁上，通常邻近泉水或河道。与水相近的位置或可体现萨珊王朝与水神阿纳希塔间的紧密联系。阿纳希塔神殿位于法尔斯的埃斯塔赫，由阿尔达希尔的先祖掌管。水在琐罗亚斯德教神话中亦为"灵光"所居之处，意义重大。与世隔绝、难以到达的选址，表明浮雕的宣传或叙事功能弱于其象征性及仪式性。目前伊朗已知的浮雕有36处，通常再加上塔克·波斯坦主伊万的两侧壁浮雕，另有1处在20世纪80年代发现于今阿富汗的巴克特里亚（图58）。伊朗境内多达30处浮雕位于帝国摇篮法尔斯，4处位于库尔德斯坦的塔克·波斯坦，1处位于西阿塞拜疆的萨勒马斯，1处位于德黑兰附近的雷伊。除塔克·波斯坦主伊万两侧壁为萨珊晚期（库思老二世及其继任者？）外，其余年代均在开国君主阿尔达希尔一世与沙普尔三世之间，集中于公元3、4世纪。没有发现萨珊中期浮雕，或因当时的政治、经济局势困难。仅10处浮雕

伊朗萨珊时期的建筑与艺术

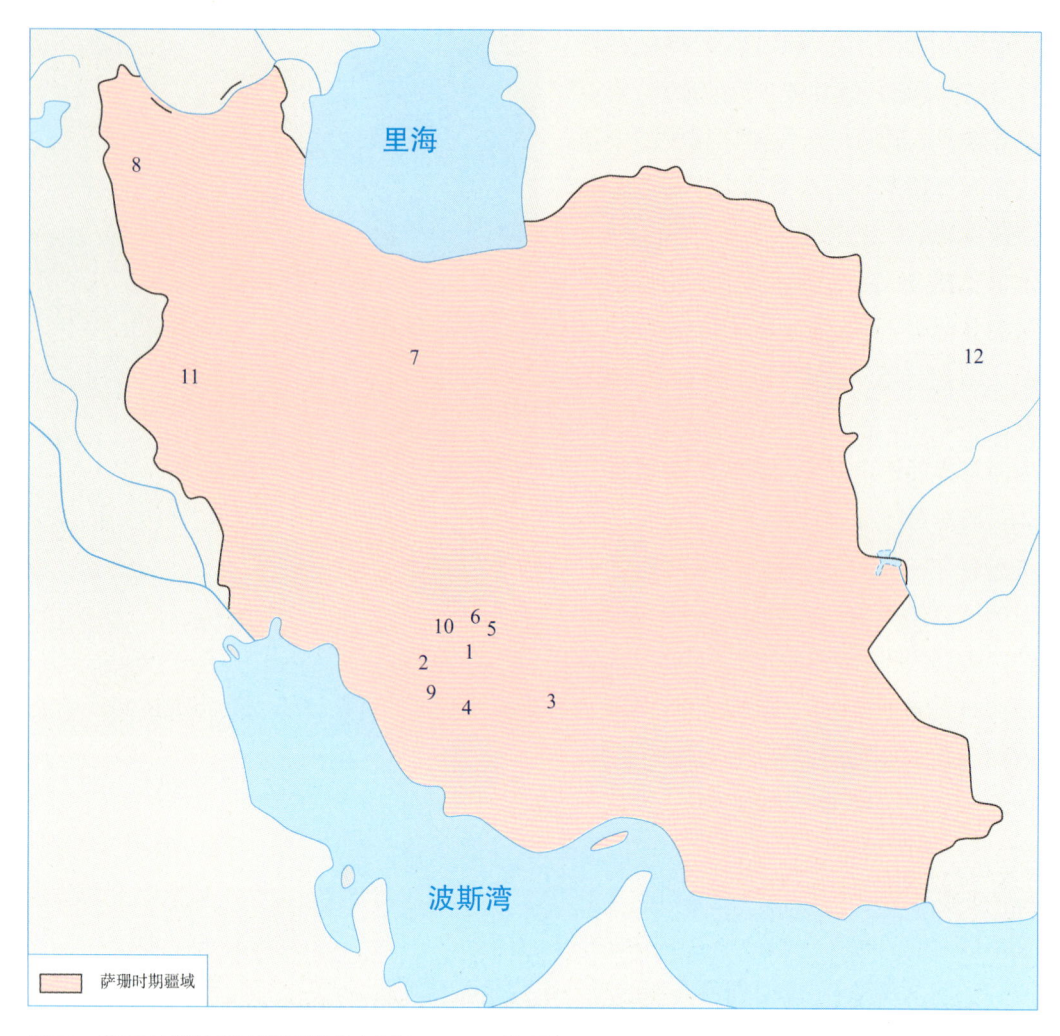

图58 萨珊时期伊朗摩崖浮雕分布图（A. Eghra绘图）

1. 巴尔姆·德拉克	5. 纳克什·拉加卜	9. 萨尔·马沙德
2. 比沙普尔	6. 纳克什·鲁斯塔姆	10. 萨拉卜·巴赫拉姆
3. 达拉卜	7. 雷伊	11. 塔克·波斯坦
4. 菲鲁扎巴德—坦格·阿卜	8. 萨勒马斯	12. 拉格·比比

有铭文，其中仅5道铭文与国王像相关。其余铭文除伊斯兰时期所刻外，还包括大祭司卡提尔的铭文，他是王室之外唯一留下直接权力证明的人物，可见其地位甚至与国王相当。

列出主题有助于理解摩崖浮雕的功能，如王权神授、克敌制胜、皇家狩猎、朝觐国王、骑士比武等。阐释图像时应考虑到，虽然场景似为历史事件，但所有主题均以象征性形式表现王权。相比之下，摩崖浮雕与图拉真柱、马可·奥勒留柱等罗马历史浮雕差异极大，罗马浮雕基于真实细致的纪年叙事，波斯浮雕则属于象征性—仪式性语境，而非复刻史实。

象征性—仪式性含义在王权神授图中体现得最为淋漓尽致。国王头戴王冠,已被穆贝德加冕,他从阿胡拉·马兹达(1处浮雕中为阿纳希塔,1处为阿胡拉·马兹达与阿纳希塔,还有1处为阿胡拉·马兹达或国王父亲,而3处浮雕中密特拉神均在场)手中接过一个绶带圆环。圆环通常被视作"灵光"的象征,即国祚,安息时期已出现,例如在伊朗国家博物馆所藏的盘子上,描绘阿尔达班四世向苏萨总督赫瓦萨克授权的场景,据阿拉姆语铭文定为公元215年。凯姆则认为圆环象征神祇与国王间的契约。无论圆环作何解释,场景并非描绘加冕的历史时刻,而是象征性地表现神授王权。神祇与国王十分相似,似乎成了赞美后者的陪衬,而国王才是画面主体。在站姿王权神授图中,神与国王一样站立。在马背王权神授图中,阿胡拉·马兹达亦与国王姿态一致,脚踏地上的恶神阿赫里曼,正如国王脚踏落败的敌人——安息国王阿尔达班四世或罗马皇帝戈尔迪安三世。

几乎所有的早期萨珊国王都有王权神授图,巴赫拉姆二世除外,他出现在许多其他题材的浮雕中。但也有学者认为,法尔斯古亚姆1处未完成的浮雕即为巴赫拉姆二世的王权神授图。在阿尔达希尔一世的两幅王权神授图中,站姿图位于菲鲁扎巴德(图59),马背图位于纳克什·鲁斯塔姆(图60)——大流士一世及其继任者的崖墓以及卡巴耶·扎尔达什特(琐罗亚斯德的方石塔)所在圣地。沙普尔一世在比沙普尔留下一幅马背王权神授图与克敌制胜图结合的浮雕(Ⅰ号浮雕,图61),敌人(或为戈尔迪安三

图59 菲鲁扎巴德,菲鲁扎巴德Ⅱ号浮雕:阿尔达希尔一世站姿王权神授图(@ Callieri)

图 60 纳克什·鲁斯塔姆,纳克什·鲁斯塔姆 I 号浮雕:阿尔达希尔一世马背王权神授图(@Callieri)

世)在他马蹄下的场景对应阿胡拉·马兹达脚踏阿赫里曼的场景,此外,另有一位下跪乞求的罗马皇帝(阿拉伯人菲利普?)。在比沙普尔,还有一幅巴赫拉姆一世马背王权神授图(Ⅳ号浮雕,图62),后纳赛赫将铭文中的巴赫拉姆一世换作自己的名字,并补刻了一名倒在国王马蹄下的人物(或为贵族瓦赫拉姆,他辅佐纳赛赫的侄子巴赫拉姆三世登基,在后者被推翻后被纳赛赫处死)。纳赛赫的站姿王权神授图位于纳克什·鲁斯塔姆(图63),依据传统解读,他从阿纳希塔而非阿胡拉·马兹达手上接过"灵光"。另有一种解读,即浮雕内容是庆祝罗马人交还在亚美尼亚惨败时被伽列里乌斯皇帝俘虏的波斯王室,塞萨洛尼基的凯旋门即为庆祝这次战功所建,故该女性应为纳赛赫的王后。但我以为可能性不大。塔克·波斯坦崖壁上的王权神授图尚存争议(图64),站立的国王既像沙普尔二世之子沙普尔三世,又像沙普尔二世的儿子或兄弟,即阿尔达希尔二世,与沙普尔三世是对手。一位戴壁形王冠、可能为阿胡拉·马兹达或沙普尔二世的人物将胜利圆环交给国王。还有一人倒在前两人脚下,可能为阿赫里曼或"背教者"尤利安,后者曾败于沙普尔二世。无论国王是沙普尔三世还是阿尔达希尔二世,其身后为契约之神密特拉,立于盛开的莲花上,手持巴尔萨姆枝,以确保即位的合法性。塔克·波斯坦小伊万的正壁两侧为沙普尔二世及沙普尔三世的图像,可由铭文确定国王

图61 比沙普尔，比沙普尔Ⅰ号浮雕：沙普尔一世马背王权神授图，及战胜戈尔迪安三世、阿拉伯人菲利普两位罗马皇帝的克敌制胜图（@ Callieri）

图62 比沙普尔，比沙普尔Ⅴ号浮雕：巴赫拉姆一世马背王权神授图，后被纳赛赫重新使用，并在右下方补刻其中古波斯语姓名铭文及其敌人瓦赫拉姆，还可能用石膏改造了王冠（@ Callieri）

图63 纳克什·鲁斯塔姆,纳克什·鲁斯塔姆Ⅷ号浮雕:或为阿纳希塔向纳赛赫的王权神授图,或表现波斯败于俘虏纳赛赫妻子的伽列里乌斯皇帝后的王室(@ Callieri)

图64 塔克·波斯坦,塔克·波斯坦Ⅰ号浮雕:表现国王从沙普尔二世或阿胡拉·马兹达手中接过胜利圆环,密特拉神为见证者(@ Callieri)

图65 塔克·波斯坦，塔克·波斯坦Ⅱ号浮雕：通过中古波斯语铭文辨认，其上人物为沙普尔二世与沙普尔三世（A. Eghra供图）

身份，风格与塔克·波斯坦王权神授图相似（图65）。最后一幅萨珊王权神授图位于塔克·波斯坦主伊万的正壁上部（图66），中央的国王为库思老二世或其继任者，他从左侧阿胡拉·马兹达及右侧阿纳希塔手上接过两个绶带圆环，同时阿纳希塔将罐中的水倾出。

克敌制胜主题对于理解萨珊浮雕的象征性—仪式性含义同样十分关键。阿尔达希尔一世、沙普尔一世及沙普尔二世（？）均留下胜敌图浮雕，其中以沙普尔一世战胜罗马皇帝的浮雕最为著名。阿尔达希尔一世的唯一一处胜敌图浮雕位于菲鲁扎巴德（图67、68），场景表现其战胜阿尔达班四世，后者从马上摔下。该浮雕同时表现阿尔达希尔一世的儿子沙普尔战胜安息皇储，以及一位萨珊将领战胜安息将领的场景。比沙普尔Ⅵ号浮雕描绘了沙普尔二世（一说纳赛赫）战胜罗马人（？）及基督徒（？）的场景（图69）。有人向国王呈上戴着王子专属的兽首帽的首级，旺当贝格根据文献将该血腥画面阐释为毕尔·古什纳卜殉道（古什纳卜是沙普尔二世的侄子，后改信基督教）。

伊朗萨珊时期的建筑与艺术

图66 塔克·波斯坦，塔克·波斯坦Ⅲ号浮雕：位于伊万的正壁上部，或为阿胡拉·马兹达（画面左侧）及阿纳希塔（右侧）对库思老二世的王权神授图（@ Callieri）

图67 菲鲁扎巴德，菲鲁扎巴德Ⅰ号浮雕，阿尔达希尔一世战胜安息国王阿尔达班四世：阿尔达希尔将阿尔达班从马上摔下（A. Eghra供图）

图68 菲鲁扎巴德，菲鲁扎巴德Ⅰ号浮雕，阿尔达希尔一世战胜安息国王阿尔达班四世：沙普尔将阿尔达班之子从马上摔下（A. Eghra供图）

伊朗萨珊时期的建筑与艺术

图69 比沙普尔，比沙普尔Ⅵ号浮雕：右下方为向国王呈上首级的场景（@ Callieri）

表现沙普尔一世战功的浮雕共有5处。约公元242—260年，他在西部边疆打了三场胜仗，先是击败戈尔迪安三世，并使阿拉伯人菲利普签订条约、丧权求和（242—244年），后击败罗马人（252—256年），最后俘虏瓦勒良皇帝（260年）。达拉卜·盖尔达浮雕年代或为最早（图70），因图中国王头戴阿尔达希尔一世的王冠，可能由沙普尔为其父所造。一说浮雕为阿尔达希尔所造，但据史载，由他发动的与罗马人的战事在他死后、沙普尔即位时才获得胜利。余下4处年代顺序仍未确定的浮雕中，3处位于比沙普尔，1处位于纳克什·鲁斯塔姆，所绘制的罗马皇帝数量及浮雕构图各不相同。在纳克什·鲁斯塔姆Ⅵ号浮雕中（图71），一位罗马皇帝跪在沙普尔身前，另一位皇帝站立，沙普尔将手置于其头顶。沙普尔身后为大祭司卡提尔及其铭文，年代较晚。比沙普尔Ⅰ号王权神授及克敌制胜浮雕中，一名罗马人跪地求饶，另一罗马人倒在国王马下，对应着阿赫里曼倒在阿胡拉·马兹达马下。比沙普尔Ⅱ号浮雕中（图72），中央画面左侧为上下两排波斯骑士，右侧为上下两排共五个步兵，服饰、武器各不相同，或为波斯盟军。画面正中为马背上的沙普尔一世从一个有翼小天使手上接过胜利圆环，小天使为希腊化胜利女神在伊朗的男性化身形象。在两位波斯高官的见证下，沙普尔脚踏一位罗马皇帝的尸体，抓住身后另一位罗马皇帝的手，第三位罗马皇帝跪在其身前。

图70 达拉卜·盖尔达：俯瞰池塘的摩崖浮雕（@ Callieri）

图71 纳克什·鲁斯塔姆,纳克什·鲁斯塔姆Ⅵ号浮雕:沙普尔一世战胜两位罗马皇帝(@ Callieri)

图72 比沙普尔,比沙普尔Ⅱ号浮雕:沙普尔一世战胜三位罗马皇帝(@ Callieri)

比沙普尔Ⅲ号浮雕最为壮观（图73），壁面为弧形，形象较其他浮雕更小，分列若干排，效果宏伟。沙普尔一世及三位罗马皇帝位于高底座、即偏右侧的未雕刻饰带上。国王左侧为上下五排波斯骑士，面朝国王，右侧五排描绘掠夺战利品、军队落败及抓获俘虏的场景。底部右侧壁面上的人物背朝观者、面向国王，营造出动态效果，与左侧静止的骑兵形成对比。三位罗马皇帝的身份是争论的热门，本文对此持保留意见。将地上的罗马人尸体定为戈尔迪安三世，即三人中唯一被杀死的皇帝，应较为可信，尽管浮雕皇帝像面部并没有罗马钱币皇帝像上的胡须。至于被沙普尔一世抓住手或将手放在头顶的人，以及跪在沙普尔一世面前的人的身份，学者意见不一。一人为不战而签订丧权和平条约的阿拉伯人菲利普，另一人为出战但被俘虏致死的瓦勒良。有人认为，阿拉伯人菲利普与沙普尔一世执手，瓦勒良跪地。亦有人称，没有出战的阿拉伯人菲利普为屈辱跪姿，而瓦勒良尽管被俘，却仍受到英勇战士应有的待遇。

从风格角度看，萨珊时期的摩崖浮雕虽然数量有限，但存在明显的演变趋势：从扁平、几无突出人物的线刻，如菲鲁扎巴德战胜阿尔达班四世图，演变至立体、接近自然主义特点的沙普尔一世及巴赫拉姆一世浮雕。而在同一名国王的浮雕中，也明显存在不

图73 比沙普尔，比沙普尔Ⅲ号浮雕：沙普尔一世及其马队战胜三位罗马皇帝及其军队（@ Callieri）

同的艺术流派,不仅与年代相关,也与分布在不同地区、年代相近的艺术中心、作坊或学院相关。将自阿尔达希尔一世至纳赛赫(224—302年)王权神授图的纳克什·鲁斯塔姆浮雕,与自沙普尔一世至巴赫拉姆二世(240—293年)的比沙普尔浮雕整体比对,可发现同一遗址不同时期的浮雕,比两个遗址同一时期的浮雕更为相近。"自然主义"趋势——虽然为纯粹的萨珊设计——似在比沙普尔盛行,在巴赫拉姆一世的王权神授图中最为突出。该趋势或源自西方。比沙普尔Ⅰ至Ⅲ号浮雕中,人物构图安排与躯体、衣物的立体效果体现出希腊化—罗马风格的影响,或与叙利亚工匠制作比沙普尔的马赛克或建造苏萨水利工程为同一时期。比沙普尔Ⅱ、Ⅲ号浮雕的中央画面,与位于罗马保守宫、表现马可·奥勒留的宽恕的浮雕构图相似。未完成或未施灰泥的比沙普尔Ⅵ号浮雕,或为沙普尔二世战胜基督徒的画面,表面扁平,与塔克·波斯坦两个小伊万类似,但细节(褶皱、头发等)更为丰富,采取线刻而非立体手法。塔克·波斯坦大伊万的萨珊晚期浮雕中出现了两种对立的风格趋势,似为不同功能:其一分布在正壁的两排雕像上,立体而柔和,人物体量使其脱离背景,接近圆雕;其二分布在两侧壁上,更为扁平,接近线刻,以雕像形式呈现岩石挖凿而成的伊万中可能原有的壁画。

本书第二部分第四章将开创性地探讨如下问题:摩崖浮雕的起源,工匠及作坊的诞生地,不同艺术中心的技术风格特点,高度专业化的技术传统及其在萨珊晚期复兴的传承方式。

金属器

萨珊王朝的影响亦体现在艺术品及手工艺品中。

大量阿契美尼德宫廷风格的工艺品,尤其是珍贵的器皿、武器,出现在离法尔斯较远的地区,为波斯国王赠予友邻的奢侈品,由此提高他们的声望。宫廷风格工艺品将皇家的典型图像与品位传播到宫外。萨珊时期亦是如此,发展出与宫廷相关的贵重器皿,这一关联体现在国王像中。阿契美尼德人的贵金属为黄金,而萨珊人几乎不使用黄金,他们的贵金属为银,亦用于铸币。

银器主要出土于中亚斯基泰的王陵中[1]。斯基泰人生活在伊朗高原以北地区,是萨珊王朝的心腹大患,而馈赠礼品是与他们交好的方式之一。因此银器出现在伊朗高原外的游牧民族首领大型陵墓(库尔干)中,后宫众人、武器、马匹亦一同殉葬在隐蔽处。

---

[1] 斯基泰人指约公元前6至前4世纪生活在黑海、高加索以北地区的游牧民族,其后的伊朗游牧民族为萨迦人、萨尔马提亚人、丹人等。

遗物保存完好,现陈列于俄罗斯的博物馆中。

古时,银器已具有以重量计算的高价。许多器皿点字中,除物主名字外,还有器皿重量。值得注意的是,许多形制相似的器皿具有相同的重量。

银器主要以银为基底金属,施加浮凸或刻划装饰。另有包银或包金技术,即在低价银铜合金或铜的主体上施加一层更贵重的纯银或纯金。鎏金技术则是用水银混合物涂在器皿上,加热使水银挥发,留下一层薄薄的金黄镀层。

从形制类型来看,银器既受地中海地区影响,也受远东地区影响。从图像学角度看,最典型的器型为银盘。银壶所饰图像来源各异,而银盘则因其表面为圆形,可呈现完整而精美的画面,通常与王室相关。银盘制作始于公元3世纪,其时银壶沿袭帕提亚传统,壶底为一个徽章式贵族半身像。而银盘母题主要为宫廷专属的皇家狩猎纹,因唯有国王能在围场狩猎;萨珊晚期或之后的盘上才出现国王以外的狩猎者。猎物通常为代表国祚的野兽,即野猪、公羊或瞪羚。苏联学者卢科宁指出,国王猎捕上述野兽以寻求国运昌盛,但亦有学者持异议。在4世纪后半叶及5世纪,银盘数量减少,仍为宫廷专用。5世纪马兹达克运动后,狩猎纹银盘开始大量生产、分发,远达各行省。国王正面坐朝母题亦被引入,后影响了拜占庭的"基督全能者"图像。

银盘上的国王王冠主要可分为两组图像,与钱币上相同的王冠,以及衍生自钱币但并非完全相同的王冠。与图像学研究相比,科技考古能更清晰地得到两组银壶中的成分差异,通过分析微量元素,可确定金属间的异同。饰有与钱币相同王冠的银壶,由与钱币相同的矿石制成,故制作银币与银器的工匠活动应处于王朝的直接控制之下,为"都城"生产,因其直接出自萨珊帝国中央。饰有衍生自钱币而非完全相同的王冠的银壶,则称为"行省"生产,出自行省的次等作坊,或许不受王朝的严格控制,使用含混合物的银矿石。

阐释萨珊晚期国王像银盘的问题在于,银盘是产自宫廷、在贵族间流传,抑或是由贵族生产的国王像工艺品?诸多萨珊晚期银盘上都有与钱币上相同的王冠,是属于"都城"生产,或是不受皇家控制的伊朗生产中心,还是外部的"行省"产品?鉴于银器制作在萨珊王朝覆灭后持续了一个世纪,部分产品或产自萨珊以后。正是"行省"生产中心,使萨珊王室灭亡后银盘制作仍可持续。

除内壁有装饰、外壁素净或是仅圈足有装饰的银盘外,常见的形制为:

- 槽纹外壁银盘,承袭希腊化传统,盘内底心通常饰动物纹;
- 梨形银壶,矮足,细圆颈,唇口,壶身饰有酒神题材、(拱下)着衣或裸体女性人像、舞者、葡萄藤、动物母题、虚构或象征性生物;
- 酒壶,亦称来通杯,形似兽角,底部为兽首;
- 水壶,古典晚期地中海典型器型,圆鼓腹,圈足饰有纹样,细圆颈,弧壁,与陶器相似;

• 带足银碗，十分常见，普遍素净无纹，有时碗内底心为刻划鸟纹，源自地中海；

• 球腹银碗，无足，为公元前1千纪西亚、中亚地区常见器型，外壁饰浮凸纹或线刻纹，主题包括葡萄涡卷纹、神秘的"塞穆鲁"鸟、乐师、搏斗者等，多出自公元6、7世纪；

• 椭球腹碗，除少数碗内有涡卷纹外，通常无纹，外壁则饰有纹样，仅出现于5世纪末；部分铭文称其为"船碗"，或由东亚传入；

• 椭球瓣纹碗，为5—12世纪在亚欧大陆广泛流传的器型；萨珊椭球瓣纹碗可分为三型：第一型为各瓣不相连（5世纪末至6世纪初）；第二型为四瓣不相连，两瓣相连（6世纪）；第三型为三瓣相连，短轴上两瓣不相连（7世纪）。

玻璃器

玻璃器在萨珊时期的伊朗占有重要地位。玻璃虽为无机材料，却相对不易保存。

学界对安息—萨珊玻璃器及美索不达米亚萨珊晚期遗址出土的玻璃器有一定的认识。目前已发现截然不同的制造工艺：使用钳子或模具吹制，该技法于公元前1世纪发明于叙利亚—巴勒斯坦；吹制后加以刻划、打磨、抛光或贴丝、贴花纹样。

玻璃器几乎都为无色或淡绿色，但器型与纹样都饶有趣味。

装饰纹样通常为几何形，可分为三组：凹球面与直线元素的组合（年代较早，在安息时期的杜拉欧罗普斯已出现）；数排凹球面纹，有时呈梅花形；圆形浮凸纹。

陶　器

萨珊时期的伊朗陶器沿袭自铁器时代的传统，呈现出显著的地区差异。相关研究数量、质量参差不齐。最新成果主要集中在萨珊帝国东北疆的马尔吉亚那和波斯湾。萨珊早期的陶器与安息时期存在延续性，而萨珊晚期与伊斯兰早期的陶器生产中心则逐渐合并。由此，本文不作详细阐明。

纺织品

有关纺织品的论述十分复杂。金属器、陶器、玻璃器的大量生产使学者得以研究其形制、材质。陶器可以借助地层学进行可靠的断代。而纺织品则不然。

纺织品主要分为两类：一类为图像，包括塔克·波斯坦的主伊万浮雕在内的所有相关资料；另一类为主要在埃及安底诺伊发现的实物，以及切赫拉巴德（赞詹，伊朗西北部）盐矿中逝者身上的衣物纤维。

安底诺伊为哈德良（117—138年）沿尼罗河建立的城市，公元619—628年由萨珊波斯统治，毁于公元640年。墓地发现的织物中，有部分由伊朗工匠在伊朗或安底诺伊生产。由于源自伊朗本土的遗物较少，该发现可作为研究萨珊织物的参考。

除棉、羊毛等织物外，丝绸占萨珊纺织品的比重最大。丝绸在亚洲极其贵重，可与黄金媲美，故用于物品交换或官方赠赐。丝绸亦是东西方贸易的主要货物之一，商贸路线被称作"丝绸之路"，尽管商品并非只有丝绸，如在阿富汗贝格拉姆遗址的仓库中发现了印度象牙、罗马玻璃、中国铜镜及制作金属器所用的希腊化—罗马灰泥模具。

丝绸的生产长期为中国所垄断，仅在拜占庭时期传至西方，因此十分依赖进口。而萨珊时期的伊朗已开始自主生产丝绸。萨珊丝绸与伊斯兰时期的仿萨珊丝绸难以区分，仅织物上的图像不足以鉴别，需要借助显微镜对纤维及纺织技艺进行检验。

纺织品图案多为皇家狩猎图、国王像、琐罗亚斯德教动物像及占星学象征等典型的萨珊艺术题材。

中世纪欧洲的圣物以珍贵的萨珊或仿萨珊织物包裹，促进了伊朗图像母题在欧洲中世纪艺术中的传播。

印　章

"glyptics"由希腊语glypho（雕划）演化而来，字面含义包括所有加工过的半宝石，包括雪花石膏瓶。但该术语通常指半宝石等材料制作的古代印章，也包括印记。就印章而言，英文单词"sphragistic"似乎更为准确，由希腊语sphragis（印章）演化而来。但该术语通常指中世纪及现代印章，材质多为金属。

印章的普及与书写有关。在古代伊朗，书写不普及，仅祭司会书写，因此印章被广泛使用。印章代表私人面向公众的唯一身份标识，等同于签名。除私人印章外亦有公章，以表明官员职位。

底格里斯河畔塞琉西亚的希腊化时期档案馆中发现了黏土封泥（cretule），作为收据或盐税豁免证明。意大利学者菲安德拉最先研究斐斯托斯的米诺斯遗址档案馆的封泥背面，即封泥所封存物体材料的痕迹。

封泥可分为：

1）"挂印"，除印章戳记外仅有绳索痕迹。印在封存文件或其他物品的挂绳上，封泥悬挂。又名bullae，球形，上有穿绳的小孔。此类萨珊封泥可达较大尺寸，因其上有数个戳记。

2）"盖印"，除印章戳记外，背面还有被印物体的痕迹。印在门或箱子等平坦表面上。门上封泥表示仓库被封存管控，门上盖印表明有相关负责官员（因祭司亦承担官员职责，现多从商业角度进行阐释）。进入仓库必须破坏封泥，故这一做法可保证物品完整无缺。箱子、瓶子等容器上的封泥则体现官方对贸易的控制，有时会遗留遮盖容器的织物痕迹。伊朗最重要的封泥出土于塔克斯特·苏莱曼与喀斯尔·阿卜纳斯尔，近10年来，又发现了更多遗存。

回到印章本身，最早的实物由模具制成。公元前3千纪至公元前1千纪初，滚筒印章在美索不达米亚传播。楔形文字在泥板上书写，而滚筒印章则可以盖印整块泥板。随着阿拉姆语广泛使用，泥板不再适用，因为文字可写在纸上，随后封存、盖印。故平面印章重新流行，很快在美索不达米亚取代了滚筒印章。阿契美尼德时期，滚筒印章复兴，尤其是在宫廷印章中。但帝国各地区仍然制作平面印章。安息时期仅制作平面印章，而萨珊印章承袭了安息的传统。

与前朝相比，萨珊时期的印章在社会中流传更广。

印章由"坚石"制成，硬度以莫氏硬度表示。钻石最为坚硬，莫氏硬度7以上称为"坚石"，包括了所有石英（玉髓、玛瑙）和石榴石。坚石不能直接刻划，而要通过金刚砂即钻石粉末粒子在砂轮滚动下高速运动，缓慢地"雕琢"。因仅使用弓钻，制造印章时间较长。

鉴于印章图案极小，而细节刻划准确，倘若没有放大镜，则印章应由高度近视的工匠制作，因为他们比视力正常的人更容易近距离对焦。另有人称，尽管古代玻璃的透明度不如现代，利用盛水的玻璃碗也可放大图像。

萨珊印章的形状依据石料不同而有较大差异，包括：1）戒面，即镶嵌在金属托座中的宝石；2）戒圈，全由石头制成；3）类似戒指的印章，有一个小孔可供绳子穿过，将印章悬在印主身上；4）圆锥形印。

1）戒面为圆形或椭圆形，极少为正方形或长方形，截面为平、凸或凹面。

2—3）从形状上可分为两类：半椭球形或指形，区别在于雕刻表面长度与反面高度之比（半椭球形的高度大于长度）。

4）有时在反面饰有几何母题。

萨珊印章图像包括人像与动物像、植物、符号纹样，以及动作各异的场景。有学者认为动物像是神祇的象征。另有类似印章的工艺品，上为魔鬼图像，不具有真印章的功能，用作护身符。

许多印章上有短铭文，多为巴列维语。

由于大多数萨珊印章并非通过科学发掘所得,博物馆展览中或有赝品,难以辨别[1]。

从社会角度看,印章可属私人(男、女)、祭司、官员或官府所有。在公章中仅刻官府名称而非官员姓名。一类特殊的萨珊印章为基督教印章,或产自基督教会盛行的苏萨、木鹿等地。由于印章为私人制作,不受王室控制,若干明显不同于正统琐罗亚斯德教的宗教印章可能为民间琐罗亚斯德教众所有。

判定萨珊印章的年代十分困难,可依据的标准为印章形状及古文字学,即若干文字的字形。亦有人通过风格学断代,但并不可靠,因为价格较低的印章制作时间较短,比较粗糙。而用于镶嵌的印章使用更贵重的矿石,多为自然主义风格,受希腊化—罗马艺术影响。非镶嵌印章则有截然不同的风格趋势。

因此,系统研究诸多萨珊印章的根本在于研究作坊。本书第二部分第五章将提出潜力巨大的新方法论。

在古代,半宝石具有与魔法相关的属性,至今依然如此。老普林尼的《自然史》中便提及半宝石的魔法属性与东方起源。在此之前,亚里士多德的弟子泰奥弗拉斯托斯亦撰写了《石头论》。此外,希腊化时期、古典晚期的迦勒底人和巴比伦人撰写了魔法书籍,他们的传统十分重要[2]。由此,在选择刻章所用石料时,必然会考虑其魔法属性,印章与魔法之间必然有现今无从得知的联系。此外,石料的选择或许也与印主的偏好相关,但仍缺乏证据支撑。

钱　币

尽管在其他地区有多个地方王朝私自铸币,但萨珊帝国对铸币的中央集权控制十分严格。钱币最能代表王权,因此钱币制造质量极高。

银币亦称德拉克马(从希腊语drachme演化而来),重约4克,质量较佳。萨珊造币所用银饼薄而大,取代了厚而小的安息银饼。罗马的基准货币为金币,但萨珊发行的金币,即代纳尔(源自denarius aureus),象征国王威望而不用于实际流通,可能用于与罗马的交易。除德拉克马银币外,萨珊还发行质量较差、流通较少的四德拉克马银币。此外

---

[1] 里克特称,只要一个印章未被证实为赝品,便不能将其视作赝品,否则形状奇怪而非赝品的印章便会被排除(Richter 1956: xlii)。
[2] "魔法师"一词的来源与如今的用法大相径庭。在希腊语中,magos为琐罗亚斯德教祭司,并不作法。而美索不达米亚地区的琐罗亚斯德教徒与迦勒底人共同生活,后者经常作法,故希腊人将其与前者混淆。比德兹与屈蒙研究了与魔法有关并被归于琐罗亚斯德教徒的希腊文献,证实其大多与迦勒底人相关。

还有青铜或红铜钱币,它们与德拉克马银币间的换算关系并不明确。

由于银矿主要分布于阿富汗东部,萨珊王朝不断向东扩张。

公元3世纪末以后,出现用特殊字母标明造币厂的现象。起初较为罕见,自5世纪始成为规范。但往往无法根据缩略字确定造币厂所在城市。亦可能存在移动造币厂,使国王可以在路途中生产钱币,补充军事所需。

只有钱币重量受到罗马的影响,而币面图像具有典型伊朗特点。钱币模具刻划与印章相似,根本区别在于印章是私人的,而钱币是国家的。在图像上,钱币正面一般为国王右侧面半身像及包含其姓名的铭文,正面像罕见。钱币背面为随年代演变的王朝圣火坛图像。阿尔达希尔一世时仅有祭坛及"阿尔达希尔之圣火"铭文;沙普尔一世时祭坛变窄变高,两侧各有一人,身份难以辨认(一为国王,一为神祇?),有时其中一人持有授权圆环;4世纪时祭坛两侧为两个相同的简约人物(持巴尔萨姆枝的祭司?);自库思老一世始,祭坛两侧人物持剑,尽管未有明确阐释。此外,还有一种钱币图像,与前述相似,但特殊之处在于火坛上有一个躯干及头颅,可能为国王或神祇。

以巴列维文字书写的中古波斯铭文很长。萨珊早期,钱币正面为国王称号,背面为王室圣火。萨珊晚期,正面则为国王姓名及其"法恩",即国祚延绵的祈愿,背面为发行日期及造币厂。公元5世纪后,正面的国王称号简化,仅以姓名结尾。自4世纪始,钱币背面偶尔出现造币厂名字,卑路斯(459—484年)以降,刻划造币厂名字成为规范,有时在名字旁刻有发行年份。5世纪(卡瓦德一世)之后,这一做法成为惯例。

下篇 专题

第一章 宫殿及贵族府邸

前　言

对萨珊时期宫殿建筑的研究仍然任重道远,且鲜少有人基于已有的平面布局解读建筑功能。正如比尔所言,问题在于现有资料的数量、质量均不足[1]。至今宫殿与宗教建筑仍常被混为一谈,而由于宫殿建筑缺乏如宗教建筑领域的重要新发现,仍无法突破传统的观点。

最早的萨珊宫殿建筑整体研究为鲁瑟在《波斯艺术综述》中的一章[2]。比尔认可其开创性,同时也指出书中"优美的插图"不足为信[3]。故1993年比尔写道:"60年后,萨珊时期宫殿建筑的真实面貌仍不得而知。"[4]克莱斯1989年的著作仅简单列举而缺乏批判性[5]。胡夫指出,一直以来,对大多数发现于20世纪中期的重要建筑群的研究以个案研究为主,不如整体研究可靠。他是唯一一位试图通过平面进行系统解读的学者。

因此,被定为宫殿或贵族府邸的许多萨珊建筑群缺乏分类所需的坚实理论基础。霍夫曼2006年于德国慕尼黑大学答辩、2008年公开的博士论文,对此作出了详细清晰的论述,但亦仅限于传统上被视作萨珊宫殿的主要建筑[6]。

本章将就此展开,目的并非详尽无遗地介绍可能为萨珊宫殿的新近发现,而是基于新思路,尤其是新发现,对共识进行鉴别。我将讨论被定为伊朗萨珊时期宫殿的主要例证,并查验与所有已知建筑相符的整体解读。

自建国起,萨珊便将国王形象与优越性作为权力表现的重点。限于篇幅,无法在此简略梳理这一复杂主题的发展脉络。在此仅强调,萨珊国王从未被神化,但被神祇授予

---

[1] Bier 1993, p. 57.
[2] Reuther 1938.
[3] Bier 1993, p. 57.
[4] Bier 1993, p. 57.
[5] Kleiss 1989. 由奥地利科学院出版。
[6] Hoffmann 2008.

特殊地位。而摩崖浮雕被大多数人视作王权神授的视觉表现[1]。历史的潮涨潮落表明,除王室外,贵族亦有显赫地位,有时甚至可影响国王权力。

依据西方人的思维方式,伊朗各地都应有宫殿及贵族府邸,而宫殿除官方接见区外,应包括专供国王及其王室居住的宽敞空间。故而考古发掘所揭示的宫殿及贵族府邸数量之稀少、规模之小,令人讶异。就现有资料而言,我不敢苟同胡夫所言:"宫殿的数量及其规模表明,相比琐罗亚斯德教神庙,萨珊国王似乎在建造宫殿上花费更高。"[2]因现有资料仅为九牛一毛,而建筑全貌可从文献中窥知一二。卡内帕在帝国意识形态的对比研究中,将萨珊与罗马喻为"世界的双眼"[3]。他认为至高无上的帝国意识形态应有与之匹配的各方面表现,包括建筑与艺术,且极富洞见地搜集了相关例证。然而正如希伦布兰德所言,伊斯兰世界在很大程度上借鉴了前伊斯兰时期的波斯,"似乎从未吸取催生了卢浮宫和白金汉宫的西方观点,即一座宫殿应永久为一个朝代的王座"[4]。这一伊斯兰世界的理念或许有助于我们理解典型中东建筑的特点。

伊朗萨珊时期的宫殿建筑和宗教建筑紧密相连,故许多建筑被视作非此即彼。1993年胡夫开创了比照宗教建筑整体阐释宫殿建筑的先例,后文将再次强调。其研究基于功能明确的建筑群,将沿单轴线分布的线性平面与复杂平面进行对比,充分论证多轴线建筑属于宗教建筑,而单轴线建筑属于宫殿建筑。此外,宫殿立面较复杂,而宗教建筑立面较简单[5]。

在胡夫基于平面分析研究普遍原则之前,克勒格尔在研究建筑与灰泥装饰的联系时已提出其阐释,而胡夫对此不置可否。克勒格尔关于萨珊灰泥装饰的奠基之作中指出,饰有灰泥的多柱大殿和伊万等空间具有与琐罗亚斯德教集会、教历节庆相关的宗教功能[6]。许多新发掘的资料按照胡夫的原则应归为宫殿,而克勒格尔仍然坚持原有阐释,将其归为宗教建筑[7]。

面对上述复杂分歧,应在萨珊宫殿及宗教建筑与前朝后代间的文化延续性元素中,寻找可支持建筑分类基本原则的证据。

关于安息与萨珊王朝之间的延续性,前文已强调,萨珊宫殿建筑资料固然不足,安息宫殿建筑资料则更为匮乏。下文将更加明确地指出,现有的少量材料整体表现出二

---

[1] Overlaet 2013 及第四章。
[2] Huff 1993, p. 50.
[3] Canepa 2009.
[4] Hillenbrand 1994, p. 377.
[5] Huff 1993, p. 50.
[6] Kröger 1982.
[7] 关于建造技术的研究——料石、碎石填充或砌砖——在这方面并无太多可借鉴之处,因为上述技术的性质特点比功能特点更突出,我已在研究萨珊时期料石工艺的应用中证明,参见 Callieri 2012。感谢勒里什在讨论中提出该问题。

者间的延续而非中断,与萨珊王朝昭告天下的说辞正相反。由于此前缺乏专门研究,我将着重论证延续性。

关于萨珊与伊斯兰王朝之间的延续性,比尔在研究中强调:"没有证据表明早期的穆斯林王室全方位模仿萨珊宫殿","若受萨珊影响,则始终体现在行政区,更确切地说在被作家与建筑师视为萨珊王权核心的御座大殿。"[1]伊斯兰早期宫殿中出现的多柱大殿若为世俗建筑而非宗教建筑,与萨珊时期的延续性则合情合理。换言之,穆斯林贵族为何会在府邸中化用萨珊时期与宗教相关的平面布局?

阐明这一复杂问题而不陷入循环推论,最合理的方法就是基于若干代表性建筑的解读。下文在简要论述材料后,提出概括性要点。

在开始之前,应说明几点前提。

首先,要考虑对建筑有一定影响的地理环境以及各地区的传统建筑材料。萨珊时期,建筑在地理及气候截然不同的地区内发展,反映在不同的建筑传统中,差异最为明显的是美索不达米亚平原和伊朗高原。伊朗高原内的地区亦各有不同。尽管受主要意识形态的引导,宫殿建筑还是不可避免地受地理条件影响,程式化的建筑布局亦因地制宜。

其次,宫殿建筑的位置未引起足够重视,尤其是其与居住区的关系。阿尔达希尔一世的两座功能确凿的宫殿都建于阿尔达希尔—花拉城外,而非延续安息的传统,建在城内[2]。城市中心为行政专区,被三层同心圆环绕。城外选址延续至萨珊晚期,塔克·基斯拉和特尔·达哈卜等类似宫殿的建筑,不在同时期的韦—安条克—库思老城内,而位于阿斯班巴区,区内有相距较远的官式建筑[3]。

基于现有材料,可以判定宫殿大多位于城外,而不排除贵族府邸位于城内。若文献解读无误,位于泰西封老城内的"白宫"则为特例(参见下文)。

再次,阿契美尼德时期,伊朗高原的宫殿建筑已呈现出与美索不达米亚和苏萨的显著差异。波斯建筑似乎从未设立如古典时期其他国家的明确功能类别。如在宗教建筑中,"神庙"类型直至希腊化时期仍未出现。而宫殿建筑平面如帕萨尔加德和波斯波利斯,也缺少明显的住宅布局,与其说所谓的"私人"建筑为国王居所,不如说用于行政。雷米·布沙拉指出:"若波斯波利斯高台为仪式建筑和国库,而非住宅,则迄今仍未发现国王居所。"[4]由此,可联想到"行宫"概念以及王室宫帐。普鲁塔克对被亚历山大大帝占领的大流士三世帐篷的描述,似表明其排场和奢侈与王室居所相称[5]。

---

[1] Bier 1993, p. 62.
[2] Huff 2008a, pp. 41-2.
[3] Kröger 1993.
[4] Boucharlat 2010, p. 442. 感谢格勒内在讨论中提出,在尼萨古城并未发现安息国王的住处。
[5] Alexandre, 20, pp. 11-3.

阿契美尼德时期居住区让位于行政区和仪式区的特点，在萨珊时期更为明显，尤其与古典晚期和中世纪早期的西方世界相比。在考察如下的考古证据后可见。

选取以下三个不同的建筑为萨珊前的安息时期例证：亚述的帕提亚宫殿，应为安息总督府邸；卡拉·亚兹德格德，应为堡垒，属于控制横穿美索不达米亚中部和米底干道沿线交通的当地领主；卡拉·扎哈克凉亭，即与阿契美尼德类似建筑接近的"宫殿"建筑类型。

亚述的帕提亚宫殿

亚述古城为古代亚述帝国首都，安息王朝时成为控制美索不达米亚北部的要塞。因尼萨建筑用于行政而非居住，且在泰西封亦未发现安息宫殿遗迹，亚述城内的帕提亚宫殿至今仍是已知的主要安息"宫殿"建筑。亚述宫殿（图74）建于安息早期（1世纪），包含来源各异的平面单元和建造理念，体现出安息王朝对外来影响的包容性。亚述宫殿因其中有最早的宫殿伊万之一而尤为重要。伊万为长方形平面单元，其中一条短边完全敞开，两条长边上承券顶。原型为起源于公元前3千纪的美索不达米亚、半地下或地下的类似建筑[1]。亚述宫殿中有四个伊万，面朝平面不规则的大庭院四边，朝向依据太阳方位而定，冬暖夏凉。券顶均倾斜，建造过程中不需要木构架。墙上饰有灰泥。宫殿北侧为一个砖砌四柱大殿，上承三个券顶，功能尚不明确。大殿西侧为周绕回廊的正方形大殿，使人联想到尼萨古城和阿依哈努姆古城的中亚建筑；东侧为希腊化柱廊，为门厅而非中庭[2]。

卡拉·亚兹德格德和萨拉卜·穆尔特

卡拉·亚兹德格德堡垒位于高处，俯瞰泰西封至雷伊干线上的萨尔·波勒·扎哈卜一带，可追溯至安息晚期[3]。除建筑外，丰富的灰泥墙饰遗存亦十分关键。堡垒发掘于20世纪70年代，为一个"雄心勃勃的地方领主"[4]所有，令人联想到哈吉阿巴德"庄园"。建筑群包含数个房址，但已揭露部分均不足以准确判断其布局类型。

---

[1] 本书中，术语"伊万"始终作此解，而不考虑其在波斯语中其他可能的含义（Azarnoush 1994, pp. 68–70）。
[2] Andrae/Lenzen 1933; Venco Ricciardi 2002.
[3] 部分可追溯至公元2世纪，Keall 1977, p. 9；从公元2世纪末至3世纪初，Kröger 1982, p. 257；公元220年，Mathiesen 1992, pp. 177–82.
[4] Keall 2002, p. 69.

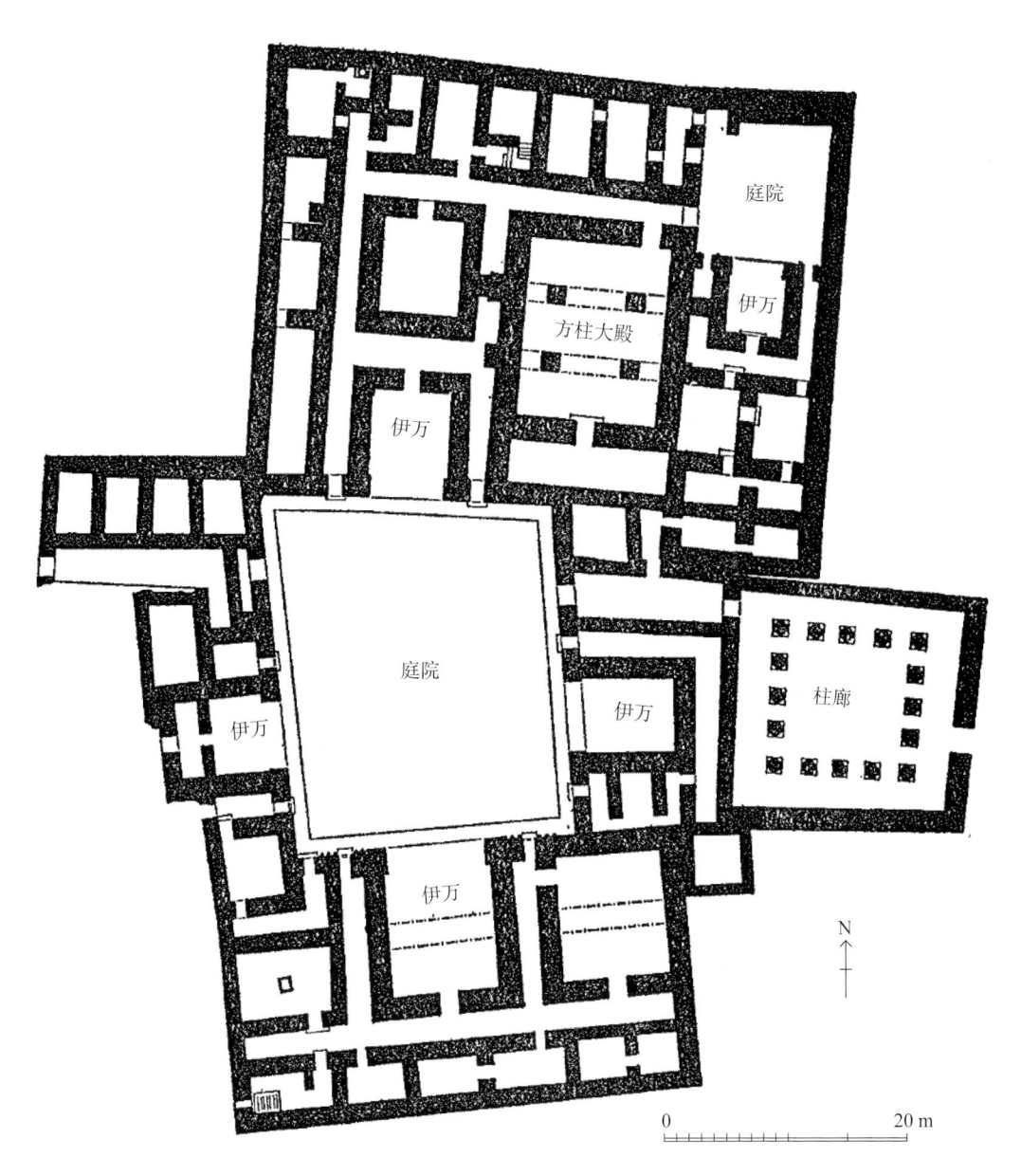

图74 亚述，帕提亚宫殿：总平面图（Schlumberger 1970, fig. 39）

与之相似的一个建筑群亦位于伊朗西部，即克尔曼沙赫西南部吉兰·阿尔卜附近的萨拉卜·穆尔特，揭露信息更丰富。其中亦有灰泥墙饰。建筑被定为"庄园"，断代假设从安息晚期至萨珊时期，莫衷一是，但直至伊尔汗国仍在使用。建筑中心为正方形券顶大殿，前有伊万，二者均周绕回廊。上述平面单元亦出现在亚述宫殿中，被视作接见区。东侧为沿墙凿出石座的庭院，及若干房间组成的行政区。伊万西侧为内有水池

73

的庭院,前为行政区。遗留通往上层或露台的楼梯[1]。

卡拉·扎哈克

卡拉·扎哈克"凉亭"位于防御护墙内,被视作萨珊时期查哈尔·卡卜的原型之一,年代为安息晚期至萨珊时期,为王室建筑而非宫殿建筑[2]。伊朗考古队揭露出一个正方形大殿(图75),内有灰泥墙饰及壁画遗存。重复利用的柱础尤为重要[3]。

至萨珊时期仍在使用的安息建筑中,既有名副其实的宫殿建筑(亚述),亦有当地贵族的建筑(卡拉·亚兹德格德)以及其他类型的王室建筑(卡拉·扎哈克)。上述例证因安息王朝的考古工作有所欠缺而显得尤为珍贵,亦成为下文论述的出发点,即

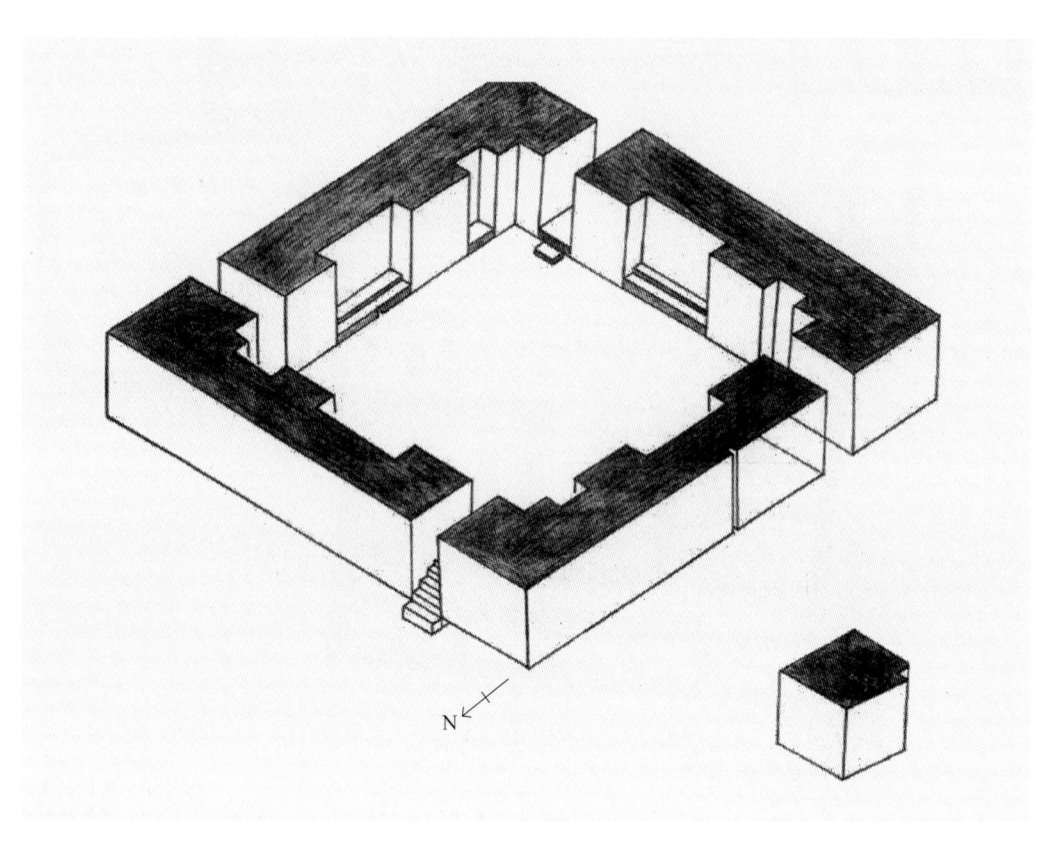

图75 卡拉·扎哈克:方形大殿平面图(Qandgar *et al.* 2004, p. 228)

---

[1] Moradi 2007.
[2] Kleiss 1973.
[3] Qandgar *et al.*, 2004.

安息建筑在萨珊建筑语言和形象语言中起到根本作用,与萨珊国王的政治宣传恰好相反。

卡拉·杜赫塔尔,菲鲁扎巴德(图76)

建筑位于山嘴上,俯瞰距坦格·阿卜河与菲鲁扎巴德平原交汇处数千米的河谷。建造工艺为典型的石膏砂浆粘接碎石。胡夫通过研究建筑与解读公元3世纪上半叶法尔斯省的政治史,确定卡拉·杜赫塔尔为宫殿,年代自萨珊开国君主阿尔达希尔一世即位始,至阿尔达希尔一世战胜阿尔达班四世以前。或有一座年代更早的同类建筑卡拉·沙内辛,用于防御,为阿尔达希尔在达拉卜·盖尔达平原边缘的山嘴上所建,位于三角城外[1]。但仍缺乏考古证据。

卡拉·杜赫塔尔是真正意义上的城堡,四周被防御工事环绕,以延缓攻势。故阿尔达希尔可在多个阵线戍守,击败对手,赢得对法尔斯省的直接控制,并与安息国王抗衡。

建筑思路较为创新,但承载能力不足,故年代应早于被称作"阿泰什卡代"的菲鲁扎巴德平原宫殿等建筑。城堡分为沿山脊上升的三层单轴线平台,包括前院、被若干谒见厅和一个讲坛所环绕的中庭(图77)以及建筑中枢。建筑中枢为突角拱支撑的正方形穹隆顶大殿(图78),四周环绕圆形、三角形房间,位于圆形护墙内。大殿前为部分嵌入护墙的伊万。大殿旁的狭窄螺旋楼梯通向上层(图79)。上层为环绕穹隆顶的狭窄回廊,以及与支撑穹隆顶的突角拱对应的三角形房间。胡夫将三角形房间定为居住区,下文将具体展开。

平面布局过于大胆,开口相较墙体厚度过大,导致建筑稳定性出现问题,两侧房间被填充以作支撑。该问题是由于缺乏成熟的建造传统而导致的,在菲鲁扎巴德平原宫殿中则得到完美解决。

菲鲁扎巴德平原宫殿,又名"阿泰什卡代"

当地人误将宫殿的三个穹隆顶和琐罗亚斯德教神庙的穹隆顶混为一谈,故称宫殿为"阿泰什卡代",即"圣火之居"。此外,阿拉伯—伊斯兰文献里记载,城市附近的水源旁有一座琐罗亚斯德教神庙,许多学者至今仍被误导[2]。依据平面布局及历史,

---
[1] Huff 1995, p. 430; Huff 2008, fig. 4.
[2] Trümpelmann 1991, p. 70.

伊朗萨珊时期的建筑与艺术

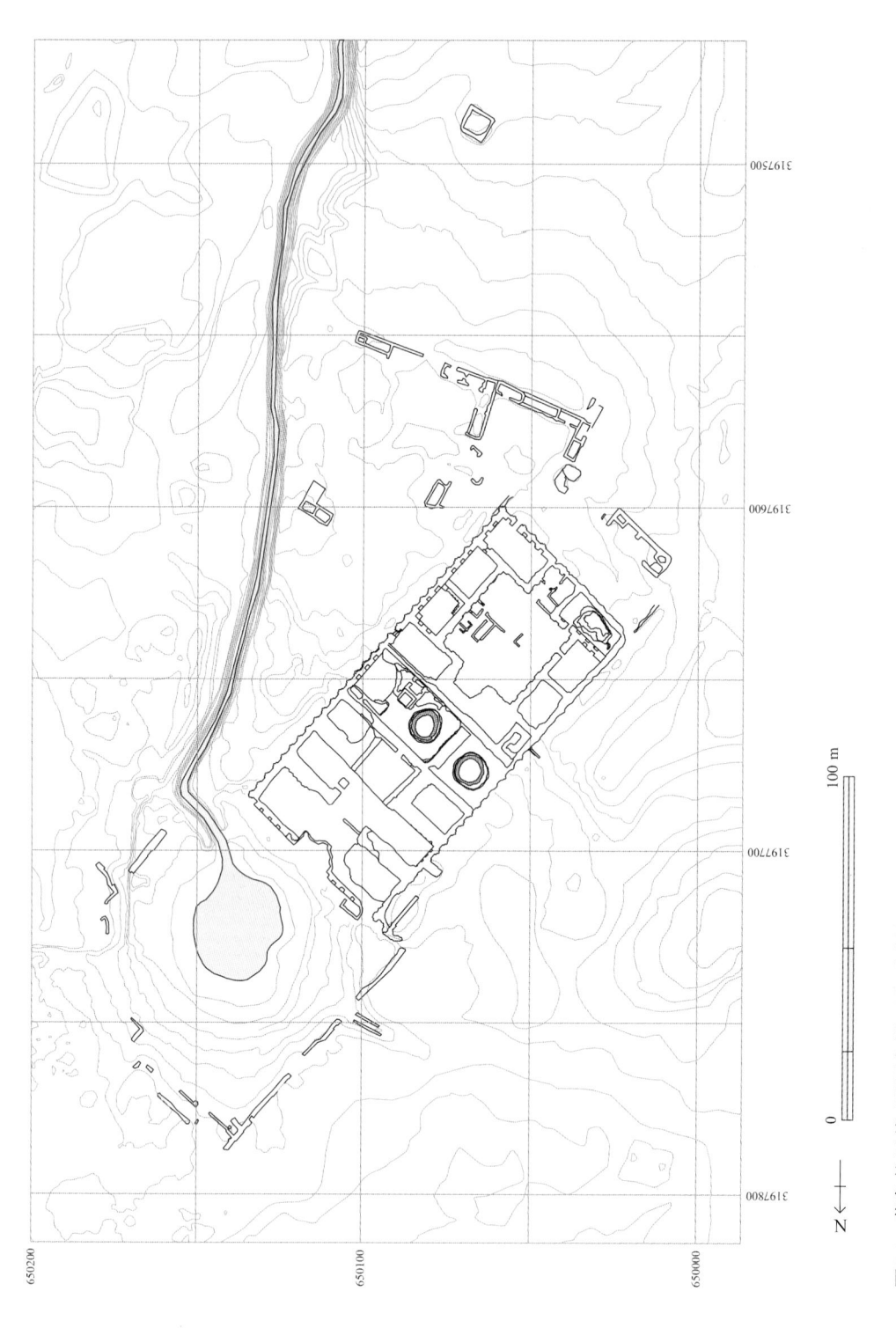

图 76 菲鲁扎巴德，平原宫殿：平面图（A. Eghra 画图）

图77 菲鲁扎巴德，卡拉·杜赫塔尔：B庭院（@ Callieri）

图78 菲鲁扎巴德，卡拉·杜赫塔尔：方形大殿，突角拱细节（@ Callieri）

图79 菲鲁扎巴德，卡拉·杜赫塔尔：通向上层的楼梯（@ Callieri）　　**图80** 菲鲁扎巴德，"阿泰什卡代"：前侧伊万现有铺地下的探测（@ Callieri）

建筑无疑属于宫殿。历经若干建造阶段的建筑群并未得到科学发掘，近期为保护结构而展开修复前，也未进行整体研究和测绘。通过在宫殿两侧的伊万中进行局部发掘，可知如今大部分地面并非原有铺地（图80），若进行系统的地层发掘，将得到更丰富的信息。

两对平行的横向伊万（A、B、C、D）位于前侧伊万（E）两侧，前为内有圆形水池（F）的正方形庭院（图81），池水引自泉水。经过前侧伊万（E）进入中央正方形大殿（G），上为突角拱支撑的穹隆顶，两侧为两个相似的大殿（H、I）。伊万正壁中的展望台较为特殊（图82），离地面高达5米，国王可从此处出现在伊万中（E）。三个穹隆顶大殿后为庭院（J），面朝庭院的房间互不相连。庭院原被视作私人住宅的一部分，胡夫指出其为半官方功能，而霍夫曼认为可能为王室专用[1]。此外，胡夫提出第三层房间应为私人区，与穹隆顶大殿相连的第二层回廊则为半官方功能。

---

[1] Hoffmann 2008, p. 139.

图81 菲鲁扎巴德,"阿泰什卡代":圆形水池(@ Callieri)

图82 菲鲁扎巴德,"阿泰什卡代":前侧伊万正壁检阅台(@ Callieri)

建筑墙体增厚,门变窄,穹隆顶增高,攻克了此前宫殿中的技术难题。

宫殿外的水池为一大特色。水池包含在围墙内,边缘经过规整,似为建筑元素之一。水对萨珊国王的重要性体现在几乎所有摩崖浮雕都临水而立上,不仅由于萨珊王朝与伊朗水神阿纳希德关系密切,亦因水与"灵光"亦即国祚有关[1]。

比沙普尔"宫殿"

位于比沙普尔城西北方的大型建筑群首先由法国考古队于20世纪30年代进行发掘,后经伊朗考古队于70年代发掘。发掘者视其为沙普尔一世的宫殿,包含若干房间和走廊。不同于其他宫殿之处,在于有多条轴线。

宫殿B房址中(图83),四道拱券上承大穹隆顶,形成类似十字形的平面,通常被视作沙普尔一世宫殿的主大殿。而阿扎尔诺什提出,B房址或为文献所记沙普尔一世的火神殿中的"查哈尔·塔克",胡夫亦认同其观点。其宗教功能应无疑义,故将在下一章中展开。但仍有必要提及比尔的假设:"若建筑群已披露的部分为宗教功能,世俗活动便应在别处进行,如面朝庭院的其中一个伊万。"[2]航拍图显示,在发掘区东侧有1处凹地,比尔将其定为长方形大庭院(约100米×150米)。庭院三边中点处可能原有伊万。

由于阿尔达希尔一世的宫殿位于城外[3],而上述建筑群位于城内,2009年,在将其视作火神庙的前提下,我试图寻找真正的沙普尔宫殿,并提出如下观点。

卡拉·杜赫塔尔,比沙普尔

此前被视作沙普尔宫殿的建筑现被定为神殿,沙普尔宫殿则应位于东北方的山上,即卡拉·杜赫塔尔[4]。该地有一座未发掘的大型建筑群(图84),以石膏砂浆粘接碎石筑成。建筑包含三层人造平台,以多个伊万的券顶作支撑,有平面、大小各异的房间。平台平均长25—30米,最大的下层平台宽170米。周绕防御工事,东南方保存较为完好,外围有两个圆形角楼及两个半圆形马面(图85)。由于部分房间归王室专用,部分用于造币厂、军队营房等公务,吉尔什曼将其定为比沙普尔卫城[5]。

---

[1] Callieri 2006c.
[2] Bier 1993, p. 58.
[3] Huff 2008a, p. 54.
[4] Callieri 1971, pp. 39, 42.
[5] Ghirshaman 1971, p. 33, pl. Ⅹ.

图83　比沙普尔，B房址：全景（@ Callieri）

图84　比沙普尔，卡拉·杜赫塔尔：全景（@ Callieri）

图85 比沙普尔,卡拉·杜赫塔尔:东南方防御工事(@ Callieri)

伊万·卡尔萨

沙普尔二世在胡齐斯坦建立的城市中[1],有一个名为塔克·伊万的重要建筑群,包括一个正方形穹隆顶大殿和相邻的长方形大殿。长方形大殿上方有一排共五个券顶,落在横跨大殿的拱券上。莫内雷·德·维拉尔提出该建造技艺源于库赫·哈加[2]。在吉尔什曼发掘的建筑群南门附近,有一座三重伊万式的凉亭,其中发现了公元4世纪后半叶的壁画遗存[3]。大殿应用于接见[4]。亦有学者将其定为伊斯兰时期[5]。

哈吉阿巴德庄园

法尔斯省东部哈吉阿巴德有一座局部发掘的土坯建筑,被阿扎尔诺什定为当地领主的庄园。庄园分为三区(图86):A区为行政区,B区为若干"贵宾套间",C区为私人

---

[1] Gyselen/Gasche 1994, p. 33, pl. X.
[2] Monneret de Villard 1954, p. 103.
[3] Ghirshaman 1952, pp. 10−12; 1962, p. 183.
[4] De Waele 2004, p. 356.
[5] Goldman/Little 1980, p. 292, n. 18.

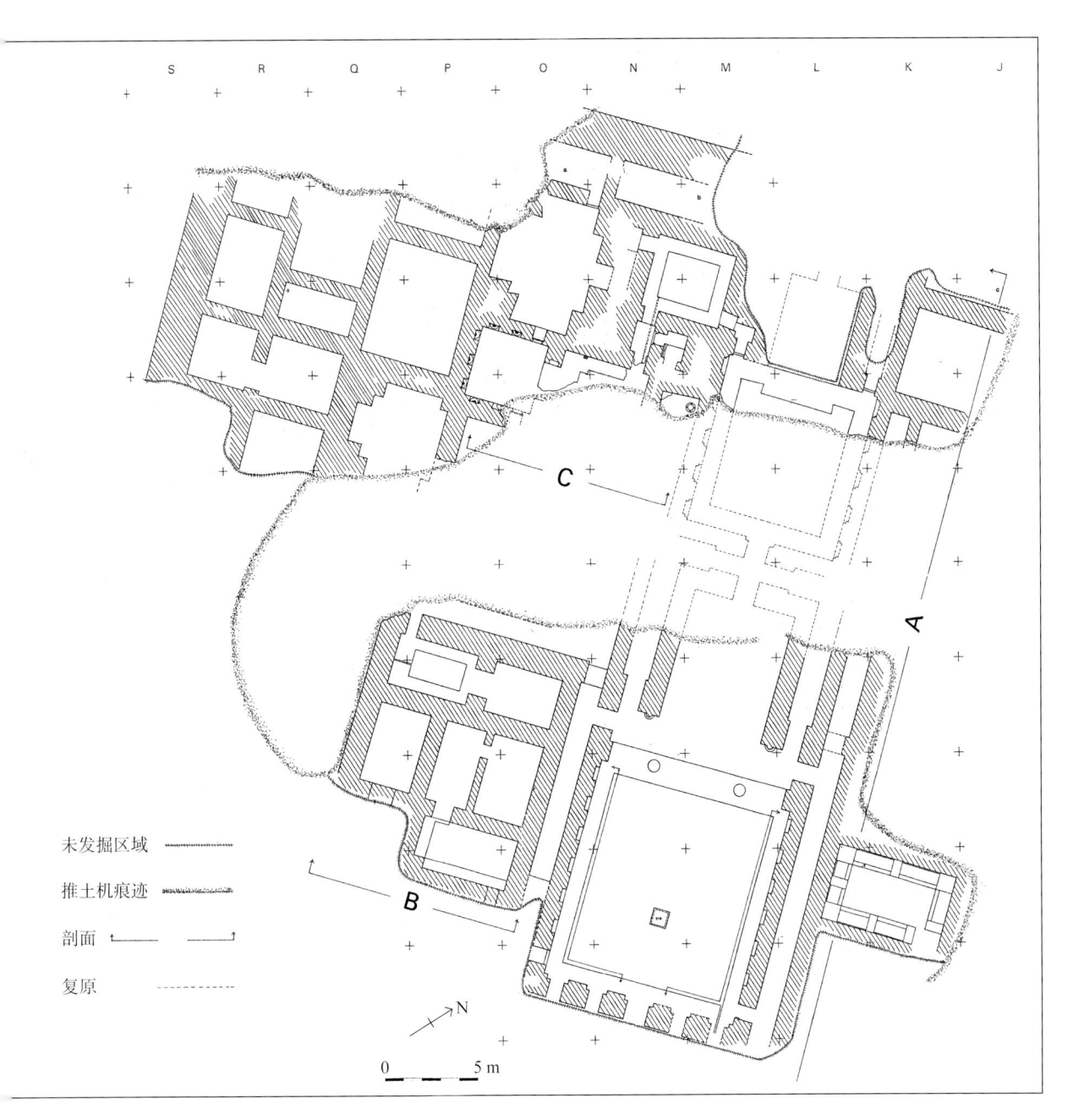

图86 哈吉阿巴德,"地主庄园":总平面图(Azarnoush 1994, pl. A)

神堂[1]。由于C区与查哈尔·塔克的十字形平面相似，宗教功能应较为确凿[2]，而A区的行政功能则需商榷。A区为突出的单轴线布局，包含接连数个面朝庭院的伊万单元。阿扎尔诺什指出，最外面的伊万是公开接见处（迪万·阿姆），最里面的伊万是私下接见处（迪万·卡斯）。值得注意的是，有两处发现了丰富的灰泥墙饰遗存，其中一处为L.178庭院（图87）及L.149伊万对面的柱廊。鉴于轴线布局出现两次，此处应为世俗行政功能，但与克勒格尔的理论相悖，即饰有灰泥的建筑应为火神庙中举办集体活动的场所。

由于庄园中发现了沙普尔二世和瓦赫拉姆二世的灰泥半身像[3]，阿扎尔诺什将其年代定为4世纪。但半身像或为祭祖之用[4]。如克勒格尔和吉钮所言，将庄园定在4—5世纪之间更为合理[5]。

图87 哈吉阿巴德，"地主庄园"：L.178庭院（Azarnoush 1994, pl. 1）

---

[1] Azarnoush 1994, p. 67.
[2] Ghanimati 2013, p. 897.
[3] Azarnoush 1994, pp. 159, 237.
[4] Kröger 1993, p. 64; 2006, p. 52.
[5] Gignoux 1995.

阐释建筑的功能时，不可忽略对灰泥装饰部分图像的分析。如A区接见区中，L.149伊万入口两侧半柱旁的两座男性半身像尤为关键（参见第二部分第三章）。

Ⅰ、Ⅱ号房址，启什

1931年由英国考古队发掘的启什两座主要房址，位于美索不达米亚平原中部、巴比伦以东，年代为公元5世纪。其时萨珊波斯正处于与嚈哒的战争中，后以卑路斯战败身亡，而波斯被中亚游牧民族征服告终。

报告中，Ⅰ、Ⅱ号遗址为两个不同的房址（图88）。而穆雷提出两者或属于同一建筑群，建筑群还包含以长方形水池为中心的第三座房址（SP-3）[1]。

Ⅰ号房址（SP-1）以庭院为中心，南侧为大伊万，前有两根立柱，北侧则有接近壁龛大小的小伊万。两个小伊万及大伊万东侧的房间内均发现了灰泥装饰遗存。在较大的Ⅱ号房址（SP-2）中，两列各三根柱子的布局将伊万变为多柱大殿（D）。大殿北侧为大庭院（B），周绕回廊。大殿南端为包含半圆形龛的十字形室（A）。大殿与庭院间的隔墙两端有狭窄门道。Ⅱ号房址中的灰泥装饰分布于大殿、半圆形龛及庭院内。庭院东、西墙十四根壁柱间形成浅龛。两个庭院中心均有水池。

基于整体布局及穆雷发现的国王半身像[2]，建筑最初被定为宫殿，而克勒格尔根据主要灰泥装饰的解读提出了质疑[3]（参见第二部分第三章）。

达斯特盖尔德，班迪扬

由拉赫巴尔发掘的A土丘位于呼罗珊·拉扎维的班迪扬，其伊万墙上所刻的中古波斯语铭文称建筑为"达斯特盖尔德"，即贵族家族领地，详见下章[4]。吉钮认为该铭文指代其所在的A土丘建筑群，并提出其余诸多论据，证明建筑并不具有宗教功能[5]。下章将一一展现。拉赫巴尔在发掘A土丘后，又发掘了与之相邻的B、C土丘。B土丘包含一个直径约20米的圆形夯土建筑，高约3米。C土丘无疑具有世俗功能[6]。由于平整土地时地形遭到严重破坏，三处土丘之间可能存在的建筑或已被毁，我认为A土丘的

---

[1] Moorey 1978, pp. 122–3.
[2] Moorey 1978, p. 135.
[3] Kröger 1982, pp. 268–70.
[4] 吉钮（2008, p. 167）提出，根据肖尔沃的观点，达斯特盖尔德可指"土地财产"及"精神财产"，而他认为在班迪扬遗址中应采用第一种释义。
[5] Gignoux 2008.
[6] Rahbar 2007.

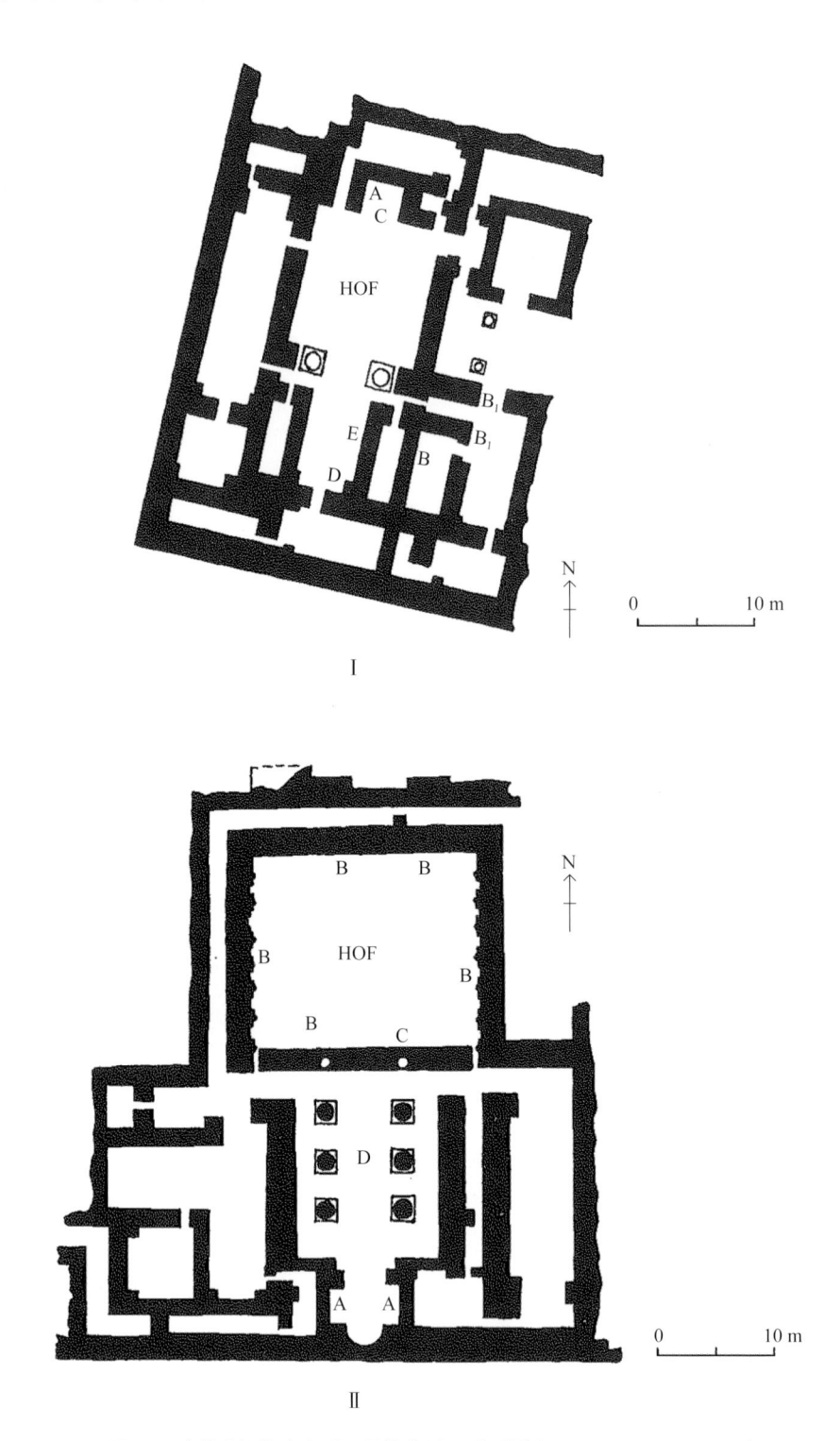

图88 启什（伊拉克），Ⅰ、Ⅱ号房址：平面图（Kröger 1982, fig. 119）

"达斯特盖尔德"（贵族家族领地）应指的是遗址整体[1]。

距A土丘约100米的C土丘原为一处宫殿建筑群，依据钱币定为库思老一世时期。两个主要建造阶段的遗迹被一层土坯覆盖，土坯上为一个伊儿汗国时期的窑址。宫殿中央为一座大殿（现存约24米×13.5米），殿内有两列各四根土坯方柱，南部已毁（图89）。大殿东侧为正门，西侧侧门与私人房间相连。大殿西北方有若干房间及与大殿相垂直的空间，后者墙上有壁柱，被定为庭院。其余房间属于第二阶段，用于手工制作和贮存。一个石膏砂浆铺地的房间被视作用于压制葡萄，另一房间中发现了一个石磨。出土一块记有行政用途的中古波斯语铭文的陶片。通过一枚硬币确定第二阶段的年代为库思老二世时期[2]。

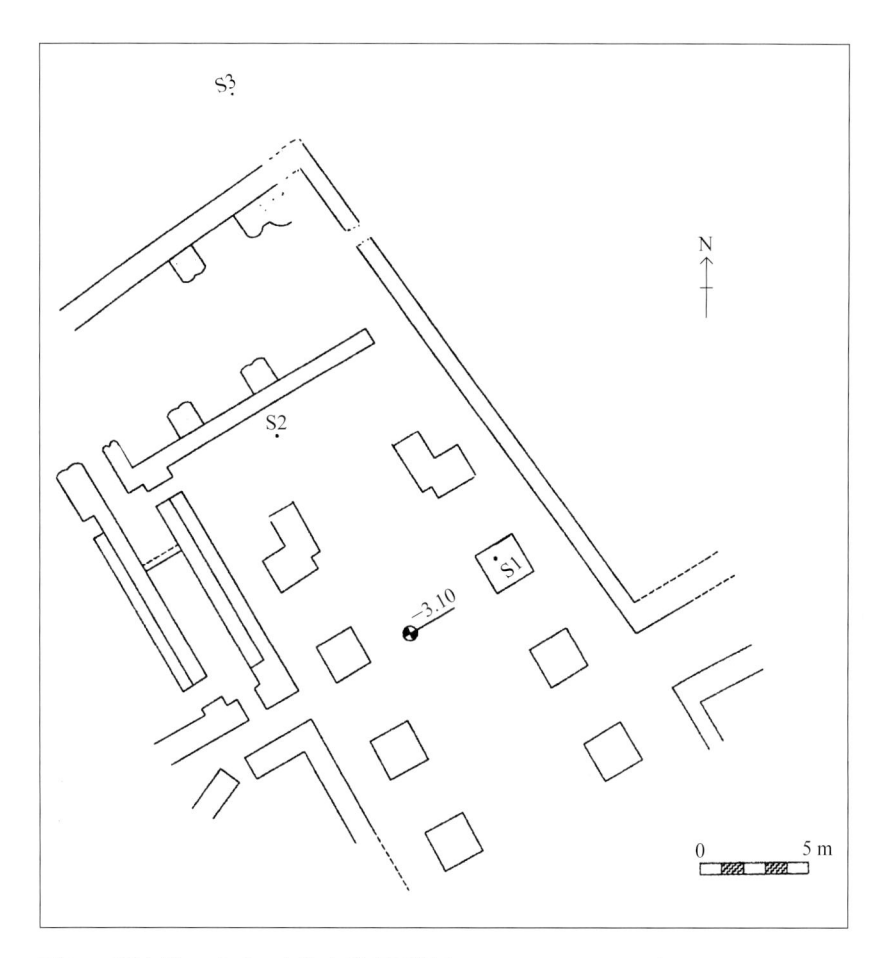

图89 班迪扬，C土丘：方柱大殿平面图（Rahbar 2007a, fig. 2）

---

[1] 尽管A土丘的主要年代为公元5世纪，而C土丘的主要年代为公元6世纪。
[2] Rahbar 2007, p. 132.

塔克·基斯拉

随着底格里斯河变迁，古都泰西封所处的美索不达米亚平原中部地貌遭到破坏，导致泰西封的资料较少，研究安息和萨珊时期官式建筑较为困难。20世纪20年代末起，在该地区展开了考古工作。地域变迁体现在阿拉伯语名称"麦达恩"中（即"麦地那[城市]"的复数形式），得名于此处发现的四处遗址。安息都城考古资料匮乏，萨珊都城信息少而零散，其重要性再强调也不为过。本章原应探讨被阿拉伯文献称为"白宫"的王室宫殿，位于麦达恩"老城"中[1]。但迄今为止尚未发现"白宫"遗址，故相关研究围绕另一宫殿展开，即塔克·基斯拉。该宫殿位于萨珊晚期的"行政城市"阿斯班巴，可能用于召见。

德国学者的发掘表明，塔克·基斯拉属于一处更大的建筑群（图90）。建筑群还包括东侧一座类似建筑，其庭院四周被埃德曼定为住宅[2]。

位于塔克·基斯拉南端以南的苏德堡（阿迪拜）遗址中，发现了非居住功能的建筑及重要灰泥装饰。装饰年代根据风格定为公元6世纪[3]。由于发现灰泥装饰，遗址最初被误作白宫。另有灰泥装饰分布于东南方名为特尔·达哈卜的正方形平台上。塔克·基斯拉原有大理石、马赛克和灰泥装饰，现残存一座大型伊万，敞开的一边有装饰性壁柱及半圆拱。伊万顶部为无构架倾斜式的抛物线大券顶，宽25.60米，高30米，深43米。伊万三面墙后各有一排小房间，两侧的小房间分别通向两个长方形房间和与之相连的正方形房间，正壁后为一个长方形房间。伊万所在轴线上没有穹隆顶大殿，故伊万似乎兼具大殿的功能。应注意的是，地基与立面细节反映出两侧房间的上层布局与菲鲁扎巴德宫殿相似。伊万和伊万正壁后的房间地基水平不同，似分属两个建造阶段，但修复券顶工作中的勘探否定了这一假设[4]。

塔克·基斯拉由库思老一世建造。而库思老二世不喜居于都城，在距此东北方100千米的达斯特盖尔德另建有一宫殿，其址现存一座宏伟堡垒[5]。公元627年，达斯特盖尔德被赫拉克利乌斯征服。

鲁瑟提出塔克·基斯拉的建筑立面源自叙利亚原型，故将其年代定为公元6世纪[6]。亦有人称建筑立面和安息时期的美索不达米亚建筑间密切相关，如亚述宫殿。

---

[1] Morony 2009.
[2] Erdmann 1969, p. 32.
[3] Kröger 1982, pp. 18–37.
[4] Keall 1987.
[5] Sarre/Herzfeld 1920, p. 76 及其后；Schippmann 1969, p. 43 及其后. 但塔巴里（Ⅰ, p. 1043）认为库思老在韦—阿尔达希尔有一座宫殿，Morony 1989, p. 93.
[6] Reuther 1938, pp. 515–6.

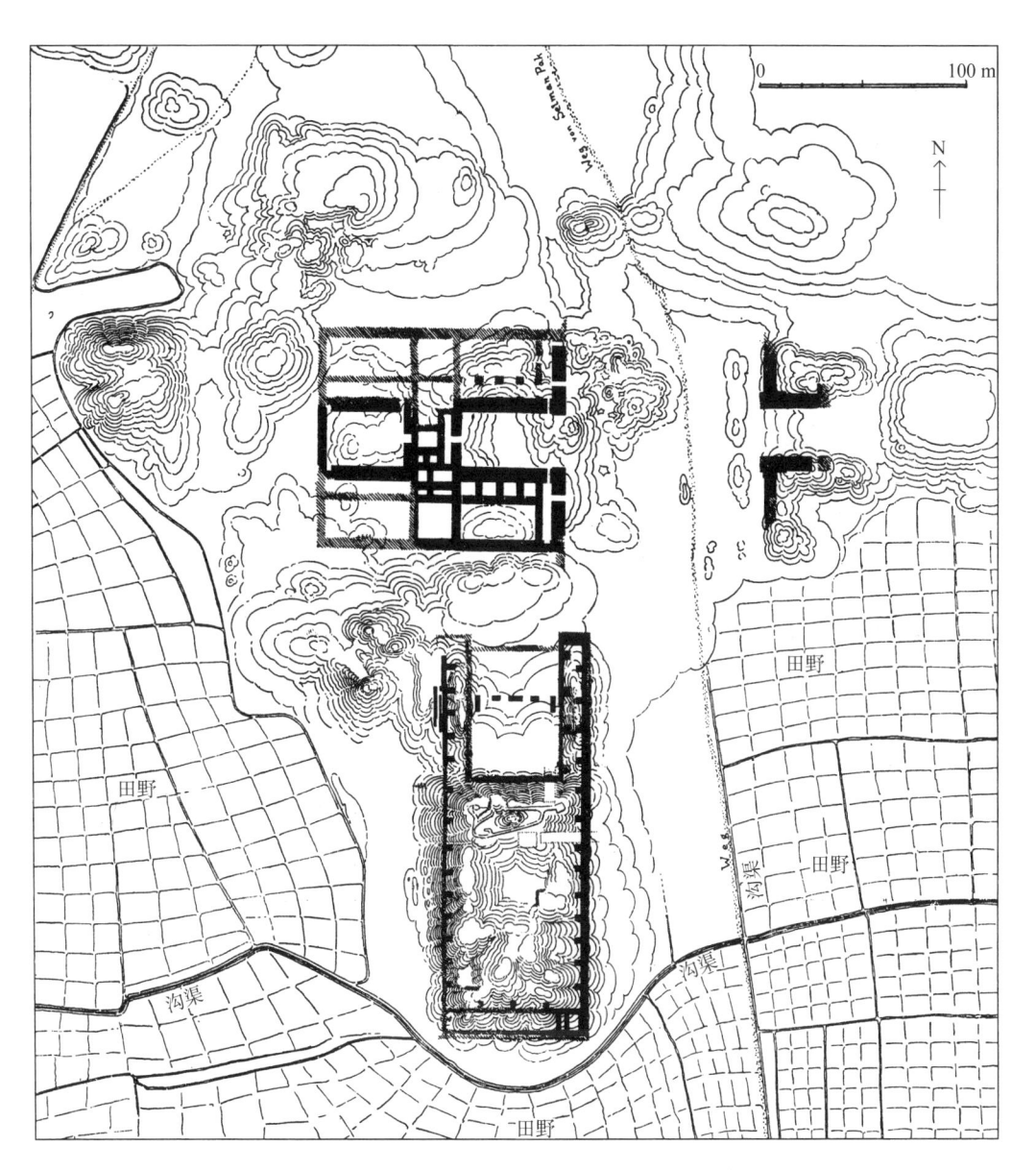

图 90 麦达恩（伊拉克），塔克·基斯拉：总平面图（Fahimi 2012, fig. 7a）

西伊万,塔克斯特·苏莱曼

塔克斯特·苏莱曼火神庙位于阿塞拜疆西部,主要建于库思老一世时期。亦包括一座宫殿,在每年朝拜王室及贵族圣火——阿杜尔·古什纳斯普时,供国王和贵族居住。宫殿为一个料石墙支撑的砖砌大型伊万(图91),其轴线与主神殿轴线相垂直,位于神殿与湖泊之间空地的西侧。伊万三侧被若干长方形小房间环绕(图92),各个阶段的铺地分层明显。胡夫指出,面朝西伊万的多柱大殿群应为宫廷所用,因其与神庙主体相隔一条狭长走廊,仅有两条窄道相通[1]。故多柱大殿的功能应与西伊万宫殿而非神庙相关。

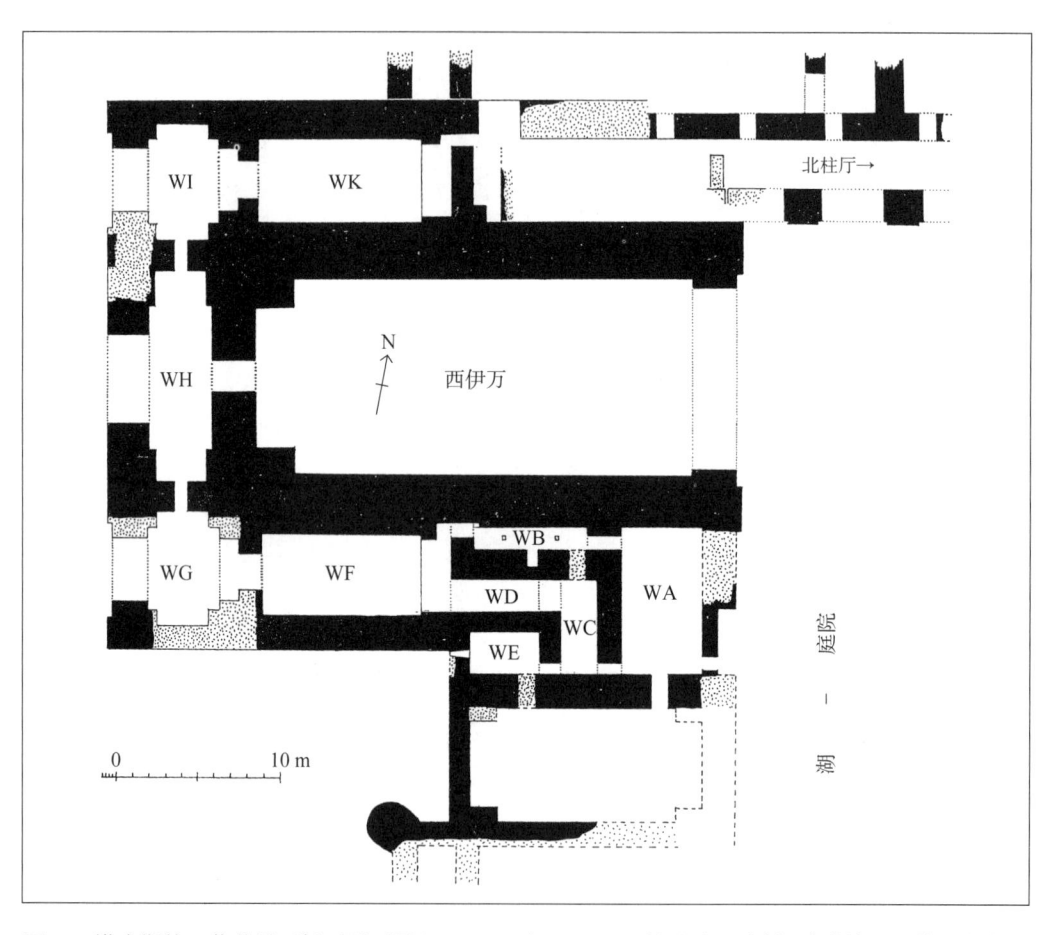

图91 塔克斯特·苏莱曼西伊万平面图(A. Eghra在W. Kleiss的基础上绘制,感谢德黑兰德国考古研究院提供)

---

[1] Huff 1993, p. 55.

图92 塔克斯特·苏莱曼,西伊万:伊万旁的长方形房间(@ Callieri)

伊朗萨珊时期的建筑与艺术

坎加瓦尔大型建筑群

位于伊朗西部坎加瓦尔的大型建筑群,原被视作文献中供奉阿娜希塔或阿尔忒弥斯的神殿,年代为塞琉古王朝[1]或安息王朝[2]。阿扎尔诺什1981年[3]及2009年的文章[4]则对其功能提出了新的解读。依据与安息墓地的地层关系、石块上的标识、建筑装饰(柱头、檐口等)以及对墙体下方一块砖头的热释光断代,他充分论证建筑年代只可能为萨珊晚期。此外,他通过阿拉伯—伊斯兰文献将建筑群定为萨珊晚期的"喀斯尔·阿卢索斯"宫殿。该观点往往连同年代学解读一起被全盘接受,但未考虑其背后的含义,即萨珊时期伊朗高原存在一种新的宫殿类型。建筑平面为东北角突出的正方形,分为两层叠压平台,下层为210米(东—西)×220米(南—北),上层为94米×94米。现仅存厚度分别为18米和9.32米的承重墙,外砌料石,内部填充泥土和碎石。靠墙南侧有两列相向台阶(图93),东侧有一列,通往下层平台顶部。依据下层平台边缘的坍塌

图93 坎加瓦尔,大型建筑群:下层平台南侧台阶(@ Callieri)

---

[1] Ghirshman 1962, p. 32.
[2] Kambaxsh Fard 1373, 1386; Mehriyar/Kabiri 1383.
[3] Azarnoush 1981.
[4] Azarnoush 2009.

图94 坎加瓦尔，大型建筑群：下层平台西侧边缘的柱廊（@ Callieri）

石质构件，可知原有一列粗壮的柱子支撑拱廊，借鉴了外来建筑元素，如爱奥尼式柱础、多立克式线脚及科林斯式顶板（图94）。若确为宫殿，这一巨大布局便意味着彻底的革新，因只有阿契美尼德时期存在类似的建筑原型，但亦仅有单层平台。1977年，卢科宁基于碑铭学确定年代为萨珊晚期，但他认为建筑群是建于安息时期阿尔忒弥斯神庙上的阿娜希塔神庙，由库思老二世敕令重修[1]。布沙拉审慎地称之为"宫殿或神殿"，亦表明对其宫殿功能的怀疑[2]。我认同霍夫曼的观点，即在缺乏台上立面遗迹的情况下，建筑功能难以判定[3]。

达姆甘

1931—1932年，在塞姆南东北地区达姆甘发掘了建筑主体，东南侧为一个大庭院。中央为长方形多柱大殿（1），被两列各三根圆柱、一根壁柱分为三开间（图95）。

---

[1] Lukonin 1977b.
[2] Bouchartat 2006, p. 50.
[3] Hoffmann 2008, p. 147.

图95 达姆甘：房址平面图（Kröger 1982, fig. 124）

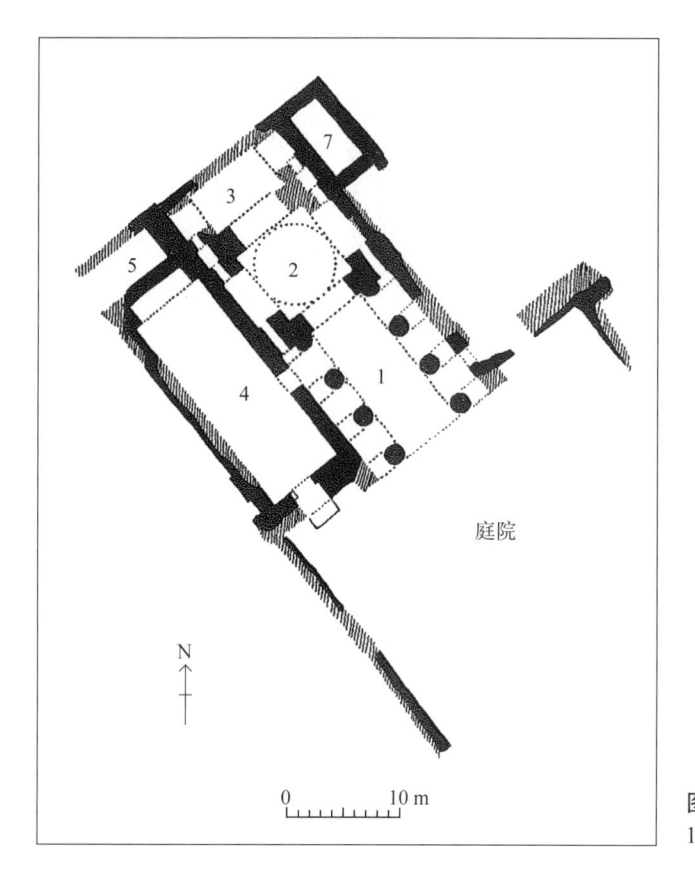

大殿后为正方形穹隆顶房间（2），周绕回廊，正壁或与一个长方形小房间连通（3）。多柱大殿和正方形房间的西南侧为一个饰有壁画的长条形房间（4），题材或为狩猎场景。东北侧可能有一个类似房间。多柱大殿的柱子、拱门饰和拱券上有大量灰泥装饰，克勒格尔参照装饰风格，将大殿年代定为6世纪后半叶[1]。发掘者将建筑定为宫殿，似有不妥。席普曼将其视作火神殿[2]。而克勒格尔则谨慎地表示，尽管雷伊·瓦拉明地区的类似建筑的确在伊斯兰早期作为住宅，在萨珊时期也可能作为地方领主的府邸或琐罗亚斯德教集会中心[3]。

1936年美国考古队在雷伊局部发掘的查拉·塔尔汉·埃什加巴德中，包含两座未完全揭露的宫殿（图96）。建筑由萨珊晚期至伊斯兰早期使用。伊斯兰早期的多次改造使原始平面难以确定。主殿（C宫殿）包含朝向东北的长方形大殿，以两列各三根圆柱隔出两侧狭窄的次开间。大殿前为露天庭院而非正方形房间。大殿东南壁有4处开口，

---

[1] Kröger 1982, p. 262; 2005b.
[2] Schippmann 1971, pp. 8-11.
[3] Kröger 2005b.

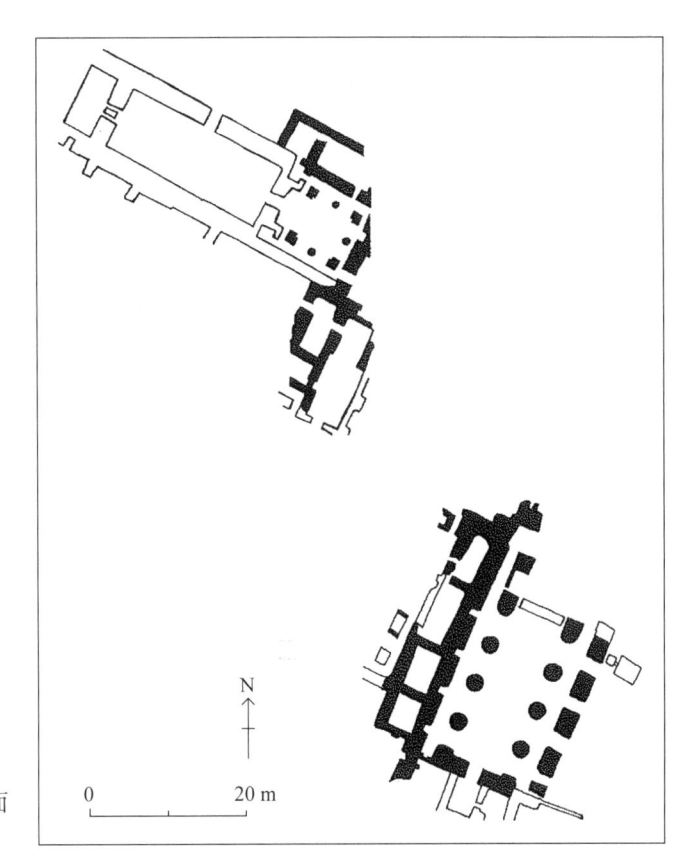

图96 查拉·塔尔汉："主殿" 平面图（Kröger 1982, fig. 130）

通往另一庭院。倭马亚王朝的改造主要集中在中央为正方形多柱大殿的偏殿（B宫殿）中，故萨珊时期的建筑结构难以复原。C宫殿的灰泥装饰大多属于倭马亚王朝，质量较高[1]。

伊马拉特·库思老，喀斯尔·席林

建筑群位于伊朗西部、萨珊首都附近，通常依据文献将其定为库思老二世所建的豪华宫殿之一[2]。

建筑群位于一个宏伟平台上（285米×91米），高于平原8米，北侧有两列与立面平行的大型台阶，东、西侧各有一列相似的台阶。贝尔参照伊拉克乌海迪尔的一座阿拔斯王朝宫殿，对建筑群进行了复原，而鲁瑟在此基础上绘制了平面图，故原始布局不明确[3]。

---

[1] Thompson 1976; Kröger 1990.
[2] Huff 1973, p. 52.
[3] Sinisi 2005, p. 390.

最新的航拍表明复原大致正确[1]。平台东侧为大型露天空间，用作花园。一个伊万面朝花园敞开，两侧有两次开间，券顶外侧落于两列柱子上。上述布局为伊朗考古队近期的科学发掘所证实（图97）。但伊万后的建筑结构尚不明确，或为另一庭院、其他伊万及相邻房间。建筑群似无穹隆顶大殿，附近一座平面相似的建筑豪什·库里亦是如此。

发掘者认为，伊马拉特·库思老是一座位于城外的阿拔斯王朝宫殿，坐落在园林中[2]。依据砖块残片的热释光分析、砖内的伊斯兰陶片，以及探沟内大量伊斯兰早期而非萨珊时期的陶片，可确定其年代。另，从建筑结构角度，与萨迈拉间的相似之处亦证实其年代为公元8世纪[3]。

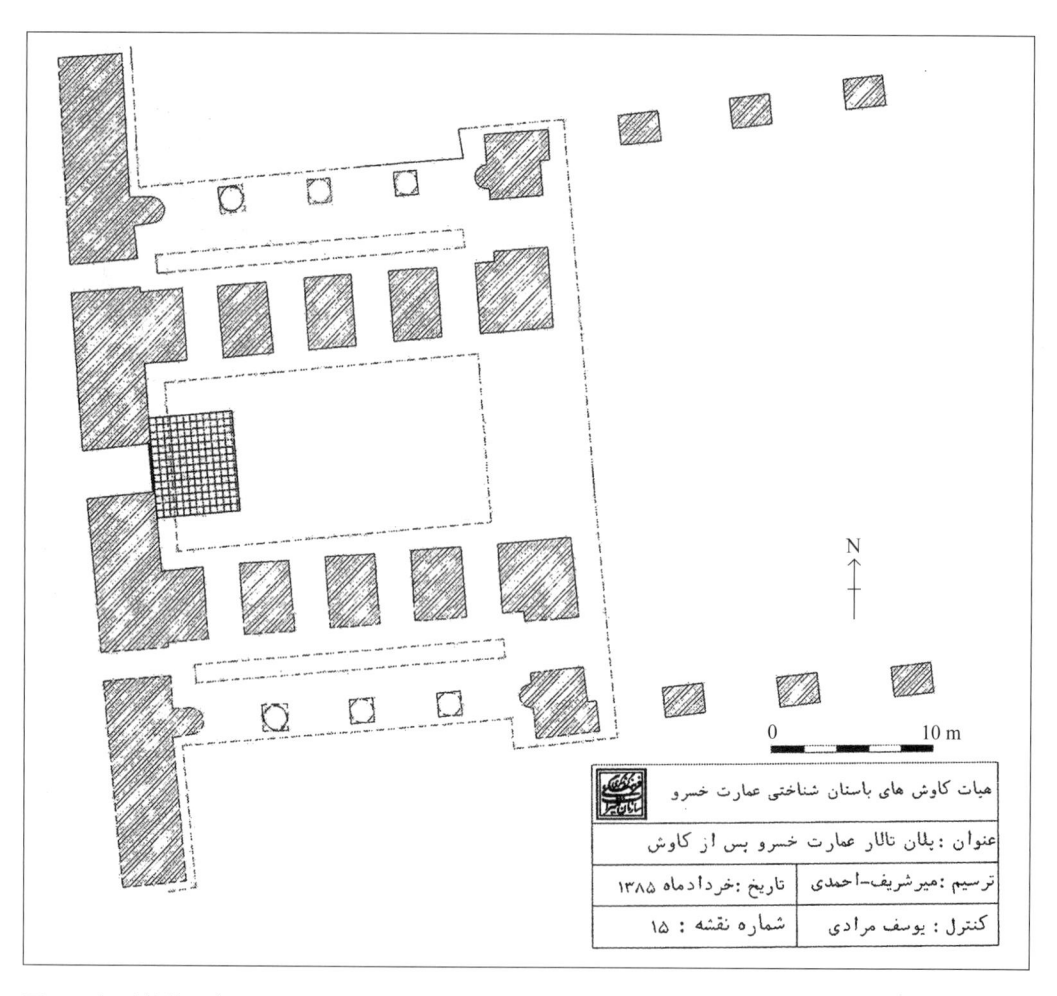

图97 伊马拉特·库思老，喀斯尔·席林：早期区域平面图（Moradi, fig. 7, p. 340）

---

[1] Hoffmann 2008, pl. 35.
[2] Bier 1993, p. 59, 比尔指出该建筑具有"明显的阿拔斯风格"，源自贝尔提出的建筑重建阶段。
[3] Moradi 2012, pp. 333-2.

萨尔韦斯坦

萨尔韦斯坦位于法尔斯省中东部,原被视作公元5世纪的宫殿[1]。而比尔对其建造技术展开严谨的研究后,将其定为建于伊斯兰早期的琐罗亚斯德教神殿[2]。

近期通过建筑周边探沟发现活动层为萨珊晚期,故建筑修建应始于萨珊晚期,竣工和使用阶段则分别为伊斯兰阿拔斯和塞尔柱王朝[3]。

从功能阐释角度,建筑的复杂平面亦异于胡夫提出的宫殿建筑典型特点,而符合比尔提出的宗教建筑特点。建筑可能为火神殿,至伊斯兰时期仍在使用,或被改造以适应新的需求。

克什克·阿尔达希尔,博兹帕尔

博兹帕尔"克什克·阿尔达希尔"大型建筑群亦同上(图98)。建筑地处与法尔斯的萨尔·马沙德区接壤的布什尔山区,离阿契美尼德晚期的古雷·杜赫塔尔古墓不远处。当地通常将其视作阿尔达希尔的宫殿。除旺当·贝格[4]和阿斯卡里·查韦尔迪[5]的简述外,建筑群未经调查研究。

建筑群包含萨珊建筑的代表性元素,屋顶则不同于前伊斯兰时期的典型做法。由于缺少实测图,难以了解建筑的复杂布局。可知建筑包括两个以走廊相隔的单元,走廊中间为两个相对的入口。第一个单元中央为长方形券顶房间,与突角拱支撑的正方形穹隆顶房间相连(图99)。第二个单元中央为长方形券顶大殿,两侧分别为券顶房间和横向长方形大殿。横向长方形大殿被有拱门的隔墙分为三间,包含半圆形后殿。

墙体的建造技术为石膏砂浆粘接碎石,故旺当·贝格将建筑定为萨珊时期,同时强调建筑平面与叙利亚及美索不达米亚的教堂相近[6]。

建筑群的年代难以确定。从穹隆顶房间前有券顶大殿来看,可能属于萨珊时期,从复杂的建筑布局和屋顶做法来看,可能属于伊斯兰时期。

---

[1] Ghirshman 1962, p. 183.
[2] Bier 1986.
[3] Askari Chaverdi 2009, pp. 62–3; 2012.
[4] Vanden Berghe 1961.
[5] Askari Chaverdi 2014, p. 161.
[6] Vanden Berghe 1961, p. 411.

图98 博兹帕尔,"克什克·阿尔达希尔":全景(@ Callieri)

图99 博兹帕尔,"克什克·阿尔达希尔":方形房间,顶部为突角拱支撑的穹隆顶(@ Callieri)

建筑单元

正方形穹隆顶大殿

就建筑单元而言，菲鲁扎巴德的阿尔达希尔一世两所宫殿中均有正方形穹隆顶大殿，显然为建筑群的意识形态核心，即御座大殿。就建筑本身而言，正方形穹隆顶大殿属于当地术语中的"查哈尔·卡卜"，即四面开门的正方形大殿。而不同于"查哈尔·塔克"，即四角方柱支撑拱券形成十字形平面。中央穹隆顶在琐罗亚斯德教建筑中以查哈尔·塔克的形式盛行，而在3世纪后功能明确的宫殿中不再出现，尤其是考虑到比沙普尔的穹隆顶大殿为宗教建筑。目前伊万·卡尔萨的功能无法确定，故唯一可能属于萨珊宫殿的穹隆顶大殿位于达姆甘，但被克勒格尔认为另作他用。

上述建筑布局演变的原因值得深思。在我看来，正方形穹隆顶大殿逐步成为火神殿的专属，而不见于世俗建筑。因此菲鲁扎巴德的塔克斯特·内辛成为后世琐罗亚斯德教建筑的典范，而阿尔达希尔的宫殿形式却未被继承下来，因穹隆顶大殿为火神殿所独有。穹隆顶（"贡巴德"）几乎只在火神殿中出现，故菲鲁扎巴德当地将阿尔达希尔的第二所宫殿称作"阿泰什卡代"，并非巧合。

萨珊中晚期宫殿建筑中不见穹隆顶大殿，也证实了萨尔韦斯坦没有居住功能。

伊万

与穹隆顶大殿相反，伊万是王室与贵族宫殿中最常见的元素，在宗教建筑中并未完全消失，而是退居次位[1]。在萨珊王室建筑历时演变中，伊万从依附于穹隆顶大殿，到逐渐成为核心并替代后者功能。伊万的次要位置体现在菲鲁扎巴德的两所宫殿中，为国王接见臣民之处，如平原宫殿中伊万正壁的检阅台。因此，萨珊早期宫殿建筑的核心元素为穹隆顶大殿与伊万的结合。

其后数世纪的宫殿建筑中无穹隆顶大殿，而伊万位处中心，应为御座所在。至少在泰西封宫殿中，文献记载御座所在的塔克·基斯拉仅有大伊万，而没有穹隆顶大殿。仔细阅读最早的考古简报中发现伊万的过程，则会发现并非仅有如今遗存的伊万，而应另有一个与之对称的伊万[2]。第二个伊万只余下少量遗迹，但足可证明其正壁厚度及开口大小都与第一个伊万相同。故并非仅有中轴线上的单个伊万，而是存在面朝同一庭院（在泰西封中未见庭院遗存）的数个伊万。亚述宫殿亦是如此，通过朝向保证冬暖夏凉。

---

[1] Hoffmann 2008, p. 130.
[2] Reuther 1929, p. 451.

另一展现王权的伊万为塔克斯特·苏莱曼的西伊万，其功能同时体现在文献资料、建筑规模以及有别于火神庙的位置中。

贵族府邸如哈吉阿巴德"庄园"中，伊万前有柱廊、面朝庭院的单元两次出现。美索不达米亚的启什Ⅰ号房址及哈姆林地区特拉卜·沙夫发掘的住宅中[1]，伊万和庭院之间亦有柱廊。

伊万的位置邻近入口，似有接见功能。其绘制或灰泥塑制的形象题材应与世俗建筑内行政区的意识形态相关。

方柱或圆柱大殿

方柱或圆柱大殿出现在伊朗高原和美索不达米亚的数个建筑群中。圆柱或方柱大多为石质，较为粗壮，足以支撑券顶重量[2]。胡夫强调，在许多大殿中，"方柱"更像是支撑券顶的墙体遗存，即开凿拱券后的墙体部分[3]。由此可进一步推断，多柱大殿源于把伊万分为三开间，至少在布局中可视作伊万的变体。多柱大殿面朝庭院的形式与伊万十分相像，与仪式和接见功能相关。考察伊万和多柱大殿的年代，会发现在公元6、7世纪时发生演替，多柱大殿的数量超过大型伊万。

除上述多柱大殿外，在（胡齐斯坦）贝赫贝汗地区阿尔甘，一次偶然发现后的发掘揭露了一座大型建筑的局部，出土了大量萨珊灰泥装饰[4]。至少三列、每列三根砖制圆柱的布局，似在模仿美索不达米亚和班迪扬C土丘的贵族府邸[5]。

萨珊时期多柱大殿的首要问题是功能，因克勒格尔依据大量灰泥装饰指出，多柱大殿并非用于贵族的世俗生活，而应为琐罗亚斯德教所用。在此假设之前，所有带有多柱大殿的建筑都被归为宫殿建筑。

克勒格尔的假设，即所有多柱大殿应归为宗教建筑[6]，似与首次出版时的考古资料一致[7]。随后他进行了较大的改动，将多柱大殿归于大地主或当地琐罗亚斯德教团体（参见第二部分第三章）[8]。班迪扬A土丘的平面不同于上述多柱大殿，并非如吉钮所说为小型宫殿（参见上文），而更接近祭拜先祖的房间，与克勒格尔的观点并不矛盾。

---

[1] al-Kassar 1979.
[2] 在讨论方柱大殿时，亦应考虑石制柱头（不仅出现在萨珊晚期），以便理解圆柱在萨珊建筑尤其是在宫殿中的作用，包括除下列平面以外的例证。
[3] Huff 1986b.
[4] Peymani 2009.
[5] Zare'/Atayi 2009.
[6] Kröger 1982, p. 272.
[7] 阿卜纳斯尔堡是特例，参见下文惠特科姆在1985年出版的著作。
[8] Kröger 2005b.

反对者则以雷伊附近伊斯兰早期的泰佩·米勒为例,其中包含方柱大殿。此外,喀斯尔·席林的伊马拉特·库思老的考古调查亦证明这一建筑单元存在,但年代从萨珊晚期往后推至阿拔斯王朝。考虑到琐罗亚斯德教在伊斯兰时期的次要地位,宏伟的伊马拉特·库思老在阿拔斯王朝时不应为宗教建筑。

再者,克勒格尔的假设与胡夫的理论相悖,后者认为单轴线布局应属于宫殿建筑,在达姆甘和查拉·塔尔汉中较为突出,而布局复杂的班迪扬是例外。

克勒格尔亦涉足泰西封贵族府邸中伊万的功能问题[1]。伊万的装饰母题与启什遗址相同,应具有宗教功能。饰有灰泥的多柱大殿与伊万不同,前者证明其所在的建筑整体具有宗教功能,而伊万所在建筑的宗教功能仅限于伊万中。

因此,克勒格尔的阐释历程是正确的,萨珊晚期饰有灰泥的多柱大殿也可能属于宫殿建筑。卡内帕在研究拜占庭与萨珊的相似性时提出,萨珊帝国的建筑与艺术以象征性为主要特点[2]。如启什Ⅱ号房址的庭院墙上饰有十四座国王半身像,应为纪念萨珊王朝及先祖荣耀之地。哈吉阿巴德庄园中,火神殿旁的小房间内有国王和贵族的徽章式灰泥半身像。在具有丧葬功能的班迪扬建筑群中,多柱大殿的图像呈现出显著的宫廷特征,尽管其中有一幅祭祀画面。而布沙拉曾经称班迪扬"只是亲王神殿"[3]。

庭院

尽管资料匮乏,庭院在保存完好的建筑布局中占有十分重要的位置。研究的主要困难在于,庭院作为开阔的露天空间,常常被粗疏的考古研究忽略。除亚述的安息宫殿与菲鲁扎巴德的两个宫殿庭院外,塔克·基斯拉大伊万前的庭院内或包含另一伊万。塔克·基斯拉庭院的南、北两侧并不明确,面积或可达10 000平方米[4]。

建筑类型

凉亭

就建筑类型而言,尤其是王室建筑,不得不提古代伊朗花园或围场里的凉亭,用

---

[1] Kröger 1982, p. 270.
[2] Canepa 2009.
[3] Boucharlat 2006, p. 49.
[4] Erdmann 1969, p. 32.

于皇家狩猎。最著名的例子为塔克·波斯坦主伊万（图100），由岩石挖凿而成。其建筑形式与砌筑伊万相似，包括立面上部波斯波利斯风格的阶梯金字塔顶饰。与塔克·波斯坦主伊万类型最接近的地面建筑是塔克·格拉的小伊万（图33），位处美索不达米亚和伊朗高原之间的要道。依据内部底座的遗迹，小伊万应用于放置雕像[1]，因空间太小，无法作其他用途[2]。塔克·波斯坦伊万两侧壁所刻的两幅狩猎浮雕，除证实伊万墙体采用不同装饰手法外，还表明狩猎场景在萨珊建筑壁画中的重要性，可追溯至安息时期[3]。另一方面亦显示出伊万与其装饰间的关系，即伊万或与皇家狩猎相关[4]。

因此，塔克·波斯坦主伊万可被视作国王狩猎的皇家园林中的凉亭[5]，尤其是在其周边发现了一座土坯建造的大型围场[6]。此外，不可忽视水与王室题材间的关联，体现

图100 塔克·波斯坦：全景（G.P. Basello供图）

---

[1] Von Gall 1971, p. 222; Callieri 2012, pp. 157-8.
[2] 近来，根据在修复中被替换的阶梯金字塔顶饰顶端燕尾榫的尺寸，胡夫重新判定该建筑年代应为伊斯兰时期。燕尾榫发现于建筑的墙根下（Huff 1986a; cf. Kambaxsh Fard 1376, pp. 426-7）。
[3] 根据苏萨壁画的最新研究，De Waele 2009.
[4] Movassat 2005.
[5] Canepa 2009, pp. 175-6.
[6] Huff 1986a.

在两幅公元4世纪、分布于王室专属圣地的摩崖浮雕中,这一关联为分析塔克·波斯坦建筑群的关键。莫瓦萨特将主伊万定义为:"胜利的纪念碑、萨珊王权的政治声明,与贤君的三重身份——国家的领袖、伟大的战士和出色的猎手。伊万是萨珊皇家园林中的避暑胜地,及春猎(诺鲁孜)、秋猎(米赫拉甘)等宫廷或宗教节庆的检阅台。"因此,皇家狩猎具有高度象征意义,与"灵光"临水圣地以及伊万正壁上接近圆雕的高浮雕相关[1]。

此外,应注意近期发现的一道猎场围墙,位于比索通摩崖浮雕下方、已被定为皇家园林的区域附近[2]。

泰西封以南的布斯坦·库思老围墙,若非库思老一世为庇护540年远征期间被俘的安塔基亚居民所建的韦—安条克—库思老新城的城墙,则应为另一皇家园林的围墙[3]。

贵族府邸

安息时期的伊朗东部已有地主府邸的先例,而哈吉阿巴德庄园为萨珊时期该建筑类型的例证,在美索不达米亚亦有局部发掘的贵族府邸。

阿扎尔诺什的解读似乎无懈可击。哈吉阿巴德的重要性在于同一建筑内包含不同的功能区,因此与班迪扬相异,后者的"达斯特盖尔德"(贵族家族领地)在我看来为相距几十米的若干建筑的整体名称。

哈吉阿巴德庄园与启什Ⅱ号房址庭院中都有壁柱,柱头分别被地主或国王半身像代替。上述发现表明萨珊建筑的两个新特点,一是半身像代替壁柱柱头,二是国王像多次出现,或与贵族府邸中的祭祖仪式相关(参见上文)。

在解读宫殿建筑各区的功能时,难点在于确定居住区的位置。胡夫提出建筑上层为私人房间,以此区分宫殿建筑与宗教建筑[4]。他随后重申该观点[5],并参考阿米耶的提议,即波斯波利斯的阿帕达那中央大殿南侧的上层房间或为居住区,并与伊斯兰时期伊朗建筑的相似布局对照[6]。在阿帕达那中,因无其他可能,胡夫的解读应为唯一的居住区位置。

---

[1] Callieri 2006.
[2] Mohammadi Ghasrian 2012.
[3] Huff 1986a.
[4] Huff 1971; 1976.
[5] Huff 2005, pp. 375-7.
[6] Huff 1999.

胡夫的假设无疑有启发性,但考虑到下列建筑群中局部完好的上层房间的大小和形状,似乎不足为信。在卡拉·杜赫塔尔中,宽约1.20米的回廊环绕穹隆顶,连接四个突角拱上方宽约4米的三角形房间[1]。如此狭小的空间不应为国王出入起居之处,尤其是萨珊王室通常为多妻制,且女性成员在萨珊社会中的地位较高。最为合理的解释是,卡拉·杜赫塔尔堡垒为国王指挥战事、维护和当地贵族关系的场所,而非国王本人或王室的住处。在中世纪欧洲,城堡亦为宫廷生活的中心,国王在此举行集会、接见大臣并制定政治决策。

　　菲鲁扎巴德平原宫殿的第二层包括宽约2—2.2米的走廊[2],对应三个正方形房间突角拱高度上的剖面[3](图101)。第三层房间位于三个穹隆顶之间,面积较大,宽2.8—3.1米(图102)。胡夫指出墙内有简易小龛,间或以薄墙分隔,以合理利用空间。1971年胡夫首次发表的文章中,鉴于第二层房间面积较小且与穹隆顶大殿相连,他将其定为半行政区,而合理地将第三层定为居住区[4]。房间大小虽可满足居住功能,但为何人所用? 鉴于宽敞的楼梯不应为通向屋顶的过道或佣人房[5],胡夫指出房间为王室私人住宅[6](图103)。为支撑其理论,胡夫还引用泰西封塔克·基斯拉的例子,即大伊万墙后的小房间有镂空砖墙遗迹。因此他提出:"毫无疑问,大小迥异、地基环绕伊万三边的房间上方,均为一层或多层王室居住区。"[7]这一观点无疑值得重视,但无法证实。

　　我认同胡夫所言,卡拉·杜赫塔尔及菲鲁扎巴德平原宫殿的底层房间面朝庭院,无疑用于接见和展示。平原宫殿的庭院虽位于御座大殿及两个相邻大殿后,但也具备上述两个功能。与其将上层的小房间定为王室居住区,不如借鉴布沙拉对波斯波利斯王室居住区的观点,即萨珊国王在菲鲁扎巴德及塔克·基斯拉的居所另有他处,至今尚未发现。埃德曼则认为,塔克·基斯拉的王室居住区位于假定的庭院的南北两侧[8]。

　　此外,在萨法维时期,上层房间亦非国王的长期住处[9]。

---

[1] 原文未提供上层房间的测量数据,上述数据采自图像资料。
[2] 原文未提供上层房间的测量数据,上述数据采自图像资料。
[3] 胡夫还指出,两侧伊万的拱券下有房间,但平面图中并未显示入口通道。
[4] Huff 1971, p. 160.
[5] Huff 2005, p. 374.
[6] Huff 2005, p. 374.
[7] Huff 2005, p. 374.
[8] Erdmann 1969, p. 32.
[9] Hillenbrand 1994, p. 433.

图 101 菲鲁扎巴德,"阿泰什卡代":二层房间(@ Callieri)
图 102 菲鲁扎巴德,"阿泰什卡代":三层房间(@ Callieri)
图 103 菲鲁扎巴德,"阿泰什卡代":通往上层的入口楼梯(@ Callieri)

结 论

　　最后总结几点要义。宫殿建筑在诸多方面仍然不甚明晰，但最新发现证实其与单轴线平面相关。穹隆顶大殿很快被宫殿建筑摒弃，而后专属于宗教建筑。宫殿建筑则以一个或多个面朝庭院各边的伊万为特点。萨珊晚期，多柱大殿自伊万演变而来，亦有大量灰泥墙饰。与其将多柱大殿解读为具有宗教功能，并将其所在建筑都归为宗教建筑，鉴于象征性艺术在萨珊王室和贵族房中的重要性，不如认为多柱大殿用于彰显贵族身份。亦不排除多柱大殿出现在琐罗亚斯德教神庙中的可能。由此，年代明确的伊斯兰早期建筑中出现多柱大殿更为合理。而萨珊宫殿建筑中的居住区与阿契美尼德时期相似，其位置仍未确定。

第二章　萨珊时期的火神庙

在古典和中世纪世界中,伊朗萨珊时期的考古发掘与地面遗存建筑至今仍没有明确的功能解读标准,或许是唯一的特例。尽管伊朗萨珊时期的宗教建筑至关重要,学界却远未在功能解读上达成一致,无论是建筑细节或特定的琐罗亚斯德教建筑空间,还是建筑群整体布局,以比沙普尔"沙普尔宫殿"的讨论为例。

其中的原因众多,常常引发争论。解读的一大难点在于,因政治与宗教权力间错综交织的紧密关系,琐罗亚斯德教建筑传统在萨珊帝国覆灭后中断。当代琐罗亚斯德教建筑主要沿袭了满足祭礼需求的层面,有助于阐释古代遗存,但却并未保留丰富的建筑形式。伊斯兰征服下拜占庭的中东基督教建筑,与伊斯兰统治下原萨珊境内的琐罗亚斯德教建筑相比,境遇云泥之别。再则,琐罗亚斯德教缺乏修道生活,也没有独立于教阶制度或政治权力的宗教建筑,故无法如伊斯兰时期的叙利亚基督教建筑一般延续[1]。然而,伊斯兰的征服并不一定意味着琐罗亚斯德教建筑传统的终止,因若干建筑似在此之后存续了至少数十年。

此外,琐罗亚斯德教建筑的整体研究屈指可数,且因缺乏遗迹,多基于不完整甚至错误解读的信息。因此,有关宗教建筑的基础资料与考古发掘的研究较少,呈现出两个极端趋势:一方面,法尔斯与洛雷斯坦等个别地区的系统考察与详细记录足以进行方法扎实的研究[2];另一方面,自东向西的整个北方地区仅有对单体建筑的简短介绍。

有限的出版物中无法一窥伊朗琐罗亚斯德教建筑的全貌。而大量多轴线、平面以查哈尔·塔克为中心的建筑群仍未被发掘。

仅以法尔斯南部莫赫地区的萨夫耶为例。遗址坐落于高原巍峨山脉下,美景如画(图104、105)。大型建筑群的外墙为规整料石,中央为查哈尔·塔克,拱券被墙体封砌,其外为石质火坛遗迹(图106)。查哈尔·塔克南、北两侧各有一个做工精细的长方形及圆角长方形大水池[3](图107),以及平面、大小各异的房间。整个遗址表面散落着大

---

[1] Guidetti 2007.
[2] Vanden Berghe 1961b, 1965, 1977; Huff 1975.
[3] 感谢阿扎尔诺什在讨论中提出:仪式中需要净水,往往从井中获取,*Revāyat ī Ādur-Farrōbay ī Farroxzādān*, 43提到阿泰什伽中有一口井。

图104　萨夫耶：遗址全貌（A. Eghra 供图）

图105　萨夫耶：遗址全貌（@ Callieri）

图106 萨夫耶：查哈尔·塔克（@ Callieri）

图107 萨夫耶：其中一个水池（@ Callieri）

量陶制高足杯残片,应为祭器[1]。同一地区不远处,另有两座面积相似的建筑群,地理与地形环境极度恶劣,荒无人烟。阿斯卡里·查韦尔迪的地表考古勘探表明,此地在过去可能更为宜居[2]。即便如此,将重要建筑建于如此偏僻之处,定然出于今人不得而知的强烈宗教动机。

我坚信,如1985年布沙拉所指出,继续对包含查哈尔·塔克的建筑进行整体测绘,可为解决上述问题提供可靠的框架。下文将看到,伊朗同侪正推进这项工作。而我以为应当共同协作,建立标准统一、包含全部有用细节的数据库。也应弥补绘图与照片的不足,尤其是考虑到修复工作以减少损坏为目标,却往往改动原有建筑结构,使研究变得更困难。

在讨论某一建筑的功能阐释之前,应注意对原始布局的解读仍有明显分歧。最典型的例子为比沙普尔B房址(图83),基奥在《伊朗百科全书》中称其为"一座十字形宫殿。边长为22米的正方形庭院上方不应如吉尔什曼所言为券顶。庭院两侧墙上有灰泥及彩绘壁龛。更保守地说,庭院应为四个伊万围合而成的露天空间"[3]。相反,法国考古学家及其后的学者认为房址上方应为大穹隆顶[4]。霍夫曼在宫殿功能假设中提出,若庭院为露天空间,就无法解释四周的回廊与粗壮的四角方柱。他赞同胡夫关于突角拱穹隆顶的提议[5],但其力学稳定性迄今未得到证实。

为了更好地阐释琐罗亚斯德教建筑的功能,应简要回顾20世纪的主要研究阶段。约1940年,两项平行而独立的研究各自提出了相似的基本观点,即火神殿由两座建筑组合而成:一座是封闭的,用于保存长明圣火,名为阿泰什伽或阿泰什卡代;另一座形如天篷,四面敞开,在仪式中可看见圣火,名为查哈尔·塔克。作为单体建筑时,查哈尔·塔克寓意着光耀四方,如黑暗中的灯塔(戈达尔所说的"信号")。戈达尔[6]与埃德曼[7]两位学者被众多在当时被视作火神殿的敞开式建筑所迷惑,而忽略了赫茨菲尔德从20世纪20年代起指出"圣火在不与外界连通的室内燃烧",且"萨珊火神殿包含四根方柱支撑的突角拱穹隆顶,周绕狭窄回廊",故不可能有敞开天篷式的琐罗亚斯德教查哈尔·塔克[8]。

---

[1] Askari Chaverdi 2011, pp. 30-1.
[2] Askari Chaverdi 2005/2006.
[3] Keall 1989, p. 288.
[4] Ghirshman 1962, p. 141, fig. 177; Boucharlat 2006, p. 48.
[5] Hoffmann 2008, p. 58.
[6] Godard 1938.
[7] Erdmann 1941.
[8] 基于在考古资料与原文考证上几无批判性的一份报告,最近一份有影响力的专业刊物重申如下观点:"阿泰什伽不一定为封闭建筑,也可能为室外点火区,伊朗历史上不同时期都有类似的考古遗迹。"(Choksy 2007, p. 262)文中还报道:"从本文中分析的材料可知,古伊朗的琐罗亚斯德教徒并非将长明不灭作为圣火神圣性的依据。"(Erdmann 1941.)

约20世纪60年代末,英国琐罗亚斯德教语言学家、历史学家博伊斯加入辩论。她基于古代文献和现代宗教仪式的历史宗教学分析,将琐罗亚斯德教圣火划分为三个等级[1]:从高至低依次为阿泰什·瓦拉赫兰(现阿泰什·巴赫拉姆)、单独的阿泰什(现阿达兰)以及特沃拉克(现阿杜鲁格或达德伽)。由古至今,从国王敕建神庙中的第一等级阿泰什·瓦拉赫兰,到私人的第三等级特沃拉克(现达德伽),三者含义或地位均不相同,代表在不同建筑中举行不同等级的祭礼。所有萨珊王室敕建的神庙应属于第一等级,如纳克什·鲁斯塔姆的铭文所示,沙普尔一世夸耀自己在各地建有大量阿泰什·瓦拉赫兰。仅第一等级的圣火长明不灭,其所需的复杂组织运作在建筑中应当有所反映[2]。不久后,格罗普同样基于现代琐罗亚斯德教研究提出,现代火神殿分为三类(阿格力、阿杜里安、达尔·梅赫)。区分标准为是否包含特点、功能各异的两个房间:其一为用于保存圣火的穹隆顶房间(阿杜里安);其二为用于举行仪式的房间(亚兹辛·伽或达尔·梅赫),通过走廊或直接与前者相连[3]。格罗普的研究明确指出不同功能的房间共存于同一神殿,而非如20世纪40年代的论点所言,分列于两所建筑中。

随后,基于建筑遗迹与相关文献的汇编,席普曼开创性地建立琐罗亚斯德教建筑的整体理论。1971年,其基础性研究《伊朗火神庙》出版,引起激烈争论,其中1975年博伊斯发表的书评尤为重要。她指出,席普曼搜集了所有现存资料乃至相关文献,但其重点并非理解建筑本质,而在于解决琐罗亚斯德教火神殿的起源问题。席普曼按地区辑录了由阿契美尼德至萨珊王朝所有被视为宗教建筑的例证,分析章节则侧重于火神殿的起源,而非对所描述的建筑进行功能解读。四十多年后再回顾,席普曼的论点略显单薄,尤其是相比胡夫随后对被视作火神殿而缺乏确切证据的建筑的研究。继早期的几篇文章后[4],胡夫以1993年旺当·贝格等人在布鲁塞尔举办的萨珊考古与艺术展览为契机,提出清晰简要的解读[5]。他认为大多数研究仅限于解读每座建筑的功能,而缺乏整体功能阐释。他提议,确定一般标准,以是否可应用于所有已知的建筑实例来检验。

这是胡夫最富创见的独到之处。上一章中提及,对许多萨珊时期建筑群功能的解读难点,在于无法明确区分世俗与宗教建筑。胡夫的阐释基于建筑的平面与立面。他提出,所有无轴线的建筑均有单层立面。而鉴于有上述特点的塔克斯特·苏莱曼神庙等建筑已确定为宗教建筑,相反的,菲鲁扎巴德宫殿与泰西封的塔克·基斯拉等包含轴对称平面与多层立面的建筑,则无疑为世俗建筑。胡夫提议将其余功能不确定的建筑

---

[1] Boyce 1968, p. 58.
[2] Boyce 1975, pp. 462-3.
[3] Gropp 1969.
[4] Huff 1972, 1975.
[5] Huff 1993.

群分为以上两类[1]。

1982年,克勒格尔在其基础性研究《萨珊时期的灰泥装饰》中,提出其一般假设,不着眼于建筑特征,而基于灰泥装饰的图像学与风格学层面。他强调,具有重要象征性—装饰性含义的灰泥装饰集中分布于建筑群中的特定空间,即伊万与多柱大殿。两者在功能确凿的宗教建筑中十分重要,如塔克斯特·苏莱曼的多柱大殿为琐罗亚斯德教节庆场所。故饰有灰泥的伊万或多柱大殿足以证明,包含以上元素的建筑具有宗教功能,即便此前被定为世俗建筑[2]。1993年,克勒格尔修正其观点,认为宗教功能仅限于饰有灰泥的建筑空间[3]。而在最新的著述中,他提出灰泥装饰大殿的使用者或为大地主,或为琐罗亚斯德教团体[4]。下一章讨论灰泥装饰时,将更详细地阐明其观点修正的原因。克勒格尔的启发性观点与胡夫的纯建筑学论证有时重合,有时相悖,如达姆甘、查拉塔尔汉等遗址。布沙拉对20世纪80年代中期所有的基础资料进行了细致的批判性分析。他指出,大小与平面各异、功能确凿的宗教建筑拥有共同建筑元素,并强调应避免将查哈尔·塔克一律视作琐罗亚斯德教火神殿[5]。20世纪90年代,伊朗再次开展大规模考古工作,基础资料随之增加。重大发现除班迪扬外,还包括相邻国家的遗址,如由波兰学者凯姆领队、在土库曼斯坦南部发现的米勒·哈拉姆神庙。

本章中将用最新的考古发现去检验上述所有假设。

首先,不应错误地认为琐罗亚斯德教仪式仅限于圣火祭礼。克雷耶布鲁克一针见血地指出,琐罗亚斯德教文献主要记载与火相关的仪式,因其较为复杂,与祭司及其等级直接相关。而与水相关的仪式不需祭司主持,属于民间宗教[6]。建筑层面亦是如此。火神殿无疑为琐罗亚斯德教建筑中最重要及常见的圣所,但神庙中亦有其他宗教活动的专区,如在比沙普尔A房址举行的仪式似乎与水相关。水在民间宗教中是至关重要的元素,且无需特定建筑,如位于卡尚附近、公元前8世纪至公元8世纪的韦什纳维石窟寺等自然圣地[7]。水亦是王权的重要元素,见于几乎所有萨珊摩崖浮雕所在地,以及菲鲁扎巴德、塔克斯特·苏莱曼等建筑群中[8]。

胡夫已阐明,许多大规模的火神庙不仅用于举行除拜火以外的仪式,还用于由祭司

---

[1] Huff 1993, p. 50.
[2] Kröger 1982, pp. 268-76.
[3] Kröger 1993, p. 65.
[4] Kröger 2005b.
[5] Boucharlat 1985.
[6] Kreyenbroek 2011, p. 160.
[7] Bagherpour Kashani/Stoellner 2011.
[8] Callieri 2006c. 感谢格内在讨论中指出,树木在粟特人的神庙中扮演重要角色,古伊朗的神庙遗迹则未延续这一传统。

主持的行政、司法等多种活动，如萨珊时期行政封泥上的祭司印章所示[1]。在此不妨引用胡夫对琐罗亚斯德教神庙的一段生动的描写。不同于大多数欧洲著作中单调且庄重的行文，他设想塔克斯特·苏莱曼前院四周"不仅有神庙管理机构或附属人员经营的办公室、档案室或写作室，还有食物摊点与贩售各种宗教用品的商人、金银作坊⋯当然还出售纪念品⋯琐罗亚斯德教神殿的前院，或与现今东方各教神庙山门前的热闹景象相似"[2]。

神庙内生动丰富的活动应反映在布局中，如塔克斯特·苏莱曼的复杂平面所示（图108）。胡夫对这一萨珊时期的主要火神庙作了详细的功能解读[3]，但因其"国家级"地位，不具备代表性[4]。

与宫殿建筑一样，应考虑宗教建筑的地形位置。就二者与城市的关系而言，阿尔达希尔与沙普尔一世将宫殿建于城外，而将火神庙分别建于阿尔达希尔—花拉和比沙普尔城内。

此外，选址的交通便利，乃是组织祭礼不可或缺的。在琐罗亚斯德教社会中，圣火的赓续这一善举，端赖于相应收益的支撑，故与周边地区有一定的联系[5]。除圣火等级外，火神庙的社会背景，即在神庙从事宗教活动的群体，亦决定了建筑规模。布沙拉指出，塔克斯特·苏莱曼的"国家级"神庙与托尔让·泰佩小神殿分列建筑规模等级的两端[6]。参见上文对法尔斯省南部火神殿的讨论。

对琐罗亚斯德教建筑史至关重要的例证为锡斯坦的库赫·哈加神庙。塔克斯特·苏莱曼无疑建于萨珊帝国的兴盛期，而据斯坦因爵士与赫茨菲尔德的研究，库赫·哈加的年代则介于安息王朝与萨珊王朝之间。因位于资料匮乏且远离政治中心的伊朗东部，其文化明显异于阿杜尔·古什纳斯普。

在21世纪出版的相关著作中，应注意加尼马提在已有资料的基础上，增添了近年伊朗考古调查提供的信息[7]。她的两个重要的碳十四年代测定并未解决纪年问题，因第一个建造阶段差幅较大，即公元80—240±50年，而第二个建造阶段范围较小，即公元540—640±50年。依据碳十四测年，第一阶段涵盖安息王朝及萨珊早期。加尼马

---

[1] Gyselen 1995.
[2] Huff 2011, p. 104.
[3] Huff 2008c.
[4] 关于锡斯坦的阿杜尔·古斯纳斯普可能的原始位置，以及东方圣地在整个西方的错位，参见 Gnoli 1971, pp. 240–1.
[5] Boyce 1968, pp. 56–65.
[6] Boucharlat 1985, pp. 469, 472.
[7] Ghanimati 2000. 相关信息亦可参见 Mousavi 2008, p. 13, 但较为简略。

伊朗萨珊时期的建筑与艺术

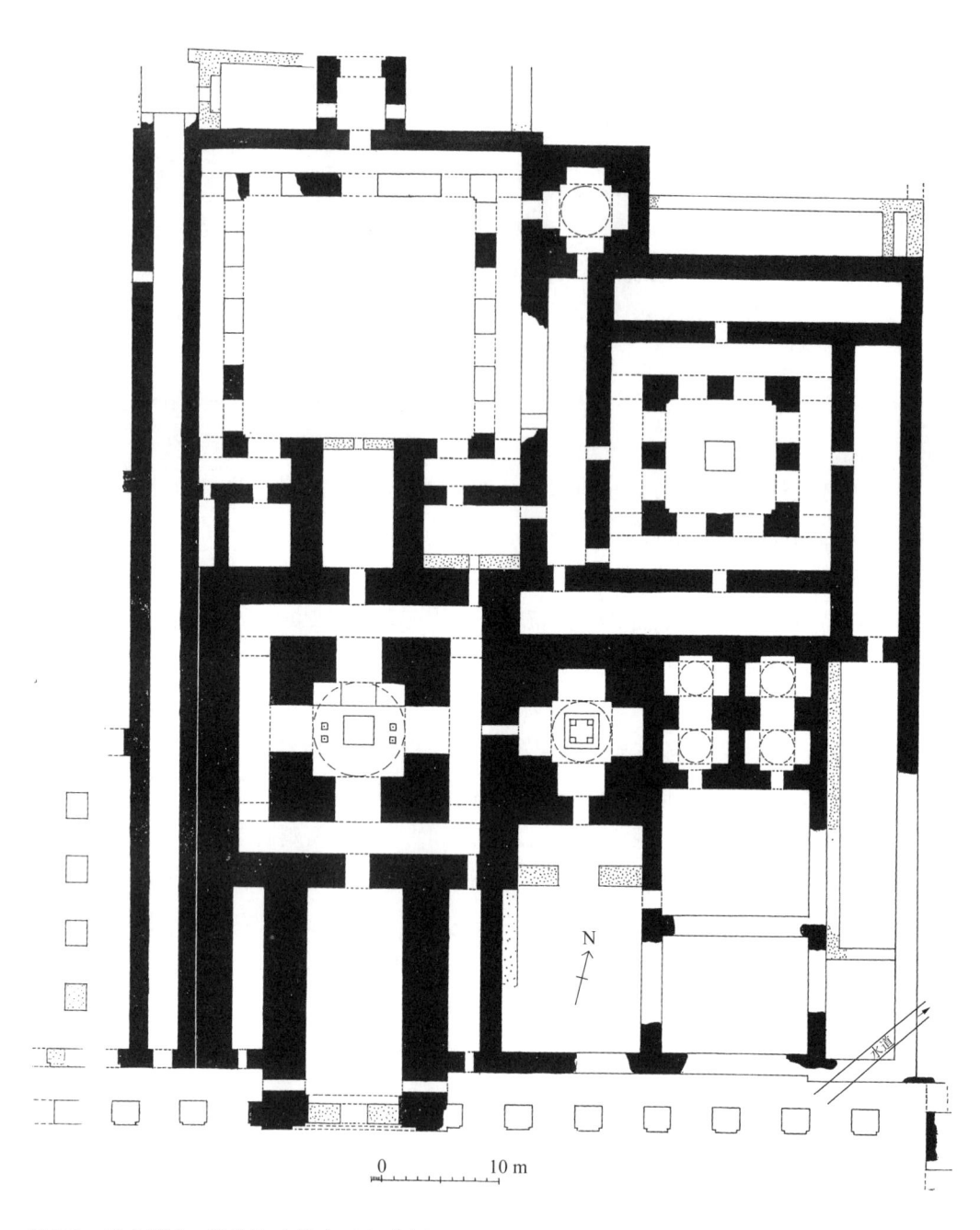

图108 塔克斯特·苏莱曼,火神庙:平面图(Naumann 1977, fig. 24)

提倾向于萨珊时期，即火神庙原型作为形式复杂的建筑整体，具有除保护圣火以外的功能，在库赫·哈加中为"埃贝德斯坦"——琐罗亚斯德教神学院，约与萨珊王朝的创立同时。将库赫·哈加保存最完好的两个阶段定为萨珊时期，而非公元1世纪（赫茨菲尔德）或公元3世纪初（施伦贝格尔），不仅对建筑，也对壁画与灰泥装饰有决定性影响。

近期，卡内帕指出，加尼马提没有提供两个碳十四年代测定的技术论据[1]。他强调，第一阶段的绘画与贵霜时期各类艺术在图像学与风格学上有相似之处，故不排除为碳十四测年范围内的安息时期[2]。

在波茨编辑的《牛津古伊朗手册》内关于琐罗亚斯德教建筑的文章中，加尼马提再次讨论年代问题，其标题《库赫·哈加与伊朗萨珊时期的宗教建筑》表明该建筑为琐罗亚斯德教建筑研究的核心[3]。文中提道："绘画、灰泥装饰与上述碳十四年代测定结果以外，库赫·哈加的土坯券顶建筑自身便体现出萨珊的建造技术与设计元素。"她进一步细化了2000年的假设，提出最早的建筑物始于阿尔达希尔一世，竣工于沙普尔一世时期[4]。

然而应强调的是，即便建筑群年代为公元3世纪，而非1—2世纪，其建立者也不一定为最初两任萨珊国王，因出土了公元3世纪的地方王朝红铜钱币。早前，苏联学者卢科宁已提出，库赫·哈加的建立者为纳克什·鲁斯塔姆的沙普尔一世铭文中所记载的萨伽沙·阿尔达希尔，他发行的红铜钱币背面的火坛图案（图109）与阿尔达希尔一世钱币背面属于同一类型[5]。萨伽沙·阿尔达希尔通常被视为统治伊朗东部与印伊边界之间领土的印度—帕提亚最后一任君主，其名号先后被读作阿达米特拉[6]与法尔恩—萨珊[7]。因此应考虑所有可能的归属，不仅限于安息或萨珊国王，亦包括印伊边界的地方王朝，而后者正与数名学者指出的库赫·哈加装饰

图109 法尔恩—萨珊铜币（Alram 2007, fig. 13）

---

[1] Canepa 2013, p. 73.
[2] Canepa 2013, p. 75.
[3] Ghanimati 2013.
[4] Ghanimati 2013, p. 892; Ghanimati 2000, pp. 144-5.
[5] Lukonin 1969, p. 40.
[6] Harper 1981, p. 104, 图29; Alram 1986, p. 269, nn. 1217-1218.
[7] Nikitin 1994; Alram, Alram/Gyselen 2003, pp. 177-8; Alram 2007, pp. 234-5. 关于这些钱币的分析结果，参见 J.-N. Barrandon, Alram/Gyselen, pp. 88-90.

中东方元素的文化背景相符。

　　总之,由于安息晚期考古资料匮乏,在研究被加尼马提判定为萨珊时期的建筑特征时,需要格外谨慎。在库赫·哈加中出现,可否作为判断查哈尔·塔克年代为萨珊时期的可靠标准? 布沙拉明智地指出,查哈尔·塔克或源于安息时期,如纳斯拉克遗址的考古资料所示[1]。建筑中发现大量安息时期由预制拱肋所建造的拱券[2],对判定其为前萨珊时期亦十分关键。尤其应注意的是,伊朗学者发现了早于第一阶段的遗迹,被加尼马提定为安息晚期[3]。上述遗迹对应古利尼提出的六号地层,但他错将其定为阿契美尼德时期[4]。卡内帕强调,这一建造阶段的布局或年代难以确定,但对建筑群的沿革十分重要[5]。

　　卡内帕指出,萨珊王朝吸收了与乌拉卡萨湖——中古波斯语中的卡扬西湖——有关的阿维斯陀传统。尽管库赫·哈加可能为安息时期,他仍将其解读为"萨珊王朝为了内化强大的阿维斯陀传统而建立的核心建筑"[6]。但因年代不确定,仅限于假设。由于第一阶段年代存疑,符合他提出的萨珊图像题材与布局的,仅有查哈尔·塔克正壁南侧毁坏严重的黏土塑骑士中楣[7](图110),碳十四年代测定为公元540—640±50年[8]。

　　此处不再详述壁画装饰的年代与阐释。法切那[9]、菲利真齐[10]及前人指出,若干画面显然有自然主义成分(图111)。与之处于同一建造阶段的还包括与萨珊早期国王摩崖浮雕明显相似的画面,如赫茨菲尔德在"画廊"第二扇窗中发现的一列

图110　库赫·哈加,火神庙:查哈尔·塔克外壁的黏土中楣(Kröger 1982, pl. 7.1)

----

[1] Boucharlat 1985, pp. 464-5.
[2] Ghanimati 2000, p. 139.
[3] Ghanimati 2000, pp. 141, 145; 2013, p. 892.
[4] Gullini 1964, p. 272.
[5] Canepa 2013, pp. 71, 73, 76.
[6] Canepa 2013, p. 77.
[7] 而非灰泥,参见Kröger 1982, p. 37。
[8] Canepa 2013, p. 77.
[9] Faccenna 1981.
[10] Filigenzi 2006.

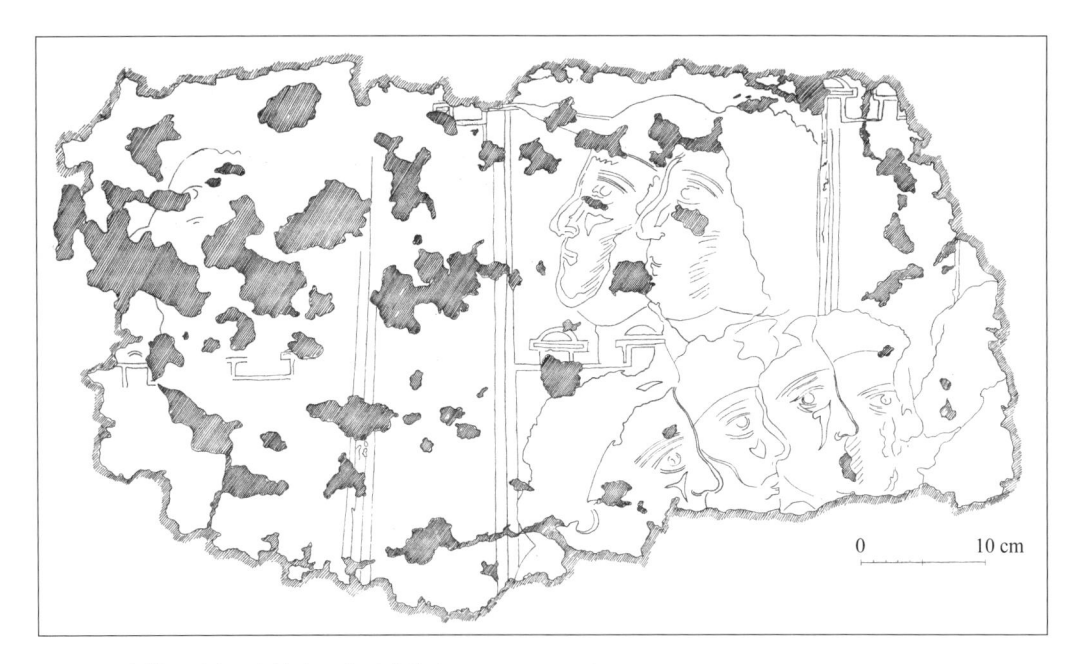

图111 库赫·哈加,火神庙:壁画残片(Faccenna 1981)

共五个右侧面人像[1]。上述图像艺术显然受希腊化影响,或追溯至公元3世纪。这一现象与伊朗高原另一端的卡拉·亚兹德格德一致,再次表明安息王朝与萨珊王朝之间的延续而非中断。

此外应注意的是,库赫·哈加建筑群为高度轴对称布局(图112)。依据胡夫的假设应为宫殿建筑特征,但此地的神圣性与火坛的发现证实了其宗教功能。目前没有事实依据可排除查哈尔·塔克如查哈尔·卡卜一般出现在宫殿建筑中的可能性(如菲鲁扎巴德),该假设似不可信,但仍待检验。因此我有意不把查哈尔·塔克列入论据,以免陷入恶性循环[2]。喀斯尔·席林的查哈尔·卡卜十分重要,依据胡夫的标准,其东西向单轴线平面属于宫殿建筑,与施密特此前的论点一致[3]。然而主轴线两侧的大殿十分突出,似乎脱离了单轴线平面,以致胡夫将其解读为萨珊最晚的火神殿之一[4]。建筑群中的核心单元为正方形大殿(16米×16米),四面厚重的墙上各有一个半圆拱门,其上为突角拱穹隆顶,因此更接近查哈尔·卡卜,而非查哈尔·塔克。周绕回廊的穹隆顶大殿位于大庭院西边,庭院四周为平面各异的房间。穹隆顶大殿以东的广阔空间中有长方形大殿,位于建筑的东—西轴线上,由东边的正门进入。喀斯尔·席林的轴对称平面与

---

[1] Kawami 1987, pp. 39-42,图18。
[2] 参见第一章。
[3] Schmidt 1978.
[4] Huff 1933, p. 55.

伊朗萨珊时期的建筑与艺术

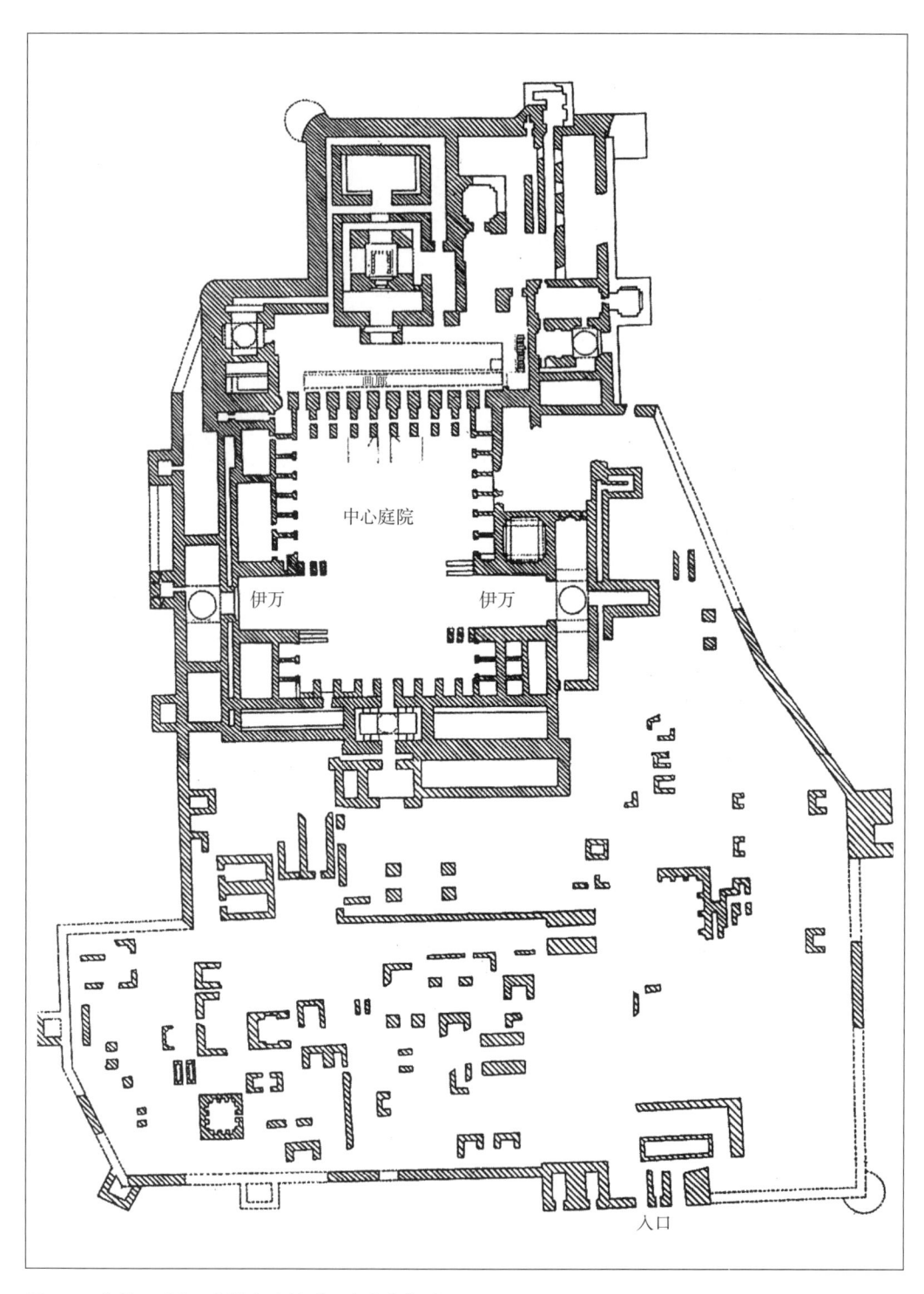

图 112　库赫·哈加,火神庙建筑群:建造末期总平面图(Mousavi 1999, fig. p.83)

库赫·哈加相差无几,前者亦有正方形穹隆顶大殿,周绕回廊,以满足琐罗亚斯德教祭礼的隔离仪轨。两者的主要差异在于大量文献记载了库赫·哈加的神圣性,而没有文献提及喀斯尔·席林火神庙[1]。如上一章所述,喀斯尔·席林的另一问题为,最新发掘证实其年代为阿拔斯王朝,而非库思老二世时期。查哈尔·卡卜不能被想当然地定为萨珊时期,故而引发了关于火神庙在伊斯兰早期数百年的存续的辩论。辩论始于比尔将萨尔韦斯坦建筑群解读为伊斯兰早期火神庙[2]。文献可证,塔克斯特·苏莱曼的宗教用途持续至第一个伊斯兰时期[3],故需探明究竟塔克斯特·苏莱曼因其与萨珊王朝之间的紧密联系成为特例,抑或火神庙在伊斯兰征服后较长时间内延续[4]。

为了正确理解琐罗亚斯德教的不同建筑形式,还应考虑位于比沙普尔城西北角的另一重要例证,即比沙普尔建筑群(图35),上文曾讨论其屋顶[5]。然而对建筑群功能的疑问并非仅由屋顶导致,因为建筑年代的解读亦不确定。相比法国考古队的发掘报告,基奥的详细分析证实萨珊晚期曾对建筑进行大规模改建,改动了原始布局。而马赛克证明早期建筑属于沙普尔时期[6]。其后,伊朗学者仅调查了A房址及伊斯兰时期建筑[7]。据载,沙普尔一世在比沙普尔城内建立了一处国家级圣火,属于阿泰什·瓦拉赫兰等级,如同其父阿尔达希尔一世此前在阿尔达希尔—花拉城中所建的圣火,即公认的塔克斯特·内辛的祭祀对象。

两座建筑最大的差异在于,塔克斯特·内辛只遗留方石砌成的大型查哈尔·塔克,其布局四边各有一个向外突出的伊万,以保护火神殿(图113、114)。而比沙普尔建筑群面积巨大,已发掘部分的尺寸、类型各不相同。此处采用法国发掘者的最初命名,作简单回顾。A房址(5)被定为"半地穴式神殿"(图115),用于与水相关的仪式,或敬奉阿娜希塔。B房址(2)为大型查哈尔·塔克,通常被视作沙普尔王宫大殿(图86)。C房址(3)为"马赛克庭院",位于上述两者之间(图116)。D房址(4)为马赛克伊万,在B房址东北边,有两处精美的马赛克铺地遗存。其余较小的房间以及东边的"瓦勒良宫殿"B宫殿(7)内,有与A房址相同的精美石灰料石墙面(图117),及已知唯一一例萨珊时期的中楣浮雕[8]。

---

[1] Schippmann 1971, p. 282.
[2] 参见第一章。
[3] Schippmann 1971, p. 321.
[4] 感谢布沙拉提出这一建议。
[5] 参见上文。
[6] Keall 1989; Canepa 2010, p. 589, n. 135.
[7] Mousavi 2008, p. 3.
[8] Bier 2009.

伊朗萨珊时期的建筑与艺术

图113 阿尔达希尔—花拉(菲鲁扎巴德),塔克斯特·内辛平面图

如上一章所述,比沙普尔的复杂布局符合胡夫关于宗教建筑的标准。"沙普尔王宫"的宗教功能最初由阿扎尔诺什在其博士论文中提出[1],胡夫在一系列著作中沿用了其观点。

B房址查哈尔·塔克周边环绕的回廊使建筑足以庇护圣火,符合隔绝、保护圣火的要求。

比沙普尔与大部分火神殿的差异在于建筑体量。B房址中央大殿边长约22米,远大于已知的火神殿。后期的火神殿如米勒·哈拉姆与班迪扬,无疑更接近现代祭礼,保存圣火的大殿只容祭司而非信徒进入,故面积较小。

---

[1] Azarnoush 1987.

图114 阿尔达希尔—花拉（菲鲁扎巴德），塔克斯特·内辛：查哈尔·塔克东南立面（D.M. Meucci 供图）

图115 比沙普尔，A 房址：西北墙，内景（A. Yazdani 供图）

图116　比沙普尔，C房址（"马赛克庭院"）：西北方全景（@ Callieri）

图117　比沙普尔，"瓦勒良宫殿"：方石墙（D.M. Meucci供图）

除比沙普尔外，萨珊早期的王朝查哈尔·塔克仅有塔克斯特·内辛，体量较大，中央穹隆顶大殿边长为14.65米，其宏伟与规模与比沙普尔B房址相差无几[1]。

此外，与两所国家级神庙的对照也十分关键。库赫·哈加虽不属于三大国家级圣火，但仍是地位崇高的朝圣场所，其查哈尔·塔克建于最后阶段，应为萨珊晚期，内部大殿边长约为7米。塔克斯特·苏莱曼神庙年代确凿，为萨珊晚期，其A查哈尔·塔克的中央大殿边长为7.65米。

因此，不能因建筑规模排除B房址为火神殿的可能性，其宏伟体量或由于其等级与塔克斯特·内辛一样为阿泰什·瓦拉赫兰，或出自国王敕建，但无疑属于建筑革新时期。

此外，比沙普尔B房址与其他火神殿的区别在于墙上均匀分布壁龛，龛中有丰富的灰泥装饰，延伸至拱门侧壁上。吉尔什曼与克勒格尔均认为灰泥装饰属于最早的建造阶段，即公元3世纪下半叶[2]。除上述装饰外，另有若干未出版的重要动物像遗存，包括穹隆顶大殿的西南拱门处一块遗留黄、黑彩绘痕迹的马头残片，以及西北拱门处可能为象头的残片[3]。殿内其余的坍塌装饰遗存属于伊斯兰早期[4]。

在库赫·哈加，装饰带沿查哈尔·塔克外立面分布；塔克斯特·内辛内部或有装饰，但未发现遗迹；而在后期的宗教建筑中，装饰集中分布于查哈尔·塔克以外，在讨论灰泥时将详述[5]。因此，比沙普尔的内部装饰亦如其宏伟体量般为特例，但并不足以排除其宗教功能。

米勒·哈拉姆火神殿位于土库曼斯坦南部（图118），由凯姆带领华沙大学发掘，可证实该建筑类型在中亚与伊朗高原接壤地区传播，横跨安息王朝及萨珊王朝主要阶段。基于该建筑，凯姆提出了可适用于其他火神殿的解读[6]。建筑由土坯建成。火坛大殿内的凹地由低矮砖墙围合，应用于阻止灰烬飘散。凹地中心为圆形无台阶祭坛基座，及截面为圆形、上覆薄石膏层的土质坛身遗存。圣火殿平面近于正方形，可能有券顶，故不同于查哈尔·塔克。圣火殿东侧通向信徒使用的券顶主殿，殿中遗留壁画。由于主殿西端有高0.9米的灰泥浮雕台座，沿两侧墙分布有低矮的灰泥装饰平台，信徒无法进入圣火殿。圣火殿西侧为长方形小室，三侧墙上均有壁龛，中央为以砖铺地的祭品放置

---

[1] 喀斯尔·席林内部查哈尔·卡卜的边长为16.15米。
[2] Kröger 1982, p. 258.
[3] Kröger 1982, p. 195.
[4] Kröger 1982, p. 258.
[5] 参见第三章。
[6] Kaim 2002; Kaim 2004.

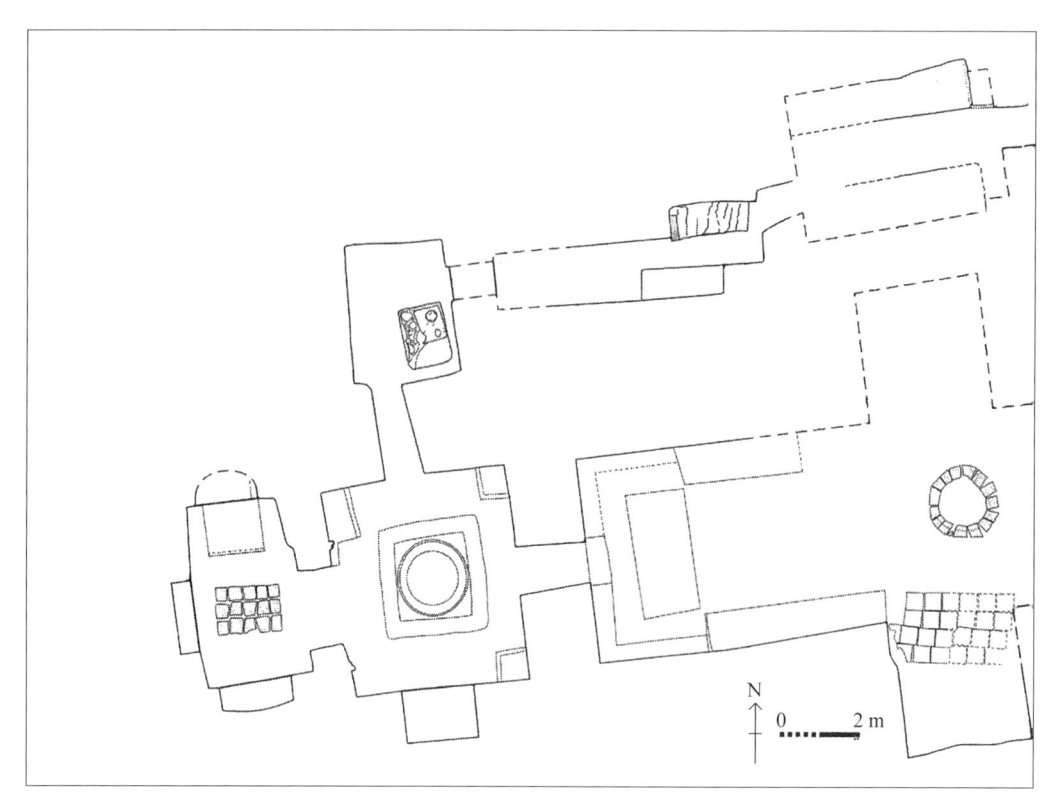

图 118 米勒·哈拉姆,火神殿：总平面图（Kaim 2013, fig. 4）

处,北侧壁龛前的平台上有炉床遗迹。与圣火殿北侧相连的长方形小室十分关键,因平台上发现了长方形火炉,用于保存重新生火所需的余烬和炭[1]。据相关发现,建筑群年代在公元1—4世纪之间,而灰泥装饰仅属于萨珊时期。

凯姆提出,圣火等级并非如胡夫所述体现在建筑布局差异上[2],而是反映在特定的祭祀装置中。米勒·哈拉姆的大殿中央凹地有一粗壮火坛,无台阶基座,与库赫·哈加、塔克斯特·苏莱曼的B查哈尔·塔克一致,可证明其等级[3]。如米勒·哈拉姆一般,库赫·哈加与塔克斯特·苏莱曼既有祭坛大殿（阿杜里安）,又有举行仪式的房间（亚兹辛—伽）[4],对应现代神庙中阿泰什·巴赫拉姆的特征,故均属最高等级。相反,所有带台阶基座的祭坛属于第二等级阿达兰。

---

[1] Kaim 2002, p. 222.
[2] Huff 1972, p. 532.
[3] Kaim 2004, p. 336.
[4] 与格罗普不同,凯姆认为塔克斯特·苏莱曼的主祭坛位于B查哈尔·塔克中,而体量更大、无凹地的A查哈尔·塔克应为亚兹辛—伽。依据其体量,PD查哈尔·塔克应为阿杜里安（Kaim 2004, p. 336）。

总体而言,凯姆的假设有其意义,但仍需更多例证判断凹地或祭坛台阶基座是否为神庙等级的依据。我以为更关键的是,阿泰什·瓦拉赫兰即长明火所在的建筑,不仅有火坛,还包含带炭炉的房间,以缓慢而节约木材的方式使火焰保持燃烧。这一现实因素在当时社会中应较为重要。

关于查哈尔·塔克中的固定装置,应参考雷兹瓦尼在希扬

图119　希扬,火神殿:查哈尔·塔克内部房间(Rezvani 2005)

发掘的建筑群(图119)。建筑群位于克尔曼沙阿省西伊斯兰阿巴德附近,出土于水坝修建工程的抢救性发掘中,目前对其仅有简短介绍[1]。围墙整体保留,共有四个轴向门道。

查哈尔·塔克的四根方柱围合的区域正中,有一处与米勒·哈拉姆相同的矮墙围合的凹地以及毁坏的装置遗迹。在凹地的一边,一道窄长的低矮平台穿过拱下,与方柱等长。

平台上残存三处低矮的台座,靠内较大的台座为圆形,其余两处为长方形,均以石灰华建造,饰有平行槽纹。圆形台座与法尔斯南部已知的祭坛相似[2],可能为火坛,但位置偏离中心。琐罗亚斯德教规定一座祭礼建筑内仅有一处圣火,故其余台座不可能为祭坛,而是用于放置祭礼所需的器具[3]。另一拱券下亦有一道低矮平台,上为若干较小的台座,其材料并未提及。上述装置布局与现已残损的塔克斯特·苏莱曼A查哈尔·塔克部分相似,后者中央大殿北侧原有一处台座[4]。

另一伊朗考古队在克尔曼沙赫省麦尔·麦拉吉发掘的查哈尔·塔克与希扬的内部装置相似,其中一道拱券下有一道台座,上为成行装置。台座与查哈尔·塔克中央的凹地或平台相接[5]。进行了抢救性发掘的帕朗盖尔德火神殿位于克尔曼沙赫省南部[6],同

---

[1] Rezvani 2005; Hozhabri 2013, p. 6, pl. 9. 感谢考古学家雷兹瓦尼与笔者慷慨分享其工作成果。
[2] 参见下文。
[3] 不固定的临时圣火存放处除外(Boyce 1968, p. 55; Huff 2008, p. 5)。
[4] Naumann 1977, p. 49.
[5] Moradi 2009.
[6] Khosravi/Rashnou 2014.

伊朗萨珊时期的建筑与艺术

样包含上述装置，台座四角浅孔为承托祭坛坛面的支柱所在。班迪扬的类似装置已被拉赫巴尔发现并正确阐释[1]。

相反，亚厄迈在博拉兹詹西北方的达雷加兹（穆罕默达巴德）发现的查哈尔·塔克中央并非凹地，且修复不当（图120）。中央平台由两级台阶可达，宽度与拱券相同，而长度超出拱券。两根方柱之间高出地面的平台正中为一正方形凹陷，并非位于建筑平面几何中心处，可惜现已完全修复。

考古学家阿斯卡里·查韦尔迪新近于伊朗出版了关于琐罗亚斯德教宗教装置的重要著作。他在法尔斯南部各地区的地面踏查中发现了大量火坛遗存，大多出自已知的遗址。最突出的是祭坛坛身，或者说遗留最多的坛身下半部分，形制相同。坛身为沙漏型，通常饰有一圈中间细两头粗、边缘为弧形的平行褶皱（图121），被阿斯卡里·查韦尔迪定为棕榈叶纹[2]。他提出，饰有棕榈叶纹的祭坛属于第二等级阿达兰，而坛身素净的祭坛属于第三等级阿杜鲁格。

图120 德赫卡伊德，火神殿：东北方全景（@ Callieri）

---

[1] Rahbar 2008, p. 18. 感谢施舍法尔。在德黑兰举办的第十二届伊朗考古专题座谈会上，当科斯瓦尼展示帕朗盖尔德遗址时，她提出，已故的阿扎尔诺什在哈吉阿巴德发掘的查哈尔·塔克，其中央台基的四角上有小孔，(此处)铜片遗存应为用作支撑的铜柱。这一发现仍未出版。
[2] Askari Chaverdi 2011.

将考古发现的祭坛与萨珊钱币背面或印章中的祭坛相比，前者多为中间细两头粗的编织纹沙漏型，而后者除赛斯坦的沙普尔二世发行的几批钱币外[1]，均为其他类型[2]。这一差异至关重要，需进一步研究。此外，应将钱币背面的祭坛视作王室圣火的象征，而非普遍意义上的祭坛。目前仅有融合了阿契美尼德御座元素的祭坛被视作王室圣火[3]，但或许适用于所有钱币上的祭坛。如果对比印章、钱币研究与凯姆的假设，即带台阶基座的火坛属于阿达兰等级，则没有一座王室神庙与阿泰什·瓦拉赫兰相符。阿斯卡里·查韦尔迪所记录的祭坛形制与约2 000千米开外的班迪扬两处祭坛相同：其一为圣火殿中央祭坛[4]（图122），因大殿晚期填土而得以保存，其二为圆柱主殿西北壁龛中心的灰泥祭坛[5]。

图121 博拉兹詹，堡垒：托勒·沙希迪火坛（Askari Chaverdi 2011, fig. 21）

班迪扬A土丘位于呼罗珊·拉扎维的达雷加兹附近，拉赫巴尔带领的伊朗考古研究所对该遗址进行了十余年的发掘。相关发现逐渐拓宽了研究视野，尤其是对建筑群各房间类型特点的功能解读。与米勒·哈拉姆神殿不同，班迪扬建筑以夯土筑成，因若干房间中有大量墙饰及装置而可提出功能解读假设。建筑群年代为萨珊中期（图123），若干图像场景似为表现波斯人抗击中亚游牧民族，即发掘者所称的嚈哒人。

主殿（A）内有四根圆柱，圆盘线脚柱础下有三层叠涩。大殿东边完全敞开，因此尽管无

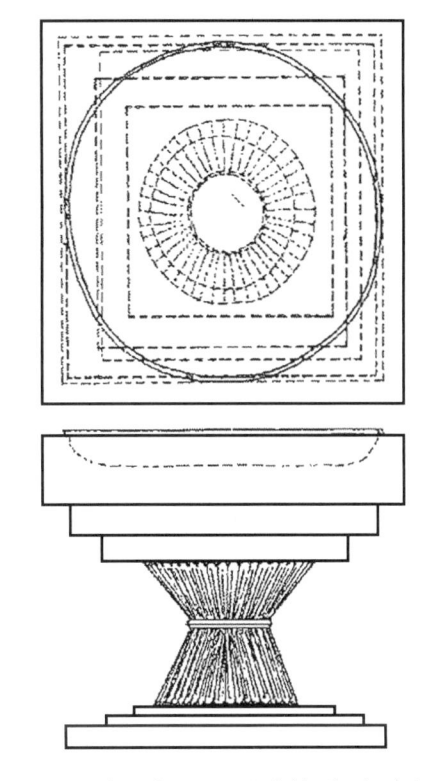

图122 班迪扬，A土丘建筑群：祭火坛（Rahbar 2004, fig. 4）

---

[1] Schindel 2004a, p. 217, Typ 2b; Schindel 2004b, p. 15.
[2] De Lillo 2012/2013, p. 89.
[3] Duchesne-Guillemin 1966, p. 66; Lukonin 1969, pp. 165-6; Harper 1979, p. 51.
[4] Rahbar 2008, pp. 17-8.
[5] Rahbar 1998, 图7, pl. Ⅸ.

伊朗萨珊时期的建筑与艺术

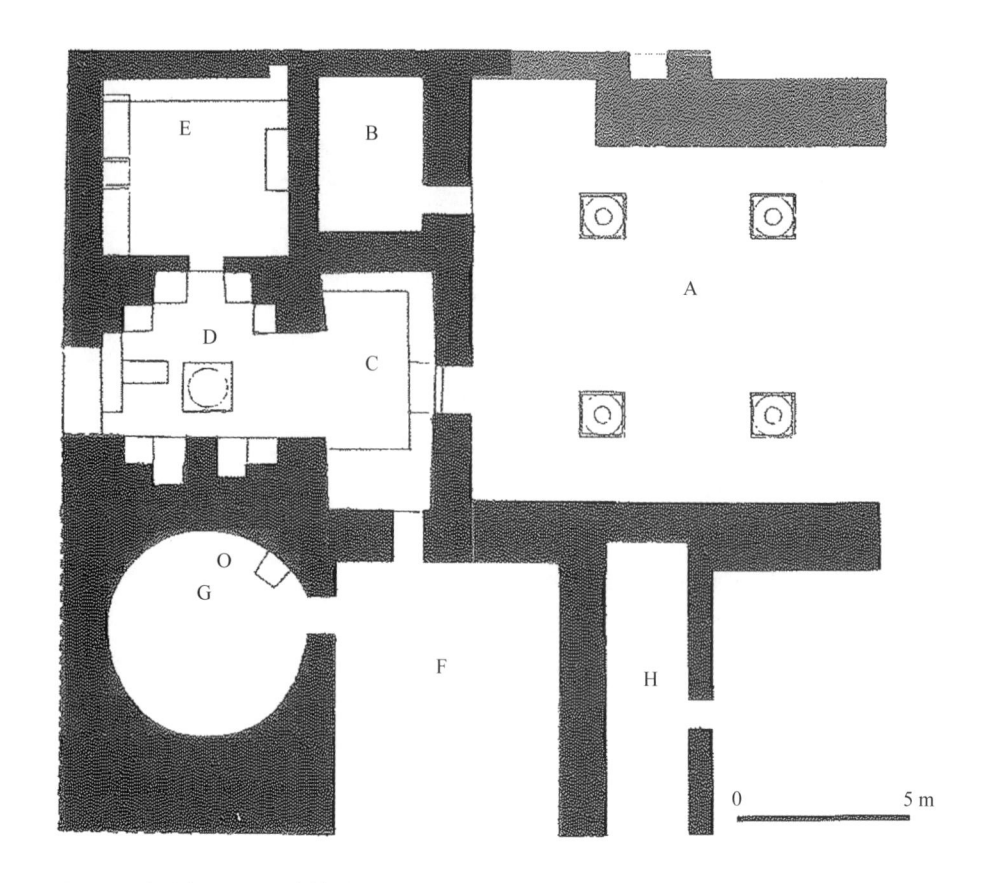

图123 班迪扬，A土丘建筑群：总平面图（Rahbar 2004, fig. 1）

中亚建筑中常见的券顶，拉赫巴尔仍称其为伊万。殿内有丰富的灰泥装饰，包括狩猎、战争、仪式、授权、宴会等场景，附有中古波斯语铭文。由主殿（A）通过以砖铺地的前殿（C）可进入圣火殿（D），圣火殿为不规则十字形平面，与查哈尔·塔克十分相似。在圣火殿（D）中央偏东南处，发现了萨珊时期唯一一个完整的火坛，因萨珊晚期大殿填土而得以保存。不同于米勒·哈拉姆的土质祭坛，班迪扬祭坛以灰泥建成[1]。与圣火殿（D）相连的房间（E）虽未发现骸骨，但其内装置被拉赫巴尔称为纳骨器。房间（B）被定为档案室，内有少量黏土封泥。另有一个圆形房间（G），发掘者视其为净化仪式之用。距建筑主体约300米处，在B土丘中发现了一个圆形建筑，被拉赫巴尔视作最早的"寂静塔"之一，用于尸体鸟葬，为晚期琐罗亚斯德教习俗，罕见于古代[2]。拉赫巴尔的首篇文章发表后，上述发现的独特性引发了以阿扎尔佩为首的激烈辩论[3]。

---

[1] Rahbar 2008, p. 17.
[2] Rahbar, 2007b.
[3] Rahbar 1997; Azarpay 1997.

拉赫巴尔关于班迪扬的首篇文章在西方面世后[1]，吉钮最先加入辩论并校订了中古波斯语铭文[2]，提出有别于伊朗语史学家巴什沙什·汉扎克的观点[3]。随后，基于逐渐累积的新材料，拉赫巴尔陆续发表了其他报告[4]。2008年，吉钮将辩论扩展至建筑的整体解读，认为其"或为一位军事指挥官（马尔兹班）的豪宅"[5]。拉赫巴尔随后逐点反驳了吉钮的论证[6]。

鉴于吉钮在中古波斯语铭文学上的深厚学识及翔实论证，其铭文及建筑历史背景为公元5世纪的解读理应无误。然而，拉赫巴尔亦作出相似的判断，但他的依据是将主殿墙面灰泥人像推定为巴赫拉姆五世与嚈哒皇帝，且按照巴什沙什·汉扎克的解读，有1处铭文提及嚈哒皇帝。我对吉钮的若干房间功能解读仍有疑虑，因此更倾向于拉赫巴尔的阐释。尽管如此，由吉钮的一个观点出发，可对整个建筑群进行可靠的解读。

如上一章中所示，吉钮提出，主殿饰有祭坛形象的壁龛左侧壁中C—D铭文提及的"达斯特盖尔德"指代铭文所在的建筑[7]，而未考虑到铭文可能指代包括A土丘在内的整个领地。C土丘的贵族府邸年代或晚于A土丘建筑群[8]，但C土丘早期地层还未完全发掘[9]，可能存在与A土丘同时期的建造阶段。

依据胡夫的标准，A土丘应为宗教建筑，而非地方领主的府邸。A土丘无主轴线，其复杂布局与其他功能明确的宗教建筑相近。此外，拉赫巴尔强调A土丘与其他具有居住功能的建筑群没有相似之处，其房间并不宜居[10]。

与米勒·哈拉姆的对比可证明班迪扬建筑并不具有世俗功能。二者有多处相似点，不可能为偶然：夯土或土坯结构，以砖铺地的祭品区，无主轴线的复杂布局，有别于查哈尔·塔克的火神殿建筑类型，沙漏型祭坛坛身，火神殿面朝大殿敞开，大殿墙上有装饰，两个建筑群装饰母题完全一致[11]。

吉钮从不同层面反驳了建筑的宗教功能阐释。在建筑层面，他提出："如为重要神殿，为何圣火不放置在圆柱大殿中？虽然大殿缺少支撑穹隆顶的拱券，但其结构明

---

[1] Rahbar 1998.
[2] Gignoux 1998.
[3] Bashshash Khanzaq 1997.
[4] Rahbar 2004, 2008.
[5] Gignoux 2008.
[6] Rahbar 2010-2011.
[7] Gignoux 2008, p. 166.
[8] 参见上文。
[9] Rahbar 2007a.
[10] Rahbar 2010-2011, p. 167.
[11] Kaim 2008.

显与查哈尔·塔克相近。"[1]然而大殿与查哈尔·塔克毫无相似之处,因其圆柱与查哈尔·塔克的方柱迥然不同,而不须考虑屋顶(查哈尔·塔克均为穹隆顶)。此外,大殿东边敞开,不符合如前所述琐罗亚斯德教的密闭要求。D房间(边长4.1米)被拉赫巴尔视作圣火殿,吉钮则认为其面积过小,不便于"祭司进行亚斯纳礼拜仪式的动作"[2],但米勒·哈拉姆的圣火殿(边长5米)并未显著大于D房间。拉赫巴尔还提出[3],琐罗亚斯德教的亚斯纳仪式中仅有一个主礼祭司(佐特)和一个助理祭司(拉斯比)[4]。且班迪扬圣火殿似为达德伽等级,仅需一个祭司主持拜火礼[5]。

吉钮提出,带有复杂石膏装置的E"仅为仓库,在农业住宅中必不可少"[6],而未考虑到只有穿过火坛所在大殿才可进入E,且E通常被土坯封堵[7],不应为仓库[8]。E的石膏外表面上刻有一个骑猎者及若干四足动物,如饰有蝎子和"卐"的瘤牛、马和山羊,更像是具有重要象征—宗教价值的狩猎图,代表王权与邪不压正[9]。在梅尔夫发现的骨瓮狩猎图亦为重要例证[10]。

在我看来,吉钮最中肯的观点与琐罗亚斯德教的洁净规定相关。他提出圣火旁不仅有一个放置纳骨器(奥斯托丹)的房间(如上所述通常是封闭的),还有一个巴雷什纳姆—伽,即净化最重的污染的场所[11]。他对内为圆形布局的G的解读,有助于阐释整个A土丘建筑群。基于博伊斯在亚兹德附近研究的类似建筑,吉钮认为:"可将G视作家族成员遗体在运到寂静塔之前的停放处,因遗体的污染无法留在'角落'里。"[12]此外,博伊斯提出:"在遗体三步开外点燃长明火(更近则是对火的污染),为另一重保护。"[13]吉钮指出,上述条件在拉赫巴尔的布局中均得到了满足。

综上,A土丘建筑群应为贵族家族领地举行丧葬仪式之用。放置圣火的达德伽前为饰有颂扬家族功勋的灰泥的仪式大殿,两侧分别为放置家族成员纳骨器的房间,以及

---

[1] Gignoux 2008, p. 165.
[2] Gignoux 2008, p. 165.
[3] Rahbar 2010-2011, p. 168.
[4] 吉钮提出圣火旁几无余烬,而F伊万中发现了余烬(Gignoux 2008, p. 166),拉赫巴尔在首篇文章中将其归因于火灾。在最新的文章中,拉赫巴尔修改了此前的阐释,将余烬解读为圣火燃烧的残留物(Rahbar 2010-2011, p. 168.)。
[5] Boyce 1968, p. 54.
[6] Gignoux 2008, p. 166.
[7] Rahbar 2010-2011, p. 169.
[8] 感谢布沙拉指出砖块填塞极易清理,因此可视为对仓库的封存。
[9] Trever/Lukonin 1987, pp. 37-8; De Waele 2004, p. 372; Rahbar 2008, p. 20; Compareti 2011, p. 12.
[10] Lukonin 1977a, p. 219.
[11] Gignoux 2008, p. 165.
[12] Gignoux 2008, p. 167.
[13] Boyce 1989, p. 149; Boyce 1968, p. 54.

举行丧事而非宗教净化的圆形房间。

此处可联想到卡内帕对纳克什·鲁斯塔姆的卡巴耶·扎尔达什特的描述："圣火庆典与遗址的丧葬（而非停尸）功能和谐共存，并另觅他处停放尸体[1]。持异议者称琐罗亚斯德教禁止圣火与王室遗体共存，却未考虑到包括此处在内的古代遗址，以及萨珊王室并非遵循正统的宗教观与祭礼[2]。"[3]

至于有图像装饰的丧葬建筑，以2005年伊朗—德国考古队于菲鲁扎巴德中心区发现、尚未出版的萨珊早期壁画为例[4]。放置陶质棺材的丧葬建筑中有一段彩绘墙体，为萨珊时期迄今未知的这一建筑类型的另一例证。

米勒·哈拉姆和班迪扬更新了学界对火神殿已有的认识。火神殿除几何与植物母题外，亦有图像母题的丰富装饰。因现有墙面装饰大多为灰泥，将在下一章讨论灰泥时详述。查哈尔·塔克的相邻大殿及查哈尔·塔克外围的装饰采用不同的媒介，如库赫·哈加的泥塑，库赫·哈加和米勒·哈拉姆的壁画[5]，比沙普尔中心查哈尔·塔克相邻的两座大殿中的马赛克（图124）。我在2001年于达勒姆演讲、2008年发表的文章中指出[6]，如果新解读将比沙普尔的十字平面大殿视作琐罗亚斯德教查哈尔·塔克，则需解释殿中马赛克为何出现酒神图像。德芒热亦独立地提出了相似观点[7]。克勒格尔认为在火神庙中，装饰往往未分布

图124 比沙普尔，C房址：X壁板（R. Ghirshman, *Bichâpour. II. Les mosaïques sassanides*, Paris 1956, pl.V.1）

---

[1] Huff 2004, pp. 595-6.
[2] Daryaee 2008.
[3] Canepa 2010, p. 584, n. 112.
[4] Huff 2008a, pp. 50-1; Compareti 2011, p. 15; Mousavi/Daryaee 2012, p. 1080.
[5] 米勒哈拉姆的发现与德瓦勒的论断相悖，他认为若不考虑库赫·哈加，则"萨珊时期的祭祀场所似无壁画"（De Waele 2004, p. 375）。
[6] Callieri 2008.
[7] Demange 2006, pp. 268-76.

于查哈尔·塔克本身,而是在其相邻房间,此为琐罗亚斯德教团体的节庆场所[1]。从这一角度,可解释酒神图像为何出现在酒占据重要地位的节庆大殿中,尽管琐罗亚斯德教文献并未提及。应注意的是,文献仅为神职人员的规范,而不一定为宗教实践[2]。

亚厄迈将他在布什尔省博拉兹詹周边发掘的两个重要建筑群定为安息时期的密特拉神殿。因两处建筑属于同一类型,却各有特点,故有此题外话。有关密特拉崇拜在萨珊时期地位的问题至关重要,众多伊朗青年考古学家虽无可靠依据,却倾向于将上述建筑定为密特拉神殿[3]。"达尔·梅赫"为指代火神殿的术语之一,可表明密特拉与火神殿之间的联系[4],即谢克德所言火神殿中对密特拉的专门礼拜[5]。

第一个建筑群位于穆罕默达巴德遗址,旧称德赫卡伊德,距上述被视作萨珊琐罗亚斯德教查哈尔·塔克的建筑西南方不远处[6]。建筑群以土坯筑成,包含两个布局相同的相邻模块(图125、126)[7]。第一模块内有两个尺寸相同的平行大殿(约5.7米×2米),西北边向另一与之垂直的长方形大殿(4)敞开。大殿(2)的两边纵向墙基各有六个半圆拱顶砖质壁龛及带线脚的拱饰。壁龛宽、深、高在65—75厘米之间,圆拱端点距龛底约30厘米处有轻微凹陷。大殿正壁有两个壁龛,共计十四个。大殿(1)仅东北壁有四个壁龛,东南正壁有两个。第二模块位于第一模块的西南方,包括与上述大殿平行的大殿(3),其西北边向与之垂直的大殿(5)敞开,而后者又与第一模块的大殿(4)相连。

遗址最初在被盗掘后被发现,面貌遭到破坏,亚厄迈依据陶片判定其年代或为安息时期[8]。与罗马圣克莱门特及其他同样无窗的密特拉神殿进行比对[9],可确定其功能[10]。遗址主要发现为地面的双耳陶罐残片,与托勒·坎达克出土的两个双耳陶罐及布什尔附近沙格阿卜墓地的大量陶罐相同[11]。

亚厄迈指出,大理石马耳叙阿斯像残片或可溯至公元3世纪,出自穆罕默达巴德密特拉神殿周边的盗掘[12]。但据拉赫巴尔所言,残片发现于托勒·坎达克相邻遗址的查哈

---

[1] Kröger 1982, pp. 268-76.
[2] Calleri 2008, p. 118.
[3] 最近一位为Hozhabri 2013, p. 16 ss。
[4] Shaked 1994, p. 46; Pourshariati 2008 p. 375.
[5] Shaked 1994, p. 46.
[6] 参见上文。
[7] Yaghmaee 2008, pl. 3-4.
[8] Yaghmaee 2008, p. 71.
[9] Yaghmaee 2008, p. 72, pl. 6.
[10] Yaghmaee 2008, p. 70.
[11] Yaghmaee 2008, p. 72.
[12] Yaghmaee 2008, p. 72, 图12。

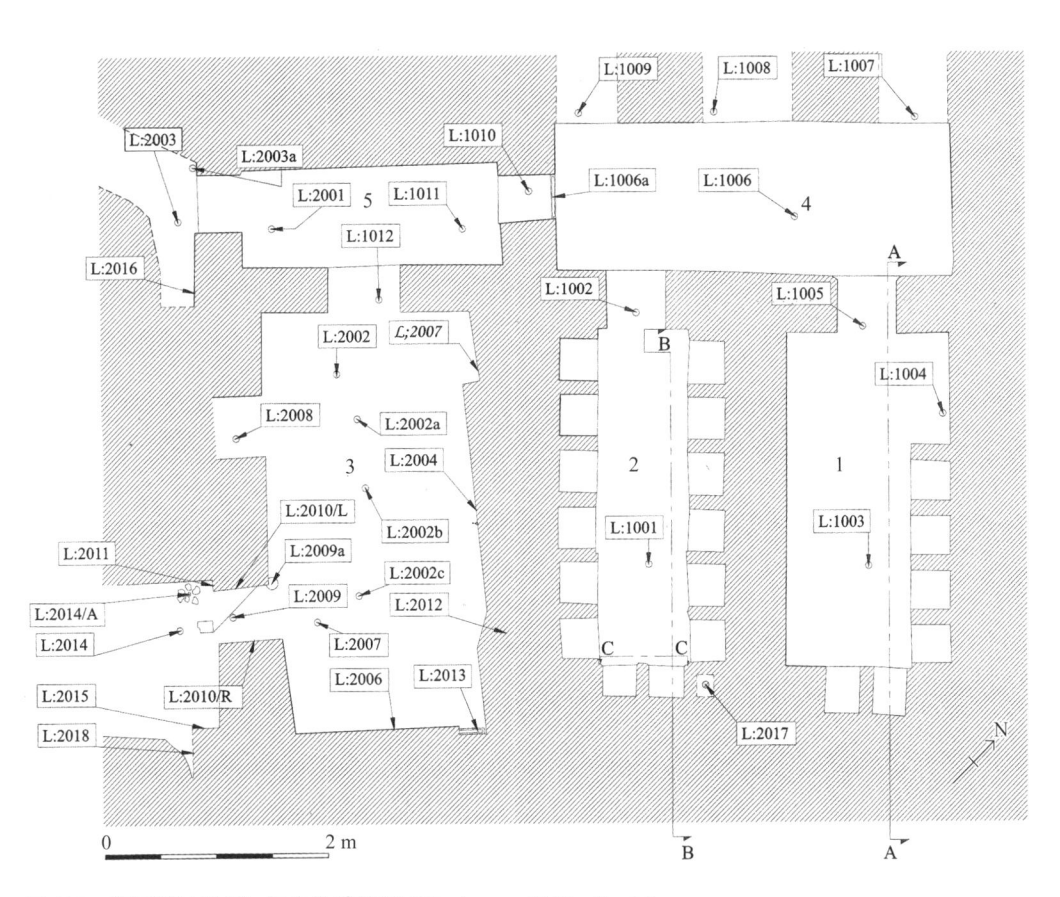

图125　穆罕默达巴德：纪念性建筑群（Yaghmaee 2008, fig. 2）

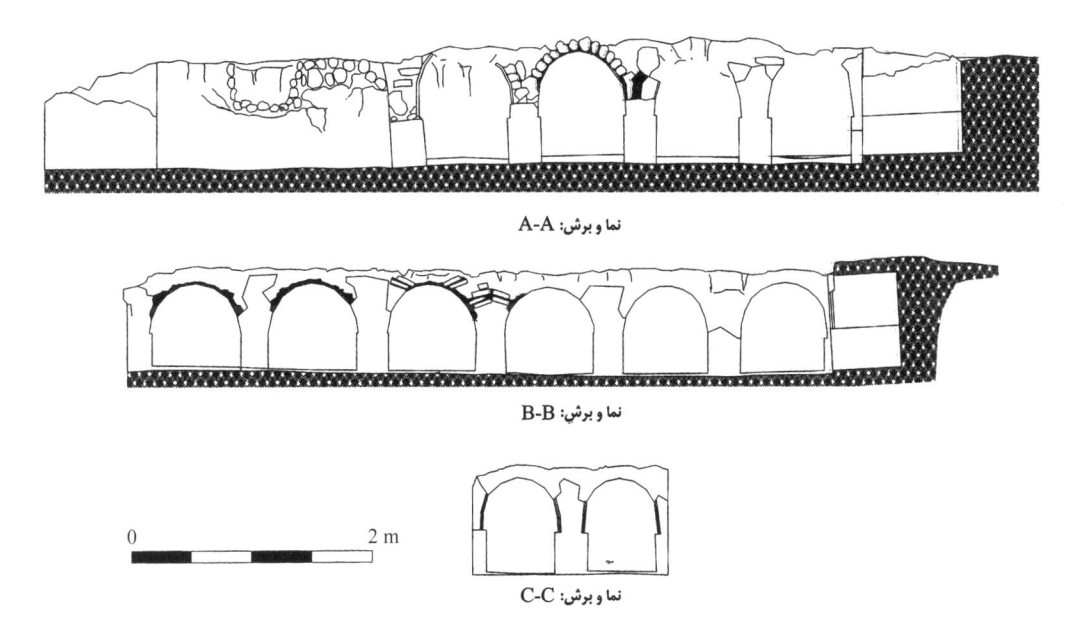

图126　穆罕默达巴德：纪念性建筑群（Yaghmaee 2008, fig. 3）

尔·塔克东南方[1]。

第二个建筑为距穆罕默达巴德约1千米的戈尔·萨依迪遗址，盗掘中发现另一长方形大殿，其壁龛与上述类型相似（图127）。大殿以石块和泥土石膏砂浆砌成，约7米×1.3米，两道纵向墙上各有七个半圆拱顶砖质壁龛（其中一边仅存五个）与带线脚的拱门饰；壁龛约73—74厘米宽，55厘米深，两侧龛壁距龛底约30厘米处有轻微凹陷；大殿正壁仅一个壁龛，共计十五个。壁龛拱顶保存完好，可知壁龛原位于距地面1米高的台座下方，台座上边缘有两层凸线脚。龛内发现若干大陶碗、一个石碗、玻璃瓶、骨头残片及一尊动物陶像[2]。

西方或杜拉欧罗普斯等近东的密特拉神殿与上述建筑截然不同[3]，仅有一个大殿，而非多个平行大殿，且沿墙台座为实心，无伊朗遗址中所见的壁龛。此外，上述建筑距查哈尔·塔克较近，尽管后者属于不同时期，我仍认为不应将建筑定为密特拉神殿，目

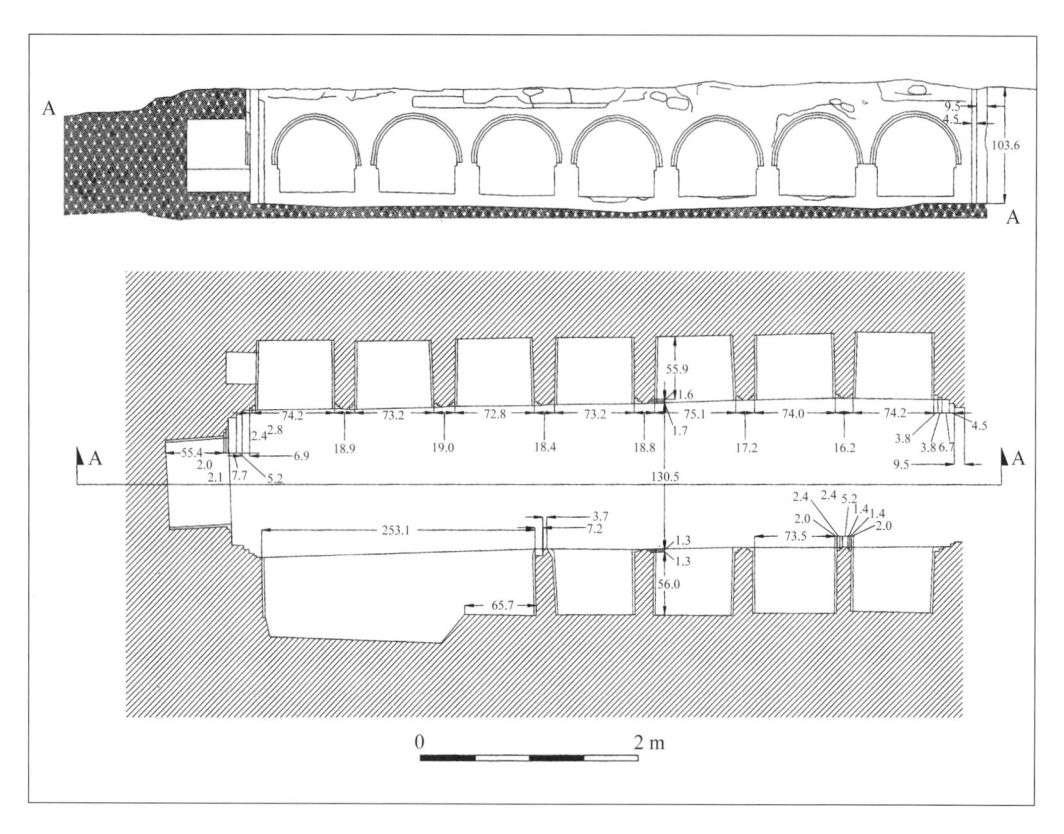

图127 戈尔·萨依迪：纪念性建筑群（Yaghmaee 2008, fig. 7）

---

[1] Callieri 2007, pp. 105–8.
[2] Yaghmaee 2008, pp. 73–5.
[3] Cumont 1975.

前的论据尚不足以支撑如此革新的神庙类型。与菲鲁扎巴德的卡拉·杜赫塔尔B庭院相邻的若干房间内，发现了包含与穆罕默达巴德及戈尔·萨依迪十分接近的拱顶壁龛的萨珊早期台座。胡夫最初将其视作仓库中的内嵌式存放处[1]。随后，尽管其中一个房间确定为仓库[2]，他又称壁龛台座为座椅[3]。其论证的不确定性使我对密特拉神殿的解读产生怀疑。基于胡夫的仓库解读及双耳陶罐和骨头残片的发现，我在此提出另一功能假设。建筑群所在区域较为平坦，四周没有如法尔斯般保存纳骨器的崖壁，故建筑可能为丧葬功能，用于保存纳骨器。在克尔曼沙赫地区帕朗盖尔德的发掘中，火神殿回廊的沿墙台座似可印证这一假设。台座被分为数格，每格正壁各有一个装饰母题。在所有方格中均发现骨头残片，故被考古学家定为纳骨器[4]。

如班迪扬所示，纳骨器置于火神殿之侧，并不违背琐罗亚斯德教的正统性[5]。

谨慎地说，目前仍需更多例子证实安息或萨珊时期伊朗高原上存在密特拉神殿，现有的新发现反而进一步证实与火神庙紧密相连的丧葬空间存在的假设。

---

[1] "Lagernischen in einem Depotraum", Huff 1976, p. 167.
[2] Huff/Gignoux 1978, p. 143.
[3] "Sitz-und Liegebänke", Huff/Gignoux 1978, p. 133.
[4] Khosrovi/Rashnou 2014, p. 178.
[5] 参见上文。

第三章　从新发现看灰泥工艺

萨珊建筑沿袭了安息时期的壁饰,除壁画外,还包括塑性的灰泥浮雕,后施彩色。萨珊时期的壁画遗存极少,而灰泥更能抵抗风化,更耐久,分布于不同阶级的建筑而不仅是王朝建筑,故其原始装饰遗留更多。

正因灰泥不为王室建筑所独有,我们得以从中窥见萨珊社会的恢宏景象。王朝专属的大型摩崖浮雕仅局限于王室意识形态的表达,相比之下,灰泥蕴含更丰富的信息。灰泥分布在各类萨珊建筑中,归属于从世俗到宗教、从王室到非统治阶级的精英。上述特点使其具有独立于重大历史事件的社会现实性,受统治者意识形态影响较小。此外,不同于金属器、纺织品、玻璃器、印章等单一的可移动工艺品,灰泥可组成大规模图像或图案程序。我们可以从中提取多元化的题材及风格样式进行深入解读,同时参照灰泥装饰与其所属建筑之间的关系。故在选择本书主题时,我认为应对灰泥略述一二,作为对世俗建筑和宗教建筑两章的补充。

1982年克勒格尔所撰《萨珊时期的灰泥装饰》至今仍为有关萨珊灰泥工艺最全面的历史艺术学与考古学著作。在该书出版时,灰泥的两大主要发现之一哈吉阿巴德仅有简报,而班迪扬仍未被发掘。本章主要通过新发现重新审视克勒格尔的结论,以证明新材料是否影响或在何种程度上影响其理论体系的准确性。他在1993年发表于"萨珊的辉煌"展览图录中的文章、2005年的若干百科全书条目及2006年"萨珊波斯"图录的短文中,未充分考虑到新发现的重要性。

在此特向非专业的读者说明,"灰泥"一词通常用于古代艺术品中,指塑性材料的墙体砌面,而不论化学成分。

在班迪扬等伊朗遗址中,灰泥大多由二水硫酸钙组成,属于石膏矿物。罗马灰泥则是作黏合剂的石灰,以及大理石、石灰华或其他石灰石粉末的钙质骨料[1]。

---

[1] 尽管如此,由于石膏砂浆远比石灰砂浆易干,灰泥类型亦与施工技术相关(Azarnoush 1994, p. 93, n. 2)。

依据其所知的例证，克勒格尔将萨珊时期的三种典型灰泥工艺定为刻划、贴塑和模制[1]。上述工艺往往同时使用，但装饰性灰泥构件越来越普遍，表明模制技术获得较大发展。他还提出，灰泥风格可分为三期，与保存更完好的摩崖浮雕分期大致相同[2]。现有遗存大多属于晚期，呈现出多种风格趋势，如泰西封灰泥同时有抽象装饰与受希腊化影响的自然主义元素[3]。中期特点为浮雕趋向扁平，装饰性图案越发重要。与此相反，早期特点为塑出立体的图像与背景，如克勒格尔所言应出自沙普尔一世时期的大量罗马工匠，而非受安息时期影响[4]。要研究这一问题，应仔细考察卡拉·亚兹德格德的图像灰泥，包括考古测定学数据。该遗址年代在发掘中断后原定为公元5世纪[5]，经过潜心研究，最终被定为安息晚期[6]。若卡拉·亚兹德格德灰泥与比沙普尔早期灰泥仅相差几十年[7]，通过列举两处灰泥包括技术在内的所有差异，可证实或推翻罗马工匠在比沙普尔参与工作的假设，也将更清晰地展现卡拉·亚兹德格德艺术与其他萨珊艺术之间的延续性。该方法亦可应用于伊朗考古队近期在卡拉·扎哈克遗址的发现[8]。

哈吉阿巴德的灰泥多为高浮雕，而班迪扬为线刻低浮雕。下文将这两个截然不同的遗址与克勒格尔的技术和风格观点进行对照。

在哈吉阿巴德，刻划灰泥罕见，多为模制或分别刻划而后贴塑，依题材而定[9]。装饰母题多为模制，有时施加贴塑元素。半身像大多为模制，仅L.149伊万两个半柱上的半身像为刻划而成（图128）。模制半身像以木制关节接合模制构件而成，随后添加各人物的五官细节。L.114房间壁龛内发现的大型女性像亦由若干模制构件接合而成（图129）。因其他遗址中仅余少量残片，哈吉阿巴德的大量高浮雕形象材料意义重大[10]。

阿扎尔诺什指出，灰泥之间存在显著的风格差异，在男性半身像的对比中尤为突出。他强调，除前述两座半柱半身像与其余半身像的技术差异外，哈吉阿巴德的半身像之间亦存在风格差异，且不仅仅与年代相关。在同被定为沙普尔二世的两座肖像中，其

---

[1] Kröger 1982, p. 209.
[2] Kröger 1982, pp. 248-55.
[3] Keall 1967, p. 121; Kröger 1982, p. 87.
[4] Kröger 1982, p. 258.
[5] Keall 1967, p. 121.
[6] Keall 1977; 也可参见 Kargar s.d., p. 46。
[7] 克勒格尔倾向于安息末期，但不排除萨珊初期的可能性（Kröger 1982, p. 257）。
[8] Qandgar et al. 2004; Kargar s.d., pp. 71-3.
[9] Azarnoush 1994, p. 155.
[10] Erdmann 1969, p. 85; Kröger 1982, pp. 249-50.

伊朗萨珊时期的建筑与艺术

一（n. 20，图130）与公元3世纪末巴赫拉姆二世时期的浮雕风格相似[1]，其二（n. 17，图131）则接近公元5世纪的启什半身像。阿扎尔诺什将原因归为灰泥的再生产可在模具制作后延续多年，在沙普尔二世漫长的任期里越发明显。故他认为风格差异与制作半身像的工匠技艺相关，而后者又与建筑群中装饰空间的重要性相关。正因如此，仅有的高超技艺刻划半身像放置在有接见功能的伊万立面[2]。为了理解风格背后的复杂成因，在此引入一个严格意义上不属于风格学的观点：克勒格尔提出，半身像具有祭拜先祖的功能，故人像年代与实际生产年代间并无确凿关联。该观点不仅关乎建筑年代判定，也影响对风格趋势演变的认识[3]。

相比之下，班迪扬灰泥工艺的出版信息更少。据发掘者拉赫巴尔称，装饰是在土坯墙上覆盖草泥后施2—4厘米厚的灰泥而成。在未直接观察的情况下，我们无法更细致地了解其制作方式，尤其是划分画面的垂带等重复元素，应由模具制成，但因其各不相同，亦可能为刻划而成。而通常被人物浮雕覆盖的画面边框，则仅可能为刻划而成。图像题材亦为刻划。图像扁平，但从满是花纹的背景中跳脱出的立体元素层次分明，呈现光影效果。生机勃勃的动态因大量细

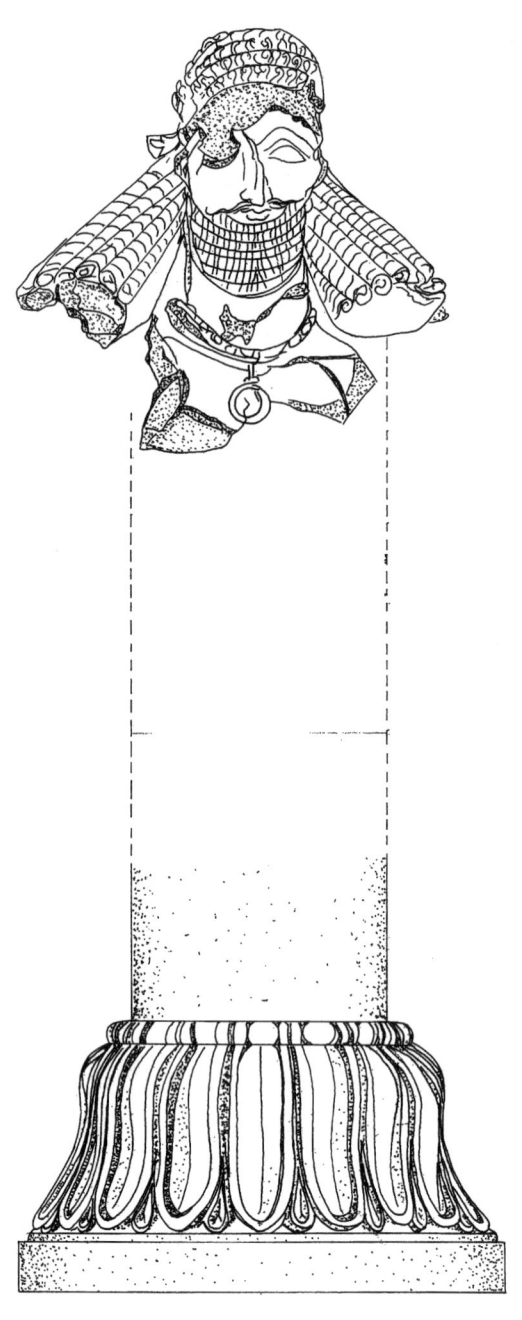

图128 哈吉阿巴德：L.149伊万立面的半柱柱顶半身像（Azarnoush 1994, fig. 143）

---

[1] 依据发现的残片，阿扎尔诺什指出该建筑中至少存在三个不同的沙普尔二世半身像。
[2] Azarnoush 1994, p. 165.
[3] Kröger 1993, p. 63.

图 129 哈吉阿巴德：L.114房间壁龛中的女性雕像（Azarnoush 1994, fig. 145）

图 130 哈吉阿巴德：20号半身像，沙普尔二世像
（Azarnoush 1994, fig. 89）

图 131 哈吉阿巴德：17号半身像，沙普尔二世像
（Azarnoush 1994, fig. 80）

节而惟妙惟肖，织物质地可与王室敕造的顶级摩崖浮雕媲美。在这方面，班迪扬亦有别于其他灰泥装饰的萨珊建筑。

此外，班迪扬还有若干尚未出版的模制人像残片，这里仅有拉赫巴尔的简要描述："一座模制石膏浮雕女性半身像左半部分的两个残片，以及若干绵羊或山羊头和羊角的模制残片。"[1]拉赫巴尔考察上述灰泥在墙面整体构图中的位置，或位于部分残存的底部饰带之上。

回到萨珊灰泥的整体论述。克勒格尔详细探讨了刻划或模制装饰与大多已消失的彩绘间的关联[2]。在某种程度上，正如建筑石刻可被视作彩绘载体，灰泥亦必须施加彩绘，安息时期便已如此[3]。

赫茨菲尔德[4]和德·维拉尔[5]先后阐明的克尔曼沙赫附近塔克·波斯坦主伊万的两侧壁，年代被冯·加尔定为库思老二世时期，可作为浮雕装饰与彩绘之间关联的关键例证[6]。伊万两侧壁为施彩绘的岩石低浮雕[7]，题材为皇家狩猎，亦见于其他萨珊建筑。右为猎鹿（图132），左为猎野猪（图133），国王形象多次出现，尺寸大于其他人物，背景中的自然环境与动物细致生动。受限于非透视的手法，两侧人物呈水平排列。两侧壁无疑为皇家敕建，但赫茨菲尔德认为其艺术形式并非摩崖浮雕，而是壁画。这也解释了为何两侧壁与其他萨珊浮雕的构图有明显差异[8]。而赫尔曼则提出两侧壁更接近灰泥建筑装饰，在班迪扬的发现公之于世后得到鲁索的证实和支持[9]。

由于壁画载体即草泥或石膏层自身的特性无法幸免于结构坍塌和腐蚀，现存萨珊时期的壁画十分稀少，无法开展大篇幅的专题研究[10]。而灰泥的塑性使其在所依附的墙体坍塌后仍可遗留。在灰泥保存相对完好的库赫·哈加、哈吉阿巴德、班迪扬和米勒哈拉姆遗址中，墙面上亦有彩绘痕迹。

如下所述，先进的分析技术可补充现有认识，辨别肉眼无法看到的颜料痕迹。

---

[1] Rahbar 2004, p. 16.
[2] Kröger 1982, pp. 216-20.
[3] Kargar s.d., pp. 51-3; Simpson 等, 2012.
[4] Herzfeld 1920, pp. 96-7.
[5] Monneret de Villard 1954, p. 84.
[6] von Gall 1990, p. 44.
[7] 依据为左侧壁顶板上雕刻的一幅场景中遗留的彩绘，年代为恺加王朝。
[8] Herrmann 2000, p. 44.
[9] Russo 2004, p. 808.
[10] De Waele 2004; Compareti 2011.

图132 塔克·波斯坦：主伊万右壁的塔克·波斯坦Ⅵ号低浮雕（@ Callieri）

图133 塔克·波斯坦：主伊万左壁的塔克·波斯坦Ⅴ号低浮雕（@ Callieri）

关于库赫·哈加，应注意其与中亚和印度西北部灰泥工艺间的联系。这一联系未得到足够重视，如下文班迪扬所示。库赫·哈加是唯一一个可用于探讨与萨珊帝国东部疆域之间联系的遗址。斯坦因之后，川见[1]与卡内帕[2]近期亦指出遗址中图像母题和风格与受贵霜影响的地区有关，尤其是巴克特里亚。

除库赫·哈加外，哈珀在1981年便提出"双线褶皱风格"或源于犍陀罗，自沙普尔二世始在萨珊金属器中传播。

萨珊帝国攻占印度次大陆西北部、即犍陀罗艺术的发源地后，波斯贵族更直接地接触到各类艺术形式，尤其是繁盛的佛教造像，后者在传播过程中借鉴灰泥并以之作为最普遍的工艺。此外，在哈吉阿巴德庄园人像中可辨认出两位贵霜沙赫，即统治萨珊东部省份的王子：灰泥制成的瓦赫拉姆[3]及绘制的霍尔米兹[4]。尽管哈吉阿巴德未体现典型东方特点，但应考虑远至犍陀罗的萨珊王土之内的贵族流动性。

前文多次提到，克勒格尔最创新的观点为灰泥装饰集中分布于两类建筑单元，并作出宗教功能阐释。他强调，灰泥装饰集中分布于多柱大殿和面向庭院敞开的伊万，其证据丰富而连贯，但仍应指出一些例外。

尽管资料并不确凿，库赫·哈加的火神殿外立面至少在萨珊晚期包含黏土浮雕装饰[5]，而查哈尔·塔克内则无装饰痕迹。即便比沙普尔B房址被证实具有宗教功能，其壁龛四周的灰泥及图像残片却是孤例，第二部分第二章中已论述其特殊性[6]。塔克斯特·苏莱曼的PD查哈尔·塔克中的残片或为另一例证[7]，但申卡尔已辨明残片为建筑群另一部分的填土材料[8]。申卡尔亦指出查哈尔·塔克无装饰的现实原因，即火神殿墙壁逐渐被烟灰覆盖，不宜施加装饰[9]。我也补充一点，查哈尔·塔克内无装饰的原因是进入人数有限，仅限主持拜火仪式的祭司，故不需投入资源装饰一间与外界隔离的阴暗房间。

近二十年的出版物整体上证实了上述情况，但不应继续认为灰泥装饰仅集中在多柱大殿与伊万中。克勒格尔在构建其理论时，显然已了解1977年发现于哈吉阿巴德、并在德黑兰举办的第六届伊朗考古研究年会上展出的灰泥残片及其简报[10]。但他并不了解

---

[1] Kawami 1987a, pp. 22–42.
[2] Canepa 2013, p. 75.
[3] Azarnoush 1994, p. 161.
[4] Azarnoush 1994, pp. 181–2.
[5] 参见第二章。
[6] Kröger 1982, p. 195.
[7] 尤其是多柱大殿建筑群的PD查哈尔·塔克中的两个男性人像残片（Kröger 1982, p. 147）。
[8] Shenkar 2015, p. 478.
[9] Shenkar 2015, p. 478.
[10] Azarnoush 1983, 1984.

阿扎尔诺什的博士论文[1]（出版于意大利都灵亚洲考古发掘与研究中心的报告中[2]）。

哈吉阿巴德建筑群中的灰泥位于L.149伊万对面的柱廊及L.178庭院，即克勒格尔指出的两类建筑单元之一。但亦有大量灰泥出自L.114小室及L.107庭院，毗邻被视作火神殿的L.104十字形大殿[3]，其数量足以使阿扎尔诺什提出完整的复原构图。从平面看，L.114小室既非伊万，亦非多柱大殿，其功能也与体量更大的上述两者毫不相干。

相反，上一章中已讨论其建筑的班迪扬和米勒·哈拉姆遗址中的灰泥完全符合克勒格尔的理论。壁饰集中于规模最大的主殿，通向祭司举行拜火仪式的无装饰小殿。班迪扬就地保存的装饰中包含图像丰富的灰泥场景。米勒·哈拉姆则仅余装饰性残片，但壁画遗存原本应属于规模更大的复杂图像画面。

在克勒格尔的阐释体系中，功能假设在当时最为轰动，但也体现出他对待考古新发现的谦虚。除包含圆柱、方柱大殿各一的塔克斯特·苏莱曼建筑群有明确的宗教功能外，多柱大殿为琐罗亚斯德教团体所用的依据为部分遗址的陶片，其上记录了葡萄酒等琐罗亚斯德教仪式祭品[4]。

20世纪30年代在设拉子周边发掘的喀斯尔·阿卜纳斯尔遗址中，若干陶片上亦记录了祭品，且与塔克斯特·苏莱曼相似，出土了或用于封存祭品的封泥。在惠特科姆出版美国考古队的发掘成果前，克勒格尔已提出假设，即喀斯尔·阿卜纳斯尔与塔克斯特·苏莱曼相似，东边平台区有一座火神庙，而西边多柱大殿建筑群有另一座火神庙，包含一个供信众使用的仪式大殿[5]。但惠特科姆认为饰有灰泥的八角形室属于布韦希时期（945—1055年），其装饰与所谓的多柱大殿无关[6]。

克勒格尔坚信灰泥装饰仅集中分布于伊万及多柱大殿中，他将多柱大殿定为"琐罗亚斯德教仪式大殿"，并在此基础上将包含上述两类单元的所有建筑群归为宗教建筑[7]。随后他对初始论点稍加改动："可以假定在饰有灰泥的建筑空间中，琐罗亚斯德教徒举行了许多关于日常事务或重大宗教节庆的集会。因此无论是宫殿、私人住宅还是火神殿，饰有灰泥的建筑的图像都具有若干相似点。"[8]在后期著作中，他的论述更加委

---

[1] Azarnoush 1987.
[2] NDT: Centre de fouilles et de recherche archéologique en Asie de Turin; Azarnoush 1994.
[3] Azarnoush 1994, p. 136 et suiv.
[4] Kröger 1982, p. 273. 关于琐罗亚斯德教仪式祭品的批判性论述，参见Huff 2011。
[5] Kröger 1982, p. 274.
[6] Whitcomb 1985, p. 43.
[7] Kröger 1982, pp. 268-76.
[8] Kröger 1993, p. 65.

婉。尽管他提出:"根据以班迪扬为主的大量新发现,此类包含灰泥大殿的建筑不应被视作宫殿或庄园,而是为琐罗亚斯德教团体所用",但紧随其后便让步道:"此类建筑亦可能属于地方领主,但许多问题仍待解决。"[1]

在最新著作中,克勒格尔仍认为灰泥装饰主要与琐罗亚斯德教团体相关:"仅琐罗亚斯德教徒使用的大殿或入口处有装饰。"[2]但他不排除大地主建筑饰有灰泥的可能性。

在我看来,新材料极大地影响了克勒格尔的解读,乃至与其出发点大相径庭,而更接近我对宫殿建筑的观察。

应当承认克勒格尔的两点突破。一方面,关于灰泥,此前仅有浅显的研究,他为深入探索其象征性意义奠定了基础。另一方面,他重新定义了琐罗亚斯德教与艺术的关联,强调艺术语言对伊朗萨珊时期的宗教意象的重要性。他指出:"至今人们仍认为琐罗亚斯德教反对形象,包括艺术语言方面,但该教在萨珊文化中的地位比此前想象的更为重要。"[3]

解读饰有灰泥的多柱大殿时,不可忽略其年代问题。克勒格尔极富洞见地提出,与琐罗亚斯德教有关的灰泥装饰及所属建筑大多属于伊斯兰初期,尤其是在雷伊地区[4]。尽管大量文献记载,琐罗亚斯德教祭祀建筑被毁坏或被改造成清真寺,伊斯兰早期亦存在继续沿用的火神庙,如塔克斯特·苏莱曼和托尔让·泰佩[5]。正如第二部分第一章中所强调的,伊斯兰时期的大规模装饰有突出的世俗含义,故其功能应与贵族而非琐罗亚斯德教团体相关。如克勒格尔所提议,应解读查拉·塔尔汉陶片上的阿拉伯语铭文,以证其内容是否与萨珊遗址中记录琐罗亚斯德教祭品的陶片相同。

克勒格尔指出的一个难点,即女性像或被定为女神,或被定为王后[6],在哈吉阿巴德尤为明显。阿扎尔诺什将该遗址中的大量着衣或裸体女性人像定为阿娜希塔女神[7],却在书评中遭到严厉驳斥[8]。伊朗学者将女性形象全部定为波斯水神的普遍趋势已在诸多场合遭到质疑[9]。吉钮提出,遗址中的形象均属于"酒神"图像题材,可由持葡萄串的爱神或狮首辨别。该观点亦与克勒格尔解读大部分灰泥装饰的节庆主题相符,故似乎比阿扎尔诺什更为可信。

---

[1] Kröger 2005a.
[2] Kröger 2006, p. 52.
[3] Kröger 1982, p. 276.关于该问题的另一观点,参见 Duchesne-Guillemin 1971。
[4] Kröger 1982, p. 274.
[5] Kröger 1982, p. 274.
[6] Kröger 1993, p. 64.
[7] Azarnoush 1994, pp. 161–3.
[8] Gignoux 1995, Huff 1995, Callieri 1996.
[9] Bier 1989.

克勒格尔提出的另一突破性主题，即启什的国王半身像属于祖先崇拜[1]，亦为20世纪80年代初德黑兰临时展览中的哈吉阿巴德遗存所证实[2]。该阐释为此前仅有文献和建筑依据的纪念逝者的论述提供了决定性的图像材料[3]。哈拉雷兹的阿克沙珊·卡拉遗址中的壁画半身像"画廊"或为重要先例，年代为公元前1世纪[4]。该阐释同时质疑了将人像归为所在建筑年代末期的观点，因人像可指代若干朝代之前的国王。哈吉阿巴德半身像的风格学分析亦支持上述解读，尽管有两个4世纪时在位的沙普尔二世像，半身像的风格却大多位于公元4—5世纪之间。

在阿扎尔诺什对L.114装饰构图的复原中（图134），墙面上方为一列持葡萄串的爱神圆板（40）。圆盾男性像位于墙的高处，每面墙有一个国王半身像（20），其下是三个较小的半身像（23—25）。下方为大型着衣女性像（34—37）所在的壁龛。阿扎尔诺什认为，小型裸体女性像（39）及连珠纹圆形狮首（41）位于国王和贵族半身像之下，着衣女性像所在的壁龛之间[5]。牛身人面卧像和公牛卧像托座支撑屋顶托梁，侧面为低浮雕，头部为圆盾像，与比沙普尔A房址中的石座相似。依据若干装饰元素的形状可确定其位置，尤其是曲线剖面三角构件（4），但大部分复原装饰构图仅为假设。无论如何，我们可大致了解毫无关联的独立元素的组合形式。

在L.149伊万前柱廊中，装饰伊万入口两侧的两根矮柱旁发现了两座男性半身像，

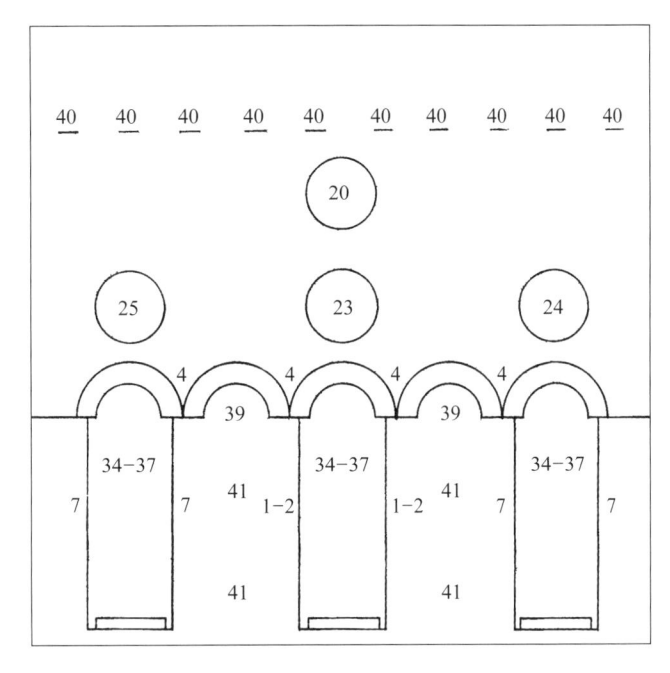

图134 哈吉阿巴德：L.114房间装饰复原示意图（Azarnoush 1994，fig. 155）。数字由上至下依次代表：40=持葡萄串的小天使；20、23、24、25=中型男性半身像；4=三角装饰构件；39=小型裸体女性像；34—37=大型着衣女性像；7=卐字及半圆饰边框；41=狮首；1—2=植物图案方形构件

---

[1] Kröger 1982, p. 265.
[2] Kröger 1993, p. 64; 2006, p. 52.
[3] Kotwal/Choksy 2004, 2013; Canepa 2010, p. 584.
[4] Kidds/Betts 2010, pp. 658-75.
[5] Azarnoush 1994, fig. 155.

阿扎尔诺什根据发掘时的位置，将其合理地置于无柱头的矮柱上。两座半身像被定为庄园主及其子[1]。这一全新的古代建筑装饰类型，与古典时期的赫耳墨斯石柱形式相似。若贝萨附近卡拉·瑙的石灰半身像年代确凿，则把半身像置于柱顶的做法在安息晚期已有先例，拙作中已指出半身像躯干的特殊形制[2]。亦有嵌入石灰墙面的半身像，如拜古里塔中发现的四个凸出于墙面的纳塞赫像，赫茨菲尔德的复原将半身像置于四壁正中央[3]。此外还有第五个半身像，残留圆盾头像的大部分，应位于更高处，但由于不能观察全表面而难以确定。该半身像现存于伊拉克库尔德地区的苏莱曼尼亚博物馆，因其恶劣的保存状况而无法移动。拜古里的四座半身像在安息时期的哈特拉有先例，证实了将肖像置于建筑中的偏好，与哈吉阿巴德的两座半身像一起构成全新的建筑装饰类型。

启什Ⅱ号房址庭院中有十四根圆壁柱，亦发现类似的半身像，证明该类型的广泛传播。十四座国王半身像高约50厘米，头戴与沙普尔二世或巴赫拉姆五世相似的王冠，身份应为后者（图135）[4]。克勒格尔引用了瓦特林的复原假设，即半身像位于沿墙均匀分布的半柱间的凹处[5]（图136）。复原假设中半柱高达墙面上边缘，沿袭古代东方传统，但不能通过半身像背面形状等客观因素证实，亦无可比较的相似布局。复原图中半身像的宽度与假定其所在的柱间凹处并不一致。德芒热提出另一假设，即半身像取代半柱柱头，距地面有一定高度[6]。这一假设同样缺乏半身像的客观特征作支撑，但与明确位于半柱上的哈

图135 启什（伊拉克）：国王半身像（Kröger 1982, pl.87.1）

---

[1] Azarnoush 1994，图143。也可参见 Harper 2008, pp. 73-4, 图2：她提出的与比沙普尔建筑的对照并不切题。
[2] Callieri 2007, p. 109. 哈珀并未注意到这一重要特点（Harper 2008, p. 77）。
[3] Herzfeld 1914，图1。
[4] Moorey 1978, p. 136; Kröger 1982, p. 223; Demange 2006, p. 53.
[5] Kröger 1982, pp. 225-6, 图122。穆雷提出这一情况下半柱的数量应为十二，Moorey 1978, p. 135。
[6] Demange 2006, p. 53.

图 136 启什（伊拉克）：瓦特林提出的Ⅱ号房址庭院装饰复原图（Kröger 1982，fig. 122）

吉阿巴德半身像相符，更为合理。启什的半柱应未达墙面上边缘，柱上为半身像。

泰西封附近特拉达拜的南侧建筑（苏德堡）中，发现了贵族男性半身像及呈奔跑状的马等动物像，被克勒格尔视作属于连续饰带的狩猎图，大型国王半身像亦属其中，但鉴于遗存的残损状况，已无法复原[1]。

---

[1] Kröger 1993b.

在克勒格尔的两部主要著作出版以前,他并未了解班迪扬遗址[1],而班迪扬的灰泥对理解各种祖先崇拜形式至关重要。如下文所示,班迪扬的人像并非孤立,而是属于整体画面,以战争与崇信琐罗亚斯德教的叙事体现对祖先的纪念。

在克勒格尔的著作中,"叙事"一词既未出现在索引中,也不作专门讨论。他所知的萨珊灰泥并非"叙事艺术",该术语也不能应用于其他萨珊时期的艺术。以有政治含义的克敌制胜摩崖浮雕为例,如菲鲁扎巴德Ⅰ号、达拉卜或比沙普尔Ⅱ号和Ⅲ号。波斯艺术与罗马艺术不同。罗马艺术通过可与年鉴写实细节相媲美的叙事来表现,例如以精妙构图将历史转变为罗马史诗的图拉真纪功柱[2]。而波斯艺术则从象征性角度表现[3],其含义并不遵从叙事逻辑[4]。萨珊艺术似为塞萨洛尼基的加莱里乌斯拱门(3世纪末至4世纪初)中轻叙事重象征特点的前奏,美国艺术史学家布里兰特将其与超越历史的永恒不变权力概念相联系[5]。萨珊唯一的建筑雕刻,即比沙普尔B宫殿的中楣,亦同此理。比尔的遗作中指出,将现存的方石视作场景的组成部分,核心主题为国王在贵族簇拥下战胜敌人,接受朝觐及贡品,或由神祇为其加冕,与摩崖浮雕同样为赞颂而非叙事[6]。

在此引用布里兰特的文字,以表现叙事艺术的若干主要元素。

> 在视觉叙事中,细节描写和场景创作等构图手法,取代了口头和文本叙事中大篇幅的讲述或思考。细节描写和构图手法可确定事件主角,将其落在时、空中,故应当是不言自明的。视觉叙事似在渲染一种现实乃至历史事件的氛围或错觉,因为它在某种意义上属于现实世界。要表现某一特定事件,就要给眼睛提供足量的信息。[7]

萨珊艺术倾向于大量增加改变事件原貌的象征性元素,而非采取上述手法。唯一的例外为班迪扬主殿的灰泥浮雕。第二部分第二章中已指出该建筑应为贵族地主举行家庭丧葬仪式之处。如前所述,班迪扬灰泥的技术手法不同于哈吉阿巴德,而更接近绘画手法。因仅有难以确定原始位置的库赫·哈加等少量遗迹,关于壁画最突出的对比并非

---

[1] Kröger 2005b.
[2] Brilliant 1984.
[3] Vanden Berghe 1983, p. 58.
[4] 我不认同哈珀所言,即摩崖浮雕战争图具有叙事特征。
[5] Brilliant 1984, p. 124; Canepa 2009, p. 98及其后。
[6] Bier 2009, pp. 12, 20.
[7] Brilliant 1984, p. 11.

位于伊朗境内,而是来自中亚,即位于科佩特山脉、伊朗高原的北部屏障以北的班迪扬所属的地理区域。

已有人指出班迪扬灰泥在图像和风格上十分接近中亚图像文化[1],但未见专门研究。值得注意的是,若干人像的半跏坐姿与粟特组画及吐火罗斯坦贵族的典型表现十分接近,马的表现手法亦为中亚地区所常见[2]。而中亚地区存在一类叙事性图像艺术传统,始于希腊化时期尼萨古城的塔式建筑精美壁画[3],延续至包含反映当时现实的仪式场景与表现文学作品的叙事场景的粟特组画[4],可追溯至公元5世纪[5]。

班迪扬艺术在萨珊帝国艺术中的独特之处,迄今仍未得到足够重视。不同于除库赫·哈加壁画外的其他萨珊艺术,班迪扬灰泥体现出了叙事性特点[6]。以下将详述其灰泥的叙事构图。

东北边敞开的伊万大殿三面墙壁下部饰有高约1米的连贯场景[7],离地面约0.6米[8]。场景边框饰有半棕榈叶纹,位于两道沿墙边缘分布的外框之间。墙上的叙事是连贯的。而西北墙壁龛场景被两列棕榈叶间的回纹垂带分割。人物时常遮挡装饰边框,呈现出三维效果,使人物朝观者的方向行进,似乎要从背景上走下来。

墙面上部现已残缺,但仍可对主题进行大致解读。首先应参考拉赫巴尔在西方发表的文章中提出[9]并随后修正的阐释[10]。他认为东南壁面由左至右依次为狩猎图、象征性战争图与胜利图。狩猎图中,两名骑兵追逐着两头鹿,其中一头负伤(图137)。狩猎图与战争图以一名立定的骑兵分隔。战争图中,两名敌方骑兵与单枪匹马的波斯骑兵交锋,后者脚踝上的饰带表明其身份为国王,众骑兵踏过有突厥特征的残缺躯体。依据摩崖浮雕中的常见构图,胜利图中应为胜利者脚踏两个倒在地上的人物(图138)[11]。

---

[1] Curatola/Scarcia 2003, p. 99.
[2] Azarpay 1981, p. 151, n. 16.
[3] Pilipko 2000.
[4] Balenitskii/Marshak 1981, p. 63; Azarpay 1981, pp. 147-50.
[5] 孔帕雷蒂认为,根据在佩肯特发现的壁画残片,当地应存在一所年代更早的粟特绘画学院,与萨珊波斯间的关系更为密切(Compareti 2011, pp. 21-3)。
[6] Azarpay 1981, pp. 90-1.
[7] Rahbar 2004, p. 16.
[8] Rahbar 2008, p. 16.
[9] Rahbar 1998.
[10] Rahbar 2008.
[11] 该场景与NRu Ⅶ号骑战双图十分相似,通常被定为巴赫拉姆二世时期,但冯·加尔将其归为巴赫拉姆四世时期(388—399年)(von Gall 1990, pp. 32, 34)。他认为战争的敌方为嚈哒帝国,与拉赫巴尔对班迪扬的阐释一致。

伊朗萨珊时期的建筑与艺术

图 137　班迪扬：大殿东南墙，狩猎图（Rahbar 1998, pls. Ⅲ — Ⅳ）

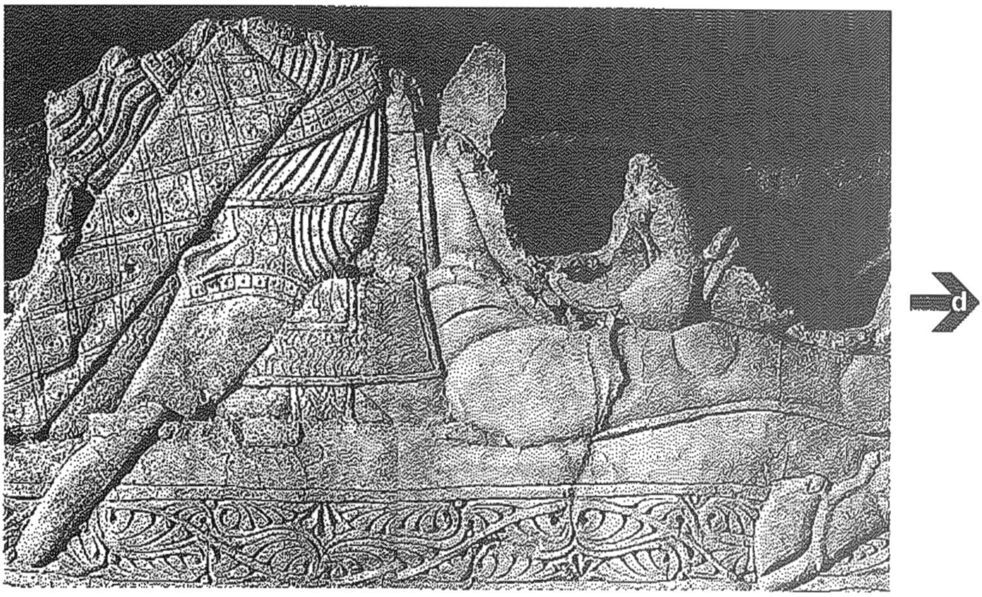

c

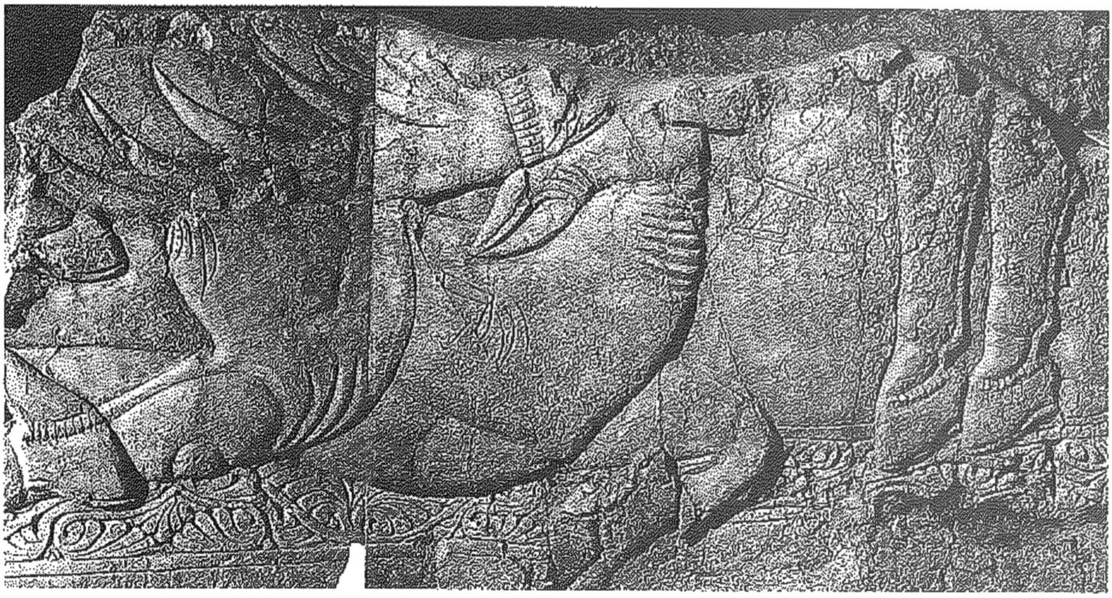

d

图 138 班迪扬：大殿东南墙，胜敌图（Rahbar 1998, pl. V）

下篇 专题

c

→ d

d

西南壁面不幸也遭损坏,仅三朵五瓣百合花的右侧遗留一个人像,被拉赫巴尔视作女性,并定为阿娜希塔女神,正将瓶中之物倒向相邻殿内,系有饰带的帘子被拉开(图139)。

西北壁靠近伊万大殿的西墙角处有一长方形壁龛,但亦只有底部装饰全部保留。龛西南壁左侧为一位着战袍的国王或英雄,坐在地毯上,右手持一巴尔萨姆枝,右臂与右腿间空白处有中古波斯语铭文(图140)[1]。右侧两列如前所述的装饰垂带之间,一人立于颈部饰有珍珠的马前,虽然与右装饰垂带的两侧铭文不符,此人应为雨神蒂尔[2]。拉赫巴尔1998年的文章指出,龛正壁为三级平台之上、两根圆柱之间的火神殿,柱间的厚帘子中部系有饰带(图141)[3]。在2004年的文章中,他合理地改称其为沙漏型坛身的圣火祭坛,中部饰系带编织纹,三级平台上边缘立有祭坛台面的木支架。祭坛整体十分接近火神殿里发现的实物[4]。祭坛两侧立有穿着各异的两人,均右手持香炉,左手持棍(巴尔萨姆枝)。一人为阿娜希塔,另一人为国王。右侧有一处中古波斯语铭文[5]。东北壁上一人立于与西南壁相似的两列装饰垂带间,应为祭司,右手持棍,左手持香炉(图142)。香炉下方有一处中古波斯语铭文[6]。

壁龛以东,伊万大殿西北壁先后为包含四个立姿人像的神授王权图(?),及至少三人坐在地毯上的接见图(?)(图143)。在四个立姿人像中,依据左起第三与第四人之间的水瓶,两人之一应为阿娜希塔。

拉赫巴尔对主题的图像阐释大体可信,但若干论据不足处仍需修改。除一些次要细节外,也应考虑西南壁面场景。拉赫巴尔提出其中的帘子对应东北边大殿的门帘[7],但我以为应表现的是沙漏型坛身,饰有与壁龛中央圣火坛相同的编织纹[8]。

拉赫巴尔对主题的阐释中有一点我无法认同,即阿娜希塔出现三次,其中两次与水瓶相关。我对吉钮将建筑群解读为世俗功能有异议[9],但我同他均反对拉赫巴尔

---

[1] Gignoux 1998, p. 254,铭文 E 为: ... BRY wyhm'... tly (t)'ywp。
[2] Gignoux 1998, p. 253, 铭文 C—D 为:Weh-Šābuhr brad ēn dastgird kard (韦沙布尔制作了这一部分)。
[3] Rahbar 1998.
[4] Rahbar 2004, p. 16.
[5] Gignoux 1998, pp. 253-4,铭文 B: Druvān-Mihr ī Yazd-Šābuhrān (Druvān-Mihr, Yarz-Šābuhrān之子)。
[6] Gignoux 1998, p. 254,铭文 A: Pahikar ēn Weh-Mihr-Šābuhr ī Weh-Šābuhr <ī?> Ardaxšīrān brād, (此图[为]Weh-Mihr-Šābuhrī,Weh-Šābuhr之子,Ardaxšīr之兄弟)。
[7] Rahbar 2008, p. 16.
[8] 感谢阿扎尔诺什证实了这一观点。她指出该场景为祭司对圣火祭坛的净化,如pl. 5 Kotwal/Boyd 1991中所示。关于壁龛中央场景,吉钮(2008, p. 169)也提出"(将两人)分隔的祭坛与一个持瓶女人所在场景的帘子十分接近",然而此处他倾向于将两幅图像视作帘子而非祭坛,与笔者的观点相反。
[9] Gignoux 2008, p. 168.

图 139 班迪扬：大殿西南墙（Rahbar 1998, pl. Ⅶ）

图140 班迪扬：大殿西北墙上壁龛，西南壁（Rahbar 1998, pl. Ⅷ）

图141 班迪扬：大殿西北墙上壁龛，西北壁（Rahbar 1998, pl. Ⅸ）

图142 班迪扬：大殿西北墙上壁龛，东北壁（Rahbar 1998, pl. Ⅹ）

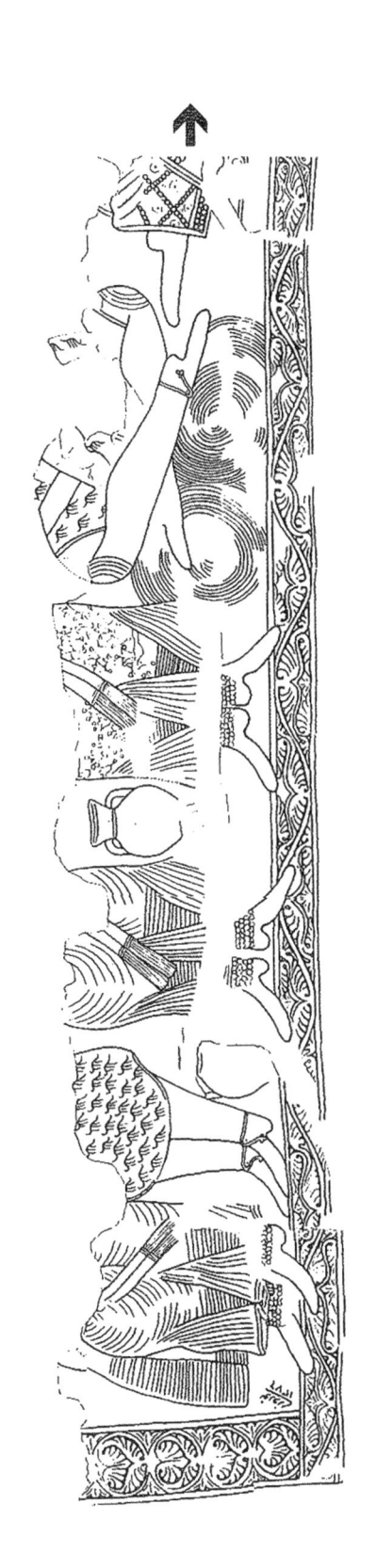

图 143 班迪扬：大殿西北墙（Rahbar 1998, figs. 9—10）

的观点，而依据与他有部分不同。首先，所谓的阿娜希塔第一次出现在西南壁时，与持瓶之人穿着相同的人应非女性，因为铭文表明其为男性，另外他的穿着不同于萨珊波斯阿娜希塔女神的典型衣物[1]。西北壁亦然，衣着相同、仅织物花纹不同的两人之间放置一瓶，故不应一为男性，一为女性。同样，壁龛正壁祭坛两边的两人，其一穿着如前所述，另一着丘尼克和长裤。将壁龛左侧壁立于马前的人定为蒂尔的论断也缺乏确凿证据。

对于若干人物所持的束棍或其他形式的标识被定为巴尔萨姆枝这一观点，我同吉钮一样持怀疑态度，包括壁龛左侧壁的坐姿一人[2]，壁龛正壁赤脚立于圣火祭坛前的两人，以及壁龛右侧壁被视作祭司的立姿一人[3]。吉钮认为祭司左手所持并非香炉，而是酒杯(？)，因其形制异于其他已知的香炉。

对于场景的阐释，应基于吉钮关于联系铭文的提议，其中一则铭文以"此图（为）"开头[4]。正因如此，他将壁龛正壁右侧的B铭文视作工匠的签名，而非如其他铭文般视作所刻人物的名称，这一提议仍需商榷[5]。

应将所有壁面视作整体，在两侧墙壁与壁龛上细分为若干场景。壁龛内人物除一处外，均附有对应的铭文[6]。铭文加强了场景的"叙事"性，突出了与人物所处时代无关的时效性。我倾向于认为壁龛用于展现举行不同仪式的家族成员。应注意壁龛的对称构图，即祭坛两侧各有一人，与两侧壁的两人以装饰垂带分隔，左侧壁坐姿的第五人遮挡了部分装饰垂带。

如上一章所述，班迪扬建筑群用于举行庆典及丧葬仪式，另一主题则为展现家族祖先的功勋，体现在伊万大殿东南壁与西北壁灰泥中。细致的人物特征使拉赫巴尔得以辨认出地上躯体的中亚长相。没有一处摩崖浮雕能如此层次丰富地表现克敌制胜，没有一件金属器能如此栩栩如生地展示狩猎场景。班迪扬的狩猎图更接近现均已残缺的壁画[7]，或是塔克·波斯坦的主伊万两侧壁的绘制手法[8]。

尽管狩猎图与制胜图的象征性含义突出，其表现形式却符合布里兰特所说的叙事艺术。

---

[1] Bier 1989.
[2] Gignoux 2008, p. 168.
[3] Gignoux 2008, p. 169.
[4] Gignoux 2008, p. 169.
[5] Gignoux 1998, p. 254.
[6] 但该处铭文也可能位于现已不存的图像上部。
[7] De Waele 2004.
[8] 参见上文。

由此可知，萨珊国土内不同艺术传统共存，与若干大区对应。班迪扬相对于其他萨珊艺术遗存所特有的叙事性，无疑因其位处中亚。同理，应重新审视美索不达米亚地区和伊朗高原灰泥间的联系，以定义萨珊艺术中，尤其是在陶瓷等其他萨珊工艺门类中公认的不同地区传统。

更广泛地说，也可扩大讨论，甚至区分伊朗西、南方的"伊朗"特点，与东、北方的"帕提亚"特点，但并非依据普沙利亚提的激进编史学[1]。从这一角度看，库赫·哈加的地理位置显然有决定性作用。

同时，也应从另一角度审视中亚艺术中目前仅限于少量图像元素的萨珊风格，若不将萨珊艺术的范围囿于王室，例证将更为丰富[2]。

在此以寄语作结。目前出版信息中通过物理—化学方法获得的分析资料仍然有限，但却逐渐成为研究的坚实基础。如前所述，克勒格尔的著作以其完整度和准确度成为典范，其中却缺少此类数据，尽管当时的古代材料研究已有涉及，如1976年汤普森关于查拉·塔尔汉灰泥的著作[3]。与银器相反，萨珊灰泥的考古测量学研究并未取得长足的进步，或由于缺乏博物馆需要甄别古玩市场物品真伪的动力。正是这一动力从20世纪70年代起促使美国考古测量学研究迅速发展[4]。因此，仅少量已知材料具备此类分析信息。

现有的少量数据预示了这一领域的巨大研究潜力。班迪扬的两块灰泥残片含有90%—92%的石膏，3%—4.5%的硅酸盐及少于0.1%的氧化铁和铝[5]。查拉·塔尔汉的八块残片则为不同的化学成分：一块含61%的石膏、24%的方解石和14%的石英，而另外七块含73%—84%的石膏、2%—3%的方解石及14%—25%的硅酸盐。

此外，对扫描电子显微镜下的小份样品进行岩相学研究，将对明确混合物的组成，尤其是少量成分大有裨益。

获取大量现有材料的分析信息后，可依据灰泥成分，结合技术—风格学方法重新分区，以定义各技术传统。亦可为未确定年代的建筑提供依据，尤其是安息至萨珊、萨珊至伊斯兰过渡期。比如沙普尔B房址的灰泥被认为并非沿袭安息，而是出自罗马工匠带来的新技艺，便可借助考古测量学数据判定。

---

[1] Pourshariati 2008.
[2] Azarpay 1981, p. 147.
[3] Thompson 1976, pp. 95–6.
[4] Gunter/Jett 1992.
[5] Rahbar 1998, p. 225.

得知柏林古代研究院与柏林伊斯兰艺术博物馆TOPOI卓越研究团队开展了泰西封灰泥装饰项目，我不胜欣慰。泰西封灰泥保存于克勒格尔主管的伊斯兰艺术博物馆。项目由克瑙特领导，为筹备由弗兰克监管的展览[1]，进行了科技考古研究，以实施新的修复工作。另一展览举办于2016年秋季，展出了TOPOI的全部研究题目，并设保护研究与物质文化的分区[2]。上述活动无疑为灰泥研究的重要转折点。

---

[1] Raumwissen 2013，与施泰因米勒的论文有关。
[2] www.topoi.org/project/c-3-1.

第四章 萨珊时期的摩崖浮雕：艺术中心

因其丰富的题材与图像母题，自研究萨珊时期的伊朗之初，学界便将摩崖浮雕作为重点。大规模的摩崖浮雕引起了早期西方旅行者的兴趣，他们为难以应对人为和自然破坏的作品留下了珍贵的记录。面对包括萨珊时期在内的摩崖浮雕日趋恶化的状况，为了奠定坚实的研究基础，德黑兰德国考古研究所开展了图像材料的"批注本"项目，即赫茨菲尔德所创立《伊朗纪念碑》系列中的《伊朗摩崖浮雕》丛书。其中仅有部分浮雕出版[1]，但仍可作为基本参考资料。除该丛书外，另有日本学者对塔克·波斯坦浮雕的数卷研究[2]，以及施密特在波斯波利斯发掘报告第三卷中提供的精美摄影资料[3]。由于近几十年岩体剥蚀导致石刻的大量细节消失，现应重拾并完善《伊朗摩崖浮雕》丛书。同时应采取针对性的保护措施，至少应尽力抑制剥蚀作用，为后世留下这一辉煌过往的记忆。无须理会拜伦在1933—1934年间游历波斯时的苛责，他简略描述比沙普尔的摩崖浮雕后总结道："只有那些欣赏蛮力不讲艺术以及重视形式甚于心灵的人，才会觉得这些石雕很美。"[4]令人欣喜的是，伊朗文化遗产、手工艺品和旅游组织已从纳克什·鲁斯塔姆和比沙普尔遗址着手，展开保护行动。

除旅行者外，古波斯研究者亦对萨珊摩崖浮雕青眼相加。万王之王的建筑中，并未遗留可与阿契美尼德时期的帕萨尔加德、苏萨及波斯波利斯比拟的装饰，因此摩崖浮雕便成为萨珊王室艺术中最丰富的考古资料之一。学界最初致力于解读母题，及辨认场景中鲜少附有铭文的人物。通过与钱币上戴特有王冠、有铭文称号的国王肖像进行比对，相对容易辨认大部分浮雕中的国王，进而可解读不同场景。相反，阐释人物姿势、发型与标识等复杂的图像语言则较为困难，因其对于时人不言自明，而现代人则不明就里，缺乏明确联系。

尽管有许多关于萨珊摩崖浮雕的研究，但无论在纯粹图像学领域，还是图像解读与表达要素的探寻，学界至今仍众说纷纭，莫衷一是。

---

[1] Trümpelmann 1975a, 1975b; Herrmann 1977, 1981a, 1989.
[2] Fukai *et al*. 1969-1984.
[3] Schmidt 1970.
[4] Byron 2000, p. 218. 译文引自顾淑馨译《远行译丛：前往阿姆河之乡》。

前人对单幅浮雕或特定主题的解读倾力颇多,改变了旺当·贝格在"古伊朗摩崖浮雕"摄影展图录中提出的"共识"[1],即:细枝末节上存在诸多分歧,但在若干基本观念上达成了一致。摄影展举办三十年后,阐释框架无疑变得更为复杂,出现了研究单幅或整体浮雕的图像母题的新角度、新方法与新解读,与先前的"共识"相去甚远。

首先,应关注新发现,尤其是巴克特里亚的拉格·比比浮雕,由格勒内作出精妙解读,将萨珊摩崖浮雕的分布范围扩大到伊朗高原的东端[2]。

其次,大量著作推动了若干特定方向的新研究,为已有的丰富资料补充了新的角度。如迈尔对阿尔达希尔一世及沙普尔一世浮雕的专题研究[3],冯·加尔在探究若干主要图像题材时[4]重申的阐释[5],均与先前的"共识"有多处不同。从整体角度,则有拙作对摩崖浮雕与河流的关联的研究[6]。

另有学者致力于图像研究,其影响之深远,甚至改变了此前关于浮雕群的"共识"。核心主题之一是原定为王权神授图的场景阐释[7],在萨珊摩崖浮雕图像中最富意识形态意味。凯姆[8]及奥弗莱特[9]先后对两个决定性的图像母题提出全新假设:一为绶环[10],"共识"将其视作"灵光",即国祚;一为手持万王之王绶环的男性人像,通常被视作阿胡拉·马兹达[11]。

创新的研究还包括索达瓦尔对艺术形式背后语言规则的辨认。他强调,整体把握萨珊艺术的图像语言,是正确解读各要素的唯一途径[12]。这一提议值得高度重视,与胡夫提出解读萨珊建筑群功能的方法不谋而合。我赞同索达瓦尔整体研究萨珊艺术语言"词汇与句法"的观点,但却认为仍有欠缺。

卡内帕以全新视角对萨珊摩崖浮雕展开整体探究的研究成果于2011年完稿,故他并未参照奥弗莱特在2013年提出的创新观点,而似乎重新趋近于1983年旺当·贝格的"共识"[13]。

---

[1] Vanden Berghe 1983.
[2] Grenet *et al.* 2007.
[3] Meyer 1990.
[4] von Gall 2008.
[5] von Gall 1990.
[6] Callieri 2006c.
[7] Vanden Berghe 1988.
[8] Kaim 2009.
[9] Overlaet 2013.
[10] 索达瓦尔(Soudavar 2003, pp. 34-5)及卡内帕(Canepa 2013, p. 863)将通常定义的"绶环"解读为绶带,与凯姆的基本理论迥然不同。私以为,该标识在摩崖浮雕中通常仅为单一圆圈元素,与系结绶带相差甚远,无论如何并非"外观柔软的"(Soudavar 2003, p. 35)。
[11] 凯姆而非奥弗莱特的假设大体可信,囿于篇幅无法展开,本文仍继续采用"王权神授图"的传统解释。
[12] Soudavar 2009.
[13] Canepa 2013.

本章无意衡量上述解读的得失[1]，而是要讨论有助于确定古代艺术中心的技术问题。对艺术中心的研究自赫茨菲尔德和卢科宁后便停滞不前。赫茨菲尔德于1941年提出，因其特点缺乏发展规律，沙普尔一世的五幅胜敌图浮雕或产自同一时期，各幅间的差异不仅受到了外来影响，还由于外国工匠团队[2]。卢科宁则在1971年的书评中强调，不仅要孤立地看待浮雕，还要关注其所属的、可能出自统一规划的浮雕群，而风格学标准对后者的定义十分关键[3]。我认为应重新审视整体性研究，尤其是在卡内帕发表最新成果后[4]。

在研究艺术中心时，应考虑摩崖浮雕制作的三个方面：设计与构图、雕刻技术与使用工具，技术—风格表现。

在第一方面，赫尔曼最早提出设计师与雕刻工匠之间的关联[5]。汤普森的探讨仅限于雕刻前的设计阶段[6]。而构图仅为可分析的因素之一，或许也是最不可信的因素，因为存在可从一个中心移交至另一个中心的设计草稿（"粉本"），凭构图不足以区分各艺术中心。汤普森的研究结果亦可证实：她将构图相似的浮雕归为一类，但同类浮雕在风格上有明显差异，如比沙普尔Ⅳ号（巴赫拉姆二世）—比沙普尔Ⅴ号（巴赫拉姆一世）—纳克什·鲁斯塔姆Ⅵ号（沙普尔一世），纳克什·拉加卜Ⅲ号（阿尔达希尔一世）—纳克什·鲁斯塔姆Ⅰ号（阿尔达希尔一世），萨拉卜·巴赫拉姆（巴赫拉姆二世）—纳克什·鲁斯塔姆Ⅷ号（纳塞赫）[7]。

第二方面即雕刻技术。首先，《伊朗摩崖浮雕》中有丰富的照片与线描资料，多处提及工具痕迹。在此之后，唯一专攻萨珊时期石作技术的是1981年赫尔曼的著作，其方法堪称典范，但止步于初期阶段。她以萨珊初期的摩崖浮雕为核心，研究不同程度的精加工。她提出，四至五幅浮雕经打磨抛光，证明阿尔达希尔一世欣赏阿契美尼德艺术并试图模仿。在菲鲁扎巴德Ⅰ号骑马战斗图中，仅人物面部抛光。在纳克什·拉加卜Ⅲ号站姿王权神授图中，除人物面部外，上半身亦抛光。纳克什·鲁斯塔姆Ⅰ号骑马授权图中的所有人物与动物、纳克什·拉加卜Ⅰ号中的沙普尔及其侍从均抛光。达拉卜浮雕则不确定[8]。总的来说，前两例中抛光见于中浮雕，另两例中抛光见于高浮雕，体现出风

---

[1] 参见注377。
[2] 五幅帝王胜敌图"严格意义上属于同一时代，同一主题。因此设计上的差异充分表明，除了外来影响，外国工匠也在这一萨珊艺术时期参与工作"（Herzfeld 1941, p. 314）。
[3] Lukonin/Dandamaev 1971, p. 159及注14。
[4] Canepa 2013.
[5] Herrmann 1981b, p. 9.
[6] Thompson 2008.
[7] Thompson 2008, p. 355. 浮雕的编号采用旺登贝格1983年的观点，图15。
[8] Herrmann 1981b, pp. 154–5.

格逐步发展。在沙普尔一世的浮雕中，仅纳克什·拉加卜Ⅰ号抛光，赫尔曼认为该浮雕年代接近阿尔达希尔浮雕中最晚的一幅，故在沙普尔浮雕中年代最早[1]。其后，工序中难度最大、耗时最长的抛光被视为不适合摩崖浮雕而遭舍弃[2]，以求扩大规模、增加场景复杂度、简化生产方法[3]。显然，上述观察对研究摩崖浮雕生产及工地组织十分关键。沙普尔一世在位初期对抛光的舍弃是重大创新，应结合生产的其他方面一起考虑。

第三方面为图像细节在不同浮雕中的呈现方式，包括形象的内外因素。分析比对同一艺术中心的元素，继而比对不同艺术中心，可确定始终在同一中心工作，或依据需求在萨珊领土内调动的工匠团队。如此，可从纯粹的技术分析研究艺术中心。

艺术中心不仅对理解各题材与母题十分重要，亦有助于理解摩崖浮雕在萨珊时期的伊朗所扮演的角色。应关注下列关键问题：生产机制与不同工作阶段的分工；仅有一个中央作坊四处调动，或是数个作坊同时工作；萨珊艺术中心的源流——摩崖浮雕在古代传统的基础上崛地而起，但因过于久远，并非直接传承。从上述角度展开的研究，可以通过可能同时存在的不同艺术中心确定地域标准。迄今为止用于摩崖浮雕分类的纯粹年代学标准，应与地域标准结合，甚至在一定程度上被后者取代。

萨珊摩崖浮雕的制作始于阿尔达希尔一世在位期间，他决定在伊朗高原上采用这一古代传统表现形式来传达帝国的意识形态。川见指出，石雕是最复杂的艺术表现形式之一，包含多种雕刻工具的使用、大规模构图的实现与复杂作坊的组织[4]。为了开创新的艺术媒介，阿尔达希尔一世显然需要一个有能力承担其委托的作坊，以催生新的传统。

为了确定这一媒介可能的起源，首先要对阿尔达希尔一世的5处浮雕进行年代排序，从最早的浮雕中寻找其原型。学界对此各执一词。唯一没有分歧的是位于阿塞拜疆奥鲁米耶湖附近的萨勒马斯浮雕（图144），同时刻画阿尔达希尔一世与沙普尔一世，可追溯至阿尔达希尔一世在位末年的共同执政时期，故年代最晚[5]。然而，萨勒马斯又是阿尔达希尔一世浮雕中最"原始"的，全部线刻而成，无立体度，出自水平较低的当地

---

[1] Herrmann 1981b, p. 156. 赫尔曼亦引用了卢科宁提出的纳克什·拉加卜Ⅰ号不早于公元262年的观点，依据为同一浮雕上铭文中的长称号与战胜瓦勒良相关（参见下文）（Herrmann 1981b, p. 158）。随后，迈尔（Meyer 1990, p. 286）与哈伊斯（Huyse 1998, p. 112）先后提出，该称号及沙普尔一世的所有胜敌图浮雕不早于262年，并为其他学者采纳（Alarm et al. 2007, p. 26）。私以为，浮雕技术比解读国王头衔中的"anērān"（非伊朗）更为关键。关于沙普尔一世的不同称号，参见Gyselen 2003, pp. 186-90。

[2] Nylander 1970, p. 32.

[3] Herrmann 1981b, p. 160.

[4] Kawami 2013, p. 751.

[5] Hinz 1969, pp. 115-43.

图 144　萨勒马斯：摩崖浮雕（Hinz 1969, pl.69）

作坊[1]。就我的方法论而言，上述公认的年代顺序是关键的先例，因其证实萨珊帝国存在数个同时工作的作坊，重要性将在之后展现。

其余4处浮雕的年代顺序众说纷纭，尤其是菲鲁扎巴德Ⅰ号阿尔达希尔一世战胜阿尔达班四世图，以及Ⅱ号站姿王权神授图，而纳克什·鲁斯塔姆Ⅰ号骑马授权图被一致认为年代最晚。

赫尔曼认为菲鲁扎巴德Ⅱ号站姿王权神授图年代最早（图145、146），她指出其简单的构图与技术相比埃兰浮雕几无长进[2]。继而是菲鲁扎巴德Ⅰ号（图147、148），她承认其起伏较小，但隆起与雕刻面的精加工极佳[3]。

相反，欣茨提出的年代顺序为菲鲁扎巴德Ⅰ号—菲鲁扎巴德Ⅱ号—纳克什·拉加卜Ⅲ号—纳克什·鲁斯塔姆Ⅰ号[4]。卢科宁指出，通过钱币上王冠间的对比可得出唯一确凿的年代学元素，故菲鲁扎巴德Ⅱ号与纳克什·拉加卜Ⅲ号（3世纪30年代末）早于

---

[1] Canepa 2013, p. 873.
[2] Huff 2008a, p. 39认为菲鲁扎巴德Ⅱ号尚未完工。
[3] Herrmann 2000, pp. 38–9.
[4] Hinz 1969, pp. 115–43.

伊朗萨珊时期的建筑与艺术

图145 菲鲁扎巴德：菲鲁扎巴德Ⅱ号浮雕（@ Callieri）

图146 菲鲁扎巴德：菲鲁扎巴德Ⅱ号浮雕示意图（而非准确测量的线图）

图147　菲鲁扎巴德：菲鲁扎巴德 I 号浮雕（@ Callieri）

纳克什·鲁斯塔姆 I 号（3世纪30年代至40年代初）。而在菲鲁扎巴德 I 号中，国王并未佩戴王冠，而是战盔[1]。1983年布鲁塞尔展览图录中的"共识"采纳了欣茨的观点[2]，卡内帕亦在其最后综述中采用[3]。

虽然我认同卢科宁所言，不能通过王冠判定菲鲁扎巴德 I 号浮雕的年代（图147），但整体风格特点表明其为萨珊浮雕生产初期，尤其是与菲鲁扎巴德 II 号浮雕的立体度相比。故我不认同赫尔曼分析精细做工与局部抛光后得出的结论。

从图像学角度看，菲鲁扎巴德 I 号浮雕仍沿袭安息时期的伊朗传统。卡内帕强调[4]，该浮雕与比索通的戈塔尔泽斯骑马胜敌图在图像上较为接近[5]，而与公认在公元

---

[1] Lukonin 1969, pp. 47–8; Lukonin 1979, pp. 18–9.
[2] Vanden Berghe 1983, p. 62.
[3] Canepa 2013, pp. 862–3.
[4] Canepa 2013, p. 862.
[5] von Gall 1990, pp. 11–3. 亦应注意该浮雕与杜拉欧罗普斯的萨珊壁画残片的相似之处（Goldman/Little 1980, p. 288; Compareti 2011），以及卡尚地区的奔驰骑兵刻划（Sowlat 2012）。

167

2—3世纪之间的埃兰摩崖浮雕在技术—风格上相似。为了制作浮雕，新上任的国王在计划建立作坊时可能借助了埃兰地区的工匠团队。实际上，法尔斯地区已有若干世纪未曾制作摩崖浮雕，在萨珊浮雕之前的雕刻——波斯波利斯的"弗拉塔拉卡"神庙与法尔斯南部的吉尔·卡尔珊浮雕——年代均早于公元前2世纪[1]。

哈珀[2]与西尼西[3]先后提出萨珊浮雕或源于埃兰工艺传统。赫尔曼则更笼统地指出阿尔达希尔一世受埃兰浮雕启发，并将这一媒介作为萨珊的帝国艺术[4]。

由于我无法近距离考察两处浮雕，寻找雕刻工具痕迹，以辨认是否存在技术相似性[5]，在此仅对比埃兰与菲鲁扎巴德Ⅰ号浮雕的图像与风格。

赫茨菲尔德指出，总体而言，无论是埃兰浮雕还是阿尔达希尔一世的首幅浮雕，主要图像雕刻模式为沿人物轮廓向下凿，使其凸显，随后采取接近线刻而非雕塑的手法[6]。除少数起伏外，图像轮廓内的细节仅使用线刻。高浮雕和立体感只体现于图像上部，尤其是人物头部。下部被完全侵蚀，或是未完工[7]。尽管浮雕试图刻画动感效果，其构图仍较为简单，三场决斗中的人物稍显凝滞。马身粗壮，四肢短小（图149），与埃兰的坦格·萨尔瓦克Ⅲ号摩崖浮雕相似（图150）[8]。后期浮雕中，马匹则为自然主义风格。我不认同赫尔曼所言，即菲鲁扎巴德Ⅰ号的构图与雕刻技艺比菲鲁扎巴德Ⅱ号王权神授图更加精湛[9]，尽管她正确地指出抛光等表面精加工质量较高。相反，菲鲁扎巴德Ⅱ号浮雕立体度更高，可证明工匠技艺有所提高。

如前所述，奥弗莱特新近对两幅站姿王权神授图，即菲鲁扎巴德Ⅱ号（图145）与纳克什·拉加卜Ⅲ号（图151）做出了启发性的解读。他创造性地提出将绶环授予国王的

---

[1] Sinisi 2013, note 127.
[2] Harper 1981b, p. 96. 她认为埃兰浮雕是"早期萨珊工匠最可能的参照，他们似将帕提亚的全平行织纹风格改编应用在摩崖浮雕与银盘上"（Harper 1981, p. 96）。
[3] Sinisi 2013.
[4] Herrmann 2000, p. 36.
[5] 如前所述，萨珊石工的专门研究仅有1981年赫尔曼的简报（Herrmann 1981a），她强调了菲鲁扎巴德Ⅰ号浮雕的精细做工与局部抛光。关于希腊化时期与安息时期的伊朗石工，则有科来奇的研究（Colledge 1979）。关于埃兰石工，近期亦有伊朗与意大利学者合著的研究（Messina/Rinaudo/Mehr Kian 2014）。
[6] Herzfeld 1941, p. 310; Goldman/Little 1980, p. 291.
[7] 冯·加尔认为整个浮雕底部都被破坏（von Gall 1990, p. 20）。而在明显倒塌的部分下方，底部边缘似乎是凸出的，也就意味着该区域可能未经加工。若这一观察属实，工作中止的原因应该是从谷底几乎看不见浮雕底部。菲鲁扎巴德Ⅰ号并非唯一一幅底部未完工的阿尔达希尔一世浮雕，纳克什·拉加卜Ⅲ号的下半部做工亦逐渐粗糙化，下边缘更是草草刻成（Trümpelmann 1991, p. 56）。赫尔曼于1969年提出标新立异的假设，即由于国王对质量不满，浮雕在完工前就已废弃，但她随后并未重提（Herrmann 1969, p. 65）。
[8] Kawami 2013, 图38.109。
[9] Herrmann 2000, p. 38.

图148 菲鲁扎巴德：菲鲁扎巴德Ⅰ号浮雕示意图

图149 菲鲁扎巴德：菲鲁扎巴德 I 号浮雕，第二场决斗细节（@ Callieri）

图150 坦格·萨尔瓦克：Ⅲ号岩壁浮雕（Vanden Berghe/Schippmann 1985, pl. 47）

图151 纳克什·拉加卜:纳克什·拉加卜Ⅲ号浮雕(Hinz 1969, pl. 57)

人物为祭司,而非如安息时期的王权神授图传统为阿胡拉·马兹达[1],但证据不足。就图像而言,两幅浮雕与公元215年苏萨石碑上的阿尔达班四世向沙瓦萨克总督授职图相似[2]。但绶环的出现也清晰地表明,浮雕与后阿契美尼德、前萨珊时期的波斯波利斯刻划相关[3]。

通过分析与波斯波利斯刻划间的关联,我得以更深入地探究两幅浮雕在阿尔达希尔一世浮雕制作中的重要性,但仅限于图像设计,因为在艺术技巧上,精美的小型线刻与大型浮雕差距过大。亦应重新审视卡内帕关于制作线刻与浮雕的工匠间关联的假设[4],但仅从纯粹的图像学角度。

---

[1] 奥弗莱特将菲鲁扎巴德Ⅱ号浮雕的年代定为公元205/206年(Overlaet 2013, p. 326),即达里亚提出的巴巴克叛乱当年,并认为纳克什·拉加卜Ⅲ号与阿尔达希尔登上法尔斯王位相关(Overlaet 2013, pp. 324, 326; Daryaee 2010, pp. 249, 251)。如卢科宁(Lukonin 1969, pp. 47-8)及阿勒拉姆(Alram/Gyselen 2003, p. 148)所言,该年代判定未考虑到两幅浮雕中的国王王冠仅在战胜阿尔达班四世后才出现在钱币中。
[2] Kawami 1987b, pp. 48-51, 164-7.
[3] Callieri 2006a; 亦可参见Canepa 2013, p. 873。
[4] Canepa 2013, p. 873.

伊朗萨珊时期的建筑与艺术

如上所述，在技术上，两幅站姿王权神授图呈现出比骑马战斗图更成熟的雕塑效果。形象立体度逐渐增加，脱离线刻，而以雕塑般的凸面为特点。尽管赫尔曼指出两幅浮雕的表面精加工逊色于菲鲁扎巴德 I 号，但在风格上对立体感的追求更突出。卡内帕合理地指出，菲鲁扎巴德 II 号与纳克什·拉加卜 III 号出自同一作坊[1]，从而将菲鲁扎巴德与法尔斯地区中部制作的浮雕联系起来。菲鲁扎巴德 II 号位处河道边的悬崖，难以近距离观察。相反，纳克什·拉加卜遗址易于到达（图152），应为圣地，毗邻水源，而卢科宁视遗址为"王朝神殿"，有最早的王权神授图，与萨珊帝国的创立相关[2]。依据现有资料，纳克什·拉加卜 III 号比菲鲁扎巴德 II 号更为成熟[3]，尽管其下部无存，仍呈现出人象完全脱离平面的效果。这一效果并非如菲鲁扎巴德 I 号般由精加工所获得，而是出自上乘的雕塑质量，而这正是菲鲁扎巴德 I 号骑马战斗图所欠缺的。纳克什·拉加卜 III 号浮雕的构图也比菲鲁扎巴德 II 号更均衡，表现出国王立于阿胡拉·马兹达前的庄严时刻，国王因冠球显得更高，而神祇实际尺寸更大，俯视国王。

图152　纳克什·拉加卜：遗址全貌（D.M. Meucci供图）

---

[1] Canepa 2013, p. 873.
[2] Lukonin/Dandamaev 1971, p. 163.
[3] 相反看法参见 Trümpelmann 1991, p. 56.

位于原古埃兰与新埃兰神庙的纳克什·鲁斯塔姆Ⅰ号岩壁西端的骑马王权神授图（图153、154），代表阿尔达希尔一世浮雕制作的最后阶段。赫尔曼认为其表明"阿尔达希尔成功创造了一种适合大规模运作的视觉语言"[1]。

若干元素可证明该浮雕在5处摩崖浮雕中年代最晚。从图像学角度看，安息国王臣服于阿尔达希尔一世马蹄下的场景，表明年代一定晚于公元224或225年的霍密兹达干战役[2]。从技术制作角度看，赫尔曼指出纳克什·鲁斯塔姆Ⅰ号为全抛光高浮雕，年代应晚于抛光更粗糙的菲鲁扎巴德Ⅱ号与纳克什·拉加卜Ⅲ号浮雕[3]。

新近研究均认可纳克什·鲁斯塔姆Ⅰ号的高水准，赫尔曼称其为"萨珊时期最精细的浮雕"[4]。我亦赞同并引用她优美的描述："画面以接近圆雕的高浮雕制成。在刻意粗糙的背景映衬下，高度抛光使图像更有戏剧性。尽管该浮雕相比骑马战斗图处于静态，飘曳的王冠饰带与神祇斗篷却蕴含动态，习习微风似由国王处拂来。"[5]卡内帕也认为该浮雕"是萨珊浮雕生产中的转折点，可称作早期'萨珊帝国古典风格'的开端"[6]。

如前人一样，卡内帕指出该浮雕与波斯波利斯的阿契美尼德雕塑以及纳克什·鲁斯塔姆的墓葬关联紧密[7]。赫尔曼认为，萨珊国王选择对雕刻进行抛光精加工，表明他欣赏并模仿阿契美尼德的艺术[8]。除全表面抛光外，若干图像细节亦可体现这一点[9]。

然而，上述研究忽略了一个根本问题，即如何从技术上实现对阿契美尼德高水平艺术的模仿。拙作中强调[10]，诸多学者已指出菲鲁扎巴德Ⅰ号与纳克什·鲁斯塔姆Ⅰ号的技术与风格存在巨大的差距，难以如卡内帕所言，仅通过对阿契美尼德雕塑的"仔细研究"便可弥补。尤其是考虑到全体浮雕制作在相对较短的时间内进行，不足以实现如阿契美尼德艺术中从帕萨尔加德R宫殿浮雕到波斯波利斯雕塑之间的技术跃进。更合理的解释为，阿尔达希尔一世征召了一位技艺高超的外来工匠，使得现有作坊技艺突飞猛进。与关于比沙普尔的"共识"相似，纳克什·鲁斯塔姆Ⅰ号浮雕应出自一位法尔斯传统以外的工匠，可能被阿尔达希尔一世在贵霜帝国西部或罗马东部的征战中掳走[11]。胡夫指出，阿尔达希尔一世于阿尔达希尔—花拉城所建的塔克斯特·内辛建筑群中，应

---

[1] Herrmann 2000, pp. 38-9.
[2] Overlaet 2013, p. 327.
[3] Herrmann 1981b, p. 156.
[4] Herrmann 2000, p. 39.
[5] Herrmann 2000, p. 39.
[6] Canepa 2013, p. 873.
[7] Canepa 2013, p. 873.
[8] Herrmann 1981b, p. 159.
[9] Trümpelmann 1977, p. 62.
[10] Callieri 2017.
[11] Kettenhofen 1995, p. 177; Edwell 2008, pp. 167, 178; Daryaee 2008b, pp. 19-20; Edwell 2013, p. 843.

伊朗萨珊时期的建筑与艺术

图153 纳克什·鲁斯塔姆：纳克什·鲁斯塔姆Ⅰ号浮雕（@ Callieri）

图154 纳克什·鲁斯塔姆：纳克什·鲁斯塔姆Ⅰ号浮雕示意图

用了罗马帝国东部的建筑尺度[1]。雕刻或同此理。我认为原因并非如卢沙伊及卡内帕所言,是纳克什·鲁斯塔姆浮雕中引入了罗马图像母题[2],而是作坊借助技术手段,在短时间内对波斯波利斯浮雕特有的图像细节进行惟妙惟肖的模仿,展现出形象设计的和谐、浮雕的立体感,并完善了石刻技术。

总而言之,阿尔达希尔一世在位时的摩崖浮雕应出自一座主要由埃兰工匠组成的作坊,他们受托制作新的图像,依据为安息的先例及波斯波利斯的前萨珊刻划传统。菲鲁扎巴德Ⅱ号与纳克什·拉加卜Ⅲ号站姿王权神授图的图像与风格相近,或体现了同一作坊的延续性。该作坊首先在菲鲁扎巴德制作菲鲁扎巴德Ⅰ号与Ⅱ号浮雕,随后迁至伊斯塔尔城。在伊斯塔尔城附近,又制作了纳克什·拉加卜Ⅲ号浮雕,并在外来工匠的帮助下,借鉴波斯波利斯,制作出高水平的纳克什·鲁斯塔姆Ⅰ号浮雕,成为后世骑马人像的范本。

在波斯工匠取得技术成就的同时,另一技艺平平的作坊在亚美尼亚的遥远疆土制作出萨勒马斯浮雕。

随着沙普尔一世继位,出现了不同情形。

关于沙普尔一世浮雕的众多研究主要围绕被其击败、往往以象征手法表现的罗马皇帝的身份上,而与现有研究中的假设相左。该问题过于复杂,无法简单概括。我推崇麦克德莫特的人物解读,尽管只是可能性之一[3],即倒在马蹄下的罗马皇帝为戈尔迪安三世,跪在地上的皇帝为阿拉伯人菲利普,被沙普尔一世抓住手的皇帝是被俘并死于狱中的瓦勒良[4]。

幸运的是,为了筹备《伊朗摩崖浮雕》丛书,学界对大多数沙普尔一世的浮雕做了仔细研究,尤其是赫尔曼[5]及特林佩尔曼[6]的基础性论述。赫尔曼基于细致的图像与技术—风格研究,分出一组约公元240年的早期浮雕,包括最初的达拉卜[7]、纳克什·拉加卜Ⅰ号与随后增加的纳克什·拉加卜Ⅳ号、比沙普尔Ⅰ号王权神授图,和一组约公元260年的晚期浮雕,包括纳克什·鲁斯塔姆Ⅵ号、比沙普尔Ⅱ号及比沙普尔Ⅲ号[8]。

---

[1] Huff 1972, pp. 539-40; Huff 2008a, p. 53.
[2] Luschey 1986, p. 379; Canepa 2009, p. 256, n. 97.
[3] 观点总结参见 Herrmann 1989, pp. 18-22;另一解读参见 Overlaet 2009。
[4] MacDermot 1954; Canepa 2013, p. 866.
[5] Herrmann 1981a, 1983, 1989.
[6] Trümpelmann 1975b.
[7] 沿着特林佩尔曼的思路(Trümpelmann 1975b, pp. 16-8),迈尔将达拉卜浮雕分为两个阶段:浮雕左半边的原始阶段(达拉卜A)及右半边的改造阶段(达拉卜B)(Meyer 1990, pp. 266-7)。
[8] Herrmann 1989, p. 22. 迈尔持不同看法。她认为除达拉卜第一阶段(达拉卜A)为沙普尔继位初期外(Meyer 1990, pp. 274-6),沙普尔一世浮雕的年代均在公元260年之后(*ibid.*, 284-6)。纳克什·拉加卜Ⅰ号浮雕抛光与其年代无关,而与质量相关(*ibid.*, 288)。冯·加尔同样将达拉卜浮雕的年代定为公元260年后(Von Gall 2008, p. 150)。

伊朗萨珊时期的建筑与艺术

赫尔曼认为，位于露天神庙左墙的纳克什·拉加卜Ⅰ号浮雕年代最早（图155），沙普尔一世骑在马上，侧身面对阿尔达希尔一世的站姿王权神授图。沙普尔身后为特殊透视的王室侍从。紧随国王的五人在不同层次上相互重叠，使浮雕具有纵深感。最后四人则鱼贯而行，分为两组，身高依岩石形状递减。当先两人身材矮小，其后两人仅从栏杆后露出上半身。

赫尔曼指出纳克什·拉加卜Ⅰ号应为最早的沙普尔一世浮雕，年代早于王权神授图。因全抛光加工相似，纳克什·拉加卜Ⅰ号浮雕应与纳克什·鲁斯塔姆Ⅰ号出自同一作坊[1]。此外，两个图像元素亦可证实：其一为长袍过膝，而在比沙普尔Ⅱ号、比沙普尔Ⅲ号及沙普尔一世以降的国王浮雕中，长袍变短；其二为马衔类型与阿尔达希尔一世及达拉卜浮雕相似，与其余沙普尔一世浮雕不同[2]。达拉卜浮雕应出自制作纳克什·拉加卜Ⅰ号的作坊（图155），主要依据为不同层次的人物塑造的透视效果，以及赫尔曼提出的技术手段的相似性[3]。

沙普尔一世浮雕中，纳克什·鲁斯塔姆Ⅵ号（图156、157）与比沙普尔的三幅浮雕间的关联存在争论。前者中，马背上的国王对面仅有两位罗马皇帝。后者则分为一幅

图155 纳克什·拉加卜：纳克什·拉加卜Ⅰ号浮雕（@ Callieri）

---

[1] Herrmann 1981b, p. 155.
[2] Herrmann 1981b, pp. 157-8.
[3] Herrmann 1989, pp. 21-2.

图 156 纳克什·鲁斯塔姆：纳克什·鲁斯塔姆Ⅵ号浮雕（@ Callieri）

图 157 纳克什·鲁斯塔姆：纳克什·鲁斯塔姆Ⅵ号浮雕示意图

包含两位战败罗马皇帝的王权神授图（比沙普尔Ⅰ号），以及两幅表现胜败双方士兵行列的凯旋图（比沙普尔Ⅱ号及Ⅲ号）。迄今为止的解读均认为上述浮雕年代不同，仅哈珀与迈尔假设为同时代不同工匠的作品[1]。他们提出，几乎所有的沙普尔一世浮雕均在十二年间制作，应同时存在数个工匠团队，可能在同一工地上活动[2]。

如前所述，赫尔曼提出比沙普尔Ⅰ号王权神授图（图158）年代早于纳克什·鲁斯塔姆Ⅵ号，而后者一定早于比沙普尔Ⅱ号（图159—161）及Ⅲ号凯旋图（图73、162、163），因为其中缺乏两幅凯旋图的创新元素[3]。

赫尔曼指出不同分组浮雕间的若干图像差异。其一为腰带类型的演变，从年代最早的达拉卜及纳克什·拉加卜Ⅰ号，到纳克什·鲁斯塔姆Ⅵ号，再到比沙普尔Ⅱ号、Ⅲ号。其二为斗篷与腰带系法，达拉卜、纳克什·拉加卜Ⅰ号及纳克什·鲁斯塔姆Ⅵ号相同[4]。赫尔曼将图像差异归为年代演变的结果，我则认为比沙普尔与纳克什·鲁斯塔姆及纳克什·拉加卜浮雕出自两个不同的艺术中心，各自的技术—风格特点在沙普尔一世后仍然延续。与其如迈尔所说，若干作坊在同一地点并行，不如说存在两个艺术中心，虽难以查明其中工匠如何参与不同项目，但均沿袭各自的传统。

自精美的阿尔达希尔一世骑马王权神授图后，从纳克什·鲁斯塔姆Ⅵ号至公元3世纪末的纳克什·鲁斯塔姆Ⅷ号浮雕中延续了突出的本土特征。尤其是设计中若干巧妙的细节处理，如横在上半身侧面的手臂，以及明显不成比例、以少数人物为中心的构图。而雕刻本身较平缓，起伏较小。类似特点亦见于纳克什·拉加卜浮雕[5]。

虽然比沙普尔Ⅱ号未完工，不同人物雕刻的精加工程度各异，并最终以灰泥完成[6]，但最早的三幅比沙普尔浮雕十分相似，而与纳克什·鲁斯塔姆浮雕截然不同。年代最早的比沙普尔Ⅰ号设计形式十分协调，而在呈现侧面人像上半身向右转动的效果时略显生涩，尤其是横在上半身的手臂。人物较为立体，若干元素呈现出接近自然主义的效果。

比沙普尔与纳克什·鲁斯塔姆浮雕相差甚远，故前者应非出自法尔斯中部的工匠。在研究比沙普尔时，多位学者引用了沙普尔一世本人在纳克什·鲁斯塔姆的铭文，提及罗马俘虏被迁至伊朗沙赫尔地区，包括法尔斯地区。最近，卡内帕提出："他选择安条克的技艺，在［比沙普尔］利用战俘，纪念在西方取得的胜利……罗马工匠应参与了摩崖

---

[1] Harper 1986, p. 586.
[2] Meyer 1990, p. 288. 距离相近的浮雕（纳克什·拉加卜，比沙普尔）在工艺上存在差异，或由于不同作坊在同一地点活动。
[3] Herrmann 1989, pp. 22–3.
[4] Herrmann 1989, p. 23.
[5] 纳克什·拉加卜Ⅳ号常被视作沙普尔一世的首幅王权神授图，而卢科宁基于其与比沙普尔Ⅴ号巴赫拉姆一世王权神授图之间的相似之处，将其定为巴赫拉姆一世时期（Lukonin 1979, pp. 18, 20）。
[6] Herrmann 1983, pp. 12–3.

图158 比沙普尔：比沙普尔Ⅰ号浮雕，细节（@ Callieri）

图159 比沙普尔：比沙普尔Ⅱ号浮雕，中央场景（@ Callieri）

伊朗萨珊时期的建筑与艺术

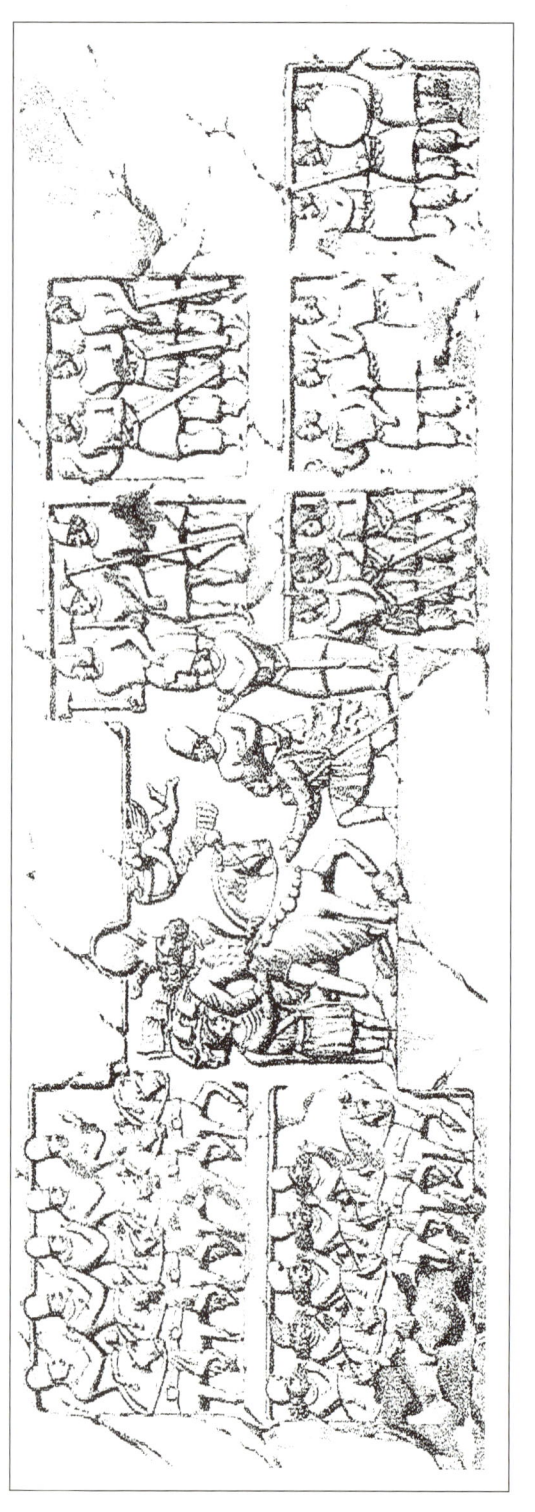

图160 比沙普尔：比沙普尔 II 号浮雕示意图

图161 比沙普尔：比沙普尔Ⅱ号浮雕，右下格壁面细节（@ Callieri）

图162 比沙普尔：比沙普尔Ⅲ号浮雕，左下格细节（@ Callieri）

图163 比沙普尔：比沙普尔Ⅲ号浮雕，右下格细节（@ Callieri）

图 164　拉格·比比（阿富汗）：摩崖浮雕（Grene 等. 2007, pl.6）

浮雕的制作，灵感源于对波斯波利斯细致的实地考察。"[1]他如前人一样，指出比沙普尔Ⅱ号及Ⅲ号体现了"罗马雕塑与构图元素对萨珊初期风格有一定影响"[2]，麦金托什亦在图像层面详尽论述了这一点[3]。

沙普尔一世统治时期被视作罗马和萨珊时期的伊朗文化交流最频繁的时期，马赛克铺地技术被引入比沙普尔，苏萨平原上建设水利工程，均由罗马帝国的专业工匠完成。在此期间，天时地利人和，罗马帝国东部的工匠加入负责制作比沙普尔的萨珊图像程序的艺术中心，在波斯人的领导下工作[4]。正是外来工匠，使比沙普尔中心的技术—风格不同于纳克什·鲁斯塔姆，上述图像细节亦可证实。

2002年在巴克特里亚发现的拉格·比比浮雕（图164），尽管保存状况不佳，仍体现出与法尔斯地区浮雕迥异的技术—风格特点[5]，如将"假体"施加于岩壁缺漏之处以达到圆雕效果的技术，未见于法尔斯[6]。尤其是接近圆雕的浮雕，形象的纵深与立体

---

[1] Canepa 2010, p. 584.
[2] Canepa 2013, p. 873.
[3] Mackintosh 1973.
[4] Canepa 2009, p. 67.
[5] Grenet *et al.* 2007.
[6] Grenet *et al.* 2007, pp. 247–8.

感,倒在地上扭曲的犀牛躯体表现的自然主义倾向,可能源于"犍陀罗佛教艺术"学派作坊或巴克特里亚当地传统[1]。因此,沙普尔一世时期应存在第三个制作摩崖浮雕的作坊。

比沙普尔中心内部的演变自沙普尔一世起,至巴赫拉姆一世(比沙普尔Ⅴ号)(图165)与巴赫拉姆二世(比沙普尔Ⅳ号)(图166),赫尔曼认为后两者中有若干图像特点与比沙普尔Ⅱ号、Ⅲ号相似。鉴于马匹有些许细节差异,她提出两幅浮雕最初应由同一人设计,而后由不同工匠制成[2]。

巴赫拉姆二世时期,比沙普尔附近的萨拉卜·巴赫拉姆等浮雕应出自比沙普尔中心(图167)[3]。无论是国王正面坐像的创新类型,还是与比沙普尔Ⅴ号、Ⅳ号相似的高立体度,都体现出该中心工匠的高超技艺。尽管萨尔·马沙德浮雕(图168)的立体度逊色于比沙普尔Ⅳ号,风格特点却十分接近,尤其是相似的国王头部处理手法以及图像在不同层次的分布,故也可将其归为比沙普尔中心的作品。其自然主义特点体现在国王挽着王后的手臂和挥舞匕首的手,以及分别表现进攻与倒毙瞬间的同一狮子的两处图像,为皇家银器中所常见。

相反,巴赫拉姆二世其余浮雕设计中没有突出的自然主义风格,人物雕刻更紧凑,更接近巴尔姆·德拉克(图169)等纳克什·鲁斯塔姆艺术中心的浮雕。

巴赫拉姆二世时期,比沙普尔与纳克什·鲁斯塔姆艺术中心之间的对比,可从纳克什·鲁斯塔姆Ⅱ号(图170)与比沙普尔Ⅳ号(图166)中的正面站立男性像切入。纳克什·鲁斯塔姆Ⅱ号创造了令人耳目一新的图像构图,宫廷侍从部分被两侧栏杆遮挡,从而凸显正面全身可见的国王,长剑垂直置于两腿间,头转向其右侧,面朝王室成员。其设计特点为正面全身,双腿对称,庞大的身躯与较小的头部不成比例,且浮雕较浅,立体度较低。不同于常见的国王侧面像,纳克什·鲁斯塔姆Ⅱ号中的巴赫拉姆二世仅一侧头发刻出,而另一侧被遮挡。

比沙普尔Ⅳ号中亦有一人身体正对前方,所持长剑垂直置于两腿间,头转向其右侧,仅刻出一束头发,为代表巴赫拉姆二世出使阿拉伯的一位波斯贵族[4]。因水道沿岩壁开凿,比沙普尔Ⅳ号人像躯干不幸全部被毁,其腿部立体度与自然主义特征较纳克什·鲁斯塔姆更突出,侧向的右腿、右脚与正对前方的左腿不对称,左脚转向外侧四分之三角度。比沙普尔艺术中心在沙普尔一世时期表现的自然主义特征贯穿其传统中。

---

[1] Grenet *et al.* 2007, p. 249.
[2] Herrmann 1981a, p. 9.
[3] 赫尔曼指出,比沙普尔附近的坦格·甘迪勒浮雕与比沙普尔地区的巴赫拉姆二世浮雕在风格上极为相似。若该浮雕的赞助人及主要人物并非国王,而是可能与王室有关的贵族,则应借助了制作王室浮雕的同一团队工匠,体现出王权的衰弱(Herrmann 1983, p. 36)。
[4] Herrmann 1981a, pp. 5-10.

图 165　比沙普尔：比沙普尔 V 号浮雕（@ Callieri）

伊朗萨珊时期的建筑与艺术

图166 比沙普尔：比沙普尔Ⅳ号浮雕（@Callieri）

图167　萨拉卜·巴赫拉姆：摩崖浮雕（Hinz 1969, pl. 128）

图168　萨尔·马沙德：摩崖浮雕（Hinz 1969, pl. 134）

伊朗萨珊时期的建筑与艺术

图169 巴尔姆·德拉克：摩崖浮雕，右侧场景（Hinz 1969, pl. 137）

图170 纳克什·鲁斯塔姆：纳克什·鲁斯塔姆Ⅱ号浮雕（D.M. Meucci供图）

纳克什·鲁斯塔姆艺术中心亦将早期浮雕作为内部参考。在纳克什·鲁斯塔姆Ⅳ号骑马战斗图中(图171),佩戴盔甲的骑兵落马,尽管姿势不同,但与菲鲁扎巴德Ⅰ号的两个骑兵有异曲同工之处。纳克什·鲁斯塔姆Ⅷ号纳塞赫图正中较小的人物(图172),或受到纳克什·拉加卜Ⅰ号阿尔达希尔一世王权神授图正中两人的启发。

比沙普尔Ⅵ号浮雕的图像及技术—风格难以解读(图173)。因雕刻尚未完工,各处完成度不一,两侧部分形象仅粗略刻出,部分形象则只欠精加工。赫尔曼研究中指出的灰泥痕迹证实了之前关于灰泥精加工的假设,但她认为最初计划并非如此,而是因工期紧迫,不得已而为之[1]。理论上,亦无法排除精加工另由其他赞助人于后期完成的可能。

若浮雕所刻国王年代为公元3或4世纪,上述论断则会有新的含义。依据岩壁上残存的王冠分析,国王身份可能为沙普尔一世、沙普尔二世、巴赫拉姆一世或纳塞赫[2]。

图171 纳克什·鲁斯塔姆:纳克什·鲁斯塔姆Ⅳ号浮雕(@ Callieri)

---

[1] Herrmann 1981a, pp. 21-2.
[2] Herrmann 1981a, p. 34,图2。

图172 纳克什·鲁斯塔姆：纳克什·鲁斯塔姆Ⅷ号浮雕（Vanden Berghe 1983, pl. 32）

图173 比沙普尔：比沙普尔Ⅵ号浮雕，左侧（@ Callieri）

赫尔曼所指出比沙普尔Ⅵ号与比沙普尔的沙普尔一世浮雕间的联系毋庸置疑，包括数栏构图（比沙普尔Ⅱ号及Ⅲ号）、部分形象的背部刻画（比沙普尔Ⅲ号）以及队列中伊朗贵族的顺序（比沙普尔Ⅱ号及Ⅲ号）。她提出，依据上述元素及岩壁的宏伟规模，可将该浮雕归为沙普尔一世时期，即与赫茨菲尔德及埃德曼意见一致。若她所言非虚，浮雕应由掌握比沙普尔Ⅱ号、Ⅲ号技艺的工匠制作，继而由于国王驾崩、工期提前等偶然因素中断，将后续工作交由灰泥工匠，以便在国王葬礼前完工[1]。这一假设大体合理，但赫尔曼无法确定两个首级的年代，其中之一无胡须，头戴王冠及"专属于王室成员"的头饰，前为翻边软帽，后为兽首（图174）[2]。赫尔曼提出该场景为镇压内乱，但未进一步明确[3]，在文献尤其是沙普尔一世铭文中未提及[4]。

与此相反，旺当·贝格通过一系列论证，将比沙普尔Ⅵ号浮雕归为沙普尔二世时期[5]，并对断头人像的身份做出了令人信服的解读。他指出，波斯殉道者叙利亚语行传

图174 比沙普尔：比沙普尔Ⅵ号浮雕，右下格细节（@ Callieri）

---

[1] Herrmann 1983, p. 26.
[2] Vanden Berghe 1980, p. 281.
[3] Herrmann 1981a, p. 37.
[4] 卡尔梅耶的解读更为详细，她将断头定为摩尼，故国王应为巴赫拉姆一世（Calmeyer 1976, pp. 63-4）。
[5] Vanden Berghe 1980, p. 277.

提及二人，一为霍尔木兹，即被流放的萨珊王子，后为尤利安军队效力；一为毕尔·古什纳斯普，即沙普尔二世同父异母兄弟的儿子，曾改信基督教并因此在十二岁时殉道[1]。两个首级似乎正对应上述两位萨珊王子，尤其是无胡须的一位[2]。仅有这一解读在文献中找到了处决王室成员的相关印证，无疑最为可信。

赫尔曼将比沙普尔Ⅵ号归为沙普尔一世时期，依据为其与比沙普尔Ⅱ号、Ⅲ号浮雕间的相似之处，但亦可能表明浮雕制作于公元4世纪。若是后者，则意味着艺术中心的传统在长期中断后改用灰泥制作细节而延续。如第二部分第三章所示，尽管哈吉阿巴德庄主的图像灰泥装饰是否可追溯到公元4世纪并无定论，但将灰泥的使用归入这一时期似无不妥。此外，选择以灰泥为雕刻作精加工的年代，与浮雕均以石质工具制作的年代相距较远，我以为更合理，尤其是考虑到未完工的Ⅱ号等比沙普尔浮雕体现出精湛的技艺水准。赫尔曼认为比沙普尔Ⅵ号年代应早于公元4世纪，依据为下摆齐平而非弧形的长袍类型。这也并不绝对。事实上，在沙普尔三世时期的塔克·波斯坦Ⅱ号中（图175），

图175 塔克·波斯坦：塔克·波斯坦Ⅱ号浮雕（Fukai/Horiuchi 1972, pl. 66）

---

[1] Hoffmann 1880, pp. 22-8; Labourt 1904, p. 79, 注1. 感谢朱利安在讨论中提出还有其他文献。
[2] Vanden Berghe 1980, p. 281; 1983, p. 90.

有两人身着弧形长袍,而塔克·波斯坦Ⅰ号中的三人中仅一人身着弧形长袍,另两人的长袍下摆齐平(图176)[1]。

若比沙普尔Ⅵ号属于沙普尔二世时期,其国王正面坐像并非创新性的构图,而是模仿了巴赫拉姆二世时比沙普尔中心在萨拉卜·巴赫拉姆制作的浮雕。

卡内帕提出[2],相比公元3世纪较强的立体呈现效果,4世纪时线刻盛行,除比沙普尔Ⅵ号外,尤其体现在塔克·波斯坦最早的两幅浮雕中,尽管其年代是否为公元4世纪末仍有争议[3]。塔克·波斯坦Ⅰ号浮雕年代在沙普尔一世(309—379年)至阿尔达希尔二世(379—383年)之间,而关于塔克·波斯坦Ⅱ号年代的假设集中于沙普尔三世时期(383—388年)。

摩崖浮雕在克尔曼沙赫地区的塔克·波斯坦崛地而起,与此前法尔斯地区的传统似无关联,因为该时期法尔斯并无此类浮雕[4]。上述浮雕与法尔斯艺术中心间的明显差异,除年代因素外,还由地形因素造成。此外,应注意此前出现在伊朗中东部的摩崖浮雕,从萨尔·波勒·扎哈卜到比索通,再到伊拉克库尔德斯坦的米尔盖里。或由于种种历史事件,或由于法尔斯与美索不达米亚核心意识形态此消彼长,位处两者之间的塔克·波斯坦的赞助人可能受到上述浮雕的启发[5]。

塔克·波斯坦浮雕主要通过向下挖凿图像四周的背景刻成,证实其为新成立的艺

图176 塔克·波斯坦:塔克·波斯坦Ⅰ号浮雕(Vanden Berghe 1983, pl. 36)

---

[1] 赫尔曼对塔克·波斯坦在该方面的论述,参见Herrmann 1976, p. 153。塔克·波斯坦Ⅰ号浮雕中,穿着弧形下摆长袍的正是接过绶环的人,无疑在三人中年龄最小者,表明相对其他二人的传统服饰,此为新颖式样。
[2] Canepa 2013, p. 873.
[3] 有关塔克·波斯坦Ⅰ号、Ⅱ号的论述,参见Tanabe 1985, Azarnoush 1986以及最新的Overlaet 2011, Overlaet 2012。
[4] 冯·加尔将纳克什·鲁斯塔姆Ⅶ号的骑马战斗双图归为巴赫拉姆四世时期(388—399年)(von Gall 1990, pp. 32-4),故将法尔斯地区的雕刻活动延长至4世纪,可纳入考量,但应注意与纳克什·鲁斯塔姆早期浮雕的联系。
[5] Harper 1999, p. 318.

伊朗萨珊时期的建筑与艺术

术中心。该手法亦出现在菲鲁扎巴德及萨勒马斯,即萨珊最早的摩崖浮雕艺术中心所在地。然而塔克·波斯坦的工匠技艺更精湛娴熟,仅人物腿部平坦无起伏,以凸显人物上半身,尤其是高浮雕头部的立体效果。此外,头部四分之三角度的轻度倾斜打破了主流的正面构图,正中人物的轴线偏向浮雕右侧,同时刻画出头部左侧细节,若拍摄时朝右偏斜,便可获得接近脸部正面的照片(图177)。这是萨珊浮雕中的全新手法,此前四分之三角度从未获得如此重视。沙普尔二世站在高一级台阶上,相比之下,其他两人位置稍低,亦是萨珊浮雕的一大创新。另一特殊手法,则是通过刻划四周以凸显倒在右侧两人脚下的一人,而没有类似左侧莲花的背景处理。从面部线条到头发、从衣着到标识的人物各方面线刻均十分精细。塔克·波斯坦中心在公元4世纪末制作出代表其最高水平的塔克·波斯坦Ⅰ号浮雕,艺术中心的精湛技艺反映在全新的风格手段中,可能借鉴了灰泥装饰。正如其他艺术中心,随之而来的是塔克·波斯坦中心起源的问题。基于塔克·波斯坦中心与萨珊主流浮雕间的差异,莫内雷·德·维拉尔提出,塔克·波斯坦Ⅱ号浮雕受到了北方邦马图拉的马特神庙中贵霜艺术的影响,但被新的年代学观点否定[1]。

与比沙普尔Ⅵ号的对比至关重要,若如上文所述,将其定为公元4世纪,则其与塔克·波斯坦浮雕的年代最为接近。而两幅浮雕迥然不同。尽管比沙普尔Ⅵ号尚未完工,但除粗略刻出的图像表面较为平坦外,几乎整个表面都具有雕塑般的立体感。浮雕整体起伏较低。由于缺乏刻划细节,浮雕无线刻元素。除国王为正面像外,其余人物头部均为侧面。塔克·波斯坦Ⅰ号中的人物则以高浮雕为特点,浮雕高处凸出于背景,形成强烈的明暗对比。仰视时,高处的立体感更为明显[2]。但低处表面均十分平坦,织物几乎仅以线刻表现。头部则呈四分之三角度。尽管塔克·波斯坦浮雕的年代与比沙普尔Ⅵ号相近,但与后者的遗存现状却并无关联,若比沙普尔Ⅵ号的灰泥精加工仍保留,则二者或有联系。总之,公元4世纪末,塔克·波斯坦中心创造出宏伟的浮雕,而技术高超的工匠来源仍待探究——他们显然对前朝的浮雕制作有所了解,尽管并未直接沿袭其艺术传统[3]。

塔克·波斯坦主伊万的塔克·波斯坦Ⅲ号、Ⅳ号浮雕证实了又一种新传统的诞生(图178),其风格不同于制作塔克·波斯坦Ⅰ号、Ⅱ号的前述艺术中心。

第二部分第三章中曾提及,我认为主伊万两侧壁并非摩崖类浮雕,其本质是以石材仿制重要建筑中的伊万的灰泥装饰[4]。尽管对伊万的全面考量应包括对王室意识形态

---

[1] Monneret de Villard 1954, p. 83.
[2] 感谢菲利真齐提出这一点。
[3] 哈珀的观点略有不同(Harper 1986)。
[4] 参见第三章及Herrmann 2000, pp. 44-5。依据穆歇的假设,侧壁与建筑其余部分完全统一,即整座塔克·波斯坦建筑源自罗马凯旋门,两小拱之间为一大拱,其中一侧小拱未完成。在伊朗,历史性叙事的罗马拱券被象征性的狩猎图所代替,如国王的头光所示(Musche 1994)。

图177 塔克・波斯坦：塔克・波斯坦 I 号浮雕，中心人物细节（Fukai/Horiuchi 1972, pl. 84）

图 178 塔克·波斯坦,主伊万:塔克·波斯坦Ⅲ号、Ⅳ号浮雕
(Vanden Berghe 1983, pl. 37)

的歌颂的探究——哈珀认为后者与两幅狩猎图所体现的美索不达米亚传统密切相关[1],但在此仅讨论塔克·波斯坦Ⅲ号、Ⅳ号浮雕。塔克·波斯坦Ⅲ号位于正壁上方,刻画出两位神祇将绶环授予正中的国王的场景。塔克·波斯坦Ⅳ号位于正壁下方,表现了身披盔甲的雄壮骑兵。

"共识"将上述浮雕的年代定为公元7世纪库思老二世[2]或阿尔达希尔三世时期[3],埃德曼[4]及其后的冯·加尔[5]则将其归为公元5世纪的卑路斯时期,但应者寥寥[6]。赫茨菲尔德提出浮雕年代为公元7世纪[7],卢沙伊于1968年总结了前者与埃德曼于1938年的争辩[8],并指出应存在三个阶段,均属于7世纪,因为篮状柱头在君士坦丁堡及波斯的出现不应早于公元6世纪[9]。而我认为,由于国王王冠间有相似之处,上述观点均缺乏决定性的内部因素。前人讨论不再赘述,以下是通过对比在制作中发挥作用的外来文化地域后得出的几点思路。

尽管有人指出拜占庭教堂半圆形后殿布局的影响,但从面容掩于头盔下的庄严骑兵[10],到立于上方台座上的正面国王像,再到国王两侧的神祇,浮雕构图均清晰地展现

---

[1] Harper 1999, p. 318.
[2] Vanden Berghe 1983, pp. 146-7.
[3] Tanabe 2006.
[4] Erdmann 1937, p. 39.
[5] von Gall 1990, pp. 38, 44-7.
[6] Russo 2004, pp. 802-3, 806.
[7] Herzfeld 1938.
[8] Luschey 1968.
[9] 鲁索坚称篮状柱头源于波斯,随后传入拜占庭,应较为可信(Russo 2004, p. 803)。故所谓的年代下限不成立(参见下文)。
[10] 关于骑兵的不同象征性解读,参见 von Gall 1990, pp. 46-7.

图179 塔克·波斯坦，主伊万：阿胡拉·马兹达，塔克·波斯坦Ⅲ号浮雕细节（@ Callieri）

图180 塔克·波斯坦，主伊万：阿娜希塔，塔克·波斯坦Ⅲ号浮雕细节（Fukai/Horiuchi 1972, pl. 24）

出偏好静态、形式雄壮的伊朗风格[1]。神祇中，阿胡拉·马兹达呈四分之三角度面朝国王（图179），斗篷扬起，尽显优雅，而阿娜希塔整体缺乏女性的优美，正面双腿分开的姿势代表王权，而非生物学上的女性特征[2]。若从近处观察阿娜希塔面部（图180），可发现其精致发型与连拱下棕榈叶母题的美丽王冠，都与浮雕整体一般精雕细琢。从图像学角度看，上述浮雕呈现出不同于以往的特征，如将三个人物置于台座上，而国王台座高于两侧神祇。神祇与国王互为镜像的萨珊传统至此中断，且高台座赋予国王塑像般的意味。从风格学角度看，两幅浮雕呈现出前所未有、高度立体的体积感。通过高浮雕与底切加工图像轮廓，位于上方的三人与下方的骑兵似从石壁上跃出，为萨珊艺术中的全新技术。在刻出饱满主体的基础上，精心制作所有浮雕或线刻细节。因此，建筑群中图像程序的灵感显然源于伊朗，并由技艺精湛、独树一帜的工匠实践。

上述浮雕或完工于公元7世纪，或完工于5世纪，自沙普尔三世以来已中断了至少

---

[1] Mackintosh 1980, p. 151.
[2] 感谢菲利真齐提出这一点。

两代，不禁令人疑惑：水平如此高超的作坊是在何种现实条件下诞生的？

塔克·波斯坦主伊万的立面为石质仿建筑，主要灵感来源无疑为同一遗址的小伊万，尽管小伊万立面未经加工。主伊万立面包含建筑装饰特有的元素，如回归伊朗传统的阶梯金字塔顶饰及两个植物装饰壁柱（图181）。鲁索强调植物纹与萨珊灰泥纹样相关，而哈珀则认为源于美索不达米亚生命树。主伊万立面与君士坦丁堡的圣波里克多教堂（524—527年）建筑装饰十分相似，其篮状柱头被许多学者视作拜占庭影响萨珊波斯的证明。鲁索则认为篮状柱头是拜占庭模仿波斯式样的结果，在君士坦丁堡工地上出现了"一个极具创造性、对萨珊艺术有直观深入了解的大师"[1]。除上述建筑装饰元素外，繁复的拱门饰两侧的有翼胜利女神被视作希腊—罗马式胜利女神与拜占庭天使糅合而成的图像（图182）[2]。胜利女神浮雕远低于伊万图像浮雕，卡内帕指出其风格接近罗马晚期象牙制品，但为材料、规模迥异的工匠传统[3]。因此，灵感源泉应为古典时代

图181 塔克·波斯坦，主伊万：立面右侧壁柱（@ Callieri）　　图182 塔克·波斯坦，主伊万：立面右侧有翼胜利女神（@ Callieri）

---

[1] Russo 2004, p. 764。我完全同意其方法："仅通过应用人员流动性以及人与环境互动的准则[…]可为突然出现在君士坦丁堡艺术中心的新装饰形式找到合理的解释。"
[2] Mackintosh 1980, p. 159.
[3] Canepa 2013, p. 873.

晚期的图像文化,对东罗马帝国与萨珊波斯均有影响[1]。

伊万正壁支撑上方浮雕(塔克·波斯坦Ⅲ号)的半圆柱柱头,对于判定伊万立面及其内部的年代关系至关重要(图183)。柱头母题与立面壁柱接近,相似的风格应出自同一团队工匠之手。尽管立面的建筑雕刻与内部图像分属不同类型的装饰程序,且图像浮雕各有差异,两者仍应属于同一时期。

如前所示,塔克·波斯坦伊万正壁浮雕的立体度极高,仅比沙普尔浮雕可与之媲美,但两者年代、地点均相去甚远。由于缺乏类似的萨珊图像艺术资料,应从立面所体现的外来影响中追溯塔克·波斯坦Ⅲ号、Ⅳ号与其余浮雕之间差异的来源,尤其是在技术水平方面[2]。图像程序则无疑沿袭自伊朗传统。

图183 塔克·波斯坦,主伊万:伊万正壁半柱柱头(Fukai/Horiuchi 1972, pl. 58)

若塔克·波斯坦的主伊万浮雕年代为公元7世纪,则在时间上,可假设与此前伊朗传统相异的风格出自东罗马工匠之手。依据或为文献所记查士丁尼一世派遣拜占庭工匠至萨珊波斯[3],或为莫里斯一世给库思老二世赠送礼物[4]——菲尔多西曾提到征召工匠以制作库思老御座的国家[5]。麦金托什则提出另一假设,与拜占庭皇帝慷慨相助无关,即库思老二世打破和平的征战使其得以模仿沙普尔一世,将技艺娴熟的工匠迁至波斯[6]。

然而,在公元7世纪时,拜占庭帝国并没有能够迁入萨珊波斯的雕塑传统。萨珊雕塑中受东罗马帝国影响的元素不可能晚于6世纪,因为当时东罗马帝国艺术中心已停止制作高浮雕[7]。虽然从历史角度看,公元7世纪拜占庭工匠相助的假设成立,但从雕塑角

---

[1] 感谢塔代伊的建议。
[2] 几乎不可能为现已失落的当地传统的传承。
[3] Canepa 2009, p. 210.
[4] Canepa 2009, p. 200.
[5] Mackintosh 1980, pp. 172, 174. 沙赫巴齐对文献的可信度持怀疑态度(Shahbazi 1990)。
[6] Mackintosh 1980, p. 176.
[7] Fıratlı 1990.

度则绝无可能,因为东罗马没有类似的艺术传统。公元7世纪时,唯一精于石刻制作的高超工匠来源是印度后笈多王朝,不仅是由于卡内帕所言狩猎图两侧壁的大象形象源于印度[1],因为伊朗早在安息时期已有将大象与王权相联系的传统[2]。这一假设理论上可行,但浮雕中缺乏来自印度的特有图像与风格元素,反而出现与东罗马有关的元素。换言之,若这一新的艺术中心得到西方的支持,塔克·波斯坦Ⅲ号、Ⅳ号浮雕的年代不可能为公元7世纪,故应考虑埃德曼与冯·加尔先后提出的卑路斯时期[3]。公元5世纪,萨珊与拜占庭间复杂的双向交流或使波斯工匠得以借助在东罗马仍然活跃的雕塑传统,在命运多舛的国王卑路斯治下,制作意义重大的图像程序[4]。这一艺术中心亦可能源于现已失落的当地传统,但我们对此知之甚少。

质言之,本章探讨了萨珊历朝历代的若干艺术中心,在建造有重大意识形态价值的图像程序的国王敕令下制作摩崖浮雕。首个艺术中心由阿尔达希尔一世于菲鲁扎巴德创立,随后迁至法尔斯地区中部的纳克什·鲁斯塔姆及纳克什·拉加卜。在阿尔达希尔一世统治下,伊朗西北部的另一艺术中心制作了简约的萨勒马斯浮雕。沙普尔一世任内,纳克什·鲁斯塔姆及纳克什·拉加卜在巩固艺术传统的基础上继续运行。其次,比沙普尔新建了一个有罗马工匠参与的艺术中心。再次,萨珊帝国东端的巴克特里亚有一个新的艺术中心,为截然不同的传统,可能不属于波斯。沙普尔一世以降,公元3世纪末、4世纪初,纳克什·鲁斯塔姆及比沙普尔中心延续各自的艺术传统,必要时亦在相邻工地活动,尤其是在巴赫拉姆二世时期。比沙普尔中心的活动先是中断,在公元4世纪年幼的沙普尔二世继位后,又制作了比沙普尔Ⅵ号浮雕。若纳克什·鲁斯塔姆Ⅶ号浮雕属于巴赫拉姆四世时期,则纳克什·鲁斯塔姆艺术中心亦是如此。公元4世纪末,摩崖浮雕的制作从法尔斯地区迁至伊朗高原与美索不达米亚间主干道上的塔克·波斯坦,两个与法尔斯迥异的艺术中心先后在此诞生。在制作了主伊万塔克·波斯坦Ⅲ号、Ⅳ号浮雕的第二个艺术中心,有人提出拜占庭工匠参与的假设,但我认为仅在浮雕年代为公元5世纪、即与伊万外立面装饰同时期的情况下成立。

---

[1] Canepa 2013, p. 874.
[2] 感谢西尼西指出,塔西佗的文章中描述弗拉特斯国王在亚美尼亚骑着大象迎战罗马军队(*Ann.*, XV, 15)。关于萨珊与印度间的比较,参见 J. Kröger 1981。
[3] von Gall 1990, pp. 44-7. 冯·加尔提出,两侧壁的帝王狩猎图源于库思老二世对伊万的重复利用。鉴于王冠间的相似之处,库思老二世改造卑路斯像,为自己所用(von Gall 1990, p. 45)。
[4] 塔克·波斯坦建筑群及毗邻水源的阿胡拉·马兹达与阿娜希塔授权图为对王权的颂扬,因为当时波斯深陷困境,骑兵雕像便体现了卑路斯抵抗嚈哒帝国的多次军事行动。阿勒比鲁尼称,卑路斯曾到供奉祭司圣火阿杜尔·法恩巴格的阿达尔库拉神庙朝圣,使一场漫长的旱灾终止,其朝圣之旅便是阿布里扎甘节的起源。这证实了卑路斯与水的关联(Atāral-bākīya, pp. 228-9, trad. pp. 215-6)。

现无法就上述艺术中心的分工安排提出假设,因为各中心只可通过若干图像选择及不同工匠参与形成的风格来大致辨别。

最后,应尤其注意萨珊时期的伊朗相对其他地区显而易见的独特之处,即上述艺术中心的活动不具有延续性。阿契美尼德时期,建筑工程需要耗费数代人的精力,居鲁士大帝与大流士一世时期创造的艺术传统几乎原封不动地保留了下来。而萨珊时期与此相反,虽为中央集权,但未刻意保持其工艺传统,在屡次创建技艺要求极高的摩崖浮雕时,不耻于招募外来工匠。由此可推断,尽管摩崖浮雕具有极高的象征性地位,在萨珊对外宣扬的王权中却并非必不可少的固定要素。

第五章　萨珊时期的印章风格与技术：生产中心

鉴于大量已发现和出版的印章与印泥印记，印章也许是萨珊时期最负盛名的工艺品。在此不得不提《伊朗研究手册》主编吉塞莲长久以来对该领域的杰出贡献。她的决定性成果体现在两方面：一是出版了严谨完备的图录，呈现出数量可观的萨珊印章与印泥，二是对印章及相应印记进行批判性研究。珠玉在前，我犹豫良久才斗胆班门弄斧。秉着奋勇方能出学问的信念，也出于对向亚尔夏特科学委员会举荐本人的吉塞莲女士的尊敬，我决定勉力一试，怀谦逊之心，行艰难之事，但愿天神不致怪罪此等傲慢！

在吉塞莲的著作出版前，学界自20世纪初已从不同角度展开对萨珊印章的研究。篇幅所限，仅列出最早系统研究萨珊印章的卢科宁、比瓦尔与布伦纳，以及于1973年首先探讨图像分类的格布尔。近来，除吉塞莲外，其他学者亦各有贡献，在此主要针对里特尔于2010年出版的《萨珊印章的古代东方传统：形状—应用—图像》提出几点批判性思考[1]。

图像学方法已在印章研究中取得重大进展。故本章并非整体性介绍，而是意在指出技术与风格研究的必要性，因其有助于初步阐明萨珊印章生产中心的问题。每个工艺品背后都有一个接受技术培训、具有特定文化身份的工匠，却往往被忽略。

首先，我将从里特尔最新的萨珊印章批判性研究切入。他强调萨珊与古代近东印章间在图像与风格上有延续性。萨珊时期，美索不达米亚的印记遗存多于印章本身，表明作坊历经希腊化时期与安息时期仍在延续。此类工艺品反而证实了萨珊时期印章刻制的繁盛。里特尔的可取之处在于，他在哈珀于亚尔夏特会议的发言后再次申明，古美索不达米亚传统存续至伊斯兰时期[2]。

我不同意里特尔所提出的延续性与"萨珊王朝"相关，因印章刻制大多为私人性质，应由此入手阐释。里特尔对此有充分的认识，但其研究有时似乎超出了美索不达米

---

[1] Die altorientalischen Traditionen der sasanidischen Glyptil. Form-Gebrauch-Ikonographie。遗憾的是，我未能拜读 K. Yamauchi, *The Vocabulary of Sasanian Seals*, Tokyo, 1993。
[2] Harper 2006.

亚印章作坊的工艺传统。他试图论证萨珊王朝在文化上整体延续了美索不达米亚传统，而几乎未考虑两个朝代间相隔数个世纪。"萨珊王朝既非外来统治者，也非模仿如影子般几不可见的旧文化的折中主义者。作为波斯本土王朝的萨珊建立了古代近东的最后一个帝国，在诸多方面沿袭了古代近东的传统。"[1]此类表述会产生误导，因里特尔的研究对象并非萨珊王朝，而是萨珊治下某地区的私人刻制的印章。

欲探究印章中的萨珊王朝文化趋向，应考察可由铭文佐证王室成员身份的少量印章。里特尔在论述古代近东传统中的王室印章与萨珊时期王室印章的资料时有所涉及[2]，但列举不全，如吉塞莲在书评中所指出的[3]。

里特尔仅编录了五枚萨珊王室印章：

1. "哥达红锆石"，藏于巴黎法国国家图书馆；
2. 双色缠丝玛瑙，藏于大英博物馆，上为巴赫拉姆四世像；
3. "德文郡宝石"，出自古玩市场，上为巴赫拉姆克尔曼沙赫像；
4. 亚兹丹·弗里·沙布赫，沙普尔三世的妃子，藏于法国国家图书馆；
5. 紫晶，藏于艾尔美塔什博物馆，上为"万后之后"德纳格像；

在此基础上，吉塞莲补充了两枚重要的王室印章：

6. 卑路斯印章，出自古玩市场；
7. 沙普尔二世半身像印章，其印记在赛义迪收藏中的印泥上。

下文对上述印章作详细介绍。

1. "哥达红锆石"是一枚希腊化风格的铁铝榴石印章（图184）[4]，富特旺格勒将其上的右侧面男性半身像定为米特里达梯一世[5]。印章原表面粗锉边缘的初始铭文已被雕刻磨去，由于称号无存，仅知为一位沙普尔国王。卢科宁将其定为沙普尔一世[6]。居里埃尔与赛里格将印章年代定为公元3世纪后半叶至4世纪初[7]，依据为如下图像细节：连珠饰王冠与数组古币及纳克什·鲁斯塔姆摩崖浮

图184 法国国家图书馆，巴黎："哥达红锆石"（Gyselen 1993, pl. XVII, 20.J.1）

---

[1] Ritter 2010, p. 230.
[2] Ritter 2010, pp. 47–9.
[3] Gyselen 2012, p. 321.
[4] Bibliothèque Nationale, Inv. 1970. 392; Gyselen 1993, p. 104, no. 20. J. 1.
[5] Furtwaengler 1900, p. 104, pl. 2. 50.
[6] Lukonin 1969, p. 68.
[7] Curiel/Seyrig 1974.

雕上的纳塞赫王冠相似；冠上飘带虽形式简化，但为萨珊国王像的必要元素；悬于耳垂的硕大梨形珍珠未见于萨珊时期以前。两位学者不排除该人物为理想化图像的可能，或为一位阿契美尼德先祖，但也认同富特旺勒将其归为希腊化风格，"因未发现任何可与这一杰作媲美的阿契美尼德凹雕"[1]。至于这一风格的来源，居里埃尔与赛里格在注解中谨慎地提出："鉴于东方国家仍在制作希腊式佛教造像，且其希腊化东方传统技艺精湛，（治印的）大师是否来自此地？"[2]公元2—3世纪的犍陀罗印章摒弃了希腊化刻制的自然主义风格，而以砣轮制成的罗马帝国刻制来表现程式化的题材[3]。故更合理的解释为，这一精美印章出自沿袭西方传统的高超工匠之手，类似作品还包括刻画沙普尔与瓦勒良决斗的凸雕。

2. 尼科罗缠丝玛瑙印章（图185）[4]，藏于伦敦大英博物馆西亚文物部[5]，上为国王左侧面站立全身像，其脚下有一人横卧在地，尺寸较小。比瓦尔依据王冠将国王定为巴赫拉姆四世[6]。刻制图像虽小，但细节丰富，精加工完整，与摩崖浮雕中的萨珊国王像惊人地相似。

3. "紫晶德文郡公爵"来自私人收藏（图186），上为戴库拉赫的右侧面男性半身像。其铭文提及一位巴赫拉姆克尔曼沙赫，比瓦尔将其定为即位前的巴赫拉姆四世

图185 大英博物馆，西亚文物部，伦敦：巴赫拉姆四世印章（Vanden Berghe, ed. 1993, n°140）

图186 "德文郡宝石"，紫晶巴赫拉姆克尔曼沙赫像（Harper 1981, fig. 7）

[1] Curiel/Seyrig 1974, p. 59.
[2] Curiel/Seyrig 1974, n. 12S.
[3] Callieri 1997, pp. 232-4, 262.
[4] 比瓦尔称其为"玉髓，石英的一种"。
[5] Inv. 119352.
[6] Bivar 1969, p. 56, no. BC1; Gyselen 2006, p. 211, cat. 173.

（388—399年）[1]。而根据风格及图像标准，卢科宁此前提出其年代应为公元3世纪至4世纪初[2]。冠上符号与刻画巴赫拉姆一世像的卡拉斯拉亚·波利亚纳银盘上的符号极为相似[3]。综上，卢科宁将其定为即位前的巴赫拉姆一世[4]，在公元262—274年间为克尔曼沙赫[5]。哈珀随后亦采用其观点[6]。

4. 亚兹丹·弗里·沙布赫印章（图187），即沙普尔三世"最宠爱的"妃子[7]，藏于法国国家图书馆[8]。印章为精美的三层缠丝玛瑙，以尼科罗制成，在红底上刻出白色主体[9]。右侧面王后像的自然主义细节丰富，躯干正面朝前，头戴连珠饰圆帽形王冠，颈后飘带由系结开始向上飘扬并逐渐变宽。王后头上饰有一双羱羊角，吉塞莲认为两角间或为一片栗树叶。帽边垂下四根发辫。

5. 紫晶印章（图188），藏于艾尔美塔什博物馆[10]，依据铭文应属于"万后之后"德纳格，上为自然主义特征明显的右侧面女性像，图像细节极其详尽[11]。赫兹菲尔德提出"万后之后"为卑路斯及霍米兹三世之母，公元457年摄政[12]。卢科宁则认为是阿尔达希尔一世的妹妹及妻子[13]。如哈珀所言，该印章与萨珊初期印章间的相似性可支持卢科宁的观点[14]。

6. 珍贵印章（图189），出自古玩市场，最初仅有铭文问世[15]，幸而整枚印章的线描也已发表[16]。上为萨珊国王右侧面半身像，根据王冠可将其定为万王之王卑路斯，除冠

图187 法国国家图书馆，巴黎：亚兹丹·弗里·沙布赫印章（Gyselen 1993, pl. IX, 20.A.1）

---

[1] Bivar 1969, pp. 2, 15.
[2] Lukonin 1960, p. 380.
[3] Lukonin 1961, p. 58.
[4] Lukonin 1969, p. 68.
[5] Lukonin 1969, p. 107.
[6] Harper 1974, p. 69 & n. 12; 1981, p. 29, fig. 7.
[7] Curiel/Gignoux 1974.
[8] Inv. 1974. 1080.
[9] Gyselen 2006, p. 207, cat. 156; 也可参见 Gignoux/Gyselen 1989a, p. 882; Gyselen 1993, p. 88, no. 20. A. 1。
[10] Inv. Gl. 979.
[11] Borisov/Lukonin 1963, no.2, p. 74.
[12] Herzfeld 1924, p. 75.
[13] Lukonin 1960; 1977, p. 154; 1979, p. 10.
[14] Harper 1974, p. 73, n.30; Gignoux 1994.
[15] Gignoux 2000; Skjævø 2003, pp. 284-6.
[16] Baratte *et al*. 2012, p. 15, fig. a.

伊朗萨珊时期的建筑与艺术

图188 艾尔美塔什博物馆，圣彼得堡："万后之后"德纳格印章（Vanden Berghe, ed. 1993, n°131）

球下新月底部的珍珠外，与卑路斯在Ⅲb型钱币上的肖像几乎完全一致[1]。边缘铭文亦可证实。

7. 赛义迪收藏中的印泥上的印记（图190），上为萨珊国王右侧面半身像，王冠及铭文均明确表明其为沙普尔二世[2]。尽管沿袭了表现侧面的传统，印章半身像与摩崖浮雕、钱币等其他材质中的肖像几乎完全一致，区别为自然主义风格的五官刻画十分准确。

图189 万王之王卑路斯印章（Baratte 等 2012, p.15, fig. a）

图190 万王之王沙普尔二世印章（Gyselen 2007b, fig. Ab）

---

[1] Schindel 2004a, p. 390; 2004b, pp. 282–3.
[2] Gyselen 2007b.

补充关于国王印章的文学作品，亦有助于了解萨珊王室印章的全貌。其中，比瓦尔所引用的马斯乌迪对"野驴"巴赫拉姆五世、库思老一世及库思老二世印章的记述尤为重要[1]。库思老一世的四枚印章仅刻有铭文。库思老二世则有不少于九枚材质各异的印章：一为国王像，一为疾驰骑兵，一为鹰，一为野猪头，其余则附有各不相同的铭文[2]。尽管具有文学性，但马斯乌迪对印章材质十分内行，其记述应较为可信，即印章上除王室半身像外还有多种形象。

里特尔将罗列的五枚王室印章统而视之，但应注意国王、王后像与克尔曼沙赫等其他王室成员肖像之间的关键差异。就图像类型而言，前者有王冠或饰带等国王、王后及其身份的特有元素，后者则显然与高官印章属于同一类型，如下文所见。而高官印章间的主要差异在于库拉赫的类型及其上的符号[3]。

吉塞莲强调，克尔曼沙赫的半身像与若干戴圆锥形冠的非王室半身像相似，故圆锥形冠显然为"一个特定社会阶层，即萨珊王室成员与国王敕封贵族的特权"[4]。鉴于戴圆锥形冠的半身像印章与若干有威望的萨珊贵族世家印章属于不同图像类型，这一特权更为明显[5]。

回到里特尔的研究。他发现王室印章均为刻半身像或全身像、原嵌于托座内的缟玛瑙、缠丝玛瑙或紫晶印章，异于大部分萨珊印章。因此他认为托座印章比无托座印章等级更高，后者主要为半椭球形及指形[6]。就风格、质量及手工技艺而言，托座印章为萨珊刻制的杰作。就图像而言，其特有元素与钱币上的王室肖像相同[7]。此外里特尔指出，未发现用于封泥的王室印章[8]。而吉塞莲在书评中提到，沙普尔二世的印章（长约4.5厘米）推翻了里特尔的结论，其封泥与萨珊典型"印珠"的封泥类型不同，正面仅有国王印记，背面似为卷轴痕迹[9]。

王室印章均不属于美索不达米亚传统的图像—风格组合。里特尔认为它们或属于"萨珊飘扬风格"，即萨珊艺术最典型的风格，尤见于沙普尔一世至瓦赫拉姆一世的摩崖浮雕、灰泥及金属器中[10]。私以为，印章与摩崖浮雕间的相似性仅限于瓦赫拉姆四世脚

---

[1] Bivar 1969, pp. 30-4.
[2] Bivar 1969, pp. 31-2.
[3] Gyselen 1989b.
[4] Gyselen 2006, p. 200.
[5] Gyselen 2006, p. 200; Gyselen 2007a, p. 67; Gyselen 2008.
[6] Gyselen 1993, pp. 30-1.
[7] Ritter 2010, p. 50.
[8] Ritter 2010, p. 50.
[9] Gyselen 2007b, p. 74, n. 12.
[10] Ritter 2010, p. 36.

踏败将的印章[1]。但应采纳里特尔指出王室印章与众多沿袭美索不达米亚传统的萨珊印章间存在明显差异的论点。正如前文所述，这一论点恰好可修正里特尔的出发点，即古美索不达米亚印章与"萨珊王朝"的延续性。

严格意义上的萨珊王室印章并不属于美索不达米亚传统，而更接近制作萨珊钱币冲头肖像的自然主义作坊，属于沿袭了希腊化传统的安息传统，亦为达官贵族采用，如下文所见。

相反，被里特尔证实沿袭了古美索不达米亚传统的印章，则归次等阶层所有，其艺术品位与技术传统历经阿契美尼德、塞琉古及安息王朝，传承至萨珊王朝。美索不达米亚为萨珊帝国重要的经济区，故大量印章或产自此地。

质言之，将"萨珊时期的印章"当作"萨珊的印章"，引起了混淆。

现在回到讨论的主题，即技术与风格。

萨珊印章呈现出多种风格趋势，从简略、模式化到技艺复杂、质量上乘的刻制[2]。

近来，里特尔等人对风格学研究能取得可靠的结果持怀疑态度，以格布尔为例："（断代中）切忌高估风格因素，再怎么强调也不为过。"[3]但回顾可知，卢科宁在20世纪60年代基于图像与风格研究萨珊早期印章的框架十分严密。由于迄今为止的萨珊印章风格体系探索均为个案研究，流于主观，是使学界对风格学研究持怀疑态度的原因之一，进而导致学者们未采用更系统的方法来研究风格，在恶性循环中变得边缘化。

比瓦尔在大英博物馆的萨珊印章图录前言中并未对风格进行介绍，但他把半身像分为一组"早期"半身像、一组"有翼半身像"与一组"模式化半身像"，以及"衰落风格""刚劲风格""'刻划'风格"和"晚期风格"，而未进一步解释术语含义[4]。

哈珀对喀斯尔·阿卜纳斯尔若干印记的风格作了恰如其分的论述，其中三枚高官印章的图像及风格特征对本章主题尤为重要。印章由当时的能工巧匠刻成，胡须与半身像的刻制手法异于公元3、4世纪的印章，故哈珀倾向于将年代定于5—6世纪之间[5]。

尽管1978年纽约大都会艺术博物馆图录的印章数量较少，布伦纳对萨珊印章风格趋势的概述仍值得一提，但缺乏可作为现代分类标准的方法论基础。他基于品质，参照比瓦尔的部分术语，将馆藏印章分为五组形象逐渐简化的风格[6]：

---

[1] 该印章为瓦赫拉姆四世战胜匈人的场景（Daryaee 2009, p. 20）。
[2] Ritter 2010, p. 36.
[3] Göbl 1973, p. 26, Ritter 2010, p. 37.
[4] Bivar 1969, pp. 50-4.
[5] Harper 1973, p. 86.
[6] Brunner 1978, pp. 131-4.

1. 自然主义。通过精细的形状与轮廓呈现写实的形象,乃至可辨别身份的特定人物肖像(图191)。

2. 模式化。刻制清晰但模式化,形状与起伏略微简化,但形象细节准确(图192)。

图191 大都会艺术博物馆,纽约:"自然主义"风格印章(Brunner 1978, n. 31, p. 54)

图192 大都会艺术博物馆,纽约:"模式化"风格印章(Brunner 1978, n. 34, p. 54)

3. 衰落。大体准确,使用钻头后未细致加工,起伏简略而不规则,线条较粗,表明次要细节被舍弃(图193)。

4. 轮廓。无精妙细节,勉强可看出形象主要元素,母题刻划不完整或有变形。常通过在粗浅的刻划上加深短线条而成(图194)。

5. 刻划。相交错的线条大致勾勒出形象,无起伏(图195)。

布伦纳总结出如下标准:"决定性因素为形象中线条的使用与起伏程度。"[1]其他学者随后从分析角度深化了他的论点[2]。应强调的是,布伦纳意识到风格与年代之间没有关联,"风格分组本身并不能作为年代学的依据",但可印证对印章的形状、母题及铭文的判断[3]。

里特尔准确地指出,布伦纳基于品质[4]划分的风格分组,本质上与雇主的经济实力相关[5]。无可否认,刻制自然主义风格的印章比刻划印章耗时更多,价格差异亦十分显著。

---

[1] Brunner 1978, p. 131.
[2] Gorelick/Gwinnet 1996, p. 79.
[3] Brunner 1978, p. 131.
[4] Ritter 2010, p. 41, n. 65.
[5] 参见下文。

图193 大都会艺术博物馆,纽约:"衰落"风格印章(Brunner 1978, n. 124, p. 57)

图194 大都会艺术博物馆,纽约:"轮廓"风格印章(Brunner 1978, n. 224, p. 58)

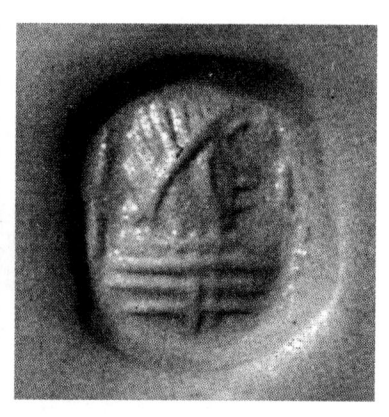

图195 大都会艺术博物馆,纽约:"刻划"风格印章(Brunner 1978, n. 148, p. 58)

在巴黎法国国家图书馆及卢浮宫博物馆的图录中,对待萨珊印章的风格问题,吉塞莲十分谨慎。前人的探索固然可贵,但她不愿沿袭其方法[1],主要原因为风格差异本质上与价格相关:"诚然,精雕细琢的印章与简单刻划的印章极易区分,但除雇主的财力外,还能反映什么?风格是否能反映其他方面的情况?萨珊晚期印泥中可清晰看到多种风格并存,证明治印工匠的技艺水平不具有年代含义。"[2]吉塞莲并未止于此,她强调,治印时"风格显然与印章'类型'相关,而后者又与形状、材质、图像等因素相关",她将重点转为整体考虑影响一枚印章最终面貌的所有因素[3]。在我看来,她由此深化的分类可作为研究风格问题的新方法的前提,详见下文。在最新著作中,她再次强调风格与图像间的关联,尤其是官印,这类图像遵循严格制作规定与等级的印章。就官印而言,某些细节差异或与风格因素相关,或出于其他原因[4]。

里特尔最初同吉塞莲一样,对风格持怀疑态度,但立场更激进,认为以风格分析探索萨珊时期印章的分期与分区不足为信。他指出,印章风格百花齐放,没有地区或年代规律的多种风格同时独立出现[5],再加上技艺杂糅,难以统一分类[6]。"因此风格分组不可取,技艺与风格分析亦无法得到有用成果。"[7]里特尔认为萨珊印章风格并非一个发展过程或结果,也不是一种年代、地域、种族或艺术趋势,而是对政治、社会、经济条

---

[1] Gyselen 1993, p. 60.
[2] Gyselen 1993, p. 60.
[3] Gyselen 1993, p. 60.
[4] Gyselen 2007a, p. 20.
[5] Ritter 2010, p. 37.
[6] Ritter 2010, p. 37.
[7] Ritter 2010, p. 37.

件的表现或反映[1]。故若要充分了解风格,解释其传播过程,应考虑技艺、艺术史及分析方法,并纳入社会学角度[2]。大众化而简略、材质与形状各异的印章图像重复出现,表明印章的使用并不局限于精英群体,但跻身显贵的社会阶层才可获得技艺精湛的作坊产品,正如公元前1000年的印章所示[3]。吉塞莲正确地指出,存在快速制作的印章,但里特尔认为并非和某一时期的艺术品位相关,而是面向社会次等阶层的量产,罕见于行政印记[4]。

回到吉塞莲的观点,我在当中提取出对风格讨论至关重要的元素。她对伊朗萨珊时期的印章图像分组的研究方法远非简单分类,而可为深化研究奠定基础。我认为还应考虑技术与风格。

最能体现吉塞莲的理论作用的是男性半身像印章,因为她在论证图像分组时引入了重要的年代因素。她的著述涉及两个层面,其一为全部萨珊印章的图像分组体系,尽管巴尔策提议修改,其分组仍应作为相关研究的参考[5]。吉塞莲将分组称为"系列","(分组)不反映风格元素,而是方便后续增加新印章,无须改变冗长的编号清单",如下[6]:

右侧面男性像,戴圆锥形冠等发冠(20.B);

右侧面男性像,长鬈发、无冠(20.C);

右侧面男性像,脸周蓄满"短"发、无冠(20.D);

右侧面男性像,"环形鬈发"(20.E);

右侧面男性像,头发"紧贴"头皮(20.F);

正面男性像(20.G);

双翼上男性像(20.H)。

由于分组标准较为笼统,各组内亦包括不尽相似的印章。故除上述"系列"外,吉塞莲依据其他图像细节及相似的印章,将男性半身像印章分为七个"类型系列"[7]:

1. 花卉半身像;

2. 星形半身像;

---

[1] Ritter 2010, p. 41.
[2] Ritter 2010, p. 37.
[3] Ritter 2010, pp. 38–9.
[4] Gyselen 1993, p. 60.
[5] 巴尔策的方法似与本章主题不一致。他的创新主要在于纳入了多人物情节的图像,而对本章所研究的男性半身像等独立题材贡献不大(W. Balzer 2007, pp. 31, 41)。
[6] Gyselen 1993, p. 44.
[7] Gyselen 1993, p. 62.

3. 洛林十字半身像；

4. 长鬈发及"卷曲鬈发"半身像；

5. 长鬈发及"编发"半身像；

6. 着细布的短发半身像；

7. 翼上半身像。

基于上述类型系列的材质、形状及铭文，吉塞莲提出了年代顺序。

就材质、形状而言，各类型系列存在明显差异。系列1至3为杂色石英，不含凸圆形；系列4与5仅为凸圆形铁铝榴石；系列6与7由多种形状及材质组成。就铭文而言，系列4至7仅为方正体，系列1至3还包括手写体；系列4、5仅有本名，而系列6、7还包括称号。系列1至3的印主多为系列4至7中从未出现的琐罗亚斯德教祭司。

将上述考量与可判断年代的印记相对照后，吉塞莲提出："系列4至7更可能为萨珊初期，而系列1至3属于萨珊晚期。"[1]

整体考虑形状、材质、铭文、图像等元素，可确定在同一时段内的印章组别。这一方法得出的结果尤为重要，因大部分萨珊印章研究对分期持怀疑态度。

过去包括比瓦尔在内的许多断代观点，都基于铭文的古文字标准。在大英博物馆的印章图录中，"依据（目前已知的）古文字资料及其他论述"，比瓦尔提出萨珊印章主要形状及其优先使用材质的年代顺序[2]。缠丝玛瑙、铁铝榴石制成的原嵌于托座内的印章为公元3—4世纪所特有；碧玉、红玉髓及其他玉髓品种制成的半椭球形印及指环在4—5世纪盛行；碧石、赤铁矿制成的半球体印常见于5—6世纪；榴石、紫晶或岩石晶体制成的长凸圆形印常见于6—7世纪[3]。但吉塞莲一方面驳斥形状作为年代学标准的可行性[4]，另一方面强调，对公元6、7世纪行政封泥的研究表明传统的古文字学并不可靠，因为主要的方正体与手写体并用，没有年代区分[5]。

卢科宁是为数不多提出可靠年代学方法的学者之一。他多次阐释其方法，在"官方肖像"中尤为有效[6]。首先，他选取几组图像元素相近的印章，随后甄别金属器、钱币等有更多年代证据的工艺品中相同的图像元素。其次，他对铭文进行了碑铭学研究，参照其他历史文献对比了姓名与称号。最后，他通过与其他材料的铭文对比，研究了印章中

---

[1] Gyselen 1993, p. 63.
[2] Bivar 1969, p. 23.
[3] Bivar 1969, p. 24.
[4] Gyselen 1979.
[5] Gyselen 1993, p. 28.
[6] Lukonin 1961, pp. 39–55; Borisov/Lukonin 1963, p. 67.

的古文字。基于该方法,卢科宁将披肩长发绺半身像、齐胸处以别针固定的大衣以及四球形半身像等元素的年代归为公元3—4世纪。库拉赫或为行政官员的弗里吉亚帽,或为祭司的弧顶帽。他还指出,公元4—5世纪的肖像变得标准化和理想化,半身像底部增加了翅膀或植物母题。公元6世纪时传统风格的官方肖像复兴,但6—7世纪尤以大量线刻的半身像(štrixovaja rez'ba)为特点[1]。

为了解决萨珊印章的断代难题,我十余年前便重述卢科宁的观点,即应研究高加索地区考古语境中绝对年代的基点,尽管我未有机会践行[2]。高加索地区曾直接或间接地受到萨珊文化与政治的辐射,与伊朗领土不同,这一地区以随葬品丰富的厚葬习俗为特点。墓葬中若有萨珊印章出土,则应与其他年代确凿的工艺品相关。石质印章历久使用,故应考虑考古语境中的绝对年代学下限[3]。

回到吉塞莲的图录,其主要贡献为通过对图像及相关材质、形状等特征进行详细分析,将几组印章分为不同的时段。从吉塞莲分析男性半身像得出的重要结论入手,可进一步深化,另辟蹊径研究生产中心,从而回归风格问题。一言以蔽之,通过研究吉塞莲依据图像划分的所有印章中若干元素的技法,可发现图像分组相异的印章来源相同。

数年前,我对犍陀罗地区(今巴基斯坦西北部)印章的研究取得了可喜成果,故据此提出探讨部分萨珊印章图像分组风格的方法。在我首开先河之际,尽管犍陀罗地区印章意义重大,却仅有少数孤立研究。通过该方法,我首次提出至今仍未过时的图像分组及技术风格分组[4],包括被新材料证实的年代顺序[5]。在此显然无法用简短语言一一尽现,故仅以若干实例证明该方法的"理论"可行性。

研究的出发点是图像分类。在这方面,吉塞莲所著《法国国家图书馆及卢浮宫博物馆藏萨珊印章、凸雕及印泥图录》中已有成熟的结果[6]。所出版印章印记均附有放大至2∶1比例的插图,可供分析研究,当中的全部图像细节即为本文的"实验"对象。

无论是同一图像分组,或是对比不同图像分组,仔细研究所有图像元素中指向特定生产中心的技法,均可证明技术—风格相似性。而生产中心性质的问题极为复杂,如古罗马生产中心的相关假设"从'工业化'或'半工业化'的量产,到较小的'家庭'作坊,再到工匠个体"[7]。辨识生产中心的第一步,即为通过形象细节的技术—风格,将图像各不相同的印章归类。

---

[1] Borisov/Lukonin 1963, p. 67.
[2] Borisov/Lukonin 1963, pp. 25–6.
[3] Callieri 2004b.
[4] Callieri 1997.
[5] Lerner 2010.
[6] Gyselen, 1993.
[7] Tassinari 2011, col. 404. 亦可参见 Sena Chiesa 1966, pp. 11, 51; 1978, pp. 44–5。

在此要向不熟悉印章制作方式的读者说明，印章所用宝石的莫氏硬度均大于5.5，故无法像石雕或金属雕刻一样以金属工具加工，而只能使用硬度更高的石料刻划。刚玉砂为两种莫氏硬度最高的石料，即金刚石或刚玉的粉末，可用于研磨莫氏硬度比其低2—3度的石料，如古代印章中最常见的榴石、玉髓及缠丝玛瑙。研磨方式：为使微小颗粒快速转动，通过手摇金属钻头转动油性混合物基质，粘接颗粒并阻止其扩散。依据不同的钻头及其与石料表面的交角，钻头旋转中，缓慢而重复的磨削可刻出圆形或长条形元素。圆形是以圆钻头垂直于石料表面刻成，长条形则由圆盘头即"砣轮"以一定倾斜角度刻成。故该技艺为"研磨"而非"雕塑"。由工匠耗费时间多少所决定的印章价格不同，刻制细节的深度与融合度不同，印记的立体度及完整度也随之不同。在上述方法制成的粗坯上，以更小的钻头刻画出与工匠耗时及技艺水平相关的细节[1]。

印章刻制为一项高度专业化的技术，因面积极小而使制作难度倍增[2]，特别是当时是否使用放大镜仍未可知，尽管在罗马帝国已有（放大镜）实物[3]。生产印章的作坊必然存在工匠直接传承技艺的传统。在此前提下可推测，每个工匠选择其呈现图像的特定手法，同时在图像上区分用于身份证明的印章。私以为，在这一专业化制作中，使用不同工具呈现的不同形象元素，几乎不可能在不同时间或地点重新出现，而更可能出自同一生产中心。换言之，该方法与语史学中的"归因"趋势相同，即英语中的"鉴赏"，为有效的历史—艺术方法的第一步。

技术—风格手法的分析始于图像，与之相辅相成，并可被验证。这类风格分组与布伦纳提出的品质，抑或德国古典印章图录中的主观评估截然不同，可辨识出图像相异的印章在制作上的客观相似性[4]。研究眼睛、眉毛、鼻子、耳朵、发型或饰物的不同刻制手法，均可发现优于图像分组的关键点，在同一图像分组中更易识别，可由此再与其他分组进行对比。需重申的是，应以同一图像分组内部的比较为出发点，随后对不同图像分组进行比较。

初步成果体现在是否可以辨识若干印章所属的或多或少的生产中心，即在整个萨珊时期及帝国领土有多少生产中心。在此条件下，若能确定至少两枚不同图像分组的印章所属的生产中心，便可证实上述研究方法的可行性。由此可借助印泥与钱币，得到具有绝对年代学基点的技术—风格分组，甚至确定其地理位置。

正如吉塞莲与里特尔所强调，在少数印泥上的印记足以辨认印章的情况下，可得出

---

[1] Callieri 1997, pp. 251-2.
[2] Callieri 1997, pp. 251-2.
[3] Beretta/Di Pasquale 2003.
[4] Zazoff 1970, 1975, 1983.

印章使用的时间与地点[1]。但仍需考虑两个问题,即档案馆中的印泥所封存的物件可能来自帝国其他地区,且萨珊晚期印泥上的印记可能出自早期印章。出自古玩市场、注明日期的巴克特里亚文献上,便使用了年代更早的印章[2]。此外,粟特地区的卡菲里·卡拉也可证明同一档案馆中存在年代相去甚远的印记[3]。

以卢科宁为代表的学者通过钱币来推定萨珊印章年代。该方法基于印章与钱币冲头制作间的相似性,尽管二者材质迥异。以印度西北部的钱币与印章为例,即便前者为国家订制,材质为金属,形制统一化,而后者为私人制作,材质为硬石,形制各不相同,二者之间仍有诸多相似之处。首先,形象均为阴刻,尺寸较小,均存在对焦的问题。其次,二者的母题都集中在较小的圆形或椭圆空间中[4]。

如在一枚钱币上发现与一组印章相同的技术—风格特征,则有充分理由确定该组印章的时代,以及与钱币生产中心相去不远的地理位置。

古钱币学家研究风格的方法简述如下。吉塞莲在收录于《萨珊钱币总集》的沙普尔一世钱币研究中,从下列问题切入风格概念:"在将一种风格归为某一作坊之前,应思考一种风格能代表什么。一种风格是否等同于一个工匠、一个生产中心,或是介于两者之间?"[5]此外,她对风格的定义包括古钱币学家赋予风格的特殊语义,实际上涉及碑铭学、钱币工艺及风格学本义,后者又分为钱币的形象布局和图像细节的刻制。但在其古钱币学分析中,纯粹的风格元素也与图像元素相混淆,如半身像服装、颈饰等。"风格"一词在古钱币学研究中具有特殊意义,包括更接近图像而非风格的元素,但不涉及呈现眼睛、鼻子、嘴巴等形象固有元素、与图像学无关的技法。吉塞莲仔细研究图像实现的技法,将沙普尔一世的钱币分为23种风格,并指出上述钱币出自多个统一化的生产中心,而部分生产中心拥有多种风格[6]。

申德尔的角度则偏向艺术创作。他将风格定义为:"一枚钱币(更准确地说是冲头)上可观察到的艺术家个性的全貌。此外,风格一词并不包括类型或物理特征。"[7]他强调,一定时期的风尚与各制钱工匠的个性相关,并指出尝试辨认工匠身份的钱币学家仅有尼基金与罗特[8]。

---

[1] Harper 1973, p. 86.
[2] Lerner 2006.
[3] Cazzoli/Cereti 2005.
[4] Callieri 2006b, p. 7.
[5] Gyselen 2003, p. 210.
[6] Gyselen 2003, p. 251.
[7] Schindel 2005, p. 288.
[8] Nikitin/Roth 1995.

现在回到印章，即我对吉塞莲1993年图录中男性半身像的分组探索。

第一个技术—风格分组包含两枚凸圆形印章。其一以红玉髓制成，被吉塞莲归为系列4，即长卷发及"卷曲鬈发"半身像（图196A）。其二以铁铝榴石制成，属于系列5，即长卷发及"编发"半身像（图196B）。尽管两枚印章分属不同类型系列，但多处技法相同，清晰可见：略长而微弯的眉毛，眼睛瞳孔和双眼睑，上眼睑长于下眼睑，鼻子，嘴，微卷胡髭的轮廓线条，和发辫一样以横向刮痕与内部斜痕表现的胡髯，以不同方式刻画的其他头发。躯干的制作亦十分相似，尽管其中一枚印记中束腰衣褶的刻画不够清晰（图196B）。二者发辫、眉弓、眼睛和鼻子均与德纳格王后印章极为相似（图188）[1]，故可归为同一水平高超的作坊，该作坊亦为宫廷服务。这有利于证明吉塞莲提出的王室印章与贵族印章之间的紧密关联（参见上文）。相似的眼睛处理亦出现在沙普尔一世发行的若干版钱币中[2]，但她的描述中并未专门提及。

第二个技术—风格分组包括以铁铝榴石制成的两枚印章（图197A、B），吉塞莲指出其相似之处，但不属于她划分的任一类型系列。有多处相似的特殊处理，如眉弓，双眼睑相隔较远、不刻出瞳孔的眼睛，流畅平直的鼻唇轮廓线。两枚印章的发型类型不同，但额前均用平行线刻画。躯干底部的图像截然不同，其一似为侧面姿势（图197A）。没有发现其他可提供年代对照的材料。

第三个技术—风格分组包括三枚印章，一枚凸圆形，两枚半椭球形，分属两种图像系列。其一由光玉髓制成，为长鬈发、无冠的男性右侧面像，因其发型复杂特殊，未被吉塞莲归入任一类型系列（图198A）。余下两枚分别以玉髓（图198B）和玛瑙（图198C）制成，属于脸周蓄满"短"发、无冠的右侧面像系列，二者在图像上有细微差异。只有一枚属于吉塞莲提出的穿着细布的短发半身像类型系列（图

图196 法国国家图书馆，巴黎：20.C.1、20.C.2印章（Gyselen 1993, pl. XI）

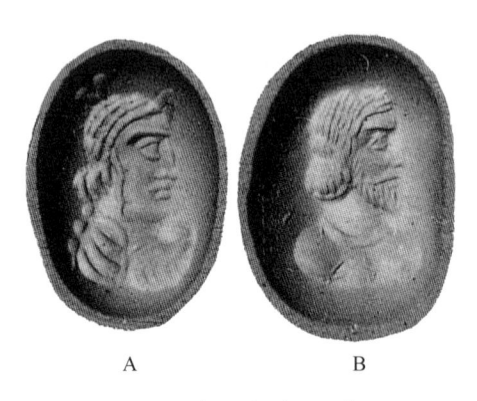

图197 法国国家图书馆，巴黎：20.B.35、20.B.36印章（Gyselen 1993, pl. XI）

---

[1] 参见上文。
[2] 如Alram/Gyselen 2003, p. 358, no. 172, Style Q, Taf. 34。

图198 法国国家图书馆,巴黎:20.C.9、20.D.8、20.D.11印章(Gyselen 1993, pls. XI, XII)

198B),但另一枚仅在发型上与其有若干图像细节差异(图198C)。虽然第一枚为光玉髓凸圆形印(图198A),造价应为最高,制作精良,轮廓精妙,但三枚印章中多处技法相同:眉弓均略长而微弯;刻出双眼睑而无瞳孔;鼻子水平轮廓笔直;嘴唇为两条平行粗线,嘴角一条近乎笔直的线表示胡髭;胡髯通过竖直排线表现,在第三枚中效果较为简略(图198C);硕大的耳环由一颗扁珠连接两颗大珠子而成。躯干处理亦相同,双肩之间为两块健硕的胸肌,织物均有不明显的三或四层褶皱,方向略有差异。没有发现其他可提供年代对照的材料。

第四个技术—风格分组包括两枚凸圆形印,分属两种图像系列:其一以铁铝榴石制成,为长鬈发、无冠的男性右侧面像,未被吉塞莲划分为任一类型系列(图199A);其二为光玉髓玛瑙,属于头发"成环形"的右侧面像类型系列(图199B)。后者的介绍中提到"半身像的刻制手法十分特殊",四个硕大的球形代表双肩和两块胸肌,前者亦是如此[1]。尽管两枚印章的图像尤其是发型有所不同,但人物均双眼圆睁,眉弓下双眼睑内为大瞳孔,鼻子无轮廓线,嘴唇为两道平行短线。此组仍然没有其他可提供年代对照的材料。

图199 法国国家图书馆,巴黎:20.C.8、20.E.10印章(Gyselen 1993, pls. XI, XIV)

第五个技术—风格分组包括:一枚原嵌于托座内的光玉髓,被吉塞莲归为类型系列6,即穿着细布的短发半身像(图200A);一枚光玉髓半椭球形印,被吉塞莲归为类型系列7,即翼上半身像(图200B)。两枚印章中胡髭的刻制技法相同,线条与上唇相交,两端明显上翘;胡髯均以密集竖排线表示;发型上部相同,但其一抹额为球形(图

---

[1] Gyselen 1993, p. 100.

图200 法国国家图书馆,巴黎:20.D.4、20.H.5 印章(Gyselen 1993, pls. XII, XV)

图201 法国国家图书馆,巴黎:20.D.5、20.D.10 印章(Gyselen 1993, pl. XII)

图202 法国国家图书馆,巴黎:20.B.10、20.E.4 印章(Gyselen 1993, pls. X, XIV)

200B),另一为椭球形(图200A);眼睛十分相似;其一鼻子无竖轮廓线(图200A)。尽管存在上述差异,两枚印章很可能出自同一作坊。

第六个技术—风格分组包含两枚印章。一枚原嵌于托座内的玛瑙,属于穿着细布的短发半身像类型系列(图201A)。一枚光玉髓半椭球形印,与前者十分接近,但未被吉塞莲纳入同一系列(图201B)。二者大致勾勒出眉弓,仅上眼睑与眼球相接;鼻子横轮廓线略超出与竖轮廓线的相交点;山羊胡以密集竖排线表现;头发为短平行线,戴椭球形宽抹额,其一抹额较大(图201B)。躯干处理亦十分相似,有两块立体胸肌。服饰差异则显然出于图像选择。

第七个技术—风格分组包括两枚玛瑙指形印。其一被吉塞莲归为类型系列3,即洛林十字半身像(图202A)。其二属于类型系列1,即花卉半身像(图202B)。尽管尺寸明显不一,较大的印章上刻制细节更为自如,但二者均有若干可证实相同来源的元素:较粗的眉弓下刻出眼睛正面,仅表现出略弯的双眼睑及略椭圆的眼球;鼻子竖轮廓线笔直,横轮廓线略带弧度;厚嘴唇由两条粗线构成;长而上翘的胡髭不与上唇相交,胡髯为粗细适中的竖排线;耳朵立体,耳环为两颗形状大小各异的珠子。二者发型类型不同,前者佩戴王冠(图202A)。领口与作装点的珍珠项链相似,但前者佩戴双层项链。此组年代因素为眼睛的技法,与库思老二世的多版钱币极其接近[1],与吉塞莲将类型系列划分为萨珊晚期相符。

---

[1] Gyselen/Kalus 1983, pl. II, n°420, 487, 517.

第八个技术—风格分组包括两枚印章，与前一组大体相似，工艺略逊色，但两者的若干共同点与前一组相异。其一为玛瑙指形印（图203A），其二为碧玉指形印（图203B）。吉塞莲仅将后者归为花卉半身像类型系列。除无胡髭外[1]，两枚印章与第七组相近，但眼睛正面较为简略粗糙，嘴唇较薄，胡髯排线较稀疏。故可推断上述两枚印章与第七组或出自同一作坊，但造价更低，抑或出自另一传统相似但技术水平较低的作坊。

图203 法国国家图书馆，巴黎：20.B.30、20.D.47 印章（Gyselen 1993, pls. XI, XIII）

第九个技术—风格分组包括五枚印章：两枚指形印（图204A、B）与三枚半椭球形印（图204C、D、E）。三枚以碧玉制成（图204A、D、E），余下两枚以玛瑙制成（图204B、C）。其一被吉塞莲归为类型系列2，即星形半身像（图204A）。另有三枚属于类型系列3，即洛林十字半身像（图204B、C、D）。除了发型与躯干的图像选择，尤其是上眼睑的手法不同外，相同的五官证明五枚印章出自同一作坊。球形眼珠的处理较为独特，其上

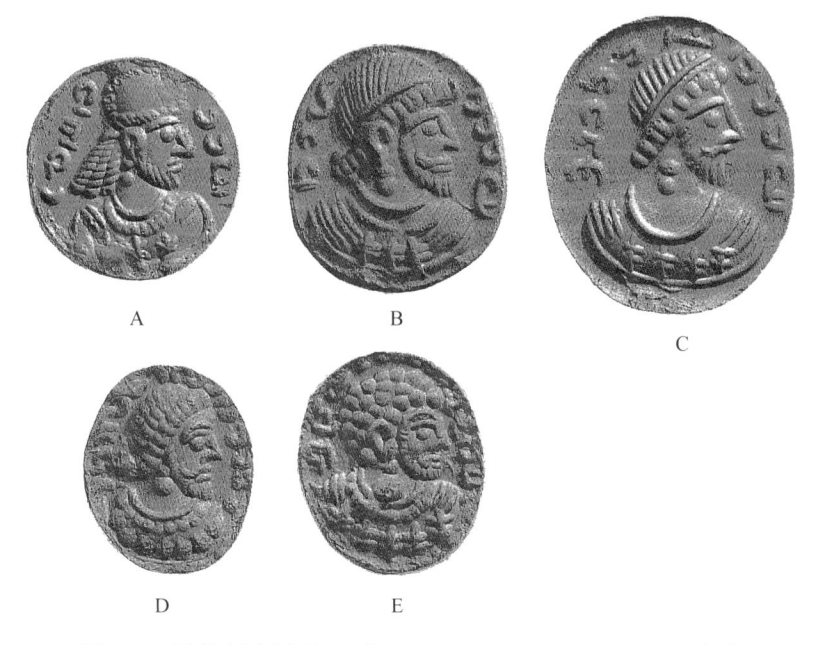

图204 法国国家图书馆，巴黎：20.B.4、20.D.38、20.E.2、20.E.6印章（Gyselen 1993, pls. X, XIII, XIV）

---

[1] 此处为图像差异，使该组少了一个突出的特征标识。

图205 法国国家图书馆,巴黎:20.D.22、20.D.29 印章(Gyselen 1993, pls. XII, XIII)

图206 法国国家图书馆,巴黎:20.B.2、20.D.43 印章(Gyselen 1993, pls. X, XIII)

或仅刻出眉弓(图204A、B、C),或为两道平行弧线构成的眉弓与上眼睑(图204D、E)。鼻子亦特点鲜明,与上眼睑的端点相接,竖直轮廓线与略弯的水平轮廓线相交。五枚印章中嘴唇均以两道平行粗线表现,两腮胡须为竖直粗排线。

第十个技术—风格分组包括一枚玛瑙半椭球形印(图205A)和一枚原嵌于托座内的光玉髓印(图205B)。除图像选择的差异外,二者眉弓下方的眼球均略椭圆;鼻子轮廓线粗,顶端成球形;嘴唇肥厚;额前鬈发由平行椭球组成;耳环为低垂于颈部的圆珠,无耳线。

第十一个技术—风格分组包括一枚指形印(图206A)和一枚半椭球形印(图206B),均以碧玉制成。吉塞莲将其一归为类型系列2,即星形半身像(图206A),另一为类型系列3,即洛林十字半身像(图206B)。二者的相同特点为横椭圆的眼球位于粗线表示的眉弓与细线表示的下眼睑之间;鼻子轮廓线较粗;胡髭与厚嘴唇重叠;耳朵较简略,但耳环相异。

除上述明确的十一个技术—风格分组外,其余诸多印章亦体现出相似的风格元素,可考虑归入上述分组,但并非采用现有方法。故此处仅讨论上述明确具有一致性的分组,若以不严谨的标准分组,恐流于主观。

总而言之,在吉塞莲图录的153枚男性半身像印章中,仅26枚可确凿无疑地分为与各个生产中心相关的技术—风格分组,即全部印章中的17%,可见印章作坊之多。吉塞莲曾提出:"显然,多数印章并非出自同一工匠。"[1] 相较已知的萨珊印章总数,我所研究的样本极少,应以更多实例验证。但不能排除如下可能,即增加样本数量后,可辨认生产中心的印章比例也基本没有提高。还应注意的是,男性半身像仅是所有萨珊印章中数量较少的一类。

我的主要成果在于证实了一个重要观点,即存在多个生产中心。如吉塞莲等学者所言,横跨萨珊王朝及辽阔疆域的大规模生产,不同于嚈哒时代(4世纪中叶至5世纪中

---

[1] Gyselen 1989b, p. 154.

叶)巴克特里亚与印度西北部,由少数作坊负责制作几乎所有的印章。

在坚实的方法学基础上,我辨认出若干生产中心。隶属于同一作坊的印章图像类型或有差异,证明可通过跨图像分组的方法确定其共同来源。通过与钱币进行比照,其中两组的年代判定比前人更为准确。

上述结论虽然有限,但意义重大,因为新方法可作为前人重要成果的补充。

最后,还应检验新方法的结论是否符合里特尔对萨珊印章风格元素的社会意义的论述。如前所述,里特尔指出印章的不同技术—风格分组与其主人的社会地位间关联紧密,我大体认同,但该论点需要与半身像印章中各图像元素的社会意义进行比照。

铭文可表示不同的贵族等级,而拥有半身像印章本身就具有标记社会阶层的含义,并通过服饰元素、决定造价的技术—风格、印章材质与形状进一步明确区分。吉塞莲便曾提到光玉髓凸圆体印属于行省高官的典型私印[1]。里特尔指出,印章形象或由官方限定、规范化,并分配到不同的社会群体,雇主可从相应范围内挑选[2]。

以男性半身像印章为例,可基于图像固有元素、发型、有无冠帽、饰物等其他标识,重新划分图像分组[3],由此与社会等级密切相关。而在进一步的细分中,与刻制时长挂钩的价格彰显其分级作用,可证实里特尔所提出风格的社会意义。

不同于此前对风格特点的品质研究,基于上述方法的技术—风格研究,与将风格和雇主社会地位相联系的方法相辅相成,亦对萨珊印章生产中心的性质提出了重要的初步设想。时间所限,我未能研究更多的印章。从定量角度看,上述研究仅为小范围样本研究,故其成果需要更多例证检验。尽管存在客观局限,仍望得到造诣更深的方家的认可。

---

[1] Gyselen 1993, p. 44.
[2] Ritter 2010, p. 35.
[3] Gyselen 1989b, 1993.

附录1 萨珊世系

国王称号	在位时间	英文名字	国王称号	在位时间	英文名字
阿尔达希尔一世	224—239/40年	Ardashir Ⅰ	巴拉什	484—488年	Valakhsh
沙普尔一世	239/40—270/72年	Shapur Ⅰ	卡瓦德一世	488—496年	Kavadh Ⅰ
霍尔木兹一世	270/72—273年	Hormizd Ⅰ	扎马斯普	496—498年	Zamasp
巴赫拉姆一世	273—276年	Bahram Ⅰ	科巴德一世	499—531年	Kavadh Ⅰ
巴赫拉姆二世	276—293年	Bahram Ⅱ	库思老一世	531—579年	Khosrow Ⅰ Anoshirvan
巴赫拉姆三世	293年	Bahram Ⅲ	霍尔木兹四世	579—590年	Hormizd Ⅳ
纳塞赫	293—302年	Narseh	库思老二世	590—628年	Khosrow Ⅱ
霍尔木兹二世	302—309年	Hormizd Ⅱ	巴赫拉姆·楚宾	590—591年	Bahrām Ⅵ Chubin
沙普尔二世	309—379年	Shapur Ⅱ	卡瓦德二世	628年	Kavadh Ⅱ
阿尔达希尔二世	379—383年	Ardashir Ⅱ	阿尔达希尔三世	628—630年	Ardashir Ⅲ
沙普尔三世	383—388年	Shapur Ⅲ	沙赫尔巴拉兹	630年	Shahrbaraz
巴赫拉姆四世	388—399年	Bahram Ⅳ	库思老三世	630年	Khosrow Ⅲ
耶兹德卡尔德一世	399—421年	Yazdegerd Ⅰ	孛兰	630—631年	Puran
巴赫拉姆五世	421—439年	Bahram V Gor	阿扎米杜赫特	631—632年	Azarmigdukht
耶兹德卡尔德二世	439—457年	Yazdegerd Ⅱ	霍尔木兹五世	631—632年	Hormizd V
霍尔木兹三世	457—459年	Hormizd Ⅲ	库思老四世	631—633年	Khosrow Ⅳ
卑路斯一世	459—484年	Peroz	伊嗣俟三世	633—651年	Yazdegerd Ⅲ

附录2 人名对照表

中　　文	其他语言	中　　文	其他语言
阿尔朗	Alram	菲利真齐	Filigenzi
阿马多里	Amadori	冯·加尔	von Gall
阿米耶	Amiet	弗兰克	Franke
阿斯卡里·查韦尔迪	Askari Chaverdi	富特旺格勒	Furtwaengler
阿扎尔诺什	Azarnoush	戈达尔	Godard
阿扎尔佩	Azarpay	格布尔	Göbl
埃德曼	Erdmann	格勒内	Grenet
奥弗莱特	Overlaet	格罗普	Gropp
巴塞洛	Basello	贡代	Gondet
拜伦	Byron	古利尼	Gullini
贝尔	Bell	哈珀	Harper
比尔	Bier	哈伊斯	Huyse
比瓦尔	Bivar	汉扎克	Khanzaq
波茨	Potts	赫茨菲尔德	Herzfeld
博伊斯	Boyce	赫尔曼	Herrmann
布里昂	Briant	胡夫	Huff
布里兰特	Brilliant	惠特科姆	Whitcomb
布伦纳	Brunner	霍夫曼	Hoffmann
布沙拉	Boucharlat	基奥	Keall
川见	Kawami	吉尔什曼	Ghirshman
达尔亚埃	Daryaee	吉钮	Gignoux
德芒热	Demange	吉塞莲	Gyselen
德瓦勒	De Waele	加尼马提	Ghanimati
法琴纳	Faccenna	居里埃尔	Curiel

续 表

中　文	其他语言	中　文	其他语言
卡尔梅耶	Calmeyer	尼基金	Nikitin
卡内帕	Canepa	普沙利亚提	Pourshariati
凯姆	Kaim	萨姆韦良	Samvelian
科斯瓦尼	Khosravi	赛里格	Seyrig
克莱斯	Kleiss	沙赫巴齐	Shahbazi
克勒格尔	Kröger	申德尔	Schindel
克雷耶布鲁克	Kreyenbroek	申卡尔	Shenkar
克瑙特	Knaut	施伦贝格尔	Schlumberger
孔帕雷蒂	Compareti	施密特	Schmidt
拉蒂菲·亚尔夏特	Latifeh Yarshater	施舍法尔	Shishefar
拉赫巴尔	Rahbar	施泰因米勒	Steinmüller
拉扎尔	Lazard	索埃	Sauer
勒里什	Leriche	索达瓦尔	Soudavar
雷兹瓦尼	Rezvani	塔巴索	Tabasso
里克特	Richter	塔代伊	Taddei
里特尔	Ritter	汤普森	Thompson
卢科宁	Lukonin	特林佩尔曼	Trümpelmann
卢沙伊	Luschey	瓦特林	Watelin
鲁瑟	Reuther	旺当·贝格	Vanden Berghe
鲁索	Russo	西尼西	Sinisi
罗特	Roth	希伦布兰德	Hillenbrand
罗慕齐	Lo Muzio	席普曼	Schippmann
迈尔	Meyer	肖尔沃	Skjærvø
麦金托什	Mackintosh	谢克德	Shaked
麦克德莫特	MacDermot	欣茨	Hinz
麦肯齐	MacKenzie	亚厄迈	Yaghma'i
梅乌奇	Meucci	亚兹丹尼	Yazdani
莫内雷·德·维拉尔	Monneret de Villard	伊赫桑·亚尔夏特	Ehsan Yarshater
莫瓦萨特	Movassat	朱埃尔	Juhel
穆雷	Moorey		

附录3 地名对照表

中　　文	其他语言	中　　文	其他语言
阿尔达希尔—花拉	Ardashir-Xwarrah	博兹帕尔	Bozpar
阿尔甘	Argan	布什尔	Bushehr
阿霍尔·鲁斯塔姆	Akhor-e Rostam	布斯坦·库思老	Bustan-e Xosrow
阿克沙珊—卡拉	Akshaxan-Kala	查拉·塔尔汉	Chal Tarxan
阿塞拜疆	Azerbaïjan	查拉·塔尔汉—埃什加巴德	Chal Tarxan-Eshqabad
阿依哈努姆	Aï Khanoum	达拉卜	Darab
埃兰	Elymaïde	达拉卜·盖尔达	Dârâbgerd
安底诺伊	Antinoe	达勒姆	Durham
安条克	Antioch	达雷加兹	Daregaz
奥鲁米耶湖	lac de Orumiyeh	达姆甘	Damghan
巴比伦	Babylone	达斯特盖尔德	Dastagerd
巴尔姆·德拉克	Barm-e Delak	德赫卡伊德	Dehqayed
巴伐利亚	Baviere	蒂尔巴尔	Tirbal
巴克特里亚	Bactriane	杜拉欧罗普斯	Doura Europos
白宫	Palais Blanc	法尔斯	Fars
拜古里	Paikuli	菲鲁扎巴德	Firuzabad
班迪扬	Bandiyan	戈尔·萨依迪	Gow Sa'idi
贝赫贝汗	Behbehan	古尔比扬	Ghulbiyan
贝萨	Bayza	古雷·杜赫塔尔	Gur-e Doxtar
比沙普尔	Bishapur	贵霜	Kouchan
比索通	Bisotun	哈吉阿巴德	Hajjiabad
波斯波利斯	Persépolis	哈拉雷兹	Xwarezm
博拉兹詹	Borazjan	哈姆林	Hamrin

225

续表

中文	其他语言	中文	其他语言
豪什·库里	Hawsh Quri	洛雷斯坦	Lorestan
胡齐斯坦	Xuzestan	麦尔·麦拉吉	Mile Milege
霍密兹达干	Hormizdagan	美索不达米亚平原	plaine mesopotamienne
吉尔·卡尔珊	Qir-Karzin	米底	Médie
犍陀罗	Gandhara	米尔盖里	Mirquli
喀斯尔·阿卜纳斯尔	Qasr-e Abu Nasr	米勒·哈拉姆	Mele Hairam
喀斯尔·阿卢索斯	qasr al-lusus	莫赫	Mohr
喀斯尔·席林	Qasr-e Shirin	木鹿	Merv
卡巴耶·扎尔达什特	Ka'be-ye Zardosht	穆罕默达巴德	Mohammadabad
卡尔萨伊万	Ivan-e Karxa	纳克什·拉卜	Naqsh-e Rajab
卡菲里·卡拉	Kafir Kala	纳克什·鲁斯塔姆	Naqsh-e Rostam
卡拉·杜赫塔尔	Qal'e-ye Doxtar	纳斯拉克	Naxlak
卡拉·瑙	Qal'e-ye Now	尼萨古城	Nisa
卡拉·沙内辛	Qal'e-ye Shah Neshin	帕朗盖尔德	Palang Gard
卡拉·亚兹德格德	Qal'e-ye Yezdegerd	帕萨尔加德	Pasargades
卡拉·扎哈克	Qal'e-ye Zahak	佩肯特	Paykend
卡拉斯拉亚·波利亚纳	Krasnaja Poljana	启什	Kish
卡尚	Kashan	切赫拉巴德	Chehrabad
卡扬西	Kayānsīh	萨尔·波勒·扎哈卜	Sar-e Pol-e Zohab
坎加瓦尔	Kangavar	萨尔·马沙德	Sar Mashhad
克尔曼沙赫	Kermanshah	萨尔韦斯坦	Sarvestan
克什克·阿尔达希尔	Koshek-e Ardashir	萨夫耶	Xafruyeh
库尔德斯坦	Kurdistan	萨拉卜·巴赫拉姆	Sarab-e Bahram
库赫·哈加	Kuh-e Xwaja	萨拉卜·穆尔特	Sarab-e Murt
拉格·比比	Rag-e Bibi	萨勒马斯	Salmas
拉伊—瓦拉明	Ray-Varamin	萨迈拉	Samarra
拉扎维呼罗珊	Xorasan-e Razavi	塞姆南	Semnan
雷伊	Ray	沙格阿卜	Shaghab

续　表

中　文	其他语言	中　文	其他语言
圣克莱门特密特拉神殿	Mithræum de Saint-Clement	托尔让塔卜	Tureng Tepe
苏德堡（阿迪拜）	Südbau（aD-Dba'i）	托勒·坎达克	Tol-e Xandaq
苏萨	Susiane	托勒·沙希迪	Toll-e Shahidi
塔克·波斯坦	Taq-e Bostan	韦—阿尔达希尔	Weh-Ardashir
塔克·格拉	Taq-e Gerra	韦—安条克—库思老	Weh-Andiyok-Xusraw
塔克·基斯拉	Taq Kisra	维什纳维	Veshnaveh
塔克·伊万	Tâq-e Eivân	乌海迪尔	Ukhaydir
塔克斯特·内辛	Taxt-e Neshin	乌拉卡萨湖	Vouru.kaša
塔克斯特·苏莱曼	Taxt-e Solayman	西吉兰	Gilan-e Gharb
泰佩·米勒	Tepe Mil	西伊斯兰阿巴德	Eslamabad-e Gharb
泰西封	Ctesiphon	希扬	Shiyan
坦格·阿卜	Tang-e Ab	锡斯坦	Siéstan
坦格·博拉吉	Tang-e Bolaghi	亚美尼亚	Armenie
坦格·甘迪勒	Tang-e Qandil	亚述	Assur
坦格·萨尔瓦克	Tang-e Sarvak	亚兹德	Yazd
特拉卜·沙夫	Tell Abu Sh'af	伊朗高原	plateau iranien
特拉达拜	Tell ad-Dba'i	伊朗沙赫尔	Eranshahr
特拉达哈卜	Tell Dahab	伊马拉特·库思老	Emarat-e Xosrow
特拉德巴伊	Tell ad-Dba'i	伊斯塔尔	Estaxr
土库曼斯坦	Turkménistan	赞詹	Zanjan

附录4 术语词汇

中　　文	其他语言	释　　义
阿达兰	Âdarân/ātaxsh	博伊斯提出古代及现代琐罗亚斯德教徒的二级圣火
阿杜里安	adurian	用于保存圣火的穹隆顶室；格罗普所言帕西人的三类火神庙之一
阿杜鲁格圣火	âdurog	博伊斯提出的三级圣火，即最低等级的私人圣火
阿格力	agyari	格罗普所言帕西人的三类火神庙之一
阿帕达那	Apadāna	古波斯语中表示谒见厅
阿斯班巴	Aspanbar	行政城市，泰西封南部
阿泰什伽/阿泰什卡代	Āteshgâh/âteshkade	戈达尔与埃德曼提出的火神庙封闭区域
阿泰什圣火	Ātakhsh, Âdarân	博伊斯提出古代及现代琐罗亚斯德教徒的二级圣火
阿维斯陀	avestique	阿维斯陀语属于伊朗语支的东伊朗语；《阿维斯陀》为琐罗亚斯德教经典
埃贝德斯坦	erbedestān	琐罗亚斯德教神学院
埃马扎代	emâmzâdeh	伊斯兰教什叶派圣人的陵墓，为信仰和朝圣的中心，被视作具有神奇的特性和治愈的能力
奥斯托丹	ostodân, ossuaire	纳骨器，陶质或石质容器或是岩洞中存放人骨的地方
巴尔萨姆枝	barsom	琐罗亚斯德教祭司用于举行神圣仪式的礼器
巴赫兰圣火	Ātakhsh Warahrān/âtash Bahrâm	博伊斯提出古代及现代琐罗亚斯德教徒的一级圣火
巴雷什纳姆伽	bareshnum-gâh	用于净化最严重的污染的地方
白宫（阿）	al-qasr al-abyad	白宫，位于老城中
布尔赞米赫圣火	Âdur Burzen Mihr	萨珊琐罗亚斯德教农民的圣火

续 表

中　　文	其他语言	释　　义
草泥	*kâhgel*	伊朗古代传统砂浆之一，由大量粘土掺杂干泥和稻草混合而成
查哈尔—卡卜	*chahâr qâpu, čahārqāpū*	"四扇门"，四面敞开的方形大厅
查哈尔—塔克	*chahâr tâq*	"四道拱"，四角筑有柱子，以拱券相连，顶端为突角拱的方形穹隆顶大厅
达尔·梅赫	*dar-e mehr*	等级较低的火神庙；格罗普所言帕西人的三类火神庙之一，亦为举办亚兹辛仪式的场所
达德伽圣火	*dâdgâh*	博伊斯提出现代琐罗亚斯德教徒的私人第三等级圣火
达斯特盖尔德	*dastgird*	贵族家庭地产
迪万·阿姆	*divân-e 'âmm*	住宅中的公开接见处
迪万·卡斯	*divân-e 'xâss*	住宅中的私下接见处
蒂尔	Tir, Tishtrya	琐罗亚斯德教中掌管带来生命的降雨和生育之神
法恩巴格圣火	*Âdur Farnbâgh*	萨珊琐罗亚斯德教祭司的圣火
非伊朗	*anērān*	中古波斯语的民族语言学术语，一般用于贬义，指伊朗和拜火教的政治和宗教敌人
弗拉塔拉卡	*fratarakā*	总督，古波斯头衔
贡巴德	*gonbâd*	穹隆顶
古什纳普圣火	*Âdur Gushnasp*	萨珊琐罗亚斯德教国王及贵族的圣火
国祚	*farn*	王朝的气运
祭司	mage (*magush, mog*)	古巴比伦及波斯帝国中的琐罗亚斯德教祭司及占星师，亦称麻葛或穆护
寂静塔	dakhma	遵循琐罗亚斯德教习俗的丧葬建筑
克尔曼沙赫	*Kermānshāh*	萨珊时期的头衔，译为"克尔曼王"；沙普尔三世之子巴赫拉姆王子在任吉尔曼省总督后被授予该头衔
克罗比罗斯	*korymbos*	萨珊国王王冠上突出的球状元素，将头顶上的一撮头发聚拢并包裹在布中而成
刻划	Kerbschnittechnik	克勒格尔提出的灰泥技艺之一
库拉赫	*kolāh*	伊朗贵族的传统头饰
拉斯比	*raspi*	琐罗亚斯德教中的助理祭司

续　表

中　　文	其他语言	释　　义
老城（阿）	*al-madina al-'atiqa*	老城，萨珊时期泰西封的一个区域
灵光	*xwarrah*	国王的吉祥、荣耀、好运
马尔兹班	*marzbân*	负责帕提亚和萨珊帝国边境省份的军事指挥官
麦达恩（阿）	Mada'en	泰西封都城的阿拉伯语名称（麦地那的复数形式）
麦地那（阿）	Madina	城市
米赫拉甘	Mihragan	大型秋猎
密特拉	Mithra, Mihr	伊朗掌管契约、光明、誓言、正义和太阳之神
密特拉神洞	*mithraeum*	天然洞穴或大地洞所改建的，或是模仿山洞的密特拉教神庙
模制	Guβtechnik	克勒格尔提出的灰泥技艺之一
南部建筑	Südbau	泰西封的南部建筑
诺鲁孜	Nowruz	大型春猎
萨伽沙	*Sakānshāh*	伊朗东部萨卡斯坦省统治者的头衔
沙赫	*shāhānshāh*	波斯语古代君主头衔的汉译名
陶片	Ostrakon (plural òstraka)	上有文字的陶器碎片
特沃拉克	*'twrlwk*	阿杜鲁格圣火，博伊斯提出的三级私人圣火
贴塑	Antragtechnik	克勒格尔提出的灰泥技艺之一
王子	*Kushānshāh*	贵霜—萨珊王国统治者的称号，该王国为前贵霜帝国在索格迪亚纳、巴克特里亚和犍陀罗地区的领土，名为贵霜沙赫，在公元3—4世纪期间被萨珊帝国占领
线刻（俄）	*štrixovaja rez'ba*	通过线刻塑造形象的技艺
亚斯纳	yasna	琐罗亚斯德教主要的礼拜仪式，仪式上需要朗诵《阿维斯陀》里的《亚斯纳》文本（"献祭"或"崇拜"）
亚兹辛—伽	*yazishn-gâh*	举行亚兹辛仪式的房间
伊万	*ivân*	长方形的大厅或空间，通常为券顶，三面有墙，一面完全敞开
园林	*paràdeisos*	源自古波斯语的希腊语术语，指代波斯皇帝的花园，一个种满树木、可以饲养动物的美好场所
佐特	*zot*	琐罗亚斯德教中的主礼祭司

插图索引

图1　库思老二世时期的萨珊帝国疆域图（图片来源于网络）·················· 4
图2　伊朗萨珊时期的行政分布图（A. Eghra绘图）·························· 6
图3　萨珊时期伊朗主要遗址分布图（A. Eghra绘图）························ 7
图4　坎儿井功能示意图（感谢俄克拉何马州立大学的Dale Lightfoot教授提供）······ 8
图5　舒什塔尔水坝桥（A. Eghra供图）···································· 8
图6　德尔本特：城市防御工事南部（感谢UNESCO提供）···················· 9
图7　菲鲁扎巴德：阿尔达希尔—花拉圆形城市鸟瞰图（A. Eghra供图）········· 10
图8　菲鲁扎巴德：阿尔达希尔—花拉圆形城市平面图（A. Eghra绘图）········ 11
图9　菲鲁扎巴德：阿尔达希尔—花拉中塔克斯特·内辛（前景）及蒂尔巴尔塔鸟
　　　瞰图（A. Eghra供图）·· 12
图10　达拉卜·盖尔达平面图（A. Eghra绘图）····························· 12
图11　比沙普尔城及其周边鸟瞰图（SALF供图）···························· 13
图12　比沙普尔城平面图（SALF绘图）···································· 14
图13　比沙普尔中心纪念堂（@ Callieri）································· 15
图14　伊万·卡尔卡老城（感谢ITTO提供）································ 15
图15　伊斯塔尔城鸟瞰图（A. Eghra供图）································· 16
图16　伊斯塔尔城平面图（A. Eghra绘图）································· 16
图17　菲鲁扎巴德：卡拉·杜赫塔尔堡鸟瞰图（A. Eghra供图）··············· 17
图18　菲鲁扎巴德：卡拉·杜赫塔尔堡平面图（A. Eghra在D. Huff的基础上绘制，
　　　感谢德黑兰德国考古研究院提供）································· 18
图19　菲鲁扎巴德：阿尔达希尔一世宫殿鸟瞰图（A. Eghra供图）············· 19
图20　菲鲁扎巴德：阿尔达希尔一世宫殿中央正方形大殿（@ Callieri）········ 19
图21　菲鲁扎巴德：阿尔达希尔一世宫殿上层，穹隆顶之间空隙处的房间
　　　（@ Callieri）·· 20
图22　菲鲁扎巴德：阿尔达希尔一世宫殿，阿契美尼德灰泥假额枋，上有埃及凹弧
　　　饰（@ Callieri）··· 20

231

图23　比沙普尔：卡拉·杜赫塔尔（@ Callieri） 21
图24　塔克·基斯拉（感谢UNESCO提供） 21
图25　塔克斯特·苏莱曼西伊万（@ Callieri） 22
图26　塔克斯特·苏莱曼西伊万平面图（A. Eghra在W. Kleiss的基础上绘制，感谢德黑兰德国考古研究院提供） 22
图27　萨尔韦斯坦鸟瞰图（A. Eghra供图） 23
图28　萨尔韦斯坦建筑平面图（L. Bier 1986: fig. 5） 24
图29　萨尔韦斯坦10号房间方柱所支撑的穹隆顶（@ Callieri） 25
图30　哈吉阿巴德：L.178庭院（Azarnoush 1994, fig. 1） 26
图31　塔克·波斯坦大伊万（A. Eghra供图） 26
图32　塔克·格拉（A. Eghra供图） 27
图33　塔克·格拉：平面图（G. Tilia绘图） 28
图34　比沙普尔：火神庙平面图（A. Eghra在D. Huff的基础上绘制，感谢德黑兰德国考古研究院提供） 30
图35　比沙普尔：火神庙2号大殿（@ Callieri） 30
图36　比沙普尔：火神庙3号房间（@ Callieri） 31
图37　比沙普尔：火神庙5号半地下式建筑（@ Callieri） 31
图38　比沙普尔："瓦勒良宫殿"（@ Callieri） 32
图39　比沙普尔博物馆："瓦勒良宫殿"的雕刻人像中楣（A. Eghra供图） 32
图40　塔克斯特·苏莱曼：遗址鸟瞰图（A. Eghra供图） 33
图41　塔克斯特·苏莱曼：查哈尔·塔克（PD）所在火神庙平面图（A. Eghra在Naumann 1977，图37的基础上绘制） 34
图42　库赫·哈加主要建筑群（A.M. Naderi Bani供图） 35
图43　比沙普尔：穆旦洞穴（@ Callieri） 36
图44　纳克什·鲁斯塔姆：东南方视角（@ Callieri） 36
图45　比索通：塔拉什·法尔哈德（@ Callieri） 37
图46　阿霍尔·鲁斯塔姆（法尔斯中部）：岩壁凹处墓穴（@ Callieri） 38
图47　纳克什·鲁斯塔姆：祭火坛形状的纳骨器（@ Callieri） 38
图48　哈吉阿巴德绘画遗存（A. Eghra供图，依据Azarnoush 1994, pl. XXXII） 39
图49　菲鲁扎巴德：阿尔达希尔—花拉中心区域出土的绘画场景（@ Callieri） 39
图50　木鹿（马尔吉亚那）：绘有形象的纳骨罐（Koshelenko 1977） 40
图51　比沙普尔：2号大殿查哈尔·塔克灰泥装饰细节（依据Kröger 1981, pl.90, 4绘制） 41

插图索引

图52 比沙普尔：2号大殿查哈尔·塔克灰泥装饰的复原，现藏于巴黎卢浮宫博物馆（图片来源于Wikimedia Commons） 42

图53 哈吉阿巴德庄园：L.114房间就地保存的灰泥装饰（Azarnoush 1994, Pl.XXVII Unit 114） 42

图54 班迪扬：建造固定住所后的A遗址全景图（@ Callieri） 43

图55 比沙普尔"马赛克庭院"：壁龛中的两幅马赛克画面（Ghirshman 1956） 45

图56 比沙普尔"马赛克庭院"：沿墙分布的两幅马赛克装饰带（Ghirshman 1956） 46

图57 穆旦洞穴：沙普尔一世雕像（@ Callieri） 47

图58 萨珊时期伊朗摩崖浮雕分布图（A. Eghra绘图） 48

图59 菲鲁扎巴德，菲鲁扎巴德Ⅱ号浮雕：阿尔达希尔一世站姿王权神授图（@ Callieri） 49

图60 纳克什·鲁斯塔姆，纳克什·鲁斯塔姆Ⅰ号浮雕：阿尔达希尔一世马背王权神授图（@ Callieri） 50

图61 比沙普尔，比沙普尔Ⅰ号浮雕：沙普尔一世马背王权神授图，及战胜戈尔迪安三世、阿拉伯人菲利普两位罗马皇帝的克敌制胜图（@ Callieri） 51

图62 比沙普尔，比沙普尔Ⅴ号浮雕：巴赫拉姆一世马背王权神授图，后被纳赛赫重新使用，并在右下方补刻其中古波斯语姓名铭文及其敌人瓦赫拉姆，还可能用石膏改造了王冠（@ Callieri） 51

图63 纳克什·鲁斯塔姆，纳克什·鲁斯塔姆Ⅷ号浮雕：或为阿纳希塔向纳赛赫的王权神授图，或表现波斯败于俘虏纳赛赫妻子的伽列里乌斯皇帝后的王室（@ Callieri） 52

图64 塔克·波斯坦，塔克·波斯坦Ⅰ号浮雕：表现国王从沙普尔二世或阿胡拉·马兹达手中接过胜利圆环，密特拉神为见证者（@ Callieri） 52

图65 塔克·波斯坦，塔克·波斯坦Ⅱ号浮雕：通过中古波斯语铭文辨认，其上人物为沙普尔二世与沙普尔三世（A. Eghra供图） 53

图66 塔克·波斯坦，塔克·波斯坦Ⅲ号浮雕：位于伊万的正壁上部，或为阿胡拉·马兹达（画面左侧）及阿纳希塔（右侧）对库思老二世的王权神授图（@ Callieri） 54

图67 菲鲁扎巴德，菲鲁扎巴德Ⅰ号浮雕，阿尔达希尔一世战胜安息国王阿尔达班四世：阿尔达希尔将阿尔达班从马上摔下（A. Eghra供图） 55

图68 菲鲁扎巴德，菲鲁扎巴德Ⅰ号浮雕，阿尔达希尔一世战胜安息国王阿尔达班四世：沙普尔将阿尔达班之子从马上摔下（A. Eghra供图） 55

233

图69　比沙普尔,比沙普尔Ⅵ号浮雕:右下方为向国王呈上首级的场景(@ Callieri) 56

图70　达拉卜·盖尔达:俯瞰池塘的摩崖浮雕(@ Callieri) 57

图71　纳克什·鲁斯塔姆,纳克什·鲁斯塔姆Ⅵ号浮雕:沙普尔一世战胜两位罗马皇帝(@ Callieri) 58

图72　比沙普尔,比沙普尔Ⅱ号浮雕:沙普尔一世战胜三位罗马皇帝(@ Callieri) 58

图73　比沙普尔,比沙普尔Ⅲ号浮雕:沙普尔一世及其马队战胜三位罗马皇帝及其军队(@ Callieri) 59

图74　亚述,帕提亚宫殿:总平面图(Schlumberger 1970, fig. 39) 73

图75　卡拉·扎哈克:方形大殿平面图(Qandgar et al. 2004, p.228) 74

图76　菲鲁扎巴德,平原宫殿:平面图(A. Eghra画图) 76

图77　菲鲁扎巴德,卡拉·杜赫塔尔:B庭院(@ Callieri) 77

图78　菲鲁扎巴德,卡拉·杜赫塔尔:方形大殿,突角拱细节(@ Callieri) 77

图79　菲鲁扎巴德,卡拉·杜赫塔尔:通向上层的楼梯(@ Callieri) 78

图80　菲鲁扎巴德,"阿泰什卡代":前侧伊万现有铺地下的探测(@ Callieri) 78

图81　菲鲁扎巴德,"阿泰什卡代":圆形水池(@ Callieri) 79

图82　菲鲁扎巴德,"阿泰什卡代":前侧伊万正壁检阅台(@ Callieri) 79

图83　比沙普尔,B房址:全景(@ Callieri) 81

图84　比沙普尔,卡拉·杜赫塔尔:全景(@ Callieri) 81

图85　比沙普尔,卡拉·杜赫塔尔:东南方防御工事(@ Callieri) 82

图86　哈吉阿巴德,"地主庄园":总平面图(Azarnoush 1994, pl. A) 83

图87　哈吉阿巴德,"地主庄园":L.178庭院(Azarnoush 1994, pl. 1) 84

图88　启什(伊拉克),Ⅰ、Ⅱ号房址:平面图(Kröger 1982, fig. 119) 86

图89　班迪扬,C土丘:方柱大殿平面图(Rahbar 2007a, fig. 2) 87

图90　麦达恩(伊拉克),塔克·基斯拉:总平面图(Fahimi 2012, fig. 7a) 89

图91　塔克斯特·苏莱曼西伊万平面图(A. Eghra在W. Kleiss的基础上绘制,感谢德黑兰德国考古研究院提供) 90

图92　塔克斯特·苏莱曼,西伊万:伊万旁的长方形房间(@ Callieri) 91

图93　坎加瓦尔,大型建筑群:下层平台南侧台阶(@ Callieri) 92

图94　坎加瓦尔,大型建筑群:下层平台西侧边缘的柱廊(@ Callieri) 93

图95　达姆甘:房址平面图(Kröger 1982, fig. 124) 94

图96　查拉·塔尔汉:"主殿"平面图(Kröger 1982, fig. 130) 95

图97　伊马拉特·库思老,喀斯尔·席林:早期区域平面图(Moradi, fig. 7, p. 340) 96

插图索引

图98　博兹帕尔，"克什克·阿尔达希尔"：全景（@ Callieri）⋯⋯⋯⋯⋯⋯⋯⋯⋯⋯⋯⋯98

图99　博兹帕尔，"克什克·阿尔达希尔"：方形房间，顶部为突角拱支撑的穹隆顶（@ Callieri）⋯⋯⋯⋯⋯⋯⋯⋯⋯⋯⋯⋯⋯⋯⋯⋯⋯⋯⋯⋯⋯⋯⋯⋯⋯⋯⋯⋯⋯⋯⋯98

图100　塔克·波斯坦：全景（G. P. Basello供图）⋯⋯⋯⋯⋯⋯⋯⋯⋯⋯⋯⋯⋯⋯⋯⋯102

图101　菲鲁扎巴德，"阿泰什卡代"：二层房间（@ Callieri）⋯⋯⋯⋯⋯⋯⋯⋯⋯⋯⋯105

图102　菲鲁扎巴德，"阿泰什卡代"：三层房间（@ Callieri）⋯⋯⋯⋯⋯⋯⋯⋯⋯⋯⋯105

图103　菲鲁扎巴德，"阿泰什卡代"：通往上层的入口楼梯（@ Callieri）⋯⋯⋯⋯⋯105

图104　萨夫耶：遗址全貌（A. Eghra供图）⋯⋯⋯⋯⋯⋯⋯⋯⋯⋯⋯⋯⋯⋯⋯⋯⋯108

图105　萨夫耶：遗址全貌（@ Callieri）⋯⋯⋯⋯⋯⋯⋯⋯⋯⋯⋯⋯⋯⋯⋯⋯⋯⋯⋯108

图106　萨夫耶：查哈尔·塔克（@ Callieri）⋯⋯⋯⋯⋯⋯⋯⋯⋯⋯⋯⋯⋯⋯⋯⋯⋯109

图107　萨夫耶：其中一个水池（@ Callieri）⋯⋯⋯⋯⋯⋯⋯⋯⋯⋯⋯⋯⋯⋯⋯⋯⋯109

图108　塔克斯特·苏莱曼，火神庙：平面图（Naumann 1977, fig. 24）⋯⋯⋯⋯⋯⋯114

图109　法尔恩—萨珊铜币（Alram 2007, fig. 13）⋯⋯⋯⋯⋯⋯⋯⋯⋯⋯⋯⋯⋯⋯115

图110　库赫·哈加，火神庙：查哈尔·塔克外壁的黏土中楣（Kröger 1982, pl. 7.1）⋯⋯⋯⋯⋯⋯⋯⋯⋯⋯⋯⋯⋯⋯⋯⋯⋯⋯⋯⋯⋯⋯⋯⋯⋯⋯⋯⋯⋯⋯⋯⋯⋯⋯⋯⋯116

图111　库赫·哈加，火神庙：壁画残片（Faccenna 1981）⋯⋯⋯⋯⋯⋯⋯⋯⋯⋯⋯117

图112　库赫·哈加，火神庙建筑群：建造末期总平面图（Mousavi 1999, fig. p.83）⋯⋯⋯⋯⋯⋯⋯⋯⋯⋯⋯⋯⋯⋯⋯⋯⋯⋯⋯⋯⋯⋯⋯⋯⋯⋯⋯⋯⋯⋯⋯⋯⋯⋯⋯⋯118

图113　阿尔达希尔—花拉（菲鲁扎巴德），塔克斯特·内辛平面图⋯⋯⋯⋯⋯⋯120

图114　阿尔达希尔—花拉（菲鲁扎巴德），塔克斯特·内辛：查哈尔·塔克东南立面（D.M. Meucci供图）⋯⋯⋯⋯⋯⋯⋯⋯⋯⋯⋯⋯⋯⋯⋯⋯⋯⋯⋯⋯⋯⋯⋯⋯⋯121

图115　比沙普尔，A房址：西北墙，内景（A. Yazdani供图）⋯⋯⋯⋯⋯⋯⋯⋯⋯121

图116　比沙普尔，C房址（"马赛克庭院"）：西北方全景（@ Callieri）⋯⋯⋯⋯⋯122

图117　比沙普尔，"瓦勒良宫殿"：方石墙（D.M. Meucci供图）⋯⋯⋯⋯⋯⋯⋯⋯122

图118　米勒·哈拉姆，火神殿：总平面图（Kaim 2013, fig. 4）⋯⋯⋯⋯⋯⋯⋯⋯124

图119　希扬，火神殿：查哈尔·塔克内部房间（Rezvani 2005）⋯⋯⋯⋯⋯⋯⋯⋯125

图120　德赫卡伊德，火神殿：东北方全景（@ Callieri）⋯⋯⋯⋯⋯⋯⋯⋯⋯⋯⋯126

图121　博拉兹詹，堡垒：托勒·沙希迪火坛（Askari Chaverdi 2011, fig. 21）⋯⋯127

图122　班迪扬，A土丘建筑群：祭火坛（Rahbar 2004, fig. 4）⋯⋯⋯⋯⋯⋯⋯⋯127

图123　班迪扬，A土丘建筑群：总平面图（Rahbar 2004, fig. 1）⋯⋯⋯⋯⋯⋯⋯128

图124　比沙普尔，C房址：X壁板（R. Ghirshman, *Bichâpour. II. Les mosaïques sassanides*, Paris 1956, pl.V.1）⋯⋯⋯⋯⋯⋯⋯⋯⋯⋯⋯⋯⋯⋯⋯⋯⋯⋯⋯⋯⋯⋯⋯131

图125　穆罕默达巴德：纪念性建筑群（Yaghmaee 2008, fig. 2）⋯⋯⋯⋯⋯⋯⋯⋯133

图126　穆罕默达巴德：纪念性建筑群（Yaghmaee 2008, fig. 3）⋯⋯⋯⋯⋯⋯⋯⋯⋯ 133

图127　戈尔·萨依迪：纪念性建筑群（Yaghmaee 2008, fig. 7）⋯⋯⋯⋯⋯⋯⋯⋯⋯ 134

图128　哈吉阿巴德：L.149伊万立面的半柱柱顶半身像（Azarnoush 1994, fig. 143）
⋯⋯⋯⋯⋯⋯⋯⋯⋯⋯⋯⋯⋯⋯⋯⋯⋯⋯⋯⋯⋯⋯⋯⋯⋯⋯⋯⋯⋯⋯⋯⋯⋯⋯ 138

图129　哈吉阿巴德：L.114房间壁龛中的女性雕像（Azarnoush 1994, fig. 145）⋯⋯⋯ 139

图130　哈吉阿巴德：20号半身像，沙普尔二世像（Azarnoush 1994, fig. 89）⋯⋯⋯ 139

图131　哈吉阿巴德：17号半身像，沙普尔二世像（Azarnoush 1994, fig. 80）⋯⋯⋯ 139

图132　塔克·波斯坦：主伊万右壁的塔克·波斯坦Ⅵ号低浮雕（@ Callieri）⋯⋯⋯ 141

图133　塔克·波斯坦：主伊万左壁的塔克·波斯坦Ⅴ号低浮雕（@ Callieri）⋯⋯⋯ 141

图134　哈吉阿巴德：L.114房间装饰复原示意图（Azarnoush 1994, fig. 155）。数字
　　　　由上至下依次代表：40=持葡萄串的小天使；20、23、24、25=中型男性半身
　　　　像；4=三角装饰构件；39=小型裸体女性像；34—37=大型着衣女性像；7=
　　　　卍字及半圆饰边框；41=狮首；1—2=植物图案方形构件 ⋯⋯⋯⋯⋯⋯⋯⋯ 145

图135　启什（伊拉克）：国王半身像（Kröger 1982, pl.87.1）⋯⋯⋯⋯⋯⋯⋯⋯⋯ 146

图136　启什（伊拉克）：瓦特林提出的Ⅱ号房址庭院装饰复原图（Kröger 1982,
　　　　fig. 122）⋯⋯⋯⋯⋯⋯⋯⋯⋯⋯⋯⋯⋯⋯⋯⋯⋯⋯⋯⋯⋯⋯⋯⋯⋯⋯⋯⋯ 147

图137　班迪扬：大殿东南墙，狩猎图（Rahbar 1998, pls. Ⅲ—Ⅳ）⋯⋯⋯⋯⋯⋯⋯ 150

图138　班迪扬：大殿东南墙，胜敌图（Rahbar 1998, pl. Ⅴ）⋯⋯⋯⋯⋯⋯⋯⋯⋯ 152

图139　班迪扬：大殿西南墙（Rahbar 1998, pl. Ⅶ）⋯⋯⋯⋯⋯⋯⋯⋯⋯⋯⋯⋯⋯ 155

图140　班迪扬：大殿西北墙上壁龛，西南壁（Rahbar 1998, pl. Ⅷ）⋯⋯⋯⋯⋯⋯ 156

图141　班迪扬：大殿西北墙上壁龛，西北壁（Rahbar 1998, pl. Ⅸ）⋯⋯⋯⋯⋯⋯ 156

图142　班迪扬：大殿西北墙上壁龛，东北壁（Rahbar 1998, pl. Ⅹ）⋯⋯⋯⋯⋯⋯ 156

图143　班迪扬：大殿西北墙（Rahbar 1998, figs. 9—10）⋯⋯⋯⋯⋯⋯⋯⋯⋯⋯⋯ 157

图144　萨勒马斯：摩崖浮雕（Hinz 1969, pl.69）⋯⋯⋯⋯⋯⋯⋯⋯⋯⋯⋯⋯⋯⋯ 165

图145　菲鲁扎巴德：菲鲁扎巴德Ⅱ号浮雕（@ Callieri）⋯⋯⋯⋯⋯⋯⋯⋯⋯⋯⋯ 166

图146　菲鲁扎巴德：菲鲁扎巴德Ⅱ号浮雕示意图（而非准确测量的线图）⋯⋯⋯⋯ 166

图147　菲鲁扎巴德：菲鲁扎巴德Ⅰ号浮雕（@ Callieri）⋯⋯⋯⋯⋯⋯⋯⋯⋯⋯⋯ 167

图148　菲鲁扎巴德：菲鲁扎巴德Ⅰ号浮雕示意图 ⋯⋯⋯⋯⋯⋯⋯⋯⋯⋯⋯⋯⋯⋯ 169

图149　菲鲁扎巴德：菲鲁扎巴德Ⅰ号浮雕，第二场决斗细节（@ Callieri）⋯⋯⋯⋯ 170

图150　坦格·萨尔瓦克：Ⅲ号岩壁浮雕（Vanden Berghe/Schippmann 1985, pl. 47）
⋯⋯⋯⋯⋯⋯⋯⋯⋯⋯⋯⋯⋯⋯⋯⋯⋯⋯⋯⋯⋯⋯⋯⋯⋯⋯⋯⋯⋯⋯⋯⋯⋯⋯ 170

图151　纳克什·拉加卜：纳克什·拉加卜Ⅲ号浮雕（Hinz 1969, pl. 57）⋯⋯⋯⋯⋯ 171

图152　纳克什·拉加卜：遗址全貌（D.M. Meucci供图）⋯⋯⋯⋯⋯⋯⋯⋯⋯⋯⋯ 172

图153	纳克什·鲁斯塔姆：纳克什·鲁斯塔姆Ⅰ号浮雕（@ Callieri）	174
图154	纳克什·鲁斯塔姆：纳克什·鲁斯塔姆Ⅰ号浮雕示意图	174
图155	纳克什·拉加卜：纳克什·拉加卜Ⅰ号浮雕（@ Callieri）	176
图156	纳克什·鲁斯塔姆：纳克什·鲁斯塔姆Ⅵ号浮雕（@ Callieri）	177
图157	纳克什·鲁斯塔姆：纳克什·鲁斯塔姆Ⅵ号浮雕示意图	177
图158	比沙普尔：比沙普尔Ⅰ号浮雕，细节（@ Callieri）	179
图159	比沙普尔：比沙普尔Ⅱ号浮雕，中央场景（@ Callieri）	179
图160	比沙普尔：比沙普尔Ⅱ号浮雕示意图	180
图161	比沙普尔：比沙普尔Ⅱ号浮雕，右下格壁面细节（@ Callieri）	181
图162	比沙普尔：比沙普尔Ⅲ号浮雕，左下格细节（@ Callieri）	182
图163	比沙普尔：比沙普尔Ⅲ号浮雕，右下格细节（@ Callieri）	182
图164	拉格·比比（阿富汗）：摩崖浮雕（Grene等. 2007, pl. 6）	183
图165	比沙普尔：比沙普尔Ⅴ号浮雕（@ Callieri）	185
图166	比沙普尔：比沙普尔Ⅳ号浮雕（@ Callieri）	186
图167	萨拉卜·巴赫拉姆：摩崖浮雕（Hinz 1969, pl. 128）	187
图168	萨尔·马沙德：摩崖浮雕（Hinz 1969, pl. 134）	187
图169	巴尔姆·德拉克：摩崖浮雕，右侧场景（Hinz 1969, pl. 137）	188
图170	纳克什·鲁斯塔姆：纳克什·鲁斯塔姆Ⅱ号浮雕（D.M. Meucci供图）	188
图171	纳克什·鲁斯塔姆：纳克什·鲁斯塔姆Ⅳ号浮雕（@ Callieri）	189
图172	纳克什·鲁斯塔姆：纳克什·鲁斯塔姆Ⅷ号浮雕（Vanden Berghe 1983, pl. 32）	190
图173	比沙普尔：比沙普尔Ⅵ号浮雕，左侧（@ Callieri）	190
图174	比沙普尔：比沙普尔Ⅵ号浮雕，右下格细节（@ Callieri）	191
图175	塔克·波斯坦：塔克·波斯坦Ⅱ号浮雕（Fukai/Horiuchi 1972, pl. 66）	192
图176	塔克·波斯坦：塔克·波斯坦Ⅰ号浮雕（Vanden Berghe 1983, pl. 36）	193
图177	塔克·波斯坦：塔克·波斯坦Ⅰ号浮雕，中心人物细节（Fukai/Horiuchi 1972, pl. 84）	195
图178	塔克·波斯坦，主伊万：塔克·波斯坦Ⅲ号、Ⅳ号浮雕（Vanden Berghe 1983, pl. 37）	196
图179	塔克·波斯坦，主伊万：阿胡拉·马兹达，塔克·波斯坦Ⅲ号浮雕细节（@ Callieri）	197
图180	塔克·波斯坦，主伊万：阿娜希塔，塔克·波斯坦Ⅲ号浮雕细节（Fukai/Horiuchi 1972, pl. 24）	197

图181　塔克·波斯坦,主伊万:立面右侧壁柱(@ Callieri) 198
图182　塔克·波斯坦,主伊万:立面右侧有翼胜利女神(@ Callieri) 198
图183　塔克·波斯坦,主伊万:伊万正壁半柱柱头(Fukai/Horiuchi 1972, pl. 58) 199
图184　法国国家图书馆,巴黎:"哥达红锆石"(Gyselen 1993, pl. XVII, 20.J.1) 203
图185　大英博物馆,西亚文物部,伦敦:巴赫拉姆四世印章(Vanden Berghe, ed. 1993, n°140) 204
图186　"德文郡宝石",紫晶巴赫拉姆克尔曼沙赫像(Harper 1981, fig. 7) 204
图187　法国国家图书馆,巴黎:亚兹丹·弗里·沙布赫印章(Gyselen 1993, pl. IX, 20.A.1) 205
图188　艾尔美塔什博物馆,圣彼得堡:"万后之后"德纳格印章(Vanden Berghe, ed. 1993, n°131) 206
图189　万王之王卑路斯印章(Baratte 等 2012, p.15, fig. a) 206
图190　万王之王沙普尔二世印章(Gyselen 2007b, fig. Ab) 206
图191　大都会艺术博物馆,纽约:"自然主义"风格印章(Brunner 1978, n. 31, p. 54) 209
图192　大都会艺术博物馆,纽约:"模式化"风格印章(Brunner 1978, n. 34, p. 54) 209
图193　大都会艺术博物馆,纽约:"衰落"风格印章(Brunner 1978, n. 124, p. 57) 210
图194　大都会艺术博物馆,纽约:"轮廓"风格印章(Brunner 1978, n. 224, p. 58) 210
图195　大都会艺术博物馆,纽约:"刻划"风格印章(Brunner 1978, n. 148, p. 58) 210
图196　法国国家图书馆,巴黎:20.C.1、20.C.2印章(Gyselen 1993, pl. XI) 216
图197　法国国家图书馆,巴黎:20.B.35、20.B.36印章(Gyselen 1993, pl. XI) 216
图198　法国国家图书馆,巴黎:20.C.9、20.D.8、20.D.11印章(Gyselen 1993, pls. XI, XII) 217
图199　法国国家图书馆,巴黎:20.C.8、20.E.10印章(Gyselen 1993, pls. XI, XIV) 217
图200　法国国家图书馆,巴黎:20.D.4、20.H.5印章(Gyselen 1993, pls. XII, XV) 218
图201　法国国家图书馆,巴黎:20.D.5、20.D.10印章(Gyselen 1993, pl. XII) 218
图202　法国国家图书馆,巴黎:20.B.10、20.E.4印章(Gyselen 1993, pls. X, XIV) 218
图203　法国国家图书馆,巴黎:20.B.30、20.D.47印章(Gyselen 1993, pls. XI, XIII) 219
图204　法国国家图书馆,巴黎:20.B.4、20.D.38、20.E.2、20.E.6印章(Gyselen 1993, pls. X, XIII, XIV) 219
图205　法国国家图书馆,巴黎:20.D.22、20.D.29印章(Gyselen 1993, pls. XII, XIII) 220
图206　法国国家图书馆,巴黎:20.B.2、20.D.43印章(Gyselen 1993, pls. X, XIII) 220

参考文献

Alram 1986

    M. Alram, *Nomina Propria Iranica in Nummis. Materialgrundlagen zu den Iranischen Personennamen auf Antiken Münzen* [Iranisches Personennamenbuch, IV], Wien, 1986.

Alram 2003

    M. Alram, "II. A. Ardashir I. (nach 205/206 bzw. 224–240)", Alram/Gyselen 2003, pp. 91–180.

Alram 2007

    M. Alram, "Ardashir's Eastern Campaign and the Numismatic Evidence", J. Cribb/G. Herrmann (edd.), *After Alexander. Central Asia before Islam* [Proceedings of the British Academy, 133], New York, 2007, pp. 227–242.

Alram 2008

    M. Alram, "Early Sasanian Coinage", V. Sarkhosh Curtis/S. Stewart (edd.), *The Sasanian Era. The Idea of Iran, Volume III*, London, 2008, pp. 17–30.

Alram *et al.* 2007

    M. Alram/M. Blet-Lemarquand/P.O. Skjærvø, "Shapur, King of Iranians and Non-Iranians", R. Gyselen (ed.), *Des Indo-Grecs aux Sassanides: Données pour l'Histoire et la Géographie Historique* [Res Orientales, XVII], Bures-sur-Yvette, 2007, pp. 11–40.

Alram/Gyselen 2003

    M. Alram/R. Gyselen, *Sylloge Nummorum Sasanidarum Paris-Berlin-Wien, Band I, Ardashir I. -Shapur I.* [Veröffentlichungen der Numismatischen Kommission, 41], Wien, Österreichische Akademie der Wissenschaften, 2003.

Andrae/Lenzen 1933

    W. Andrae/H. Lenzen, *Die Partherstadt Assur* [Wissenschaftliche Veröffentlichungen der Deutschen Orientgesellschaft, 57], Leipzig, 1933.

Askari Chaverdi 2005/2006

    A. Askari Chaverdi, "Barrasi-ye Bâstânshenâxti-ye Mohavvatehâ-ye Bâstâni-ye

Paskarânehâ-ye Xalij-e Fârs: Lâmerd va Mohr, Fârs", *Iranian Journal of Archaeology and History*, 2005/2006, pp. 3–10.

Askari Chaverdi 2009

A. Askari Chaverdi, "Kâvosh dar Banâ-ye Ma'ruf-e Kâx-e Sâsâni-ye Sarvestân, Fârs [Excavations at the so-called Sasanian Palace at Sarvestan]", *Iranian Journal of Archaeology and History*, 23, 2 (46), 2009, pp. 37–65.

Askari Chaverdi 2011

A. Askari Chaverdi, "Madârek-e az Jonub-e Fârs dar Zamine-ye Âyin-e Takrim-e Âtash dar Irân-e Bâstân [Evidence from Fārs for Fire Rituals in Ancient Iran]", *Iranian Journal of Archaeology and History*, 25, 1, no. 49, 2011, pp. 27–39.

Askari Chaverdi 2012

A. Askari Chaverdi, "Archaeological Excavations in the So-called 'Palace of Sāsān' at Sarvestān, Fārs", *Sasanika Archaeology.3.2012*, see http://www.sasanika.org/wp-content/uploads/Archaeological-Excavations-in-the-So-Called1-NXPowerLite2.pdf.

Askari Chaverdi 2014

A. Askari Chaverdi, "Esteqrârhâ-ye Doure-ye Haxâmaneshi, Farâ-haxâmaneshi dar Dashthâ-ye Rostam 1 (Fahliyân), Rostam 2, Nurâbâd, Dasht-e Bozpar (Posht-e par), Kâzerun, Borâzjân", A. Askari Chaverdi/D.T. Potts/C. Petrie, *Achaemenid and Post Achaemenid Studies. Mamasani Region, Northwestern and Western Fars, Iran*, Shiraz, 2014, pp. 143–178.

Azarnoush 1981

M. Azarnoush, "Excavations at Kangavar", *Archäologische Mitteilungen aus Iran*, n.F., XIV, 1981, pp. 69–94.

Azarnoush 1983

M. Azarnoush, "Excavations at Hâjîâbâd, 1977: First Preliminary Report", *Iranica Antiqua*, XVIII, 1983, pp. 159–176.

Azarnoush 1984

M. Azarnoush, "A New Sassanian Temple in Eastern Fars", *Iranica Antiqua*, XIX, 1984, pp. 167–200.

Azarnoush 1986

M. Azarnoush, "Sapur II, Ardasir II and Sapur III: Another Perspective", *Archäologische Mitteilungen aus Iran*, n. F., 1986, pp. 219–247.

Azarnoush 1987

    M. Azarnoush, *Sassanian Art in Eastern Fars: The excavation of a Manor House at Hajiabad, Darab, Iran*, PhD Dissertation, University microfilm, Ann Arbor, 1987.

Azarnoush 1994

    M. Azarnoush, *The Sasanian Manor House at Hajiābād, Iran* [Monografie di *Mesopotamia*, III], Firenze, 1994.

Azarnoush 2009

    M. Azarnoush, "New Evidence on the Chronology of the 'Anahita Temple'", *Iranica Antiqua*, 44, 2009, pp. 393–402.

Azarpay 1981

    G. Azarpay, *Sogdian Painting: The Pictorial Epic in Oriental Art*, Berkeley-Los Angeles-London, 1981.

Azarpay 1997

    G. Azarpay, "The Sasanian Complex at Bandian. Palace or Dynastic Shrine", *Bulletin of the Asia Institute*, n.s., 11, 1997, pp. 193–196.

Bagherpour Kashani/Stoellner 2011

    N. Bagherpour Kashani/Th. Stoellner (edd.), *Water and Caves in Ancient Iranian Religion: Aspects of Archaeology, Cultural History and Religion* [*Archäologische Mitteilungen aus Iran und Turan*, 43], Berlin, 2011.

Balzer 2007

    W. Balzer, *Siegelbildmotive und ihre Kodifizierung. Eine motivtypologische "Grammatik" der Siegel der Sasanidenzeit*, s.l., 2007.

Baratte *et al.* 2012

    F. Baratte, O. Bopearachchi, R. Gyselen, N. Sims-Williams, "Un Plat Romain Inscrit en Bactrien et *Pārsīg*", R. Gyselen (ed.), *Objects et Documents Inscrits en* Pārsīg [Res Orientales, XXI], Bures-sur-Yvette, GECMO, 2012, pp. 9–28.

Bashshash-e Kanzaq 1997

    R. Bashshash Kanzaq, "Qarâ'at-e Katibehâ-ye Bandiyân-e Darregaz 'Dastkard-e Yazdshâpurân' [Translation of Inscriptions Discovered at Bandiyān, Darreh Gaz (Dastkard-e Yazd Shāpourān)]", *Archaeological Reports of Iran*, I, 1997, pp. 33–38.

Belenitskii/Marshak 1981

    A.M. Belenitskii/B.I. Marshak, "Part One. The Paintings of Sogdiana", G. Azarpay, *Sogdian Painting: The Pictorial Epic in Oriental Art*, Berkeley-Los Angeles-London, 1981, pp. 11–77.

Beretta/Di Pasquale 2003

　　M. Beretta/G. Di Pasquale (edd.), *Vitrum. Il Vetro fra Arte e Scienza nel Mondo Romano*, Firenze, 2003, see http://brunelleschi.imss.fi.it/vitrum/evtr.asp?c=8205.

Bier 1986

　　L. Bier, *Sarvestan. A Study in Early Islamic Architecture*, Pennsylvania University Park-London, 1986.

Bier 1989

　　C. Bier, "Anāhīd iv Anāhitā in the arts", in *Encyclopaedia Iranica*, Vol. I, Fasc. 9, 1989, pp. 1009–1011, see http://www.iranicaonline.org/articles/anahid (rev. 2011).

Bier 1993

　　L. Bier, "The Sasanian Palaces and Their Influence in Early Islam", *Ars Orientalis*, 23, 1993, pp. 57–65.

Bier 2009

　　L. Bier, "Palais B at Bishapur and Its Sasanian Reliefs", R. Gyselen (ed.), *Sources pour l'Histoire et la Géographie du Monde Iranien (224–710)* [Res Orientales, XVIII], Bures-sur-Yvette, 2009, pp. 11–40.

Bivar 1969

　　A.D.H. Bivar, *Catalogue of the Western Asiatic Stamp Seals in the British Museum. Stamp Seals II : The Sassanian Dynasty*, London, 1969.

Borisov/Lukonin 1963

　　A.Ja. Borisov/V.G. Lukonin, *Sasanidskie Gemmy*, Leningrad, 1963.

Boucharlat 1985

　　R. Boucharlat, "Chahar Taq et Temple du feu Sassanide: Quelques Remarques", J.-L. Huot *et al.* (edd.), *De l'Indus aux Balkans, Recueil à la Mémoire de Jean Deshayes*, Paris, 1985, pp. 461–478.

Boucharlat 2006

　　R. Boucharlat, "L'Architecture Sassanide", F. Demange (ed.), *Les Perses Sassanides. Fastes d'un Empire Oublié (224–642)*, Paris, 2006, pp. 47–50.

Boucharlat 2010

　　R. Boucharlat, "Suse dans l'Architecture Iranienne et Moyenne-Orientale", J. Perrot (ed.), *Le Palais de Darius à Suse. Une Résidence Royale sur la Route de Persépolis à Babylone*, Paris, 2010, pp. 420–443.

Boyce 1975

　　M. Boyce, "On the Zoroastrian Temple Cult of Fire", *Journal of the American Oriental*

Society, 95, 3, 1975, pp. 454–465.

Boyce 1989

M. Boyce, *A Persian Stronghold of Zoroastrianism*, Persian Studies Series, No. 12, Lanham-New-York-London, 1989.

Brilliant 1984

R. Brilliant, *Visual Narratives. Storytelling in Etruscan and Roman Art*, Cornell University, 1984.

Brunner 1978

C.J. Brunner, *Sasanian Stamp Seals in the Metropolitan Museum of Art*, New York, 1978.

Byron 2000

R. Byron, *La Via per l'Oxiana*, Milano 2000, Italian translation of *The Road to Oxiana*, 1937.

Callieri 1996

P. Callieri, Compte-rendu de Azarnoush 1994, *East and West*, 46/3–4, 1996, pp. 504–507.

Callieri 1997

P. Callieri, *Seals and Sealings from the North-West of the Indian Subcontinent and Afghanistan (4th Century BC–11th Century AD). Local, Indian, Sasanian, Graeco-Persian, Sogdian, Roman*, with contributions by E. Errington, R. Garbini, Ph. Gignoux, N. Sims-Williams, W. Zwalf [Dissertationes, I], Naples, 1997.

Callieri 2004a

P. Callieri, "India. iv. Political and Cultural Relations: Seleucid, Parthian, Sasanian periods", in *Encyclopaedia Iranica*, Vol. XIII, Fasc. 1, 2004, pp. 13–16, see http://www.iranicaonline.org/articles/india-iv-relations (rev. 2012).

Callieri 2004b

P. Callieri, "Sasanian Glyptics in Caucasian Archaeological Contexts: Contribution on Problems of Chronology", *Atti del convegno internazionale "La Persia e Bisanzio" (Roma, 14–18 ottobre 2002)* [Atti dei Convegni Lincei, 201], Roma, Accademia Nazionale dei Lincei, 2004, pp. 923–933.

Callieri 2006a

P. Callieri, "At the Roots of Sasanian Royal Imagery: The Persepolis Graffiti", M. Compareti/P. Raffetta/G. Scarcia (eds.), *Ērān ud Anērān. Studies Presented to Boris Il'ič Maršak on the Occasion of his 70th Birthday*, Venezia, 2006, pp. 129–148.

Callieri 2006b

P. Callieri, "The Activity of Gem and Coin Die Engravers in North-West India Between the Indo-Greeks and the Kushanas", P. Callieri (ed.), *Architetti, Capomastri, Artigiani. l'Organizzazione dei Cantieri e della Produzione Artistica nell'Asia Ellenistica. Studi Offerti a Domenico Faccenna nel suo Ottantesimo Compleanno* [Serie Orientale Roma, C], Roma, IsIAO, 2006, pp. 7–16.

Callieri 2006c

P. Callieri, "Water in the Art and Architecture of the Sasanians", A. Panaino/A. Piras (edd.), *Proceedings of the 5th Conference of the Societas Iranologica Europaea*, I, Milano, 2006, pp. 339–349.

Callieri 2007

P. Callieri, *L'Archéologie du Fārs à l'Époque Hellénistique. Quatre leçons au Collège de France 8, 15, 22 et 29 mars 2007* [Persika, 11], Paris, 2007.

Callieri 2008

P. Callieri, "'Dionysiac' Iconographic Themes in the Context of Sasanian Religious Architecture", D. Kennet/P. Luft (edd.), *Current Research in Sasanian Archaeology, Art and History. Proceedings of a Conference Held at Durham University, November 3rd and 4th, 2001* [BAR International Series, 1810], Oxford, 2008, pp. 115–125.

Callieri 2009

P. Callieri, "Bishapur: The Palace and the Town", Ph. Gignoux/Ch. Jullien/F. Jullien (edd.), *Trésors d'Orient. Mélanges Offerts à Rika Gyselen*, Paris, 2009, pp. 51–65.

Callieri 2012

P. Callieri, "Some Remarks on the Use of Dressed Stone Masonry in the Architecture of Sasanian Iran", H. Fahimi/K. Alizadeh (edd.), *Nâmvarnâmeh. Papers in Honour of Massoud Azarnoush*, Tehran, 2012, pp. 153–162.

Callieri 2017

P. Callieri, "Cultural Contacts Between Rome and Persia at the Time of Ardashir I (c. AD 224–40)". *Sasanian Persia Between Rome and the Steppes of Eurasia (Edinburgh Studies in Ancient Persia)*, ed. E.W. Sauer, Edinburgh, 2017, pp. 221–238.

Canepa 2009

M.P. Canepa, *The Two Eyes of the Earth. Art and Ritual of Kingship Between Rome and Sasanian Iran*, Berkeley/Los Angeles/London, 2009.

Canepa 2010

    M.P. Canepa, "Technologies of Memory in Early Sasanian Iran: Achaemenid Sites and Sasanian Identity", *American Journal of Archaeology*, 114/4, 2010, pp. 563–596.

Canepa 2013a

    M. Canepa, "Building a New Vision of the Past in the Sasanian Empire: The Sanctuaries of Kayânsîh and the Great Fires of Iran", *Journal of Persianate Studies*, 6, 2013, pp. 64–90.

Canepa 2013b

    M.P. Canepa, "Sasanian Rock Reliefs", D.T. Potts (ed.), *The Oxford Handbook of Ancient Iran*, New York, 2013, pp. 856–877.

Cazzoli/Cereti 2005

    S. Cazzoli/C.G. Cereti, "Sealings from Kafir Kala: Preliminary Report", *Ancient Civilizations from Scythia to Siberia*, 11, 2005, pp. 133–164.

Choksy 2007

    J. Choksy, "Reassessing the Material Context of Ritual Fires in Ancient Iran", *Iranica Antiqua*, XLII, 2007, pp. 229–269.

Colledge 1979

    M.A.R. Colledge, "Sculptor's Stone Carving Techniques in Seleucid and Parthian Iran and Their Place in the 'Parthian' Cultural Milieu: Some Preliminary Observations", *East and West*, 29, 1979, pp. 221–240.

Compareti 2005–2006

    M. Compareti, "Remarks on Late Sasanian Art: The Figural Capitals at Tāq-e Bostān", *Nāme-ye Irān-e Bāstān*, 5, 1&2, 2005–2006, pp. 83–98.

Compareti 2011

    M. Compareti, "The State of Research on Sasanian Painting", *E Sasanika Archaeology* 8, see http://www.sasanika.org/esasanika/the-state-of-research-on-sasanian-painting-2/

Cumont 1975

    F. Cumont (transl. and edited by E.D. Francis), "The Dura Mithraeum", J.R. Hinnels (ed.), *Mithraic Studies. Proceedings of the first International Congress of Mithraic Studies*, I, Manchester, 1975, pp. 151–214.

Curatola/Scarcia 2003

    G. Curatola/G. Scarcia, *Iran. L'Arte Persiana*, Milano, 2003.

Curiel/Gignoux 1975

R. Curiel/Ph. Gignoux, "Sur une Intaille Sassanide du Cabinet des Médailles de Paris", *Studia Iranica*, 4, 1975, pp. 41–49.

Curiel/Seyrig 1974

R. Curiel/H. Seyrig, "Une Intaille Iranienne", D.K. Kouymjian (ed.), *Near Eastern Numismatics, Iconography, Epigraphy and History, Studies in Honor of George C. Miles*, Beirut, American University, 1974, pp. 55–59.

Daryaee 2008

T. Daryaee, "Kingship in Early Sasanian Iran", V. Sarkhosh Curtis/S. Stewart (edd.), *The Sasanian Era* [The Idea of Iran, 3], London 2008, pp. 60–70.

Daryaee 2008

T. Daryaee, *Sasanian Iran (224–651 CE). Portrait of a Late Antique Empire* [Sasanika Series, 1], Costa Mesa, Ca., 2008.

Daryaee 2009

T. Daryaee, *Sasanian Persia. The Rise and Fall of an Empire*, London-New York 2009.

Daryaee 2010

T. Daryaee, "Ardaxšīr and the Sasanians' Rise to Power", *Anabasis. Studia Classica et Orientalia*, 1, 2010, pp. 236–255.

De Lillo 2012/2013

G.M.S. De Lillo, *Gli altari del Fuoco nell'Iran Sasanide (III–VII secolo d.C.): Rituali e Testimonianze Iconografiche*, dissertation de Master, Sapienza Università di Roma, 2012/2013.

De Waele 2004

A. De Waele, "The Figurative Wall Painting of the Sasanian Period from Iran, Iraq and Syria", *Iranica Antiqua*, XXXIX, 2004, pp. 339–381.

De Waele 2009

A. De Waele, "Sasanian Wall Painting", in *Encyclopaedia Iranica*, see http://www.iranicaonline.org/articles/sasanian-wall-painting-murals-found-on-sites-within-the-territory-of-the-sasanian-empire.

Demange 2006a

F. Demange, "Buste d'un roi", F. Demange (ed.), *Les Perses Sassanides. Fastes d'un Empire Oublié (224–642)*, Paris, 2006, p. 53.

Demange 2006b

F. Demange, "Les Mosaïques de Bishapur", *Les Perses Sassanides. Fastes d'un Empire Oublié (224–642)*, Paris, 2006, pp. 63–67.

Duchesne-Guillemin 1966

J. Duchesne-Guillemin, *Symbols and Values in Zoroastrianism*, New York, 1966.

Duchesne-Guillemin 1971

J. Duchesne-Guillemin, "Art et Religion sous les Sassanides", *Atti del Convegno Internazionale sul Tema "La Persia nel Medioevo", Roma, 31 marzo-5 aprile 1970* [Accademia Nazionale dei Lincei, Quaderno n. 160], Roma, 1971, pp. 377–388.

Edwell 2008

P. Edwell, *Between Rome and Persia: The Middle Euphrates, Mesopotamia and Palmyra under Roman Control*, London/New York, 2008.

Edwell 2013

P. Edwell, "Sasanian Interactions with Rome and Byzantium", D.T. Potts (ed.), *The Oxford Handbook of Ancient Iran*, New York, 2013, pp. 840–855.

Erdmann 1937

K. Erdmann, "Das Datum des Tak-i Bustan", *Ars Islamica*, IV, 1937, pp. 79–97.

Erdmann 1941

K. Erdmann, *Das Iranische Feuerheiligtum* [Sendschrift der Deutschen Orient-Gesellschaft, 11], Leipzig, 1941.

Erdmann 1969

K. Erdmann, *Die Kunst Irans zur Zeit der Sasaniden*, revised new edition, Mainz, 1969.

Faccenna 1981

D. Faccenna, "A New Fragment of Wall-Painting from Ghâga Sahr (Kûh-i Hvaga, Sistan, Iran)", *East and West*, 31, 1–4, pp. 83–97.

Fahimi 2012

H. Fahimi, "Tâq-e Kasrâ, Aspânbar-Tisfun: Gozâresh-e Bâzdid [Taq-e Kasra, Espanbar-Ctesiphon: A Report of a Visit]", H. Fahimi/K. Alizadeh (edd.), *Nâmvarnâmeh. Papers in Honour of Massoud Azarnoush*, Tehran, 2012, pp. 226–215.

Filigenzi 2006

A. Filigenzi, "From Mind to Eye. Two-dimensional Illusions and Pictorial Suggestions at Saidu Sharif I", P. Callieri (ed.), *Architetti, Capomastri, Artigiani. L'Organizzazione dei Cantieri e della Produzione Artistica nell'Asia Ellenistica. Studi Offerti a Domenico Faccenna nel suo Ottantesimo Compleanno* [Serie Orientale Roma, C], Roma, IsIAO, 2006, pp. 17–40.

Fıratlı 1990

N. Fıratlı, *La Sculpture Byzantine Figurée au Musée Archéologique d'Istanbul* [Bibliothèque de l'Institut Français d'Études Anatoliennes d'Istanbul, XXX], Paris, 1990.

Fukai/Horiuchi 1972

S. Fukai/K, Horiuchi, *Taq-i-Bustan*. II. Plates, Tokyo, 1972.

Fukai *et al.* 1969–1984

S. Fukai/K. Horiuchi/K. Tanabe/M. Domyo, *Taq-i-Bustan I–IV*, Tokyo, 1969–1984.

Furtwaengler 1900

A. Furtwaengler, *Antike Gemmen*, Leipzig-Berlin, 1900.

Gall, von 1971

H. von Gall, "Entwicklung und Gestalt des Thrones im Vorislamischer Iran", *Archäologische Mitteilungen aus Iran*, n.F., IV, 1971, pp. 207–235.

Gall, von 1990a

H. von Gall, *Das Reiterkampfbild in der Iranischen und Iranisch Beeinflußten Kunst Parthischer und Sasanidischer Zeit* [Teheraner Forschungen, VI], Berlin, 1990.

Gall, von 1990b

H. von Gall, "The figural Capitals at Taq-i Bustan and the Questions of the So-called Investiture in Parthian and Sasanian art", *Silk Road Art and Archaeology*, 1, 1990, pp. 99–122.

Gall, von 2008

H. von Gall, "New Perspectives on Sasanian Rock Reliefs", D. Kennet/P. Luft (eds.), *Current Research in Sasanian Archaeology, Art and History. Proceedings of a Conference Held at Durham University, November 3rd and 4th, 2001* [BAR International Series 1810], Oxford, 2008, pp. 149–161.

Ghanimati 2000

S. Ghanimati, "New Perspectives on the Chronological and Functional Horizon of Kuh-e Khwaja in Sistan", *Iran*, 38, pp. 137–150.

Ghanimati 2013

S. Ghanimati, "Kuh-e Khwaja and the Religious Architecture of Sasanian Iran", D.T. Potts (ed.), *The Oxford Handbook of Ancient Iran*, New York 2013, pp. 878–908.

Ghirshman 1962

R. Ghirshman, *Iran. Parthes et Sassanides*, Paris, 1962.

Ghirshman 1971

R. Ghirshman, *Fouilles de Châpour, Bîchâpour I* [Musée du Louvre, Département d'Antiquités Orientales, Série archéologique VII], Paris, 1971.

Gignoux 1995

Ph. Gignoux, Compte-rendu de Azarnoush 1994, *Studia Iranica*, 24, 1995, pp. 147–149.

Gignoux 1998

Ph. Gignoux, "Les Inscriptions en Moyen-Perse de Bandiân", *Studia Iranica*, 27, 1998, pp. 251–258.

Gignoux 2000

Ph. Gignoux, "À Propos de l'Airiiana Vaêjah", *Studia Iranica*, 29, 2000, pp. 163–166.

Gignoux 2008

Ph. Gignoux, "Le Site de Bandiân Revisité", *Studia Iranica*, 37, 2008, pp. 163–174.

Gignoux/Gyselen 1989a

Ph. Gignoux/R. Gyselen, " La Glyptique des Femmes à l'Époque Sassanide", *Archaeologia Iranica et Orientalis. Miscellanea in Honorem Louis Vanden Berghe*, Gent, 1989, pp. 877–896.

Gignoux/Gyselen 1989b

Ph. Gignoux/R. Gyselen, "Nouveaux Sceaus Sassanides Inscrits", *Studia Iranica*, 18, 1989, pp. 199–208.

Gnoli 1971

G. Gnoli, "Politica Religiosa e Concezione della Regalità sotto i Sassanidi", *Atti del convegno internazionale sul tema "La Persia nel Medioevo", Roma, 31 marzo-5 aprile 1970* [Accademia Nazionale dei Lincei, Quaderno n. 160], Roma, 1971, pp. 225–251.

Göbl 1973

R. Göbl, *Der Sâsânidische Siegelkanon* [Handbücher der mittelasiatischen Numismatik, IV], Braunschweig, 1973.

Godard 1938

A. Godard, "Les Monuments du Feu", *Athâr-è Îrân*, III, 1938, pp. 7–80.

Goldman/Little 1980

B. Goldman/A.M.G. Little, "The Beginning of Sasanian Painting and Dura Europos", *Iranica Antiqua*, XV, 1980, pp. 283–298.

Gorelick/Gwinnet 1996

L. Gorelick/A.J. Gwinnet, "Innovative Methods in the Manufacture of Sasanian Seals", *Iran*, XXXIV, 1996, pp. 79–84.

Grabar 1963

A. Grabar, *Sculptures Byzantines de Costantinople (IVe-Xe siècle)*, Paris, 1963.

Grenet et al. 2007

F. Grenet/J. Lee/Ph. Martinez/F. Ory, "The Sasanian Relief at Rag-i Bibi (Northern Afghanistan)", J. Cribb/G. Herrmann (edd.), *After Alexander. Central Asia before Islam* [Proceedings of the British Academy, 133], New York, 2007, pp. 243–277.

Gropp 1969

G. Gropp, "Die Funktion des Feuertempels der Zoroastrier", *Archäologische Mitteilungen aus Iran*, n.F., 2, 1969, pp. 166–173.

Guidetti 2007

M. Guidetti, "Bizanzio dopo Bisanzio: Le Chiese Bizantine nel Medioevo Arabo-Musulmano", *Porphyra*, IV. X, 2007, pp. 29–53.

Gullini 1964

G. Gullini, *Architettura Iranica dagli Achemenidi ai Sasanidi: Il "palazzo" di Kuh-i Khwaja (Seistan)*, Torino, 1964.

Gunter/Jett 1992

A.C. Gunter/P. Jett, *Ancient Iranian Metalwork in the Arthur M. Sackler Gallery and the Freer Gallery of Art, Washington, DC*, Washington, 1992.

Gyselen 1979

R. Gyselen, "Les Formes Sont-elles un Critère del Datation pour les Cachets Sassanides?", *Akten des VII. Internationalen Kongresses für Iranische Kunst und Archäologie, München, 7.–10. September 1976* [*Archäologische Mitteilungen aus Iran*, Erg. 6], Berlin, 1979, pp. 352–363.

Gyselen 1989a

R. Gyselen, *La Géographie Administrative de l'Empire Sassanide. Les Témoignages Sigillographiques* [Res Orientales, 1], GECMO, Paris, 1989.

Gyselen 1989b

R. Gyselen, "La Glyptique des Hauts Fonctionnaires et Dignitaires de l'Empire Sassanide", Gyselen 1989a, pp. 149–166.

Gyselen 1993

R. Gyselen, *Catalogue des Sceaux, Camées et Bulles Sassanides de la Bibliothèque Nationale et du Musée du Louvre. I. Collection Générale*, Paris, Bibliothèque Nationale, 1993.

Gyselen 1995

R. Gyselen, "Les Sceaux des Mages de l'Iran Sassanide", R. Gyselen (ed.), *Au Carrefour des Religions: Mélanges Offerts à Philippe Gignoux* (Res Orientales, VII), Bures-sur-Yvette, 1995, pp. 121–150.

Gyselen 2003

R. Gyselen, "II. B. Shapur Ier (240–272)", Alram/Gyselen 2003, pp. 181–289.

Gyselen 2006

R. Gyselen, "L'Art Sigillaire: Camées, Sceaux et Bulles", F. Demange (ed.), *Les Perses Sassanides. Fastes d'un Empire Oublié (224–642)*, Paris, 2006, pp. 199–213.

Gyselen 2007a

R. Gyselen, *Sasanian Seals and Sealings in the A. Saeedi Collection* [Acta Iranica, 44], Lovanii, 2007.

Gyselen 2007b

R. Gyselen, "Shapur, Fils d'Ohrmazd, Petit-Fils de Narseh", R. Gyselen (ed.), *Des Indo-Grecs aux Sassanides: Données pour l'Historie et la Géographie Historique* [Res Orientales, XVII], Bures-sur-Yvette, GECMO, 2007, pp. 73–80.

Gyselen 2008

R. Gyselen, "The Great Families in the Sasanian Empire: Some Sigillographic Evidence", D. Kennet/P. Luft (edd.), *Current Research in Sasanian Archaeology, Art and History. Proceedings of a Conference Held at Durham University, November 3rd and 4th, 2001* [BAR International Series, 1810], Oxford, 2008, pp. 107–113.

Gyselen 2012

R. Gyselen, Compte-rendu de Ritter 2010, *Studia Iranica*, 41, 2012, pp. 319–323.

Gyselen/Gasche 1994

R. Gyselen/H. Gasche, "Suse et Ivān-e Kerkha, Capitale Provinciale d'Ērān-Xwarrah-Šāpūr, Note de Géographie Historique Sassanide", *Studia Iranica*, 23, 1994, pp. 19–35.

Harper 1973

P.O. Harper, "Representational Motifs on the Sealings", R.N. Frye (ed.), *Sasanian Remains from Qasr-i Abu Nasr. Seals, Sealings, and Coins* [Harvard Iranian Series, 1], Cambridge, Mass., 1973, pp. 66–87.

Harper 1974

P.O. Harper, "Sasanian Medallion Bowls with Human Busts", D.K. Kouymjian (ed.), *Near Eastern Numismatics, Iconography, Epigraphy and History, Studies in Honor of George C. Miles*, Beirut, American University, 1974, pp. 61–81.

Harper 1979

P.O. Harper, "Thrones and Enthronement Scenes in Sasanian Art", *Iran*, 17, 1979, pp. 49–64.

Harper 1981

P.O. Harper, *Silver Vessels of the Sasanian Period. Volume one: Royal Imagery*, New York, Metropolitan Museum of Art, 1981.

Harper 1986

P.O. Harper, "Art in Iran. v. Sasanian Art", in *Encyclopaedia Iranica*, vol. II, Fasc. 6, pp. 585–594, see http://www.iranicaonline.org/articles/art-in-iran-v-sasanian (revisione 2011).

Harper 1999

P.O. Harper, "Geographical Location and Significant Imagery: Taq-e Bostan", M. Alram/D.E. Klimburg-Salter (edd.), *Coins, Art, and Chronology. Essays on the pre-Islamic History of the Indo-Iranian Borderlands*, Wien, 1999, pp. 315–319.

Harper 2006

P.O. Harper, *In Search of a Cultural Identity: Monuments and Artifacts of the Sasanian Near East, 3rd to 7th Century A.D.* [Biennial Ehsan Yarshater Lecture Series, No. 2], New York, 2006.

Harper 2008

P.O. Harper, Image and Identity: Art of the Early Sasanian Dynasty, V. Sarkhosh Curtis/S. Stewart (edd.), *The Sasanian Era. The Idea of Iran, Volume III*, London, 2008, pp. 71–87.

Herrmann 1969

G. Herrmann, The Dārābgird Relief — Ardashīr or Shāhpūr? A Discussion in the Context of Early Sasanian Sculpture", *Iran*, VII, 1969, pp. 63–88.

Herrmann 1976

G. Herrmann, "The Sasanian Rock Reliefs: Some Significant Details", *The Memorial Volume of the VIth International Congress of Iranian Art & Archaeology, Oxford, September 11th–16th 1972*, Tehran, 1976, pp. 151–161.

Herrmann 1977

G. Herrmann, *Naqsh-i Rustam 5 and 8. Sasanian Attributed to Hormuzd II and Narseh* [Iranische Felsreliefs, D. Iranische Denkmäler, Lieferung 8 enthaltend Reihe II], Berlin, 1977.

Herrmann 1980

G. Herrmann, *The Sasanian Rock Reliefs at Bishapur: Part 1. Bishapur III, Triumph Attributed to Shapur I* [Iranische Felsreliefs, E. Iranische Denkmäler, Lieferung 9 enthaltend Reihe II], Berlin, 1980.

Herrmann 1981a

G. Herrmann, *The Sasanian Rock Reliefs at Bishapur: Part 2. Bishapur IV, Bahram II receving a Delegation. Bishapur V, The Investiture of Bahram I. Bishapur VI, The Enthroned King* [Iranische Felsreliefs, F. Iranische Denkmäler, Lieferung 10 enthaltend Reihe II], Berlin, 1981.

Herrmann 1981b

G. Herrmann, "Early Sasanian Stoneworking: A Preliminary Report", *Iranica Antiqua*, XVI, 1981, pp. 151–160.

Herrmann 1983

G. Herrmann, *The Sasanian Rock Reliefs at Bishapur: Part 3. Bishapur I, The Investiture/Triumph of Shapur I?. Bishapur II, Triumph of Shapur I and Sarab-i Bahram, Bahram II enthroned. The Rock Relief at Tang-i Qandil. Inscription by D.N. MacKenzie* [Iranische Felsreliefs, G. Iranische Denkmäler, Lieferung 11 enthaltend Reihe II], Berlin, 1983.

Herrmann 1989

G. Herrmann, "Description and Commentary", *The Sasanian Rock Reliefs at Naqsh-i Rustam. Naqsh-i Rustam 6, The Triumph of Shapur I (together with an account of the representation of Kerdir). * [Iranische Felsreliefs, I. Iranische Denkmäler, Lieferung 13 enthaltend Reihe II], Berlin, 1989, pp. 13–33.

Herrmann 2000

G. Herrmann, "The Rock Reliefs of Sasanian Iran", J. Curtis (ed.), *Mesopotamia and Iran in the Parthian and Sasanian Periods: Rejection and Revival c. 238 BC–AD 642. Proceedings of a Seminar in Memory of Vladimir G. Lukonin*, London, British Museum, 2000, pp. 35–45.

Herzfeld 1914

E. Herzfeld, *Die Aufnahme des Sasanidischen Denkmals von Paikuli* [Abhandlungen Akademie Berlin, Phil.-Hist. Klasse 1914.1], Berlin, 1914.

Herzfeld 1920

 E. Herzfeld, *Am Tor von Asien. Felsdenkmale aus Irans Heldenzeit*, Berlin, 1920.

Herzfeld 1924

 E. Herzfeld, *Paikuli. Momument and Inscription of the Early History of the Sassanian Empire*, I–II, Berlin, 1924.

Herzfeld 1935

 E. Herzfeld, *Archaeological History of Iran*, London, 1935.

Herzfeld 1938

 E. Herzfeld, "Khusrau Parwez und der Taq i Vastan", *Archäologische Mitteilungen aus Iran*, 9, 1938, pp. 91–158.

Herzfeld 1941

 E. Herzfeld, *Iran in the Ancient East*, New York-Oxford, 1941.

Hillenbrand 1994

 R. Hillenbrand, *Islamic Architecture*, Edinburgh, 1994.

Hinz 1969

 W. Hinz, *Altiranische Funde und Forschungen*, Berlin, 1969.

Hoffmann 1880

 G. Hoffmann, *Auszüge aus Syrische Akten Persischer Märtyrer* [Abhandlungen für die Kunde des Morgenlandes, VII, 3], Leipzig, 1880 (repr. Kraus, Liechtenstein, 1966).

Hoffmann 2008

 M.-I. Hoffmann, *Sasanidische Palastarchitektur. Forschung-Grundlagen-Funktion*, thèse de doctorat, Ludwig-Maximilians-Universität, Münich, 2008.

Hozhabri 2013

 A. Hozhabri, "The Evolution of Religious Architecture in the Sasanian Period", *Archaeology 18, Sasanika*, pp. 1–40, see http://www.sasanika.org/wp-content/uploads/e-sas-AR-18-The-EvolutionofReligiousArchitecture.pdf

Huff 1971

 D. Huff, "Qal'a-ye Dukhtar bei Firuzabad. Ein Beitrag zu Sasanidischen Palastarchitektur", *Archäologische Mitteilungen aus Iran*, n.F., 4, 1971, pp. 127–171.

Huff 1972

 D. Huff, "Der Takht-i Nishin in Firuzabad. Mass-Systeme Sasanidischer Bauwerke I", *Archäologischer Anzeiger*, 1972, pp. 517–540.

Huff 1975

D. Huff, "'Sasanian' Čahār Tāqs in Fārs", *Proceedings of the 3rd Annual Symposium on Archaeological Research in Iran, Tehran 23rd 10–1st 11, 1974*, Tehran, 1975, pp. 243–254.

Huff 1976

D. Huff, "Ausgrabungen auf Qalʻa-ye Dukhtar 1975", *Archäologische Mitteilungen aus Iran*, n.F. 9, 1976, pp. 157–173.

Huff 1978

D. Huff, "Ausgrabungen auf Qalʻa-ye Dukhtar bei Firuzabad, 1976", *Archäologische Mitteilungen aus Iran*, n. F., 11, 1978, pp. 117–147.

Huff 1982

D. Huff, "Das Imamzadeh Sayyid Husein und E. Herzfelds Theorie über den sasanidischen Feuertempel", *Studia Iranica*, 11, 1982, pp. 197–212.

Huff 1986a

D. Huff, "Archeology iv. Sasanian", in *Encyclopaedia Iranica*, II, 3, 1986, pp. 302–308, see http://www.iranicaonline.org/articles/archeology-iv (rev. 2011).

Huff 1986b

D. Huff, "Architecture iii. Sasanian", in *Encyclopaedia Iranica*, II, 3, 1986, pp. 329–334, see http://www.iranicaonline.org/articles/architecture-iii (rev.2011).

Huff 1993

D. Huff, "Architecture Sassanide", *Splendeur des Sassanides. L'Empire Perse entre Rome et la Chine [224–642]*, Bruxelles, Musées Royaux d'Art et d'Histoire, 1993, pp. 45–61.

Huff 1995

D. Huff, Compte-Rendu de Azarnoush 1994, *Mesopotamia*, XXX, 1995, pp. 352–363.

Huff 1999

D. Huff, "Traditionen Iranischer Palastarchitektur in Vorislamischer und Islamischer Zeit", B. Finster/Ch. Fragner/H. Hafenrichter (edd.), *Rezeption in der Islamischen Kunst*, Beirut, 1999, pp. 141–160.

Huff 2004

D. Huff, "Archaeological Evidence of Zoroastrian Funerary Practices", M. Stausberg (ed.), *Zoroastrian Rituals in Context*, Leiden-Boston, 2004, pp. 593–630.

Huff 2005

D. Huff, "From Median to Achaemenian Palace Architecture", *Iranica Antiqua*, XL, 2005, pp. 371–395.

Huff 2008a

D. Huff, "Formation and Ideology of the Sasanian State in the Context of Archaeological Evidence", V. Sarkhosh Curtis/S. Stewart (edd.), *The Sasanian Era. The Idea of Iran, Volume III*, London 2008, pp. 31–59.

Huff 2008b

D. Huff, "Palace Architecture", in *Encyclopaedia Iranica,* see http://www.iranicaonline.org/articles/palace-architecture.

Huff 2008c

D. Huff, "The Functional Layout of the Fire Sanctuary at Takht-i Sulaimān", D. Kennet/P. Luft (edd.), *Current Research in Sasanian Archaeology, Art and History. Proceedings of a Conference Held at Durham University, November 3rd and 4th, 2001* (BAR International Series 1810), Oxford, pp. 1–13.

Huff 2011

D. Huff, "Problems of Votive Offerings in Zoroastrian Iran", Bagherpour Kashani/Stoellner 2011, pp. 79–111.

Huff/Gignoux 1978

D. Huff/Ph. Gignoux, "Ausgrabungen auf Qal'a-ye Dukhtar bei Firuzabad, 1976. A. Vorläufiger Grabungsberichte, B. Pithos-Inschriften von Qal'a-ye Dukhtar", *Archäologische Mitteilungen aus Iran*, 11, 1978, pp. 117–150.

Huyse 1998

Ph. Huyse, "Kerdir and the First Sasanians", N. Sims-Williams (ed.), *Proceedings of the Third European Conference of Iranian Studies. Part 1. Old and Middle Iranian Studies*, Wiesbaden, 1998, pp. 109–120.

Kaim 2002

B. Kaim, "Un Temple du feu Sassanide Découvert à Mele Hairam, Turkménistan Méridional", *Studia Iranica*, 31, 2002, pp. 215–230.

Kaim 2004

B. Kaim, "Ancient Fire Temples in the Light of the Discovery at Mele Hairam", *Iranica Antiqua*, XXXIX, 2004, pp. 323–337.

Kaim 2009

B. Kaim, "Investiture or *Mithra*. Towards a New Interpretation of the so called Investiture Scenes in Parthian and Sasanian Art", *Iranica Antiqua*, XLIV, 2009, pp. 403–415.

Kaim 2012

B. Kaim, "Most Ancient Fire Temples: Wishful Thinking Versus Reality", H. Fahimi/ K. Alizadeh (edd.), *Nâmvarnâmeh. Papers in Honour of Massoud Azarnoush*, Tehran, 2012, pp. 131–138.

Kambaxsh Fard 1373

S. Kâmbaxsh Fars, *Ma'bad-e Ânâhitâ, Kangâvar. Kavoshhâ va Pazhuheshhâ-ye Bâstânshenâsi va Bâzsâzi va Ahyâ-ye Me'mâri-ye Ma'bad-e Nâhid va Tâq-e Gerrâ*, Tehran, 1373.

Kambaxsh Fard 1386

S. Kâmbaxhs Fard, *Kavoshhâ va Pazhuheshhâ-ye Bâstânshenâsi ve Ahyâ-ye Me'mâri-ye Ma'bad-e Anâhitâ-ye Kangâvar va Tâq-e Gerrâ, 1* [Archaeological Excavations and Research at Anahita Temple and Taq-e Gara (Kermanshah)], 2 vols., Tehran, 1386.

Kargar 2005

M.R. Kargar (ed.), *Decorative Architectural Stucco from the Parthian and Sassanid Eras*, National Museum of Iran, Tehran, s.d., 2005.

Kassar, al- 1979

A. al-Kassar, "Tell Abu Sh'af", *Sumer*, 35, 1979, pp. 468–475.

Kawami 1987a

T.S. Kawami, "Kuh-e Khwaja, Iran, and Its Wall Painting: The Records of Ernst Herzfeld", *Metropolitan Museum Journal*, 22, 1987, pp. 13–52.

Kawami 1987b

T.S Kawami, *Monumental Art of the Parthian Period in Iran* [Acta Iranica, 26], Leiden, 1987.

Kawami 2013

T.S. Kawami, "Parthian and Elymaean Rock Reliefs", D.T. Potts (ed.), *The Oxford Handbook of Ancient Iran*, New York, 2013, pp. 751–765.

Keall 1967

E.J. Keall, "Qal'eh-i Yazdigird. A Sasanian Palace Stronghold in Persian Kurdistan", *Iran*, 5, 1967, pp. 99–121.

Keall 1977

E.J. Keall, "Qal'eh-i Yazdigird: The Question of its date", *Iran*, 15, 1977, pp. 1–9.

Keall 1982

E.J. Keall, "Qal'eh-i Yazdigird. An Overview of the Monumental Architecture", *Iran*, 20, 1982, pp. 51–72.

Keall 1987

E.J. Keall, "Ayvān-e Kesrā", in *Encyclopaedia Iranica*, III, 2, 1987, pp. 155–159, see http://www.iranicaonline.org/articles/ayvan-e-kesra-palace-of-kosrow-at-ctesiphon (rev. 2011).

Keall 1989

E.J. Keall, "Bīšāpūr", in *Encyclopaedia Iranica*, IV, 3, 1989, pp. 287–289, see http://www.iranicaonline.org/articles/bisapur-town.

Keall 2002

E.J. Keall, "Qal'eh-i Yazdigird", R. Boucharlat (ed.), *Les Parthes : L'Histoire d'un Empire Méconnu, Rival de Rome* [*Dossiers d'Archéologie*, n° 271], Dijon, 2002, pp. 64–71.

Kettenhofen 1995

E. Kettenhofen, "Die Eroberung von Nisibis und Karrhai durch die Sasaniden in der Zeit Kaiser Maximins (235/236 n. Chr.)", *Iranica Antiqua*, 30, pp. 159–177.

Khosrovi/Rashnou 2014

Sh. Khosrovi/A. Rashnou, "Kâvosh-e Ezterâri-ye Mohavvate-ye Palang Gerd-e Shahrestân-e Eslâmâbâd, Kermânshâh", *Brief Articles 12th Annual Symposium on the Iranian Archaeology, 19–21 May 2014*, ICAR, Tehran, 2014, pp. 177–179.

Kidds/Betts 2010

F.J. Kidds/A.V.G. Betts, "Entre la Fleuve et la Steppe : Les Nouvelles Perspectives sur le Khorezm Ancien", *CRAI*, 2010, II, avril-juin, pp. 637–686.

Kimball 1937

F. Kimball, The Sassanian Building at Tepe Hissar Schmidt 1937, p. 327 ff.

Kleiss 1989

W. Kleiss, *Die Entwicklung von Palästen und Palastartigen Wohnbauten in Iran* [Österreichische Akademie der Wissenschaften, Philosophisch-historische Klasse, Sitzungsberichte, 524], Wien.

Kotwal/Choksy 2004

F.M. Kotwal/J.K. Choksy, "To Praise the Souls of the Deceased and the Immortal

Spirits of the Righteous Ones: The Staomi or Stûm Ritual's History and Functions", M. Stausberg (ed.), *Zoroastrian Rituals in Context* [Studies in the History of Religions, 102], Leiden, 2004, pp. 389–401.

Kotwal/Choksy 2012

F.M. Kotwal/J.K. Choksy, "Stūm", in *Encyclopaedia Iranica*, see http://www.iranicaonline.org/articles/stum-ritual

Kreyenbroek 2011

Ph.G. Kreyenbroek, "Some Remarks on Water and Caves in pre-Islamic Iranian Religions", Bagherpour Kashani/Stoellner 2011, pp. 157–163.

Kröger 1981

J. Kröger, "Sasanian Iran and India: Questions of Interactions", H. Härtel (ed.), *South Asian Archaeology 1979*, Berlin, 1981, pp. 441–448.

Kröger 1982

J. Kröger, *Sasanidischer Stuckdekor* [Baghdader Forschungen, 5], Mainz, 1982.

Kröger 1990

J. Kröger, "Čāl Tarkān", in *Encyclopaedia Iranica*, IV, 6, pp. 654–655, see http://www.iranicaonline.org/articles/cal-tarkan-cal-tarkan-esqabad-a-site-about-20-km-southeast-of-ray-with-remains-from-the-late-sasanian-and-early

Kröger 1993

J. Kröger, "Ctesiphon", in *Encyclopaedia Iranica*, VI, 4, pp. 446–448, see http://www.iranicaonline.org/articles/ctesiphon (rev. 2011).

Kröger 2005a

J. Kröger, "Stucco Decoration in Iranian Architecture", in *Encyclopaedia Iranica,* à lire sur http://www.iranicaonline.org/articles/stucco-decoration-in-iranian-architecture

Kröger 2005b

J. Kröger, "Damghan", in *Enciclopedia Archeologica. Asia*, Roma, 2005, p. 387.

Kröger 2006

J. Kröger, "Les Stucs", F. Demange (ed.), *Les Perses sassanides. Fastes d'un Empire Oublié (224–642)*, Paris, 2006, pp. 51–61.

Labaf Khaniki/Labaf Khaniki 2012

R.A. Labaf Khaniki/M. Labaf Khaniki, "Me'mâri-ye Kohandezh-e Nishâbur dar Doure-ye Sâsâni [Sasanid Architecture of Kohandezh, Nishapur]", H. Fahimi/K. Alizadeh (edd.), *Nâmvarnâmeh. Papers in Honour of Massoud Azarnoush*, Tehran, 2012, pp. 319–328.

Labourt 1904

J. Labourt, *Le Christianisme dans l'Empire Perse*, Paris, 1904.

Lerner 2006

J. Lerner, "An Introduction to the Sealings on the Bactrian Documents in the Khalili Collection", M. Compareti/P. Raffetta/G. Scarcia (edd.), *Ērān ud Anērān: Studies Presented to Boris Il'ič Maršak on the Occasion of His 70th Birthday*, Venezia, 2006, pp. 371–386.

Lerner 2010

J. Lerner, "Observations on the Typology and Style of Seals and Selaings from Bactria and the Indo-Iranian Borderlands", M. Alram/D. Klimburg-Salter/M. Inaba/M. Pfisterer (edd.), *Coins, Art and Chronology Ⅱ. The First Millennium C.E. in the Indo-Iranian Borderlands* [Österreichische Akademie der Wissenschaften, Veröffentlichungen der numismatischen Kommission, 50], Wien, 2010, pp. 245–266.

Lukonin 1960

V.G. Lukonin, "Reznoj Ametist s Izobrazheniem Caricy Caric Denak", *Issledovanija po Istorii Kul'tury Narodov Vostoka*, Moskva-Leningrad, 1960, p. 380 ss. (未参阅).

Lukonin 1961

V.G. Lukonin, *Iran v Epokhu Pervykh Sasanidov*, Leningrad, 1961.

Lukonin 1969

V.G. Lukonin, *Kul'tura Sasanidskogo Irana. Iran v III—V vv. Ocerki po istorii kul'tury*, Moskva, 1969.

Lukonin 1977a

V.G. Lukonin, *Iskusstvo Drevnego Irana*, Moskva, 1977.

Lukonin 1977b

V.G. Lukonin, "Xram Anaxity v Kangavare", *Vestnik Drevnej Istorii*, 1977, 2, pp. 105–111.

Lukonin 1979

V.G. Lukonin, *Iran v III veke. Novye Materialy i Opyt Istoričeskoj Rekonstrukcii*, Moskva, 1979.

Lukonin/Dandamaev 1971

V.G. Lukonin/M.A. Dandamaev, Compte-rendu de Hinz 1969, *Vestnik Drevnej Istorii*, 1971, 3, pp. 157–165.

Lusehey 1968

H. Lusehey, "Zur Datierung der Sasanidischen Kapitelle aus Bisutun and des Monuments von Taq-i-Bostan", *Archäologische Mitteilungen aus Iran*, n. F., I, 1968, pp. 129–142.

Luschey 1989

H. Luschey, "Bisotun ii. Archeology", in *Encyclopaedia Iranica*, IV, 3, 1989, pp. 291–299, see http://www.iranicaonline.org/articles/bisotun-ii (rev. 2013).

MacDermot 1954

B.C. MacDermot, "Roman Emperors in the Sasanian Reliefs", *Journal of Roman Studies*, 44, 1954, pp. 76–80.

Mackintosh 1973

M.C. Mackintosh, "Roman Influences on the Victory Reliefs of Shapur I of Persia", *California Studies in Classical Antiquity*, 6, 1973, pp. 181–203. o 63–88.

Mackintosh 1980

M.C. Mackintosh, "Taq-i Bustan and Byzantine Art. A case for Early Byzantine Influence on the Reliefs of Taq-i Bustan", *Iranica Antiqua*, XIII, 1980, pp. 149–177.

Mehriyar/Kabiri 1383

M. Mehriyâr/A. Kabiri, *Edâme-ye Kankâshhâ dar Ma'bad-e Ânâhitâ Kangâvar*, Tehran, 1383.

Messina/Rinaudo/Mehr Kian 2014

V. Messina/F. Rinaudo/J. Mehr Kian, "3D Laser Scanning of Parthian Sculptural Reliefs: The Experience of the Iranian-Italian Joint Expedition in Khuzestan (Iran)", *Journal of Field Archaeology*, 39/2, 2014, pp. 151–161.

Meyer 1990

M. Meyer, "Die Felsbilder Shapurs I.", *Jahrbuch des Deutschen Archäologischen Instituts*, 105, 1990, pp. 237–302.

Mohammadi Ghasrian 2012

S. Mohammadi Ghasrian, "Naxchirgâh-i Nowyâfte az Bisotun. Shenâsâ'i-ye Divârhâ-ye Târixi-ye Pardisi az Dowre-ye Sâsâni (?) dar Kermânshâh [A Newly Found Hunting-Ground in Bisutun (Kermanshah)]", *Bastanpazhuhi*, 2012, pp. 20–24.

Mohammedifar/Motarjem 2012

Y. Mohammedifar/A. Motarjem, "Julian: A Newly Discovered Fire-Temple in Âbdânân", *Sasanika Archaeology*, 4, 2012, see http://www.sasanika.org/wp-content/uploads/Archaeological-04-mohammedifar.pdf

Monneret de Villard 1936

U. Monneret de Villard, "The Fire Temples", *Bulletin of the American Institute for Persian Art and Archaeology*, 5, 1936, pp. 175–184.

Monneret de Villard 1954

U. Monneret de Villard, *L'Arte Iranica* [Biblioteca Moderna Mondadori, CCCXCVIII], Milano, 1954.

Moorey 1978

P.R.S. Moorey, *Kish Excavations 1913–1933*, Oxford, 1978.

Moradi 2007

Y. Moradi, Rapport lu au *9th Annual Symposium on Iranian Archaeology*, Tehran. 2007, information see http://www.cais-soas.com/News/2007/May2007/06-05.htm

Moradi 2009

Y. Moradi, "The *Chahartaq* of Mile Milehgeh: A Fire Temple of the Sasanid Period", *Motâle'ât-e Bâstânshenâsi,* a journal of the College of Literature and Human Sciences, University of Tehran, Vol. 1, No. 1, Spring and Summer 1388 (2009), pp. 155–185 (in Persian).

Moradi 2012

Y. Moradi, "Emârat-e Xosrow dar Partu-ye Noxostin Fasl-e Kavoshhâ-ye Bâstânshenâxti [Imarat-e Khosrow in View of the First Season of the Archaeological Excavations]", H. Fahimi/K. Alizadeh (edd.), *Nâmvarnâmeh. Papers in Honour of Massoud Azarnoush*, Tehran, 2012, pp. 329–350.

Morony 2009

M. Morony, "Madâ'en", in *Encyclopaedia Iranica*, see http://www.iranicaonline.org/articles/madaen-sasanian-metropolitan-area.

Mousavi 1999

M. Mousavi, "Kuh-e Khadjeh. Un Complex Religieux de l'Est Iranien", *Empires Perses d'Alexandre aux Sassanides* [Dossiers d'archéologie, n° 243], Dijon, 1999, pp. 81–84.

Mousavi 2008

A. Mousavi, "A Survey of the Archaeology of the Sasanian Period during the Past Three Decades", *E-Sasanika. Archaeology.1.2008*, see http://www.sasanika.org/wp-content/uploads/e-sasanika-Arch-1-Mousavi.pdf

Mousavi/Daryaee 2012

A. Mousavi/T. Daryaee, "The Sasanian Empire: An Archaeological Survey, c. AD 220–640", D.T. Potts (ed.), *A Companion to the Archaeology of the Ancient Near East*,

Oxford, 2012, pp. 1076–1094.

Movassat 2005

J.D. Movassat, *The Large Vault at Taq-i Bustan: A Study in Late Sasanian Royal Art*, Lewiston, 2005 (未参阅).

Musche 1994

B. Musche, "Römische Einflusse auf den Taq-e Bostan", P. Calmeyer/K. Hecker/L. Jakob-Rost/C.B.F. Walker (edd.), *Beiträge zur Altorientalischen Archäologie und Altertumskunde. Festschrift für Barthel Hrouda zum 65. Geburtstag*, Wiesbaden, 1994, pp. 193–199.

Naumann 1977

R. Naumann, *Die Ruinen von Tacht-e Suleiman und Zendan-e Suleiman und Umgebung* [DAI, Abteilung Tehran, Führer zu archäologischen Plätzen in Iran, II], Berlin, 1977.

Nikitin 1994

A. Nikitin, "Coins of the Last Indo-Parthian King of Sakastan (A Farewell to Ardamitra)", *South Asian Studies*, 10, 1994, pp. 67–69.

Nikitin/Roth 1995

A. Nikitin/G. Roth, "The Earliest Arab-Sasanian Coins", *The Numismatic Chronicle*, 155, 1995, pp. 131–137.

Nylander 1970

C. Nylander, *Ionians in Pasargadae. Studies in Old Persian Architecture* [Acta Universitatis Upsaliensis-Boreas. Uppsala Studies in Ancient Mediterranean and Near Eastern Civilizations, 1], Uppsala, 1970.

Overlaet 2009

B. Overlaet, "A Roman Emperor at Bishapur and Darabgird: Uranius Antoninus and the Black Stone of Emesa", *Iranica Antiqua*, XLIV, 2009, pp. 461–530.

Overlaet 2011

B. Overlaet, "Ardashir II or Shapur III? Reflections of the Identity of a King in the Smaller Grotto at Taq-i Bustan", *Iranica Antiqua*, XLVI, 2011, pp. 235–250.

Overlaet 2012

B. Overlaet, "Ahura Mazda and Shapur II? A Note on Taq-e Bustan I, the Investiture of Ardashir II (379–383)", *Iranica Antiqua*, XLVII, 2012, pp. 133–151.

Overlaet 2013

B. Overlaet, "And Man Created God? Kings, Priests and Gods on Sasanian Investiture Reliefs", *Iranica Antiqua*, XLVIII, 2013, pp. 313–354.

Peymani 2009 [2011]

    A. Peymani, "Gachbari-ye Rustâ-ye Asadâbâd-e Behbehân [Stucco from Asadabad village]", *Bastanpazhuhi*, vol. 4, no. 7, 2009 [2011], pp. 133–134.

Pilipko 2000

    V.N. Pilipko, "On the Wall-Paintings from the Tower Building of Old Nisa", *Parthica*, 2, 2000, pp. 69–86.

Pourshariati 2008

    P. Pourshariati, *Decline and Fall of the Sasanian Empire. The Sasanian-Parthian Confederacy and the Arab Conquest of Iran*, London, 2008.

Qandgar *et al.* 2004

    J. Qandgar/H. Esmaili/M. Rahmatpour, "Kâvoshhâ-ye Bâstânshenâxti-ye Qal'e-ye Azhdahâk Hashtrud", M. Azarnoush (ed.), *Proceedings of the International Symposium on Iranian Archaeology, Northwestern Region*, Tehran, 2004, pp. 193–228.

Rahbar 1997

    M. Rahbar, "Kâvoshhâ-ye Bâstanshenâsi-ye Bandiyân-e Darregaz [Excavations at Bandiyan, Darreh Gaz, Khorasan]", *Archaeological Reports of Iran*, I, 1997, pp. 9–32.

Rahbar 1998

    M. Rahbar, "Découverte d'un Monument d'Époque Sassanide à Bandian, Dargaz (Nord-Khorassan). Fouilles 1994 et 1995", *Studia Iranica*, 27, 1998, pp. 213–250.

Rahbar 2004

    M. Rahbar, "Le Monument Sassanide de Bandiân, Dargaz: Un Temple du feu d'Après les Dernières Découvertes 1996–98", *Studia Iranica*, 32, 2004, pp. 7–30.

Rahbar 2007a

    M. Rahbar, "Bandiyân-e Daregaz dar fasl-e Yâzdahom-e Kâvoshhâ-ye Bâstânshenâxti", H. Fazeli Nashli (ed.), *Archaeological Reports (7). On the Occasion of the 9th Annual Symposium on Iranian Archaeology*, vol. 2, Tehran, 2007, pp. 129–154.

Rahbar 2007b

    M. Rahbar, "A Tower of Silence of the Sasanian Period at Bandiyan: Some Observations about *Dakhmas* in Zoroastrian Religion", J. Cribb/G. Herrmann (edd.), *After Alexander. Central Asia before Islam* [Proceedings of the British Academy, 133], New York, 2007, pp. 455–473.

Rahbar 2008

    M. Rahbar, "The Discovery of a Sasanian Period Fire Temple at Bandiyan, Dargaz",

D. Kennet/P. Luft (edd.), *Current Research in Sasanian Archaeology, Art and History. Proceedings of a Conference Held at Durham University, November 3rd and 4th, 2001* [BAR International Series, 1810], Oxford, 2008, pp. 15–40.

Rahbar 2010–2011

M. Rahbar, "Âteshkade-ye Bandiyân-e Daregaz: yek bâr-e digar", *Pazhuheshhâ-ye Bâstânshenâsi-ye Modares — Modares Archaeological Research*, vol. 1 & 2, nos. 4 & 5, 2010–2011, pp. 167–177.

Raumwissen 2013

Raumwissen, "Material Culture and Object Studies", *Raumwissen* (*TOPOI Excellence Cluster*), 5.11, 2013, pp. 28–34.

Reuther 1929

O. Reuther, "The German Excavation at Ctesiphon", *Antiquity*, III, 1929, pp. 434–451.

Reuther 1938

O. Reuther, "Sâsânian Architecture. A. History", A.U. Pope/Ph. Ackerman (edd.), *A Survey of Persian Art*, 2, London 1938, pp. 493–578.

Rezvani 2005

H. Rezvani, *Âteshkade-ye Shiyân*, ICHHTO, Kermanshah/Qasr-e Shirin, s.d. [2005].

Ritter 2010

N.C. Ritter, *Die Altorientalischen Traditionen der Sasanidischen Glyptik. Form-Gebrauch-Ikonographie* [Wiener Offene Orientalistik, 9], Wien-Berlin, 2010.

Russo 2004

E. Russo, " La Scultura di S. Polieucto e la Presenza della Persia nella Cultura Artistica di Costantinopoli nel VI secolo", *Atti del Convegno Internazionale "La Persia e Bisanzio" (Roma, 14–18 ottobre 2002)* [Atti dei Convegni Lincei, 201], Roma, Accademia Nazionale dei Lincei, 2004, pp. 737–826.

Sarre/Herzfeld 1920

F. Sarre/E. Herzfeld, *Archäologische Reise im Euphrat-und Tigrisgebiet* II, Berlin, 1920.

Schindel 2004a

N. Schindel, *Sylloge Nummorum Sasanidarum Paris-Berlin-Wien, Band III /1, Shapur II . Kawad I./2. Regierung* [Österreichische Akademie der Wissenschaften, Veröffentlichungen der numismatischen Kommission, 42], Wien 2004.

Schindel 2004b

N. Schindel, *Sylloge Nummorum Sasanidarum Paris-Berlin-Wien, Band III /2, Shapur II . Kawad I./2. Regierung. Katalog* [Österreichische Akademie der Wissenschaften, Veröffentlichungen der numismatischen Kommission, 42], Wien 2004.

Schindel 2005

N. Schindel, "Sasanian Mint Abbreviations: The Evidence of Style", *The Numismatic Chronicle*, 2005, pp. 287–299.

Schippmann 1969

K. Schippmann, "Dastagird", *Bulletin of the Asia Institute*, 1, 1969, pp. 43–47.

Schlumberger 1970

D. Schlumberger, *L'Orient Hellénisé. L'Art Grec et ses Héritiers dans l'Asie non-Méditerranéenne*, Paris, 1970.

Schmidt 1937

E.F. Schmidt, *Excavations at Tepe Hissar*, Damghan, Philadelphia, 1937.

Schmidt 1970

E.F. Schmidt, *Persepolis III. The Royal Tombs and Other Monuments* [Oriental Institute Publications, 70], Chicago, 1970.

Schmidt 1978

J. Schmidt, "Qasr-e Sirin. Feuertempel oder Palast", *Baghdader Mitteilungen*, 9, 1978, pp. 39–47.

Sena Chiesa 1966

G. Sena Chiesa, *Gemme del Museo Nazionale di Aquileia*, Padova, 1966.

Sena Chiesa 1978

G. Sena Chiesa, *Gemme di Luni*, Roma, 1978.

Shabazi 1990

A.Sh. Shahbazi, "Byzantine-Iranian Relations", in *Encyclopaedia Iranica*, IV, 6, 1990, pp. 599–599, see http://www.iranicaonline.org/articles/byzantine-iranian-relations

Shaked 1994

Sh. Shaked, *Dualism in Transformation. Varieties of Religion in Sasanian Iran* [Jordan Lectures in Comparative Religion, 16], London, 1994.

Shenkar 2015

M. Shenkar, Rethinking Sasanian Iconoclasm. *Journal of the American Oriental Society*, 135(3), pp. 471–498.

Shokoohy 1983

M. Shokoohy, "The Sasanian Caravanserai of Dayr-i Gachîn, South of Ray, Iran", *Bulletin of the School of Oriental and African Studies*, XLVI/3, 1983, pp. 445–461.

Simpson *et al.* 2012

St J. Simpson/J. Ambers/G. Verri/Th. Deviese/J. Kirby, "Painted Parthian Stuccoes from Southern Iraq", R. Matthews/J. Curtis (edd.), *7 ICAANE. Proceedings of the 7th International Congress on the Archaeology of the Ancient Near East, 12–16 April 2010, the British Museum and UCL, London. Volume 2: Ancient & Modern Issues in Cultural Heritage, Colour & Light in Architecture, Art & Material Culture, Islamic Archaeology*, London, 2012, pp. 209–220.

Sinisi 2005

F. Sinisi, "Qasr-e Shirin", in *Enciclopedia Archeologica. Asia*, Roma, 2005, pp. 390–391.

Sinisi 2013

F. Sinisi, "Sources for the History of Art of the Parthian Period: Arsacid coinage as evidence for continuity of imperial art in Iran", *Parthica* 16, 2014, pp. 9–59.

Skjærvø 2003

P.O. Skjærvø, "The great seal of Pêrôz", *Studia Iranica*, 32, 2003, pp. 281–286.

Soudavar 2003

A. Soudavar, *The Aura of Kings. Legitimacy and Divine Sanction in Iranian Kingship*, Costa Mesa, Ca., 2003.

Soudavar 2009

A. Soudavar, "The Vocabulary and Syntax of Iconography in Sasanian Iran", *Iranica Antiqua*, XLIV, 2009, pp. 417–460.

Sowlat 2012

F. Sowlat, "Nowyâfteha'i az Dowre-ye Sâsâni dar Kâshân [New Sassanid Finds from Kashan Area]", *Bastanpazhuhi*, 4–5, 8–9, 2012, pp. 97–102.

Tanabe 1985

K. Tanabe, "Date and Significance of the so-called Investiture of Ardashir II and the Images of Shapur II and III at Taq-e Bustan", *Orient*, XXI, 1985, pp. 102–121.

Tassinari 2008

G. Tassinari, "La Produzione Glittica a Roma: La Questione delle Officine nel Mondo Romano in Epoca Imperiale", *Rivista di Studi Liguri*, 74, 2008, pp. 251–317.

Tassinari 2011

G. Tassinari, "Le Pubblicazioni di Glittica (2007–2011): Una Guida Critica", *Aquileia Nostra*, LXXXII, 2011, col. 385–472.

Thompson 1976

D. Thompson, *Stucco from Chal Tarkhan-Eshqabad near Rayy*, Warminster, 1976.

Thompson 2008

E. Thompson, "Composition and Continuity in Sasanian Rock Reliefs", *Iranica Antiqua*, XLIII, 2008, pp. 299–358.

Trever/Lukonin 1987

K.V. Trever/V.G. Lukonin, *Sasanidskoe serebro. Sobranie Gosudarstvennogo Ermitazha. Xudozhestvennaja kul'tura Irana III–VIII vekov*, Moskva 1987.

Trümpelmann 1975a

L. Trümpelmann, *Das Sasanidische Felsrelief von Sar Mashad* [Iranische Felsreliefs, A. Iranische Denkmäler, Lieferung 5 enthaltend Reihe II], Berlin, 1975.

Trümpelmann 1975b

L. Trümpelmann, *Das Sasanidische Felsrelief von Darab* [Iranische Felsreliefs, B. Iranische Denkmäler, Lieferung 6 enthaltend Reihe II], Berlin, 1975.

Trümpelmann 1991

L. Trümpelmann, *Zwischen Persepolis und Firuzabad. Gräber, Paläste und Felsreliefs im alten Persien*, Mainz, 1991.

Vanden Berghe 1961a

L. Vanden Berghe, "Neuentdeckte Archäologische Denkmäler in Süd-Iran", *Zeitschrift der Deutschen Morgenländischen Gesellschaft*, 111, 1961, pp. 410–412.

Vanden Berghe 1961b

L. Vanden Berghe, "Récentes Découvertes de Monuments Sasanides dans le Fars", *Iranica Antiqua*, I, 1961, pp. 163–198.

Vanden Berghe 1965

L. Vanden Berghe, "Nouvelles Découvertes de Monuments du feu d'Époque Sasanide", *Iranica Antiqua*, V, 1965, pp. 128–147.

Vanden Berghe 1977

L. Vanden Berghe, "Les Chahar Taqs du Pusht-i Kuh Luristan", *Iranica Antiqua*, XII, 1977, pp. 175–190.

Vanden Berghe 1980

L. Vanden Berghe, "Lumière Nouvelle sur l'Interprétation de Reliefs Sassanides", *Iranica Antiqua*, XV, 1980, pp. 269–282.

Vanden Berghe 1983

L. Vanden Berghe, ed., *Reliefs Rupestres de l'Iran Ancien*, Bruxelles, 1983.

Vanden Berghe 1988

L. Vande Berghe, "Les Scènes d'Investiture sur les Reliefs Rupestres de l'Iran Ancien: Évolution et Signification", G. Gnoli/L. Lanciotti (edd.), *Orientalia Iosephi Tucci Memoriae Dicata*, III [Serie Orientale Roma, LVI, 3], Roma, IsMEO, 1988, pp. 1511–1531.

Vanden Berghe 1993

L. Vanden Berghe (ed.), *Splendeur des Sassanides: L'Empire Perse entre Rome et la Chine [224–642]*, Bruxelles, 12 février-25 avril 1993, Bruxelles, 1993.

Venco Ricciardi 2002

R. Venco Ricciardi, "Hatra et Assour", *Les Parthes: L'Histoire d'un Empire Méconnu, Rival de Rome* [*Dossiers d'Archéologie*, 271], Paris, 2002, pp. 72–79.

Whitcomb 1985

D.S. Whitcomb, *Before the Roses and Nightingales. Excavations at Qasr-i Abu Nasr, Old Shiraz*, New York, 1985.

Yaghma'i 2008 [2010]

E. Yaghma'i, "Kavoshhâ-ye Bastânshenâsi dar Mehrkade-ye Mohammadâbâd (Dashtestân, Borâzjân) [Archaeological excavations at Mithra temple of Mohammad Abad (Dashtestan-Borazjan)]", *Bâstânpâzhuhi*, vol. 3, no. 6, 2008 [2010], pp. 56–76.

Zare'/Atayi 2009 [2011]

Sh. Zare'/M.T. Atayi, "Kushk-e Sâsâni-ye? Argan [Sasanian Pavilion of Argan]", *Bâstânpâzhuhi*, vol. 4, no. 7, 2009 [2011], pp. 135–137.

Zazoff 1970

P. Zazoff, *Antike Gemmen in Deutschen Sammlungen. III. Braunschweig, Göttingen, Kassel*, Wiesbaden, 1970.

Zazoff 1975

P. Zazoff, *Antike Gemmen in Deutschen Sammlungen. IV. Hannover. Kestner-Museum. Hamburg, Museum für Kunst und Gewerbe*, Wiesbaden, 1975.

Zazoff 1983

P. Zazoff, *Die Antiken Gemmen*, München, 1983.

英文摘要

1. Form and function of the residences of kings and nobles.

Our knowledge of the typologies of the Sasanian palace architecture remains far from satisfactory as yet. This is due first of all to the fact that the available documentation is insufficient in both quantity and quality. Besides, the study of the various important architectural complexes, already largely known by the mid-20th century, has always been based on individual approaches, much less reliable than comprehensive views.

This chapter proposes some new reflections on the subject. It does not aim to offer a complete picture of all the new evidence on the possible Sasanian palace architecture, but sets out to verify the theories commonly circulating in the light of new observations and, in particular, the new discoveries.

In its representation of power the Sasanian dynasty focussed its strategy from the outset on the image of the king and his role, superior to those of all other human beings. The historical events, on the other hand, show that the aristocracy also enjoyed a prestigious position and during some periods could condition the royal power. Oddly enough, archaeology yields few aristocratic mansions and relatively simple royal palaces. It is clear that we can rely on few fragments of a picture which was originally much richer, partly illustrated by written sources.

For Sasanian Iran, the interpretation of the secular architecture is closely connected to that of the religious architecture, given that many of the most important architectural complexes have been assigned alternatively to both categories. D. Huff proposed the first attempt at a comprehensive interpretation of palace and religious architecture. He based his study on the complexes having a reliable functional interpretation, stressing the simplicity in plan of some buildings, arranged along one axis only, while others are distributed along more axes, and he argued on sound bases that the buildings with multiple axes belong to religious architecture whereas those on one single axis belong to palace architecture. These features of the plans find correspondence in the presence of a number of storeys in palaces, and the ground floor only in religious complexes.

Huff's proposal, which is based on analysis of the plans, is to be compared with a different interpretation previously proposed by J. Kröger on the basis of the relationship between structures and stucco decoration. This author had suggested that the areas decorated with stucco, mainly halls with columns/pillars and *ivân*s, should have a ritual function linked to the needs of the Zoroastrian communities. According to this hypothesis, therefore, many of the architectural complexes attributed to palace architecture according to Huff's principle should belong to religious architecture.

The importance of possible elements of cultural continuity with similar structures of the preceeding and successive epochs is one fact thta must be stressed. As regards the relationship between the architecture of the Arsacid period and that of the Sasanian period, the limited evidence available points nevertheless towards continuity, despite the strong Sasanian propaganda suggesting the contrary. As regards continuity with the Islamic epoch, a study by L. Bier suggests that "there is no evidence that early Muslim princes sought to imitate the Sasanian palace in a comprehensive sense", and that "when Sasanian influence is evident at all, it is invariably seen in the official portions, more specifically in the throne-rooms ensemble which must have embodied for writers and builders alike the essence of Sasanian imperium". Furthermore, if also appear in the Early Islamic palaces columned halls, their continuity with the preceding period could be better understood if the original models had also belonged to the civil and not the religious architecture: why should the Muslim nobles have incorporated in their residences portions which were used for cult in the Sasanian world?

To bring some light to bear on a complicated matter, the first chapter discusses some relevant monuments, and goes on to offer a few conclusive remarks.

Some introductory remarks precede this section. The first regards the importance of the geographical contexts, and indeed of the traditional building materials used in each region, which also influence the architecture. The second aspect, not sufficiently discussed, is the topographical context of palaces, particularly as regards their position inside or outside the inhabited settlements. Thirdly, there is a preliminary observation to make regarding the fact that the world of the Persians, in the Sasanian period as earlier in the Achaemenid period, does not completely fit in with the functional categories valid for the rest of the Ancient world: for the period of the Sasanians, as compared to other areas of the Late Antique and Early Medieval world, areas with a clearly residential function are significantly less extensive and visible than those with official and ceremonial functions.

After the overview of the main monuments, the chapter goes on to offer a few remarks on the planimetric modules which are singled out. Among these, the square domed hall is relevant in the Early Sasanian period: in the two Ardashir palaces at Firuzabad this clearly serves as ideological centre of the complex, i.e. the throne hall. From a structural point of view, this hall corresponds to the *chahâr qâpu* of the local terminology, a square hall with openings in the four sides. The domed room does not, however, remain a feature of the palace architecture safely identified after the 3rd century AD for very long, while it has better fortune in the religious architecture with the *cahâr tâq* form. This could be due to the fact that the domed hall was entirely taken over in fire temple architecture, so that its use in secular architecture was excluded.

Unlike the domed hall, the *ivân* represents the architectural module more widely adopted in the palace architecture, from that of the Kings of Kings to that of the nobility, even though still appearing in the religious architecture also, in a secondary role. The *ivân*, which was ancillary to the domed hall in the 3rd century AD, gradually incorporated the function of the latter. In the preserved examples of palace architecture later than the 3rd century, the *ivân* represented the centre of the building and is likely to have housed the royal throne. However, close study of the remains brought to light at Ctesiphon points to the possibility that the *ivân* preserved today was not isolated but that the monument included a second *ivân* symmetrical to the first. In this case we would no longer have an isolated and axial *ivân*, but the presence of a number of *ivân*s giving onto a court, seen in the Parthian palace at Assur, would be repeated here. Further evidence of the *ivân* as a place linked to the presence of the King is represented by the West Ivân of Taxt-e Solayman. In the aristocratic mansions, moreover, such as at Hajjiabad, the *ivân* is found twice opening onto a court, preceded by a porch.

The *ivân*, given its position near the entrance, is likely to have had an official reception function; the figural imagery of its decoration, painted or in stucco, must be related to the ideological message of the official sectors within the civil architectural complexes.

Halls with columns/pillars characterize various complexes of the Iranian plateau and Mesopotamia. The columns and pillars are mainly built in masonry, and have dimensions large enough to bear the weight of vaulted ceilings, thus usually being somewhat squat. In many of these halls the pillars appear as the remains of walls supporting the vaults crossed by arches rather than true pillars. On this evidence, we can suggest that this module originated as division of the *ivân* into three aisles and that it can be seen as a variant of the *ivân*, at least as far as its position in the whole plan is concerned. Indeed, the halls with columns/pillars open onto a courtyard in the same way as the *ivân*s, as areas serving for reception and ceremony. On turning to the chronology of *ivân*s and halls with columns/pillars, we observe a sort of succession around the 6th-7th century, when the latter took the place of the monumental *ivân*s.

The main question that arises over the halls with columns/pillars in the Sasanian period concerns their function: stressing the importance of their stucco decoration, J. Kröger advanced the hypothesis that they were not used by the nobles in their secular life but by the Zoroastrian communities. Before this attractive hypothesis almost all the buildings having halls with columns/pillars had been classified within secular architecture. However, in terms of their plan, this hypothesis clashed with Huff's theory that the complexes with an axial plan belonged to secular architecture. Kröger's hypothesis was then gradually softened and eventually he came to associate the halls showing columns/pillars with important landowners or the Zoroastrian local communities.

Therefore, in the late Sasanian epoch the halls with columns/pillars also, where stucco decoration was concentrated, could belong to palace buildings. Indeed, reference to symbolic imagery is one of the strongest aspects of the art and architecture of Sasanian kingship.

A final remark remains to be made about the court, which in the best preserved plans shows considerable importance, superior to that generally attributed on the basis of the scanty evidence: as large open spaces, in fact, the courts are usually neglected by the less searching investigations.

Discussion of the building categories must also take into consideration the pavilion set in a garden or enclosure dedicated to the King's hunting, which represents a category of ancient Iranian tradition belonging to the royal architecture. The most famous representation of it is the Main Ivân at Taq-e Bostan. This structure, cut into the rock, repeats in its architectural forms the appearance of a built *ivân*, with typical elements such as the crowning stepped merlons of Persepolitan descent. The Main Ivân, thanks also to the large mudbrick enclosure nearby, can thus be interpreted as a pavilion belonging to a royal *paradeisos* where the King of Kings engaged in his important hunting activity.

The complex at Hajjiabad is instead an example of a manor house of the landed aristocracy: it provides evidence for the existence of this typology in the Sasanian period in the Iranian plateau, adding to the rich mansions brought to light at various Mesopotamian sites. The interpretation proposed by M. Azarnoush for this building seems to remain valid. Hajjiabad importance resides in the fact that it includes sectors with different functions in the same building: thus it differs from Bandiyan, where the definition of *dastgird*, i.e. "estate", must be applied to the whole of the site including complexes some dozens of metres apart.

Comparison of the Hajjiabad Manor House with Kish Building II highlights in both the buildings the presence in the court of semi-columns supporting a male bust in the place of a capital: at Kish representing the King, at Hajjiabad the owners of the mansion. These findings highlight two new aspects of Sasanian architecture: on one hand, the existence of semi-columns supporting a bust instead of a capital, and on the other the presence of several repeated images of Kings, possibly linked to an ancestor cult within the aristocratic residences.

A question arising over the functional interpretation of the various sectors of the palaces safely identified concerns the location of the residential areas proper. D. Huff suggests locating the rooms with private character in the upper storeys, the presence of which he sees as distinguishing secular from religious architecture. This interesting hypothesis shows its weakness when we take into consideration the dimensions and characteristic of the rooms on the upper storeys in the buildings where they are, even if only partially, preserved. It is true that the rooms opening onto the courtyards in the two palaces of Qal'e-ye Doxtar and Atehskade (Firuzabad) cannot have had a residential function and must certainly have served an official reception function; but rather than locating the private residence of the King and his family in the narrow rooms of the upper storeys, as Huff proposes, it seems wise to follow the prudent position of R. Boucharlat regarding the private residences at Persepolis and to accept the possibility that the private residence of the Sasanian King, at Firuzabad as at Ctesiphon, may be elsewhere, in some unidentified place. Indeed, also in the Safavid period the rooms on the upper storeys were not conceived as a permanent place of residence for the kings.

The chapter concludes with some summary remarks. Palace architecture remains obscure in many of its aspects, but its connection to strongly axial plans is also borne out by the new findings. Having abandoned the domed hall, which was very soon to be restricted to religious architecture, palace architecture concentrated on the *ivân* opening onto a courtyard, at least in some instances repeated on more than one side of the latter. In the late Sasanian epoch the hall with columns/pillars derived from the *ivân*, characterized like the *ivân* by profuse stucco wall decoration. Rather than interpreting this module as a part with an exclusively religious function and thus classifying as cult buildings all the complexes containing it, on the basis of the importance that symbolic imagery has in the Sasanian art of dynastic and princely environment, it may reasonably be hypothesised that these halls were intended for a function connected with a celebration of nobility, without excluding their presence in the most important fire sanctuaries. This interpretation would better account for the presence of halls with columns/pillars in buildings securely dated to the Early Islamic period. Therefore, the location of the areas having a residential function proper remains problematic, as indeed it is for the Achaemenid period.

2. The fire sanctuary of the Sasanian period: questions of interpretation.

Despite the great importance which the subject of religious architecture of Sasanian Iran bears, to date we are still far from a general consensus on the functional interpretation not only of architectural details or particular rooms within the field of Zoroastrian architecture of Sasanian age, but also of whole complexes, as the discussion on the so-called Shapur Palace at Bishapur shows. The reasons are many and have frequently been discussed. One of the main causes of the trouble in interpretation has been seen in the interruption of the Zoroastrian architectural tradition following the fall of the Sasanian empire, which given the close relationship between politics and religion, plunged Zoroastrianism into crisis. It must nevertheless be stressed that we are not sure of the full correspondence between the Muslim conquest and the end of the Zoroastrian monumental tradition, which would appear to have continued at least for some decades at some sites.

In addition to the discussion of the functional interpretation of this or that building, at times substantial disagreement remains regarding the original form they had, as for example in the case of the Building B at Bishapur: E.J. Keall considers it centred on an open court with four *ivân* enclosures, while other scholars, including the present author, see this central element as an imposing domed *chahâr tâq*.

At the same time the few attempts at a global interpretation had to take into account a serious shortcoming in the documentation. The limits of studies and excavations of religious building are evident, showing a marked difference between few areas where careful surveys recording every detail useful for a proposal of functional interpretation were carried out, such as namely some districts of Lorestan and Fars, and areas where the information consists in more or less detailed description of some individual buildings only, such as the whole Northern region, from East to West. This chapter proposes the example of an area of Southern Fars, in the district of Mohr, in a geographic and topographic context totally inhospitable today: even admitting an environment originally less hostile, the presence of important religious sites in such a singularly isolated area can only be attributable to strong reasons of a religious nature, which elude us today.

Continuation of the complete survey of the *chahâr tâq* structures, as proposed by R. Boucharlat in 1985, would certainly afford a rather more reliable overview of the subject.

The chapter briefly illustrates the main steps in research on the Zoroastrian religious architecture in the 20th century, including M. Boyce's contribution on the classification of Zoroastrian fires into three hierarchical categories stemming from the historico-religious analyses associating ancient sources and modern rituals. It is necessary to stress the importance of the new archaeological evidence which came to light starting from the 1990's and the need to verify the compatibility of the hypotheses so far proposed with the new information.

Not all the Zoroastrian rituals were centred on the fire cult, as attested by the sanctuary at Veshnaveh near Kashan as well as the presence within the Zoroastrian fire sanctuaries of areas dedicated to other cults. In addition, as D. Huff has demonstrated, in the main fire sanctuaries all the wide range of activities attributed to the Zoroastrian clergy were carried out, also in the administrative and juridical fields, as indicated by the frequent presence of impressions of seals of the clergy on the administrative sealings of late Sasanian age. This abundance of activities within the sanctuary must have found at least partial confirmation in the layout, as is the case in the large and well-structured sanctuary of Taxt-e Solayman.

As in the case of the palace architecture, topographic contexts are also extremely important for the religious architecture, particularly in terms of the relationships with the inhabited settlements. The topographic location in more or less accessible areas represents an important aspect for a cult which needed good organization. The social context of the fire sanctuary, in addition to the hierarchical level of the fire itself, may possibly have influenced the dimensions of the building, reflecting the proportions of community which could make use of it.

Of the monuments well-known since the beginning of the 20th century, two monuments are particularly important for the history of Zoroastrian religious architecture: the sanctuary at Kuh-e Xwaja in Sistan, the dating of which ranges between the Arsacid and the Sasanian periods, and the complex at Bishapur, traditionally interpreted as Shapur I's Palace.

Regarding the first monument, the chapter discusses in detail the chronological problems of the first two structural phases, following upon the important contributions by S. Ghanimati. This scholar assigns the first phase to the Early Sasanian period based on various reflections, including the results of C14 dating (AD 80–240 ± 50), which unfortunately is not decisive; she also highlights the importance of an earlier phase of Arsacid date, brought to light by recent Iranian excavations and likely to correspond to the level excavated by the IsMEO Italian Mission in the 1960s, erroneously dated by them to the Achaemenid period. Given the information available to date, it is more reasonable to follow M. Canepa in avoiding peremptory exclusion of an Arsacid date for the first monumental phase of the building, which would well accord with the naturalistic character of some of the wall paintings. However, if a Sasanian date were to be confirmed, the consequences on stylistic evaluation for the Sasanian periods would be remarkable. There is also a second reason of special interest in the Kuh-e Xwaja complex, which is represented by its markedly axial plan. A similar planimetry, interpreted in the light of D. Huff's general theory, characterized the palace complexes, and yet we have clear evidence in favour of attributing the Kuh-e Xwaja complex to religious architecture in the sacred character of the place and the discovery of a fire altar. A similar axial plan also characterizes the Chahar Qapu at Qasr-e Shirin, for which the recent Abbasid dating of the near Emarat-e Xosrow suggests great caution in proposing Sasanian attribution.

As regards the so-called Palace at Bishapur, which had been interpreted as a fire sanctuary for the first time in 1989 by M. Azarnoush, there are two particular aspects that need to be highlighted: the large dimensions of the *chahâr tâq*, which has a side length of c. 22 m, and the fact that this is decorated. These peculiarities can be accounted for with dating to an early phase of Sasanian architecture and with the fact that the monument was a royal foundation. At the same time, the fact that its plans correspond perfectly with the general parameters pinpointed by D. Huff for religious architecture is to be taken into consideration.

Discussion then moves on to monuments of more recent discovery, such as the sanctuary at Mele Hairam, in Southern Turkmenistan, or the many sanctuaries brought to light by Iranian archaeologists: Shyan, Mile Milege, Palang Gerd in Western Iran, and Dehqayed in the Borazjan district of Southern Iran. These monuments, thanks to the many unmovable installations placed within the *chahâr tâq*, in the perimeter corridor and in the other loci, increase the possibility of more reliable functional interpretations. Discussion focuses in particular on the remains of fire altar bases found *in situ*.

Regarding Mele Hairam, the Polish excavator who worked on it, B. Kaim, believes that the hierarchy of sacred fires is not revealed by differences in plan but in cult installations. She suggests that the presence at this sanctuary of a massive fire altar with no stepped base, set within a basin-like depression at the centre of the fire temple, is a good indicator of a hierarchic level superior to that of the fire altars with stepped base. On the whole the hypothesis has very interesting elements, although further comparative verification is needed if the presence of the basin-like depression and the absence of stepped base are to be taken as safe hierarchical indicators. What is more important for us is the possibility to locate a fire *ataxsh Warahrân*, i.e. perennial, in a complex such as that at Mele Hairam, which in addition to the fire altar also has a room with an oven for embers — a structure which helps keep a fire perpetually burning with slower combustion and lesser consumption of wood: a practical feature which nevertheless must have had a great importance in the society of the epoch.

The discussion on fire altars reached a new level with the numerous other fragments of fire altars found by A. Askari Chaverdi in Southern Fars, showing by large the predominance of the hourglass type decorated with a cloth tied at the middle of the shaft: the chapter includes a brief discussion on the significant difference found between the fire altars known through archaeology and the fire altars represented on the Sasanian coinage.

The complex at Bandiyan, in Razavi Xorasan, is essential to the debate. Here a fire altar having the same hourglass shape as the other altars mentioned above was unearthed intact in one of the loci brought to light by M. Rahbar; there is also a representation of an altar of the same type in the stucco decoration of the main columned hall. This chapter dwells upon the interpretation of the architectural features, leaving that of the stucco decoration to Chapter 3.

The two main viewpoints proposed to date, which differ in the functional interpretation but converge in dating to the 5th century, are those of the Iranian excavator, M. Rahbar, and of the French epigraphist Ph. Gignoux, who has proposed a new and sounder interpretation of the Middle Persian inscriptions published in the first Iranian contribution. The Iranian archaeologist considers the complex on the Tepe A as the fire temple of the estate (*dastgird*) mentioned in one of the inscriptions, which would also include the palace on the Tepe C and the funerary structure on the Tepe B. The French epigraphist, on the contrary, considers the complex on the Tepe A as the lavish residence of a local aristocrat, denying its cultual function.

The functional interpretation which the French colleague proposes for many of the loci of the building appears on the whole weaker than that of the Iranian excavator. That the complex on the Tepe A may have been a ritual building rather than the residence of the landlord is suggested first of all by the general parameter identified by D. Huff for the characterization of the cult buildings: the building at Bandiyan, in fact, does not show a main axis but rather extends with a complexity similar to that of other buildings of sure religious function. In support of a function other than secular, comparison between the two complexes at Bandiyan and Mele Hairam highlights a series of similarities which can hardly be accidental: the structure in pressed earth or mud-brick; the complexity of a non-axial plan; the presence of areas with floors in baked bricks for offerings to be placed; the architectural typology of the fire temple, differing from a *chahâr tâq* proper; the hourglass shape of the fire altar shaft; the fact that the fire temple opens onto a large hall; the fact that this hall has decorated walls; and, finally, exact correspondence between the decorative motifs on both monuments.

At the same time, the way towards a partly new interpretation of the whole complex has been opened thanks precisely to a remark by Gignoux. Gignoux's more relevant remarks regard the purity rules of Zoroastrianism, namely how to account for the proximity of a sacred fire not so much to a room containing *ostodâns*, which was usually walled-up, but also to a *bareshnum-gâh*, a place dedicated to purification from the heaviest pollutions. In this case, the interpretation which the French scholar proposes for room G, characterized by the circular plan of the inner space, can integrate the interpretation of the whole complex on Tepe A. If it seems reasonable to accept the hypothesis that this room was the place where the dead of the family were laid out before the continuation of the other funerary rituals, Gignoux recalls that according to M. Boyce "for added protection, a fire was kept burning within three paces of the <dead> body (nearer would be a pollution for the fire)": this description corresponds exactly to the plan of our building.

What emerges from the evidence as a whole is, therefore, that the building on Tepe A can be considered, more than a proper fire sanctuary for the Zoroastrian cult, the structure dedicated to the funerary rituals of the *dastgird*, where the *dâdgâh* in which the sacred fire was lit — with the function of keeping evil away during the funerary rituals -, communicated through an intermediate vestibule for offerings with a ceremonial hall with figural stucco decorations celebrating the family deeds, and flanked by a room containing the *ostodâns* for the members of the family, and by a second, circular, room devoted more to the funerary rituals than to the purification rituals.

To this interpretation, which explains the presence of a fire altar in a funerary context, we can add some considerations on the presence of figural decorations in this setting, recalling the pursuit unpublished discovery of wall paintings in a probable funerary context in the site of Ardashir-Xwarrah. Similarly, the presence of figural representations in Zoroastrian religious architecture has to be linked to J. Kröger's important remarks on their connection with the feasts celebrated by the Zoroastrian communities inside the fire sanctuaries: the subject is further dealt with in Chapter 3.

The chapter closes with close analysis of two architectural complexes discovered by E. Yaghma'i near Borazjan and interpreted by him as mithraea of Arsacid date. The two buildings, not far from the *chahâr tâq* at Dehqayed mentioned above, are characterized by the presence of rooms of rectangular plan showing at the base of their walls long benches in which open shallow niches with vaulted ceilings, and which Yaghma'i interprets as seats for the devotees of the Mithraic cult. On the basis of the marked difference between these two buildings and the mithraea discovered in the Roman world, from Syria to Britain, and in consideration of the find of fragments of torpedo jars and human bones, as well as of comparison with similar installations found in the perimeter corridor of the *chahâr tâq* at Palang Gard, containing bone remains, the two complexes may instead have had a funerary function as a place for collection and conservation of *ostodâns* in close topographic association with Zoroastrian cult places: in fact these complexes rise in a plain, devoid of rock faces which could be used to conserve *ostodâns*, as was, by contrast, a widespread practice in the mountains of Fars.

3. The craft of stucco modelling in Sasanian Iran in the light of recent finds

The architecture of the Sasanian period inherited from that of the Arsacid epoch the frequent use of a wall decoration, in the form of not only wall painting but also relief decoration on plaster, which was then painted. While the remains of Sasanian period painting are indeed scanty, thanks to the better resistance of stucco to the action of time and atmospheric agents many more fragments of the original relief decorations, which embellished buildings belonging to different social levels in addition to the dynasty, have survived.

Precisely due to the fact that they belonged to non-exclusively imperial architecture, the Sasanian age stuccos represent for us an extraordinary window on the visual imagery of the society of the Sasanian empire, offering far more evidence than the monumental craft of rock reliefs, which was limited to a dynastic environment. Indeed, stuccos appear in various contexts of Sasanian age architecture, from the secular to the religious, from the dynastic to social strata evidently wealthy but not necessarily belonging to the political sphere.

To this aspect we must add that, unlike other movable productions such as metalware, textiles, glass and glyptics, which regard individual items only, the stuccos gave birth to wide-ranging figurative programmes. These programmes often display an abundance of themes and styles open to relevant interpretative approaches, and with the value added of the relationship existing between the stuccos and the architecture originally bearing them.

When J. Kröger in 1982 published his masterly *Sasanidischer Stuckdekor*, representing even today the most complete art historical and archaeological overview of Sasanian age stucco production, of the two main discoveries in this class of materials, Hajjiabad and Bandiyan, the former was known only through a preliminary publication, while discovery of the latter would only come years later. Kröger's subsequent publications only partially incorporate the new information.

The main aim of this chapter is therefore to take a new look at Kröger's conclusions in the light of the latest discoveries, in order to verify whether the new data have affected the solidity of the German scholar's construction, and if so to what extent.

The term "stucco" is generally used in the study of the ancient crafts with reference to the technique of coating a wall with plastic material, regardless of the chemical composition of the mortar.

After a summary of Kröger's remarks on the techniques of stucco manufacturing in the Sasanian epoch and its main stylistic phases, the chapter dwells on the importance of the relationship between the Proto Sasanian materials and the Late Parthian production illustrated by the stuccos from Qal'e-ye Yezdegerd and Qal'e-ye Zahak.

Kröger's remarks on technique and style are then considered in relation to the information obtained from the two sites of Hajjiabad and Bandiyan, which moreover show considerable differences: while the stuccos from Hajjiabad are characterized by a prevailing relief modelling of three-dimensional aspect, Bandiyan shows a drawing rendering, with rather low relief. However, we must remember that at Bandiyan, too, there are some fragments of moulded figures in relief, still unpublished apart from a brief description by M. Rahbar.

Kröger illustrates in detail the relationship between the sculpted or modelled decoration and its colouring, which has largely disappeared. From a certain perspective, just as the architectural sculpture in stone has to be imagined as a relief support to be completed with colour, so also for the stuccos the chromatic aspect was a necessary integration, as indeed it already was in the Arsacid period. In this respect the two side panels of the Main Ivân at Taq-e Bostan represent an outstanding example of the relationship between relief decoration and colour decoration, as already pointed out by E. Herzfeld and then U. Monneret de Villard: the art production which the two panels recall is not rock relief but painting. This accounts for the remarkable difference between these two panels and the rest of Sasanian reliefs.

If the remains of wall painting from the Sasanian period are so scanty today, it is due solely to the intrinsic weakness of support for the painting. At all the sites where the stuccos are better preserved, traces of wall paintings are also preserved, at Kuh-e Xwaja, Hajiiabad, Bandiyan and Mele Hairam. As we shall see in the final considerations, we could piece together far more of the picture with the use of updated analytical methods which, in the case of colours, can detect traces of paint invisible to the naked eye.

The relationship with the production of Central Asia and the North-West of the Indo-Pakistan subcontinent is also to be considered with closer attention than hitherto. The only site which had in fact prompted exploration of the connections with the areas East of the Sasanian empire is Kuh-e Xwaja. The Sasanian conquest of Kushanshahr must have brought Persian élites into direct contact with various art forms, and in particular the flourishing Buddhist sculpture which, as it expanded, took to stucco as the most used technical medium.

Among the most innovative features of Kröger's volume are the attention drawn to the concentration of stucco decoration in two particular architectural modules and the functional interpretation of a religious nature proposed for them. The German scholar pointed out that stucco decoration was concentrated in halls with columns/pillars and in *ivân*s opening onto a court. The publications of the last twenty years confirm this situation on the whole, but no longer justify considering it exclusive, and not only for the exceptions of the sites of Kuh-e Xwaja, Bishapur and Taxt-e Solayman, where stucco decoration is also to be seen outside or inside a *chahâr tâq*. Indeed, while it is true that at Hajjiabad stuccos have been retrieved in the porch in front of *ivân* L. 149 and in the court L. 178, i.e. in one of the two modules indicated by Kröger, it is also true that many other stucco fragments come from the small room L. 114 and from court L. 107, adjacent to the cruciform room L. 104 interpreted as the fire temple. These loci correspond neither to an *ivân* nor to a columned hall, nor can their function be associated with that of the two modules, of much larger dimensions. The finds from Bandiyan and Mele Hairam, on the contrary, fit in with Kröger's general theory. At both sites the wall decoration is concentrated in the largest room, onto which opens a small fire temple devoid of decoration. At Bandiyan the decoration preserved *in situ* includes figural scenes of great iconographic abundance in stucco; at Mele Hairam the recovered stucco fragments are only decorative, but the fragments of pictorial decoration suggest an area of larger dimensions.

Within the interpretation proposed by Kröger, it is the functional aspect that had the most impact when it was published, but it is also the aspect which the scholar has with great open-mindedness revised in the light of the information derived from the new excavation. The attribution of the columned hall to use by the Zoroastrian communities was based not only on the ascertained function of the complex at Taxt-e Solayman, which has a hall with columns and a hall with pillars, but also on the mention of wine and other products, interpreted as cultic offerings, in *ostraka* retrieved in some of the sites considered. Kröger, convinced of the exclusive concentration of stucco decoration in *ivân*s and columned halls on the basis of their interpretation as "Zeremonialhalle der Zoroastrier", initially assigns all the architectural complexes containing these two modules to religious architecture. The initial position is then softened and the German scholar maintains that "it seems possible that the buildings were also connected to a local landlord, but many questions are still unsolved". The most recent evidence has strongly influenced this evolution, which corresponds to what is proposed in Chapter 1 on palace architecture.

At any rate Kröger has laid the bases for far greater consideration of the symbolic aspects of a production which was previously read superficially, and has formulated a new interpretation of the relationship between Zoroastrianism and art, stressing the importance of the religious imagery of Iran during the Sasanian period.

Linked to the discussion on the interpretation of the columned halls with stucco decoration is the problem of their chronology. Kröger perceptively highlights the problem of Zoroastrian affiliation and Proto-Islamic chronology which ample portions of stucco decoration and of the structures themselves share, particularly in the sites of the Ray region. The sources on the destruction or transformation into mosques of Zoroastrian cultic buildings are indeed many, but there are examples of fire sanctuaries which survived during the early Islamic period, such as Taxt-e Solayman and Tureng Tepe. The construction in Islamic age of decorative compositions of great importance has strong social implications, within which a function linked to the (Zoroastrian ?) nobility rather than Zoroastrian communities would simplify interpretation. A point well made by the German scholar concerns the difficulty in the interpretation of female figures, who have been considered either divinities or queens: this difficulty is clear at Hajjiabad, where M. Azarnoush has proposed identification of all the many different representations of female figures at that site as images of the goddess Anahid. This interpretation has been criticized by some of the scholars who wrote reviews on his publication. The tendency to identify every female figure as the Persian goddess of water, widespread among Iranian archaeologists, has been questioned on many occasions. In the case of Hajjiabad, Gignoux's suggestion that these images be seen as belonging on the whole to a Dionysiac environment, identifiable by virtue of the putti bearing grapes or the lion protomes, accords well with the feast theme to which Kröger attributes much of the stucco production, and seems preferable to Azarnoush's proposal.

The finds from Hajjiabad also involve one of the other subjects which Kröger treated with great originality, i.e. the attribution of the busts of kings found at Kish to an ancestor cult, reaffirmed with the discoveries from Hajjiabad. This interpretation provides unique iconographic documentation, introducing decisive elements for the discussion on funerary devotion, which was previously based on textual and architectural evidence alone: an important precedent could be represented by the "gallery" of busts appearing on the wall painting at Akshaxan-Kala in Xwarezm, dated to the 1st century BC. At the same time, this possible interpretation casts serious doubts on the use of identification of the figures represented for dating their complexes, given that the images may refer to kings belonging to a few generations earlier.

The reconstruction proposed by Azarnoush for the two male busts found in the porch facing *ivân* L. 149, close by the two semi-columns decorating the sides of the access to the *ivân*, seems to be acceptable: according to him, the busts were set on top of the semi-columns in the place of capitals. This positioning of a bust on top of a column/semi-column finds a precedent in the Late Arsacid age, if the dating to this age of the limestone bust from Qal'a-ye Now near Bayza should be confirmed. That it was a more widespread practice could also be borne out with verification of the new interpretation proposed by F. Demange for the busts discovered at Kish in the court of Building II.

The chapter then moves on to the discussion of the stuccos brought to light at Bandiyan after the publication of Kröger's main contributions. At Bandiyan we do not have isolated figures but whole scenes: the homage to the deceased is offered through a "narration" of their deeds as fighters and their actions as Zoroastrian devotees. If for all the known production of Sasanian stuccos, as also for all the other art productions of this age, it is not possible to use the term "narrative" in the sense attributed by R. Brilliant, the stucco reliefs in the main hall at Bandiyan Tepe A represent an important exception: the close iconographic and stylistic relationships with Central Asian figural culture constitute the basic reference.

It is the narrative element that marks out the art of Bandiyan, which the chapter describes in detail on the basis of the description provided by the excavator M. Rahbar. On the whole the Iranian scholar's iconographic reading seems acceptable, although his interpretation needs modifying in a few points where it lacks the support of sufficiently sound evidence.

For interpretation of the scenes, Ph. Gignoux's suggestion to link it to the texts of the inscriptions added onto some of the representations is fundamental, given that one of them begins with the sentence "this image (is that of) ...". We have to consider the figural complex as a whole, subdivided into the scenes on the long walls of the hall and those on the walls of the niche. The presence of the inscriptions is an element which supports the "narrative" interpretation of the scenes, showing how novel they actually were irrespective of the precise period the figures may be attributed to.

If, as was proposed in Chapter 2, the complex represented a place for the funerary rituals, in addition to the rites which were celebrated here, another theme should be the deeds of the deceased members of the family: to them the two long walls on the south-east and north-west sides of the halls were dedicated. Here we have to stress the detailed characterization of the figures, on the basis of which Rahbar has been able to identify the bodies lying lifeless on the ground as belonging to Central Asian peoples. None of the rock reliefs represents the victory on the enemy with so much taste for the description of the event, none of the metal vessels depicts a hunt scene with such lively emotional participation: even though the symbolic aspects are to be considered strong, for a hunt scene as well as for a victory scene, the manner of depiction fits in with the definition which Brilliant gives of narrative art.

All this adds up to evidence of the simultaneous presence in the territories of the Sasanian empires of different art traditions, corresponding to the various macro-regions: it may also be necessary to reappraise the relationships between the productions of Mesopotamia and of the Iranian plateau.

Chapter 3 ends with some reflections on the insufficient availability of analytical information on Sasanian stuccos. With such information for a larger part of the known materials the technical and stylistic approach could be integrated with data on possible topographic grouping based on the material composition, casting light on the various technical traditions; at the same time this would provide a further element for chronological attribution of those complexes not yet safely dated, both as regards the transition between the Arsacid and the Sassanian periods and between the Sasanian and the Islamic periods. A good omen arrives with the presentation of a project at the Museum für Islamische Kunst in Berlin on the stuccos from Ctesiphon, which includes archaeometric analyses, with a view to new conservation and exhibition activities.

4. Sasanian rock reliefs: birth and development of the artistic centres.

Sasanian rock reliefs constitute one of the areas of artistic production which the activities of researchers have concentrated on from the very first phases of investigations on Sasanian Iran. The introductory part of the chapter outlines the main publishing initiatives which have offered detailed documentation for many of the reliefs, with particular emphasis on the series *Iranische Felsreliefs*, published by the German Archaeological Institute in Tehran. The role of this class of artefacts is fundamental for the study of Sasanian royal ideology, given the lack of preserved figural compositions in the imperial buildings. Obviously, the aspects which first drew the attention of scholars efforts were mainly interpretation of the figural motifs and identification of the figures represented, rarely with the support of inscriptions. Thanks to comparison with the coinage portraits, for the majority of the reliefs it was easy to identify the King and thus to propose interpretations for the various depictions. However, the complex figural expression given to hairstyle, attributes and gestures, which was no doubt clear to the peers, often remains obscure to modern observers.

Despite the many studies on the subject, wide consensus on many of the aspects concerning Sasanian rock reliefs, from the mere reading of the iconography to interpretation of it and recognition of its expressive code, is still a long way off. The more generally accepted opinion was proposed by L. Vanden Berghe and reflected in the catalogue of the photographic exhibition *Reliefs rupestres de l'Iran ancien*, which took as proved at least some basic notions. However, new perspectives, new approaches, new interpretations of isolated motifs or of whole reliefs have altered this picture.

Outstanding among the new discoveries is the relief at Rag-e Bibi in Bactria, presented in a masterly interpretation by F. Grenet: it has extended the recognised diffusion area of Sasanian rock reliefs to the easternmost frontier of the Iranian plateau. A series of contributions have focused attention on new researches on particular aspects, adding interesting perspectives to the existing mass of information. One of the main aspects addressed in these is interpretation of the scenes which were traditionally taken to be of royal investiture; in the repertory of Sasanian rock reliefs these constitute the part richest in ideological implications, and they have recently been reinterpreted. Sharable lays the stress on the need to investigate the expressive code as a whole, i.e. the language of Sasanian art in its "lexical and syntactic" aspects, proposed by A. Soudavar.

However, the chapter is not dedicated to these questions, but rather to identification of the ancient production centres, in their three fields of drawing and composition, as well as the sculptural technique and the instruments used for it, and finally technical-stylistic rendering. On the first two fields there are important contributions, notably by G. Herrmann; the third field needs further study given the possibility it offers to cast light on the activities of different groups of craftsmen.

Study of the production centres is therefore of the utmost importance for an understanding of the role which this production had in Sasanian Iran. The following questions are in fact all important, and merit appropriate response: understanding the production mechanisms, the partition of the various phases of the work among the craftsmen; understanding if there was a centralized workshop or if there existed a number of workshops operating at the same time; understanding the dynamics of the birth and development of the production centres, given that the Sasanian dynasty created ex-novo rock reliefs when the previous tradition was too distant in time to have played a continuity role. One of the outcomes of our approach is that the mainly chronological criterion applied so far in ordering the Sasanian reliefs can be integrated with and partially replaced by a topographic criterion, emerging from identification of the various artistic centres which operated in parallel.

The chapter proceeds with illustration of the main artistic centres which can be singled out thanks to detailed examination of the reliefs produced during the reigns of the various Sasanian kings. Due attention must be paid to the technical aspects of creation and organization of the workshops necessary for a production requiring considerable technical competence, which could only have been established within a solid craft tradition.

In order to identify the possible origins of the production of the first Sasanian king it is fundamental to recognize a possible chronological sequence among the five reliefs representing Ardashir I, so as to examine the earliest one for evidence of possible precedents. The chapter reviews the various positions taken to date, which agree only in placing the Salmas relief at the end of the reign, although it is the least refined: it is commonly attributed to a local workshop in Armenia. The earliest relief seems to be that of Firuzabad I celebrating Ardashir's victory over Artaban IV: its technical-stylistic rendering is very similar to that of the Elymaean rock reliefs commonly dated between the 2nd and the 3rd century AD, and craftsmen from that region could have been enlisted in the creation of the new workshop. The same workshop produced progressively more refined reliefs, culminating with the scene of investiture on horseback at Naqsh-e Rostam I: in order to account for a basic change in a very short span of time it seems reasonable to hypothesize the use of more experienced craftsmen from regions with sounder sculptural traditions, and in the first place the Eastern regions of the Roman Empire, which had also definitely provided masons contributing to the building of the Taxt-e Neshin at Ardashir-Xwarrah.

The relevance of the pre-Sasanian graffiti at Persepolis to the creation of the Ardashir I's reliefs must, on the other hand, be reappraised, for the only connection is to the iconographical elaboration, the two techniques of rock relief and graffito being in fact quite different.

Summing up, Ardashir I's reliefs must be attributed to a workshop grafted onto the proficiency of Elymaean craftsmen: this workshop was entrusted with elaboration of a new imagery deriving from Arsacid age precedents, but also from the graphic tradition of the Persepolis graffiti. On the evidence of the iconographical and stylistic similarities between the two Firuzabad II and Naqsh-e Rajab III reliefs with investiture scenes we can identify the continuity in activity of the same workshop, which apparently started at Firuzabad and then moved to Estaxr: in the vicinity of this city it appears to have produced the Naqsh-e Rajab III relief and, with the integration of foreign experienced craftsmen able to imitate Persepolis Achaemenid reliefs, reached the apex of its formal perfection in the Naqsh-e Rostam I relief. In parallel to this technical achievement of Persian craftsmen, a second workshop must have produced, showing inferior technical ability, the Salmas relief in the region of Armenia, distant from the heartland of Fars.

A number of studies have been dedicated to the production of rock reliefs by Shapur I, dealing mainly with identification of the Roman emperors defeated by this king. On the basis of differences of an iconographical and stylistic nature, which G. Herrmann associates with a chronological evolution, it is however possible to propose attribution of the Bishapur and Naqsh-e Rostam/Naqsh-e Rajab reliefs to two different production centres: these two centres can be pinpointed through technical and stylistic characteristics enduring in time, also during the reigns of the successors of Shapur I. It was not a matter of a number of workshops working simultaneously in the same centres, as proposed by M. Mayer, but rather two different centres, within which it is difficult to suggest the roles of the various craftsmen participating in the various projects, while nevertheless operating along the lines of the two traditions.

Indeed the differences between the two groups of reliefs are so marked that it is difficult to imagine that the same craftsmen employed in the sites of Central Fars also worked at Bishapur. With regard to the Bishapur site, more than one scholar has recalled what Shapur himself relates in his inscription at Naqsh-e Rostam on the Roman prisoners also deported, among other areas of Eranshahr, to Fars: under this king there existed the historical conditions to include sculptors from the Eastern Regions of the Roman Empire in the artistic centre entrusted with execution of the Sasanian figural programmes at Bishapur, obviously guided by Persian inspiration. This presence can be identified as the origin of the technical and stylistic peculiarities of the Bishapur centre as compared to the Naqsh-e Rostam centre, confirmed also by relevant iconographical peculiarities.

The Rag-e Bibi relief, discovered in 2002 in Bactria, shows technical and stylistic peculiarities which differentiate it profoundly from the reliefs of Fars: the tendency it shows to a rendering of naturalistic type, on account of which it is to be attributed to a different artistic centre, could find its origin in a workshop of the so-called Buddhist art of Gandhara or in the local Bactrian tradition.

The development of the two main artistic centres in the reigns following Shapur I can be followed up to the Bishapur VI relief, of very difficult iconographic but also technical-stylistic interpretation. In fact, this relief is not finished in its sculpted work, left at different stages to be finished with stucco. This situation takes on different implications according as to whether attribution is to a king of the 3rd or the 4th century. The attribution to Shapur II, proposed by L. Vanden Berghe, seems more grounded than all the others, being the only one which provides an explanation borne out in sources regarding the execution of a member of the royal family depicted in the relief.

The first two reliefs of Taq-e Bostan are dated to the end of the 4th century. The sudden and unprecedented creation of rock reliefs in this site of the Kermanshah district in Western Iran seems not to be linked in any way with the earlier production of Fars: on the contrary, it is important to recall the existence in Western Iran of rock reliefs of earlier epochs, which can have stimulated the inspiration of the clients, in connection both to the different historical situation and to the loss of ideological centrality undergone by Fars in favour of Mesopotamia, on the road to which Taq-e Bostan is situated.

The technical-stylistic characteristics suggest that Taq-e Bostan was a newly created artistic centre, possibly inspired by stucco production, giving of its best in the Taq-e Bostan I relief.

At the same site, the reliefs on the back wall of the Main Ivân point for the second time to the birth of a new tradition which appears stylistically very different from that of the centre which produced the first two reliefs. For these the commonly accepted dating is now to the 7th century, with different attributions to Khusro II or Ardashir III, while the attribution to Peroz (5th century) finds few supporters. However, there are no decisive elements in favour of one or the other position, given the fact that the crowns of these kings show certain similarities.

The compositional project, despite the presumed influence from the organization of the apses of Byzantine churches, shows a genuine Iranian taste for massive and static forms. At the iconographic and stylistic level, some peculiarities mark it out from the previous production: the reliefs are characterised by volumetric rendering of great plasticity, completely unknown to the previous Sasanian relief production. The three figures in the upper register, like the horseman in the lower register, seem to stand out from the background, thanks not only to the very high relief but also to the undercutting applied to almost all the outlines of the figures, a technique completely new in Sasanian art. Particularly rich modelling combines with great care in the depiction of all the details, in relief or incised. On the whole the figural programme is genuinely Persian, performed by sculptors of great skill and originality.

Considering that the reliefs, be they datable to the 7th or to the 5th century, were produced after an interruption of at least two generations from the Shapur III relief, one cannot but wonder what the practical conditions could have been for the development of a workshop that displayed such remarkable skill.

The façade of the *ivân* represents a pseudo-architectural element in stone, with various features proper to architectural decoration: the crowning stepped merlons, representing reference to the Iranian tradition, as well as the two pilasters with floral (vegetal) decoration, which shows similarities both with the decorative repertory of Sasanian stuccos and with the architectural decoration of the church of S. Polyeuktos at Costantinople (AD 524–527). To these decorative features we may add the two figures of winged Victories at the sides of the rich archway, the origins of which are in the Late Antique figural culture influencing both the Eastern Roman Empire and Sasanian Persia. The capitals of the semi-columns on the *ivân* end wall bear motifs similar to those of the façade pilasters, rendered in a style so similar as to suggest production by the same craftsmen, in turn showing that the two parts of the monument should belong to the same period. Since there are no figural representations of the kind in Sasanian art, the origins of the originality of the reliefs of the Main Ivân, particularly as regards technical execution, may better be sought elsewhere, in the same external influences which can be detected in the façade. However, in the 7th century the Byzantine Empire no longer showed such sculptural excellence as may have found its way to Sasanian Persia: the features suggesting a relationship with the Eastern-Roman world cannot go back to an epoch prior to the 5th-6th century, when the sculptural production in high relief came to an end in that area. Therefore, if the new artistic centre enjoyed an external contribution and if this contribution arrived from the West, we must take into consideration the attribution to Peroz: in the 5th century, in fact, the complex and mutual exchanges with Costantinople would have benefitted from a sculptural tradition still flourishing in the Eastern-Roman world.

The chapter continues with a summary of the activity of the various artistic centres engaged in the production of rock reliefs throughout the entire span of the Sasanian dynasty. The first artistic centre appeared at Firuzabad thanks to the initiative of Ardashir I, then following the King moved to Naqsh-e Rajab and Naqsh-e Rostam in Central Fars; under the same sovereign a second artistic centre produced the simple relief at Salmas in North-Western Iran. Under Shapur I, the artistic centre of Central Fars continued activity at Naqsh-e Rostam and Naqsh-e Rajab, on the basis of a tradition which was consolidated; a second artistic centre was developed, at Bishapur, in which the presence of Roman craftsmen can be detected; a third centre of very different tradition, presumably non-Persian, was active in the Sasanian Far East, i.e. Bactria. Under Shapur I's successors, in the last quarter of the 3rd and the beginning of the 4th century, the two centres at Naqsh-e Rostam and Bishapur continued their intense activity along the lines of their respective traditions, where necessary bringing their work to nearby sites, particularly during the reign of Wahram II. In the 4th century, with the ascent to throne of a very young Shapur II, we see the production of reliefs interrupted at Bishapur, followed by a sole episode of revival, if the attribution to Shapur II of the Bishapur VI relief should find confirmation. A similar situation appears to have recurred at Naqsh-e Rostam, should the Naqsh-e Rostam VII relief be attributed to Wahram IV. With the end of the 4th century the production of rock reliefs abandoned Fars and moved to a centre on the main road between the Iranian plateau and Meopotamia, Taq-e Bostan, where two new artistic centres were created, both very different from the Fars centres. The conjectured presence of Byzantine craftsmen in the workshop which produced the relief on the end wall of the Main Ivân could be possible only if the reliefs belonged to the 5th rather than to the 7th century, as also applies to the decoration of the *ivân* façade.

It is absolutely impossible to propose hypotheses as to the organization of these artistic centres, which can be identified only broadly on the basis of certain iconographical choices and a general stylistic approach which must have seen the activity of a number of of various different sculptors.

What has to be stressed is the discontinuity in the activity of these centres: unlike the Achamenians, the Sasanian dynasty, despite its commitment to centralization, did not consider it necessary to ensure continuity in the tradition of its craftsmen, who thus on various occasions were faced with the challenging task of reviving a technically complex production, that of rock sculpture. Notwithstanding the clear symbolic importance of the rock reliefs, they cannot have represented an essential and permanent component of the external display of Sasanian kingship.

5. Questions of technique and style in the production of seals of the Sasanian age: the production centres.

The production of seals of the Sasanian age is perhaps the best known of all the craft classes of that culture, thanks to the large number of seals and seal impressions present on sealings which have been published. In this field the role played by R. Gyselen, with the publication of a several *corpora* of seals and sealings together with critical contributions on these materials, has proved seminal.

Rather than presenting a general picture, this chapter is dedicated to a few reflections on technique and style — two aspects that could bring further light to bear on the production centres of Sasanian seals.

Having reviewed a series of contributions by several scholars, including V.G. Lukonin, A.D.H. Bivar, Ch. Brunner and R. Göbl, the chapter dwells on the recent book by N.C. Ritter, *Die altorientalischen Traditionen der sasanidischen Glyptik. Form-Gebrauch-Ikonographie*. This work stresses the iconographic and stylistic continuity between the glyptics of the Sasanian period and that of the Ancient Near East. In the seals of Mesopotamian production and Sasanian age, various features attest to the undeniable continuity in the activity of the workshops through the Hellenistic and Arsacid periods. Ritter's work, therefore, is praiseworthy for having demonstrated the survival of the ancient Mesopotamian traditions up to the arrival of Islam in those lands. However we cannot share Ritter's opinion that this continuity should be assigned to the "Sasanians", given that the seal production is by large of a private nature and is to be interpreted accordingly. For discussion of the cultural orientations of the dynasty regarding glyptics it is necessary to concentrate on the few seals which the inscriptions attribute to members of the royal family and which Ritter mentions in an incomplete list, completed by R. Gyselen in her review of Ritter's volume.

The following seven seals are illustrated and discussed in detail:

1 — The so-called Gotha Hyacinth in the Bibliothèque Nationale, Paris;

2 — A bichrome onyx in the British Museum representing Wahram IV;

3 — The so-called Devonshire Gem, on the antiquarian market, with a representation of one Wahram *Kermanshah*;

4 — The seal of Yazdan-Friy-Shabuhr, one of the spouses of Shabuhr III, in the Bibliothèque Nationale;

5 — The amethyst in the Hermitage with the portrait of the "Queen of queens" Denag;

6 — The impression of the seal of Peroz on the antiquarian market;

7 — The impression of the seal of Shapur II on a sealing in the Saeedi collection.

The picture of Sasanian royal glyptics is also completed with some literary sources on seals belonging to the Sasanian kings.

The royal seals represent busts or whole figures and, unlike most of the Sasanian seals, are ring-bezels in onyx, sardonyx and amethyst. In terms of stylistic, qualitative and technical-stylistic rendering, these seals are among the masterpieces of Sasanian age stone engraving, while their iconography is similar to that of the royal images on coinage. Not a single one of them belongs to the groups of Mesopotamian tradition. The glyptics of the Sasanians, in other words of the kings, is not that of Mesopotamian tradition, but originates in workshops of naturalistic approach showing close connections with the Sasanian coin portraits, belonging to a tradition deriving from that of the Arsacid period, in turn connected to the Hellenistic tradition. The same tradition was also widespread among the upper hierarchies of the administration and aristocracy.

The production showing marked continuity with the ancient Mesopotamian tradition, as effectively evidenced by Ritter, is on the contrary that pertaining to other, lower social strata, which retained their tastes and technical traditions up to the Sasanian age through the Achaemenid, Seleucid and Arsacid periods. We should not underestimate the significance of the fact that Mesopotamia enjoyed the major economic importance within the Sasanian empire, and that most of these seals should have been produced there. Misinterpretation derives from defining as "Sasanian glyptics" what should more correctly be called "glyptics of the Sasanian age".

The main focus in this chapter is on the technical and stylistic aspects. The seal production of the Sasanian age is characterized by the presence of various stylistic trends, ranging from swift, schematic rendering of the image to engravings of great technical complexity and artistic value. Common to the most recent studies is a profound diffidence about the possibility of obtaining sufficiently reliable results from the study of stylistic aspects. However, the overview proposed by V.G. Lukonin in the 1960s for the seal production of the first centuries of the Sasanian empire, based on iconography and style, still appears valid. The major weakness of other attempts at a stylistic overview, such as those by A.D.H. Bivar and Ch. Brunner, lay largely in their lack of a global approach and in the fact that the stylistic categories pinpointed are fundamentally linked to the economic means of the client. This view is shared by both Ritter and Gyselen. Ritter believes it impossible to rely on stylistic analysis to follow the chronological and geographical development of the vast seal production of the Sasanian period. He stresses the large number of different styles, the simultaneous and independent appearance of different style varieties showing no regional or chronological logic, and also the presence of combinations of various techniques, making global classification a challenging task; according to Ritter, style in the seal production of the Sasanian age is not, in fact, so much a process or result of a chronological, regional, ethnical or artistic development or trend, as an expression or mirror of social and economic conditions. The existence of seals produced with rapid techniques, as already reasonably proposed by R. Gyselen, is not linked to an artistic taste typical of a given period, but to the nature of mass production intended for the lower social strata — seals which, moreover, appear less frequently in the administrative sealings.

R. Gyselen shifts discussion to the entirety of the categories which may have contributed to the final aspect of a seal: this approach leads the scholar to an important step in classification, which preludes a new attitude towards stylistic questions. Her approach to the iconographical types of Iranian glyptics of the Sasanian age, far from being a mere taxonomic instrument, represents the basis for further in-depth analyses which allow for the inclusion of matters of technique and style, too.

The group of seals, which Gyselen's findings can best be applied to, is that of the male busts. Her critical observations on iconographic classification introduce some interesting elements of chronology.

R. Gyselen operates on two levels. The first is performed within her system of iconographic classification of the entire set of seals of Sasanian dating in "series". Since the definition of these groupings is rather broad, they include materials which may be somewhat dissimilar. Therefore, in addition to the general classification, the Belgian scholar identifies in the seals representing male busts seven "typological series" based on further iconographic features and including similar seals. The observations arrived at in examination of the material, form and epigraphy within these "typological series" lead the scholar to propose a chronological context for them. All these considerations are verified in the light of the impressions on sealings, which have a more objective possibility of being dated. Thus, on the basis of a combination of characteristics, form, material, inscription and iconography it is possible to define the production of groups belonging to the same chronological horizon. The result of this approach is of extraordinary interest, given the scepticism shared by most of the studies on seals of Sasanian period regarding their chronology, subsequent to Bivar's and Lukonin's attempts.

A fundamental aspect of Gyselen's contribution is therefore the fact that some groups of seals can be assigned to different chronological horizons on the basis of detailed analysis of iconography and of various physical features.

It is possible to start from these results for further in-depth analysis, this time turning to investigation of the production centres, leading also to questions of style with a different approach. If we compare the ways of rendering the various features which form the images of all the seals which have been classified according to iconography by R. Gyselen, we can identify a common origin also among seals belonging to different iconographic groups.

For this line of study I used the same method which I followed in the past to study the seals collected in the Gandharan region of today's Pakistan: on the present occasion obvious reasons of time compelled me to confine study to the sole verification of the possibility to apply the method on the basis of a sample. The object of the present test are the male busts in the Bibliothèque National, published by R. Gyselen in 1993 with excellent illustrations which, enlarged from scale 1:1 to scale 2:1, allow for analytical study of the features forming the image.

With detailed study of the way of engraving the various features, both within similar iconographic groups and in comparison between different groups, it is possible to highlight similarities of a technical-stylistic nature, associated with the production technique, which are significant enough to suggest their correspondence with shared production centres, although it remains impossible to clarify the nature of these production centres.

The first step in the recognition of these production centres is identification of groups of seals that, despite despite showing different iconographic motifs, are to be equated on the basis of the same technical-stylistic rendering of the image features. Seal engraving is a highly specialized technique, also because the difficulty is all the greater due to the miniaturistic character of the engraving. Workshops producing seals must necessarily have been depending on a direct tradition which made it possible for the masters to hand down the technical know-how: within this general frame, each engraver would possibly have chosen his own characteristic ways of rendering the images, despite the need to diversify each of his products at an iconographic level to make identification possible, necessary for practical use as a seal. It is for this reason that we can suggest that a particular way of rendering the image through a particular use of the tools should not be due to chance repetition in various moments and places, but should more likely correspond to a specific production centre.

The analysis of the technical-stylistic rendering starts from study of the iconography, which is integral to it and provides it with the possibility of verification. It is a stylistic classification very different from classifications of a qualitative type and, unlike them, allows for identification of objective links between seals of different iconographies.

The first conclusions can be drawn on the basis of the greater or lesser possibility to identify production centres shared by a more or less large number of seals, i.e. the existence of many or few production centres, bearing in mind the long duration of the Sasanian period and its considerable extension. The possibility to identify even a few production centres as common origin for a limited number of seals represents confirmation of the method's effectiveness.

The technical-stylistic groups identified on this basis can in some cases find anchoring in an absolute chronology and possibly also in topographic localization on the basis of comparable sealings and coins.

As regards coins, it is interesting to consider the approach which the coin specialists follow on style. The term "style" in numismatic studies includes aspects of an iconographic more than a strictly stylistic nature, while it does not usually take into consideration the way of rendering the intrinsic features of the image such as eye, nose and mouth, apart from the iconographic choice.

The chapter then illustrates the technical-stylistic groups which have been identified among the seals showing a male bust published by Gyselen in 1993, which amount to eleven groups including 26 seals.

On the whole, therefore, for only 26 of the 153 seals representing male busts in Gyselen's catalogue has it been possible to identify technical-stylistic groups with sufficient certainty, corresponding no doubt to unitary production centres. The percentage amounts to 17% and highlights a great diversification in the production. One of the main results of this test has been the proposed identification of some production centres, to which also seals with different motifs belong: the possibility to recognize a common origin even among seals of different iconographic classification has been demonstrated. The results, attesting to the plurality of production centres, are quantitatively mediocre but have great methodological significance in that they point to the possibility of a new approach which will be able to add to the noteworthy results obtained already.

The results of this new approach are to be considered in relation to Ritter's sociological perspective in evaluating the stylistic aspects of the Sasanian seals. The strong link existing between the stylistic aspects of seals and the social position of their owners in the case of the seals representing busts must be compared with the value of the features of the image as status symbol.

If also the epigraphical texts point to the existence of various levels in the aristocracy, the possibility cannot be ruled out that owning a seal representing a bust may have signified strong social distinction: this distinction might have further been illustrated by the clothing features and the technical-stylistic qualities connected to the seal's value and perhaps also the material and form. The seals representing male busts are grouped on the basis of iconographical features closely connected to an idea of social hierarchy: any further classification based on aspects of production levels confirms Ritter's remarks on the sociological implications of style.

The technical-stylistic in-depth analysis based on the methodology proposed in the chapter, unlike the previous evaluation of stylistic aspects of a qualitative nature, integrates well in an approach stressing the relationship between style and the social position of the owner, in addition to offering the first, decidedly interesting information on the nature of the production centres of Sasanian seals. Here it has not been possible to extend the study to a larger number of seals for lack of time, while from the quantitative viewpoint the results of this investigation represent only a small sample and need to be confirmed on a sounder statistical basis.

译后记

魏正中教授将卡列宁教授的《伊朗萨珊时期的建筑与艺术》交给译者翻译时，我非常忐忑，自知自不量力，但依然鼓足勇气接下重任，将法文转译成中文，希望这部重要的著作被更多人看见。

翻译与校对此书的过程中，得到了作者卡列宁教授的全力支持，他不厌其烦地解答了我提出的许多"外行"问题。中文本并不仅限于将法文与中文的转译。除原本的内容外，卡列宁教授还专门撰写了第一部分全面且丰富的导论，并增添了大量精美的图片，以更好地与第二部分的专题相衔接，以此献给渴望深入了解萨珊时期的伊朗的中国读者。

我还要向魏正中教授致以衷心的谢意，他不仅为此书问世积极奔走，更付出宝贵的个人时间，逐页、再三审校字词用语，直到确认无论从内容思想还是语言表达都达到了出版的标准。

感谢梁源、郭美玲、王实和雷小菲，为我解答建筑、考古等领域的专业问题，并细致地推敲、校对了第一部分的导论。感谢父母家人一直以来的支持。

承蒙上海古籍出版社编辑认真审阅和细心修改，谨致谢忱。

最后需要声明的是，译者虽与作者仔细反复核对，以求忠实于原文，但译者主要研究并非萨珊考古领域，其中不足之处在所难免，恳请行家里手不吝赐教。

吴 筱

2024 年末于佛山

作者简介

卡列宁
意大利博洛尼亚大学教授,意大利驻巴基斯坦斯瓦特地区考古项目前任负责人。

译者简介

吴 筱
毕业于北京大学考古文博学院,现于法国高等研究实践学院攻读博士学位,主要研究领域为意大利文艺复兴时期的建筑。

亚欧丛书

◈ 梵天佛地（全八册）
　　［意］图齐 著，魏正中、萨尔吉 主编

◈ 探寻西藏的心灵
　　图齐及其西藏行迹
　　魏正中、萨尔吉 编译

◈ 犍陀罗石刻术语分类汇编
　　以意大利亚非研究院巴基斯坦斯瓦特考古项目所出资料为基础
　　［意］多米尼克·法切那、安娜·菲利真齐 著，魏正中、王姝婧、王倩 译

◈ 犍陀罗艺术探源
　　［意］卡列宁、菲利真齐、奥里威利 编著，魏正中、王倩 编译

◈ 龟兹寻幽
　　考古重建与视觉再现
　　何恩之、魏正中 著，王倩 译

◈ 丝路探险
　　1902～1914年德国考察队吐鲁番行记
　　［德］卡恩·德雷尔 著，陈婷婷 译

◈ 高昌遗珍
　　古代丝绸之路上的木构建筑寻踪
　　［匈］毕丽兰、［德］孔扎克-纳格 主编，刘韬 译，王倩、方笑天 审校

◈ 龟兹早期寺院中的说一切有部遗迹探真
　　［意］魏正中、［日］桧山智美、［德］基弗尔-普尔兹、［日］谷口阳子 著，王倩 译

◈ **伊朗萨珊时期的建筑与艺术**
　　［意］卡列宁 著，吴筱 译，魏正中 审校

◈ 西域考古：青铜时代至公元9世纪
　　［意］罗慕齐 著，王倩、达吾力江·叶尔哈力克 译

上海古籍出版社

图书在版编目(CIP)数据

伊朗萨珊时期的建筑与艺术 / (意)卡列宁著；吴筱译. -- 上海：上海古籍出版社，2025.6. -- (亚欧丛书). -- ISBN 978-7-5732-1516-1

I. K883.73

中国国家版本馆CIP数据核字第20250ZH710号

责任编辑：缪　丹
装帧设计：王楠莹
技术编辑：耿莹祎

亚欧丛书
伊朗萨珊时期的建筑与艺术
［意］卡列宁　著
吴　筱　译　　［意］魏正中　审校

上海古籍出版社出版发行

（上海市闵行区号景路159弄1-5号A座5F　邮政编码201101）

（1）网址：www.guji.com.cn

（2）E-mail: guji1@guji.com.cn

上海雅昌艺术印刷有限公司印刷

开本 787×1092　1/16　印张 19.5　插页 6　字数 381,000

2025年6月第1版　2025年6月第1次印刷

ISBN 978-7-5732-1516-1/K·3810

审图号：GS（2005）2204号　定价：138.00元

如有质量问题，请与承印公司联系